Protestant Missionaries in the Philippines,
1898–1916

Protestant Missionaries in the Philippines, 1898–1916

An Inquiry into the American Colonial Mentality

Kenton J. Clymer

University of Illinois Press
Urbana and Chicago

Publication of this work was supported in part by a grant
from the Andrew W. Mellon Foundation.

Library of Congress Cataloging in Publication Data

Clymer, Kenton J.
    Protestant missionaries in the Philippines, 1898–1916.

    Bibliography: p.
    Includes index.
    1. Protestant churches—Missions— Philippines—History
—20th century.   2. Missionaries—Philippines—History—
20th century.   3. Nationalism—Philippines—History—20th
century.   4. Philippines—Politics and government—
1898–1935.   5. Philippines—Civilization—American
influences.   6. Americans—Philippines—History—20th
century.   I. Title.
BV3380.C58   1986   266'.023'730599   85-1278
ISBN 0-252-01210-0

For Marlee

Contents

Preface

My interest in American relations with the Philippines was first sparked when doing research on John Hay, who was secretary of state when the islands were acquired. Subsequent reading led to the realization that, while many prominent diplomatic historians have examined the phenomenon of American imperial expansion at the turn of the century, including the acquisition of the Philippines, very few of these scholars subsequently explored what happened in the new colonies under American rule. The Philippines had commanded the attention of a few historians of Southeast Asia, but the state of historical inquiry in Philippine-American history was aptly summarized in 1972 by Peter W. Stanley as "The Forgotten Philippines."

Fortunately, the last decade has seen a blossoming of significant books and articles on Philippine-American history. Much remains to be done, particularly on the impact of American rule on Philippine society. But Philippine-American history is no longer forgotten. It is my hope that the present study will advance further our understanding of American colonialism by exploring the attitudes, ideas, and ideals of one important group of American colonizers.

I am deeply indebted to many people who assisted in the preparation of this book. Richard E. Welch, Jr., Gerald H. Anderson, Henry Warner Bowden, Bradford Perkins, and Michael Cullinane read all, or substantial portions, of the manuscript. Their comments were very helpful. Peter W. Stanley organized extraordinarily stimulating workshops on Philippine-American history at Harvard University in the summers of 1977 and 1978. The conference participants, including Michael Cullinane, Bernardita Reyes Churchill, Ronald Edgerton, Theodore Friend, Frank Golay, Reynaldo Ileto, John Larkin, Glenn May, Stuart Creighton Miller, Alfred McCoy, Michael Onorato, Norman Owen, Bonifacio Salamanca, Shiro Saito, and Richard E. Welch, Jr., were subjected to an essay that became chapter seven of the present work. The manuscript was advanced considerably under their guidance, as was my knowledge of Philippine-American relations.

Gerald H. Anderson first encouraged me to spend some time in the Philippines. At the time such a possibility seemed out of the question. But a Fulbright grant in 1977–78 permitted my family and me to spend several months at Silliman University in Dumaguete City, as well as a few weeks in Manila. The Fulbright program also sponsored speaking engagements at other Philippine universities, for which I am most grateful.

The staff, faculty, and students at Silliman University were superb. The late Luz Ausejo, a fellow historian and dean of the college of arts and sciences, was especially helpful. She possessed a keen intellect, boundless energy, and a humane vision, and we are all diminished by her premature death in October 1984. In addition to Luz, Quintin and Pearl Doromal, Caridad Rodriguez, Carlos Magtolis, Dale and Rosita Law, Proceso and Leonora Udarbe, MacArthur Corsino, Tjaard and Anne Hommes, Judy and Rowland Van Es, Eulalio Maturan, Angel Alcala, Salvador Vista, T. Valentino Sitoy, Florence Jubela, and many others shared with us their knowledge of Philippine society, religion, and culture. Mariano Apilado, the author of a distinguished study of the missionaries, also offered helpful criticism of one of the chapters, as did Bishop Pedro Raterta of the United Church of Christ in the Philippines. I am also grateful to William Henry Scott, who shared with me his knowledge of the Episcopalian missionaries, to the late Peter G. Gowing, who invited us to visit him in Marawi City, where he introduced us to Muslim culture in the islands, and to Fr. John Schumacher, with whom I discussed the study. Whatever value the present book has owes much to these people and to the months spent in the islands.

The librarians and archivists at all of the repositories visited were, without exception, cordial, professional, and helpful. I would particularly like to mention Doris Powell and Carol Wilson of the Baptist Historical Society in Rochester, New York; John R. Ness, Jr., secretary of the Commission on Archives and History of the United Methodist Church; William Beal, archivist, and Louise Queen, librarian, at the Methodist collections, then housed at Lake Junaluska, North Carolina (now located at Drew University in Madison, New Jersey); and Nelle V. Bellamy, archivist, and Elinor S. Hearn, librarian, of the Episcopalian archives in Austin, Texas. Bishop Paul Locke A. Granadosin of the United Methodist Church in the Philippines kindly allowed me to consult the Rebecca Parrish Papers in his personal possession. David Rambo corresponded with me about the mission of the Christian and Missionary Alliance. Charles W. Forman made his New Haven apartment available to me during the summer of 1976 so that I could consult the valuable holdings of the Day Missions Library at the Yale University Divinity School. Stephen L. Peterson, the librarian, could not have been more helpful.

Permission to quote from unpublished sources has been obtained from the American Baptist Historical Society, the Houghton Library (for the records of the American Board and the W. Cameron Forbes Papers), the United Church Board for World Ministries (for the American Board records), the Board of Global Ministries of the United Methodist Church (for the Methodist-Episcopal and the United Brethren in Christ records), the Presbyterian Historical Society, the Archives and Historical Collections of the Episcopal Church, the Disciples of Christ Historical Society, the General Conference of Seventh-day Adventists, the Young Men's Christian Association, Bishop Paul Locke A. Granadosin (for the Rebecca Parrish Papers and the Harry Farmer diary), and Herbert S. Damon (for the letters of his father, Herbert M. Damon, in the records of the General Missionary Conference of the Free Methodist Church). When quoting from manuscript materials, all errors and peculiarities of style, grammar, spelling, and the like have been retained without the use of *sic*.

Portions of this book have appeared previously in the *Pacific Historical Review*, *Church History*, *Methodist History*, *Philippine Studies*, and *Kabar Seberang* and are included herein with permission. In addition, a slightly different version of chapter seven appears in Peter W. Stanley, ed., *Reappraising an Empire: New Perspectives in Philippine American History*, Harvard Studies in American–East Asian Relations (Cambridge: Harvard University Press, 1984). It appears in this book with the permission of the editor and publisher.

I am also deeply grateful to the American Philosophical Society, the Henry R. Luce Foundation, and the University Research Institute, Dean Michael Austin of the Graduate School, and Dean Diana Natalicio of the College of Liberal Arts at the University of Texas at El Paso for financial support to conduct the research and prepare the manuscript for publication. Helen Wheatley typed the first draft, while Florence Dick prepared the final manuscript on a word processor. Mrs. Dick, an accomplished stylist and copy editor, also improved the manuscript in innumerable ways. To both I wish to express my appreciation for their professional attitude and cheerful disposition in the light of unreasonable demands made upon them.

My wife, Marlee, helped in the research and patiently listened to each draft of each chapter. The manuscript is better for her contributions.

Protestant Missionaries in the Philippines,
1898–1916

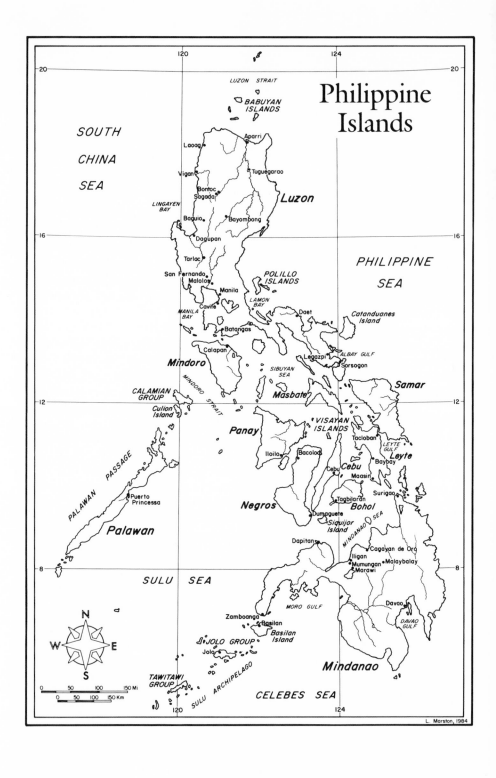

Philippine Islands

SOUTH

CHINA

SEA

LUZON STRAIT

*BABUYAN
ISLANDS*

Aparri

Laoag

Luzon

Vigan

Tuguegarao

Bontoc
Sagada

*LINGAYEN
BAY*

Baguio

Bayombong

Dagupan

PHILIPPINE

SEA

Tarlac

San Fernando
Malolos

*POLILLO
ISLANDS*

Manila

Cavite

*LAMON
BAY*

Daet

Catanduanes
Island

*MANILA
BAY*

Batangas

Calapan

Mindoro

Legazpi

ALBAY GULF

Sorsogon

*SIBUYAN
SEA*

Samar

*CALAMIAN
GROUP*

MINDORO STRAIT

Masbate

Culion
Island

*VISAYAN
ISLANDS*

Tacloban

*LEYTE
GULF*

Panay

Iloilo

Bacolod

Cebu

Cebu

Leyte

Baybay

Maasin

PALAWAN PASSAGE

Puerto
Princessa

Negros

Surigao

Tagbilaran

Bohol

Dumaguete

Siquijor
Island

Palawan

Dapitan

MINDANAO SEA

Cagayan de Oro

Iligan

Mumungan

Malaybalay

Marawi

SULU SEA

Davao

*DAVAO
GULF*

MORO GULF

Zamboanga

Basilan

Basilan
Island

JOLO GROUP

Jolo

Mindanao

*TAWITAWI
GROUP*

SULU ARCHIPELAGO

CELEBES SEA

N
W E
S

0   50   100   150 Mi
0   50   100   150 Km

L. Marston, 1984

1

Introduction

In 1521 a Portuguese explorer sailing under the Spanish flag landed on the islands that a later adventurer was to name *las Islas Filipinas*. Ferdinand Magellan became embroiled in a local feud and was killed on Mactan Island, near Cebu, by the forces of Lapu-lapu, a Filipino chieftain. Some of Magellan's forces managed to escape and returned to Spain, thus becoming the first men to circumnavigate the globe.

For several decades after Magellan's discovery, the Spanish did little to secure control of the islands. But in 1565 Miguel Lopez de Legazpi established a permanent Spanish settlement, and within a few years much of the Philippines was brought under Spanish rule, though sovereignty was never very effective in some of the remoter areas of the islands and in the Muslim areas of the South.

Spain ruled the islands for well over three hundred years, but in the last century of her rule, by which time her empire had been reduced to a shadow of its former self, new economic and political ideas began to disrupt the pattern of Philippine life. Discontent grew, an educated mestizo elite emerged, an incipient form of Filipino nationalism developed, and Spanish rule was increasingly precarious. In the last quarter of the nineteenth century a reform movement led by such patriots as Jose Rizal and Marcelo del Pilar began to demand constitutional reforms and more Filipino involvement in affairs of state. In the 1890s reformism shaded into revolution, and in 1896 fighting broke out. The hostilities ended temporarily in 1897 with the peace of Biak-na-bato but resumed shortly thereafter.

Had the Philippine revolution taken place fifty years earlier, Americans might have been more interested in it than they were in 1898, for in the early and middle parts of the century American commercial interests were second only to those of the British in the Philippines. But as the American merchant marine deteriorated in the years after the Civil War, contacts lessened. In 1876 the great American firm of Russell and Sturgis failed in the Philippines. This failure was followed in 1887 by the bankruptcy of Peale, Hubbell and Company.[1] Thereafter, although the United States maintained a consulate in the capital city, few Americans had any connections with the islands. Most could not have located them easily on a globe.[2]

Eventually, though, the United States almost certainly would have taken an interest in the Philippines, for the 1890s was a decade of expansion. With the deep depression that began in 1893, American firms began to look overseas to find new markets for their surplus products. China was the big hope for American exporters, and the Philippines were invitingly close to China. A whole range of noneconomic reasons also drove Americans toward expansion. The bitter domestic strife of the decade led some to suggest that overseas adventures might distract attention from internal problems. As Cecil Rhodes, the great English imperialist, was supposed to have said in 1895, "if you want to avoid civil war, you must become imperialists."[3] Others saw a need to expand for essentially Darwinian reasons. Virile civilizations and races expanded, the less fitted stagnated and died. Others wanted the United States to break out of its traditional isolation and become a great power. Finally, there were the humanitarian imperialists, those who thought the country had a duty to uplift and civilize the "lesser breeds."

While such currents of thought were circulating in the United States, the Cubans renewed their rebellion against Spain. The Americans instinctively sided with the rebels. Had Spain been able to end the rebellion quickly, the crisis that soon developed in Spanish-American relations might have passed. But she could not. The fighting dragged on, becoming brutal on both sides. Newspaper correspondents reported seeing hundreds of bodies along railroad tracks. Eventually President William McKinley, unable to get meaningful concessions from Spain and subjected to strong public and partisan pressures, led the nation into war in April 1898.

It is most unlikely that McKinley went to war to obtain Spanish possessions, particularly in the Far East. His purpose was to throw the Spanish out of Cuba. Nor, in all probability, was there a conspiracy of well placed imperialists to seize the Philippines once the war began, a story widely believed for many years.[4] Yet acquisition of the islands admittedly appeared conspiratorial. Less than two weeks after the war started, the commander of the American Asiatic fleet, Commodore George Dewey, sailed into Manila Bay and devastated the ships under the command of Admiral Patricio Montojo. Two weeks later American soldiers began preparations to sail for the islands, and on August 13 Spain surrendered the city of Manila after a sham battle (which, however, left six Americans and forty-nine Spaniards dead). The Americans, keeping the Filipino forces under Emilio Aguinaldo at arm's length, then entered the city and occupied it.

Conspiracy or not, these events brought the Philippines squarely into the American consciousness. Dewey became an instant hero. "You may fire when ready, Gridley," entered the American vocabulary. Opinion to keep the islands seemed to grow by the hour. Business interests noted their proximity to those 400 million potential Chinese customers, while reports of immense amounts of gold in the islands themselves circulated in some circles. Those who wanted Americans to break from their isolationist past saw a golden opportunity for the United States to establish itself as a major world power. Humanitarians could not think of turning the islands back to "cruel" Spain. Diplomats argued that it would be silly for the United States to withdraw, for this would only lead to German, Japanese, or possibly British control of the islands. Politicians feared the consequences of lowering the flag, and all agreed that the Filipinos could not govern themselves. There would be unstinting civil war for fifty years, it was widely thought, if the Filipinos had no oversight. There seemed no choice. As McKinley was reported to have said to a group of visiting Methodists, "there was nothing left for us to do but to take them all, and to educate the Filipinos, and uplift them and civilize and Christianize them, and by God's grace do the very best we could by them, as our fellowmen for whom Christ also died."[5] It came as no surprise, then, that the Treaty of Paris, which ended the war, transferred the Philippine Islands to the United States. In return the United States paid Spain $20 million, ostensibly to cover a portion of the islands' public debt.

Throughout these exciting months most Protestant churches encouraged an expansionist outlook. They supported the war against Spain, then lobbied for the acquisition of the Philippine Islands.[6] The Protestants wanted the United States to rescue the Cubans and the Filipinos from what they perceived as Spanish misrule. But they also realized that American control of the Spanish islands would open the way for the Protestant message to be preached in areas from which it had hitherto been excluded.

In spite of President McKinley's desire to Christianize the natives, most Filipinos were, of course, already Christians, though of the Roman Catholic persuasion. The friars traveling with Magellan had performed the first mass in the Philippines on Easter Sunday, 1521. As Spain established her authority in the ensuing years she brought with her the state's religion.

Spain succeeded admirably in her task. The tenacious Moros in the south held fast to Islam, and many Igorots and other mountain and forest people retained their traditional animistic faiths. But the rest of the population (the great majority) adopted Spanish Catholicism, though with distinctly Filipino nuances. Here, as elsewhere, a syncretic Catholicism emerged.

As in Spanish America, the clergy in the Philippines sometimes raised fundamental, often embarrassing, questions. Did the crown even have the right to establish sovereignty over the islands? If it did, did not the agents of the state have some obligation to treat the people fairly and kindly? To some extent the clergy served to mitigate the harsher aspects of Spanish colonialism.[7] But the church could also be oppressive, and the origins of the discontent in the nineteenth century can be traced to Filipino resentment at ecclesiastical, as well as political, abuses. The various orders, for example, seldom trained Filipinos for the priesthood.[8] The friars in particular were the targets of the nineteenth-century reformers and revolutionaries, so much that in January 1899 Aguinaldo ordered the friars expelled from the territory he controlled.[9]

Regardless of what judgments are made about the quality and character of Catholicism in the islands, it is scarcely disputable that Protestantism was virtually unknown in the islands before 1898. The Spanish maintained strict control of reading matter entering the islands, and it was a crime to propagandize on behalf of any faith other than Roman Catholicism. Even when the British occupied Manila for two years (1762–64) during the Seven Years War, they made no effort to introduce Anglicanism or to interfere very much at all with the established faith.[10]

In the nineteenth century Protestants made occasional attempts to smuggle Bibles into the Philippines, the first such effort occurring in 1828 under the auspices of the American Bible Society.[11] The most serious attempt to create a Protestant presence occurred in 1889, when Nicolas Manrique Alonso Lallave, a former Dominican priest in the Philippines who had become a Protestant minister in Spain, and Francisco de P. Castells, who came from a business family in Spain and who had also become a Protestant minister, traveled to the Philippines with the intention of distributing Scriptures in the Spanish and Pangasinan languages. Lallave himself had translated the Scriptures into the latter language. Owing to a newly published circular that seemed to promise religious liberty, the pair hoped to work openly and applied for a permit to distribute their wares, most of which the customs authorities had confiscated. They probably also intended to engage in more far-reaching evangelistic efforts. But the authorities stalled, the permit never came, and both Lallave and Castells became ill, perhaps, many Protestants later thought, the victims of a plot to poison them. Lallave in fact died. Castells attempted to carry on but was jailed in Bilibid prison for a few days, then bailed out and allowed to leave the country on the condition that he never return.[12]

As a result of the sporadic efforts of the Bible societies and committed individuals, there may have been a very few Filipinos by the late nineteenth century who believed in something like Protestantism. There was without doubt a Masonic movement, which, if not Protestant, was at least antifriar. But it was only with the coming of the Americans and the promise of religious freedom that Protestantism became significant.

Officers of the Young Men's Christian Association (YMCA) and army chaplains led the earliest Protestant services on Philippine soil, the first being held exactly one week after the occupation of Manila.[13] The YMCA remained in the islands first working with American troops but later establishing facilities for American and Filipino civilians. Though its officials were not technically missionaries, they considered the Y an evangelical organization and maintained close ties with the missions.

Two Bible societies, the American Bible Society and the British and Foreign Bible Society, were active in the islands very soon after the American occupation of Manila. The American Bible Society, in fact, had a man in the capital city late in September 1898.[14] The following year it appointed the Reverend Jay C. Goodrich, a Methodist minister, as its first official representative. Both Bible societies served as allies of the missions by translating the Scriptures into the various Filipino languages and by distributing them. Relations were sometimes tense between the two societies, however,[15] and in 1919 the British society withdrew and left the Philippines entirely in the hands of its American counterpart.

Aside from the Y officials, the chaplains, and perhaps the first Bible society agent, the first Protestant "missionaries" in the islands were probably Mr. and Mrs. Arthur W. Prautch. Prautch had been a Methodist Episcopal missionary in India, but when he arrived in Manila shortly after the Americans took the capital he was no longer affiliated with the mission board. He came apparently as a businessman, but evangelism and Christian social action were close to his heart. In cooperation with one of the chaplains, he and his wife opened a "Soldier's Institute"; subsequently he preached before Filipino audiences as well. An energetic and controversial man, "Deacon" Prautch maintained connections with several of the Protestant missions, as well as with the Philippine Independent Church, a schismatic Catholic church that broke away from the Roman communion in 1902.

The first official Methodist Episcopal missionary representative to arrive was Bishop James M. Thoburn, who as bishop of India and Southeast Asia had long wanted to open evangelistic work in the Philippines.[16] He arrived in Manila just as the Philippine American War broke out, opened a church, licensed Prautch as a local preacher, and left after about two weeks. Apparently the first full-time Methodist missionaries to arrive were women from the Women's Foreign Missionary Society. Arriving in February 1900, they edged out male missionaries affiliated with the Board of Foreign Missions who arrived a few weeks later.[17]

The Methodist mission soon became the largest mission in the Philippines. By 1916 at least fifty missionaries had served in the mission, and the church claimed about 45,000 members. By 1925 the figure was over 65,000.[18]

The mission board of the Presbyterian Church in the U.S.A. sent William H. Lingle to the islands in 1898 to study the feasibility of establishing a mission station there. Because of growing tensions between Filipinos and Americans and because of greater needs elsewhere, Lingle advised against sending missionaries to the Philippines.[19] The board, however, had already planned to begin work there and sent James B. Rodgers and his wife to the Philippines. They arrived in April 1899, about the time Lingle's report arrived in the United States. The Rodgerses were probably the first fully accredited, permanent Protestant missionaries in the islands. They stayed nearly forty years and began what was the second largest mission in the Philippines. At least sixty-five missionaries served in the islands between 1899 and 1916, and by 1925 the Presbyterians could claim a membership of about 15,700.[20]

The Episcopalians were represented very early in the islands, with several army chaplains. The same year Rodgers arrived, the Brotherhood of St. Andrew sent the Reverend James L. Smiley to the islands. He subsequently accepted appointment as the first missionary of the Domestic and Foreign Missionary Society of the Episcopal Church, but soon had to return to the United States.[21] Only in November 1901 did the Episcopalians establish permanent work, with the arrival of John A. Staunton, Jr., and Walter C. Clapp, both of whom remained for several years.

About the time Staunton and Clapp arrived, Charles Henry Brent accepted an offer to be Episcopal missionary bishop of the Philippines. Brent left for the islands on May 17, 1902, in the company of William Howard Taft, who was the first civil governor of the Philippines. After a leisurely trip by way of Europe and the Suez Canal (including a lengthy stopover in Rome), the bishop arrived in Manila on August 24, 1902. He retained his post until 1918 but managed numerous trips to the United States and elsewhere. Some of his coreligionists joked that Brent was the bishop *from* the Philippines rather than bishop *of* the Philippines. Nevertheless, Brent maintained the closest ties of any missionary with the American authorities. The Episcopal mission, never very large, confined its work primarily to the American and European community, the Chinese, and the non-Christian Filipinos of the mountains.

In 1900 both the American Baptist Missionary Union and the Christian and Missionary Alliance sent missionaries to the Philippines. The Baptists, who established a relatively small mission on Panay and Negros, actually had the longest ties with the Philippines. Alonso Lallave and other Spanish and Filipino Protestants in Spain had for some years maintained close connections with Baptist work in that country. The first Baptist missionary to arrive, in fact, was Eric Lund, a Swedish Baptist who had been in Spain for many years. In 1898 he converted Braulio Manikan, a Filipino from Capiz

Province, who had once been trained for the priesthood.[22] When Lund arrived in the Philippines in April 1900, Manikan was with him.

The Alliance was less successful in establishing a permanent foothold. Its first missionary, Elizabeth White, remained in Manila and worked with the Presbyterian mission. In 1901 she married a Presbyterian missionary and transferred her credentials to her husband's church. The Alliance revived its work in 1902 when John McKee, a former soldier in the islands, went to Mindanao under the board's auspices. His death the following year ended Alliance work for the time being. Only in 1907 did the Alliance resume work. It did so by absorbing a small Peniel mission that had existed for several years in Zamboanga. Begun by the middle of 1902, if not before, by an Apache Indian named William Abel, the Peniel mission attracted a few independent missionaries before it was taken over by the Alliance.[23] Though the Alliance mission was small, it was energetic and, according to Frank Laubach, accomplished near miracles considering its small staff and meager finances.[24]

The year 1901 saw the arrival of missionaries from the United Brethren in Christ, a group that confined its work to the Ilocano province of La Union, and the Disciples of Christ (Foreign Christian Missionary Society), which worked in various parts of Luzon. By 1925 the United Brethren counted some 2,858 converts, including the illustrious Camilo Osias, who became an important figure in Philippine education. The Disciples claimed 7,326 members, making that church the third largest Protestant denomination in the country.[25]

In 1902 the first representative of the American Board, Robert F. Black, went to Davao to open a mission station. He and his wife were the only Congregationalists in the islands until 1908, when Dr. and Mrs. Charles T. Sibley arrived to reinforce the work and to open a hospital. It was another seven years before more American Board missionaries arrived, including the eminent Frank Laubach, who roundly lambasted the board for its neglect of an important mission field.

The Seventh-day Adventists sent a colporteur to the Philippines in 1905 and established a permanent presence in 1908 with the arrival of Elder L. V. Finster and his wife. Something of a thorn in the side of the other Protestant missionaries, the Adventists claimed 2,924 members by 1925.[26]

In addition to the accredited missionaries, school teachers Herbert M. Damon and his wife served in Laoag as unofficial missionaries of the Free Methodist Church. They left in 1908 to become official Free Methodist missionaries in India.[27] Also operating in Manila were at least one Christian Science Society (though whether it attempted to convert Filipinos is not known) and perhaps a few Mormons.[28]

The missionaries constituted an important and articulate segment of the

American colonial population. They helped shape attitudes in the Philippines and in the United States about Filipino culture and about the American presence in the islands; on occasion they helped shape policy as well. They helped reconcile Filipinos to their new fate and were allies of the government in what both perceived as a "civilizing" mission. At the same time, they viewed themselves as the conscience of the American experiment and did not hesitate to judge other Americans harshly for not living up to what they believed was the best in the American tradition. An examination of their ideas, attitudes, and perceptions, then, helps us understand better the American colonial experience and the colonial mentality.

The study covers the years from 1898, when the United States first entered the Philippines, through 1916. The later date was selected primarily because it was in that year that the United States Congress passed the Jones Act, which for the first time made it clear that independence was the ultimate goal of American policy. The year 1916 also marks, in a rough sort of way, the end of the first generation of American missionaries. By then some of the most outspoken missionaries, men like Homer C. Stuntz of the Methodist mission, Stealy B. Rossiter, pastor to the English-speaking Presbyterian church in Manila, and Mercer G. Johnston, rector of the Episcopal cathedral, had already left the islands. Bishop Brent would leave in a year. At the same time younger missionaries, like Frank Laubach who arrived in 1915, brought new ideas to the islands. Finally, intellectual forces were at work in the missionary community at large that would, by the 1920s, throw the entire movement into confusion and disarray. Such forces were weakly apparent by 1916, but they had not yet disturbed the overall consensus.

PART I

Missionary Motivations and Interrelationships

2

Missionary Motivations

He may smite the hand that blesses him, but he must be blessed.
We want to do it [even] if he doesn't want it done.

> Bruce Kershner, missionary
> of the Disciples of Christ

Unless *the Philippines* are saved we shall lose Asia.

> Frank Laubach, missionary
> of the American Board

The Protestant missionary crusade of the late nineteenth century had both secular and religious roots. It was part of the bumptious spirit of nationalism that seemed to grip the nation in the years after the Civil War, and to many Americans Protestant beliefs were very much a part of American nationalism.[1] In the 1890s, the most obvious expression of national spirit was overseas expansion. Though not everyone was pleased with the new aggressiveness that characterized the country and its foreign policy, it seemed to appeal to a majority, particularly to the younger generation. Combined with nationalistic expansion was a spirit of humanitarianism. A seeming paradox, humanitarian sentiment encouraged expansion, even war. It helped propel the United States into a war for the liberation of Cuba and was an ingredient in the imperialism that followed.[2] True believers in the "white man's burden" attested to the strength of humanitarian sentiment in imperial expansion.

Implicit in all of these forces—nationalism, humanitarianism, imperialism—was a sense of mission. Though the concept of mission was often defined in a patriotic and secular way, the atmosphere was surely such as to encourage the religiously inclined to expand their horizons.[3]

The more direct root of the missionary crusade reached to the revivals of the famed evangelist, Dwight L. Moody, and his followers. Beginning in the 1870s, Moody and his colleagues crossed the continent and urged sinful men and women to surrender themselves to Christ. Young people seemed especially open to Moody's simple message, and some of them felt compelled to devote their lives to spreading the Word around the world. That the revivals had a direct effect on the subsequent missionary movement in the Philippines is attested to by James B. Rodgers, the leader of the Presbyterian mission, who in 1919, after twenty years in the Philippines, expressed his hope that a Filipino would arise who would "be the Moody of his country."[4]

In addition to stirring up interest generally in religion and missions, the Moody revivals contributed to the missionary crusade by laying the groundwork for new missionary support institutions, of which the Student Volunteer Movement (SVM) was the most important. The idea for such an organization arose in 1886 when a group of religious enthusiasts persuaded Moody himself to invite two hundred college and seminary students to Northfield, Massachusetts, for a Bible study conference. By the time the conference ended, half of the participants had declared their intention to become foreign missionaries.

Out of the Northfield meeting emerged the Volunteers. Formally organized in 1888 by students from the Young Men's Christian Association and three related organizations, the SVM encouraged students to apply to established mission boards for overseas service. John R. Mott of the YMCA became the movement's leading light and served as chairman until his retirement in the 1930s. Under Mott's energetic and able direction, the Volunteers had by 1893 established 136 mission study groups across the country. By 1910 the figure had risen to 2,084 with 25,208 students enrolled. In 1914 over 40,000 students were associated with the SVM.[5]

Though the larger significance of the Student Volunteer Movement has recently been questioned,[6] there is little doubt that it and kindred organizations like the YMCA influenced many people to apply for missionary service. Many of those who ultimately went to the Philippines had been Volunteers or active in Y work.[7]

In addition to the influence of revivals and the missionary support organizations they produced, aspiring missionaries often testified to the influence of those already in the field. Episcopalian Mercer Johnston recalled the influence of a friend in college who became a missionary in China. Corwin Francis Hartzell decided to apply to the Methodist board after hearing an appeal from a missionary in the Philippines. Methodist missionary Bishop William F. Oldham influenced Daniel H. Klinefelter to apply, while Marvin Rader left his pulpit for the islands at the request of Homer C. Stuntz, the presiding elder of the Methodist mission. Grace Myrtle Edmonson, betrothed to a prospective missionary, was deeply influenced by her aunt, a missionary in Persia. The one Free Methodist missionary in the islands stated that he had felt a call to the mission field ever since an acquaintance went to Africa when he was a child.[8]

Of course, all missionary applicants professed to feel called by God. The revivals, the missionary statesmen, the missionaries in the field were but God's agents. Often the prospective missionary tested the call, sometimes for a matter of weeks, sometimes for several years, to assure himself of its validity. Such was the case with F. David Sholin, a missionary of the Christian and Missionary Alliance, who fortunately left behind one of the most detailed, publicly available (most missionary personnel records are closed to researchers) accounts of the process by which he became a missionary in the Philippines.

Sholin's experience appears to be entirely typical. Like most missionary applicants, Sholin spent several years in religious work at home before he applied. He worked with young people in Portland, Oregon, where in 1906 he joined the Alliance. He took an ever increasing interest in the work of his church, and in 1910 began to work full time for the Alliance in eastern Washington.

Like many other applicants, Sholin was directly influenced by a missionary. In 1911, at the Alliance's spring convention in Everett, Washington, Sholin encountered the strong-willed Hulda Lund, on leave from her post in Zamboanga, the largest city on Mindanao. Though Sholin had never before considered missionary service in the Philippines, Lund's suggestion that he go to Zamboanga took hold of him. He prayed over the matter, consulted with church officials, and tentatively decided to go. When his provisional decision became known, he was asked to sing a hymn entitled, "Christ for the Philippines," which left him "so wrought upon I could hardly contain myself. After I had finished singing my heart overflowed and such peace as came into my soul can never be expressed." He tested his feelings further, was convinced that the call was genuine, and was soon with the Alliance mission in the Philippines.[9]

Sholin never discussed his deeper purposes in accepting a missionary assignment. There was, however, a comfortable certainty about the missionary undertaking in those days. Arthur J. Brown, secretary of the Presbyterian board and a prolific writer, concluded that there were three primary motivations for mission work (in a book later called a classic on the subject). First, there was "the soul's experience in Christ." If, like Sholin and the others, one had a deep and genuine spiritual experience, there arose "an overmastering impulse to communicate it to others." Second, Brown pointed to "the world's need of Christ." Though Brown included elements of the Social Gospel in this category, the most important need was to save the souls of the unchurched and thus prepare them "for eternal companionship with God." Though Brown conceded that non-Christians might in theory be saved, few in fact were, he felt. "Taking non-christian peoples as we know them," he wrote, ". . . it is sorrowfully, irrefutably true that they are living in known sin, and that by no possible stretch of charity can they be considered beyond the necessity for the revealed gospel." Third, there was the "command of Christ." The Great Commission, Brown wrote, was "not a request; not a suggestion. It leaves nothing to choice. It is an order," he insisted, "comprehensive and unequivocal, a clear, peremptory, categorical imperative: 'Go!'"[10] Though David Sholin did not say so in so many words, he almost certainly shared the motivations Brown analyzed.

Evangelism at home was, of course, an important duty, and social service was not to be ignored. But mission spokespersons considered foreign evangelism more important. God's "love seeks the most distant," wrote Brown. Christians needed to share His message with "the oppressed blacks of Africa and the starving millions of India." The fundamental reason for this was the greater spiritual deprivation in heathen lands. Without accepting Christ, there was no hope. "It was the spiritual need which made the unevangelized Chinese more abjectly to be pitied than the tubercular sweatshop seamstress or the starving Navajo," writes one scholar. To go abroad was the most sacrificial and complete manner of meeting the duty incumbent upon a Christian.[11]

Among the Philippine missionaries, the desire to save the heathen from perdition emerges most clearly in the letters of Herbert M. Damon, an unofficial missionary of the Free Methodist Church who lived in Laoag. Ever since he was a child, Damon had felt a call to mission work. After several years of introspection and prayer, he eventually "felt the load of the heathen" upon him and experienced "an intense burden for the lost." The desire to spread the Good News to those who had not heard of the Lord was overpowering. In the Philippines, Damon's position as a school teacher limited his effectiveness as a missionary, but informally he attempted to evangelize the people around him. He apparently enjoyed some success, for he wrote that he had seen his prayers answered "in the conversion of some souls and one brought out in the light of entire holiness."[12]

Missionaries of the Christian and Missionary Alliance also tended to view their task largely in terms of saving the heathen. As Elizabeth White, the first official Alliance missionary put it in 1900, the hope was to make known "the fourfold Gospel . . . to these people." John McKee, the first active Alliance missionary, testified that he had prayed for more than a dozen years "to be sent to the heathen." McKee died of cholera in 1903, leaving the Alliance without any representative for a few years. Eventually, however, the Alliance absorbed the already existing Peniel mission in Zamboanga. Like the Alliance personnel, the Peniel missionaries were primarily concerned with the salvation of souls; and there was little if any ideological adjustment necessary when they became a part of the Alliance. In account after account, the Zamboanga-based missionaries emphasized the need to spread the Gospel to Roman Catholic, Moro, and pagan alike.

Hulda Lund, for example, voiced great concern for the "40,000 souls" of a nearby mountain tribe (probably the Subanos). "They must hear, if the Great Commission is to be fully carried out. . . ," she wrote. "They are dear to His heart." [13]

Still, explicit references to "saving the heathen" are relatively rare in the Philippine missionary records. In part, this was probably due to the embarrassing fact that most Filipinos were at least nominal Roman Catholic Christians, thus making the term *heathen* inappropriate—except in the minds of those missionaries who considered Latin Catholicism unchristian. Reluctance to use the phrase also resulted, one suspects, from the fact that the missionaries entered the Philippines at precisely the time when religious thinkers were beginning to see more value in non-Western religions than they had previously. Equally significant in undermining the older rhetoric was the fact that the Social Gospel was beginning to have an impact on American Protestantism just as the missionaries began arriving in the islands. Since the Social Gospel emphasized institutional sin and the need for societal transformation, instead of the regeneration of individuals, the idea of "saving the heathen" began to sound a bit archaic. [14]

Nevertheless, the early missionary thrust into the islands still emphasized the conversion of individuals to the Protestant faith, as opposed to the concerns of the Social Gospel. On balance, this was true not just for the more theologically conservative groups but for all the missions. To some, the desire to save souls was so compelling that they felt duty bound to persist even when they met with entrenched resistance. "He may smite the hand that blesses him," wrote Bruce Kershner, a Disciples missionary, "but he must be blessed. We want to do it [even] if he doesn't want it done." [15]

As Kershner implied, many of the missionaries felt a sense of urgency about saving souls. To the traditionalists, of course, the need for haste was always apparent, since the soul would perish unless Christ had been accepted before death. Those who believed in the imminent Second Coming were likewise driven by a sense of dire necessity. "Let us remember, and believe, that the coming of the Lord draweth nigh," wrote Hulda Lund, "and what remains to be done, must needs be done speedily." The Seventh-day Adventists, tracing their origins back to the millennialist teachings of William Miller, were the most committed theologically to the imminent Second Coming. The most important reason to go to the Philippines, wrote an Adventist in 1906, was "that the coming of Christ is near at hand." The fact that the Adventists had scarcely begun work in the islands several years after the American occupation opened the territory to Protestants was therefore a matter of embarrassment for their church. [16]

Others, not so affected by a belief in the imminent Second Coming, felt compelled to work quickly on the grounds that God would keep the doors open for an undefined, but nevertheless short, period of time. "Now is the time for us as Christians to go in and possess this land," wrote a Baptist, "for the time may come when they will not endure sound doctrine & when the forces of evil will be gathered and arrayed against us." Charles W. Briggs, the Baptist leader, was similarly convinced that missionaries must strike in full force at once. "The whole game is either going to be won or lost during the first three innings!" he wrote in 1903.[17]

To others, the sense of urgency sprang more from political and cultural realities than from direct providential involvement. Many missionaries, for example, while welcoming the American presence in the Philippines, feared the consequences of the sudden impact of secular American civilization on the allegedly unformed Filipino character. Under American-inspired changes, a nation of infidels was probable, they feared, unless the missionaries worked quickly to produce a population that could resist the corruption of secular Western culture. Though such thought was present in various missions,[18] it was most prominent in the Episcopalian.

To be sure, the Episcopalian mission included men and women who were motivated by traditional evangelical concerns. But the *urgent* need to save primitive souls from eternal perdition was alien to the Episcopalian mind. Episcopalian missionaries believed, of course, that the non-Christian Igorots who lived in the mountains of central Luzon needed to be evangelized, to learn of and accept the Christian God, but not because they feared that God would condemn them to everlasting punishment if they were not converted at once. Their God was a more humane, rational, loving Father. "It might be—I think it probably so—that pagan superstitions are measureably adequate for the religious needs of tribes who are wholly excluded from outside contacts," wrote Bishop Charles Henry Brent in an exceptionally well argued essay. "It is due to God's ordering and not man's that such peoples are in the main what they are and where they are. Their twilight beliefs are God's witness to Himself, and by their loyalty to the dim knowledge they possess they must be judged." When one old Igorot woman declined baptism on the grounds that she was too old to change her ways, she was asked, "But what will you say to Christ after death, when He asks you why you were not baptized?" "I will say," she replied, "'Because I was too old—and He will understand.'"[19]

Still, the Episcopalians felt they must move quickly to prepare these "children of nature" for the inevitable contact with the corrupting, debilitating aspects of advancing "civilization." As Mercer Johnston put it, the Igorot, "naked in soul and body," was about to "fight the great fight with the ungloved forces of what we are pleased to call civilization, which is marching on him, battle-hand foremost." Brent felt that the fate of the mountain people would be even worse than that of the American Indians if the missionaries failed to invigorate their spiritual and moral character. Irving Spencer, stationed in Mindanao, felt the same way about the Bagobo people who inhabited the slopes of Mt. Apo. "The vital necessity," he wrote in 1905, "is to make our entry before any hurtful white element arrives for trading purposes with the vices of the civilized West at present all unknown here." [20]

To protect the Filipinos, it was important not only to invigorate their character but to elevate the spiritual and moral qualities of the American population in the islands. Several missions made efforts along these lines, but only the Episcopalian saw this as its first priority. The main purpose of Episcopalian work, wrote Mercer Johnston, was "to try to keep Americans in the Philippine Islands mindful of Baptismal vows made by them, or for them, in the United States, so that they will be an example of godly living to the whole Filipino population." If the character of the Americans in the islands was not of a high quality, Bishop Brent told a missionary convention in 1904, "then I say American civilization . . . is an unwarranted interference." Walter C. Clapp, who was assigned to the Episcopalian mission station in Baguio, agreed. It was the Church's task in the Philippines, he wrote, "to do all she can to hallow our contact with these people, by preserving our own countrymen from that colonial degeneration which belies religion and contaminates the bewildered native." [21]

For several missionaries, the need for haste concerned issues that went well beyond the fate of the islands themselves. To these persons the entrance of the United States into the Orient as a colonial power had ramifications far beyond the Philippines. Small though the new territory was, these missionaries, like some other Americans, felt that it held the key to "the mammoth Oriental drama now presenting itself on the world's stage." Victory for Protestantism and Americanism in the Philippines meant a better chance for success in the Orient as a whole. As Frank Laubach put it, "unless *the Philippines* are saved, we shall lose Asia." [22]

To missionaries of this persuasion, the Philippines were tremendously alluring. In other Asian nations, with their "hoary and revered civilizations," the missionaries were fortunate if they could report a handful of converts even after decades of effort, and then they were seldom certain if the conversions were genuine. By contrast, in the Philippines they saw "a barefooted nation, paddling in its ricefields with primitive tools, building its house with bamboo slats." Its civilization was fluid, open to new ideas. [23] Instead of a handful of converts, the missionaries anticipated hundreds of thousands, perhaps even millions.

Preaching the Gospel—the traditional evangelical method—was the primary means of reaching individuals. But many missionaries thought that their work entailed more. They raised up churches and kept detailed statistics on conversions, but they also established a wide variety of philanthropic institutions including hospitals, dispensaries, orphanages, dormitories, schools, colleges, libraries, community centers, settlement houses, and social clubs. The missionaries usually insisted that these institutional ministries supplemented preaching. The ultimate end of missionary work, they insisted, remained individual salvation. "This must never be forgotten," said Bruce Kershner in 1908. "Educational, medical, literary or any other kind of work is carried on for the contribution it makes to this first end."[24]

Of all their institutional undertakings, the missionaries were the most defensive about medical work, and to justify using the board's scarce money to send a physician and finance a hospital—instead of supporting a "regular" missionary—they virtually had to contend that medical work contributed far more than healed bodies. It had to deliver souls as well. Thus, missionaries were quick to point out that patients received Bibles in the hospitals in the hope that conversions might take place even before they were discharged.[25] They also argued that, having ministered to the physical needs of the people, they had better access to their homes for more direct evangelism. In 1906, for example, a Baptist wrote that medical work was valuable in keeping "their hearts open until the seed of the Gospel can take root." Even Episcopalian Bishop Brent insisted that medical missions were ultimately evangelical tools. "I do not care to have a hospital, or a dispensary—for that matter—where the mere exercise of scientific skill is the sum total of treatment," he wrote in 1907. "If we haven't physicians who can bring into play in an active manner the potent influences of divine power in connection with their operative skill," he explained, "we had better not attempt medical missionary work."[26]

Most of the missionary physicians in the Philippines were, in fact, men and women of deep spiritual commitment who considered evangelism one of their most important responsibilities. None was more committed in this regard than Rebecca Parrish, a Methodist physician who arrived in Manila in 1906 to establish the still functioning Mary Johnston Hospital in the slums of Tondo. She remained in the islands until World War II. Parrish insisted on high quality medical care. Physicians associated with the hospital had to be members of the American Medical Association and its Manila affiliate. But Parrish's concerns went far beyond caring for the physical needs of her patients, for she was an active evangelist. "In foreign mission work," she wrote, "we are ever on the lookout for new ways to present the gospel." Virtually every day she displayed a new religious poster near the hospital's front gate for passersby to read. Vesper services were held on the hospital lawn. Daily Bible lessons were given in the clinic. Religious

songs were translated, and religious meetings were held on the plaza. Sunday school papers were distributed not only to the churches but to nearby public schools. "Scattering the Gospel Seed—PAYS!!" she exclaimed. One night, after an exhausting day in the hospital, Parrish went down to the seawall to rest, only to encounter two Filipino boys who wanted to know about Jesus. "So," she related, "away out there 10,000 miles from home, in a tropic midnight, I fought my weariness; and for an hour, I told those Filipino Boys about Jesus!"[27] Surely Rebecca Parrish must have satisfied even the most hardened critic of medical missions!

Looking back after twenty years in the Philippines, Presbyterian James B. Rodgers recalled that "the spirit of preaching the Gospel, of genuine untiring evangelism [was] the dominant note. It is true that Silliman [a Presbyterian school] had started and that Drs. Hall and Langheim were doing their excellent medical work," he added, "but even their work was subordinated to the breaking of the ground for the evangelistic work." The measure of success, then, lay not in better living conditions, a transformed culture, improved education, or even in healed bodies, but in conversions. The Presbyterian goal was to double the membership annually.[28]

Yet the Social Gospel and Progressive Movement, with their emphasis on societal transformation and humanitarian reform, were not without impact on the missionaries. As early as 1908, Arthur J. Brown acknowledged that a number of "secondary motivations" influenced the missionaries. In addition to saving souls, the missionary often thought of himself as an "advance agent of civilization" who spoke out against such remnants of barbarism as slavery, polygamy, and cannibalism, and who taught the Horatio Alger virtues of honesty, sobriety, thriftiness, purity, and industriousness. Such motives, thought Brown, appealed "particularly to persons of the intellectual type." The "emotional type" of person was more likely to exhibit another of the secondary motivations, the philanthropic. Medical and educational undertakings were the most prominent results of the philanthropic mind, Brown thought. Brown considered such motivations legitimate for missionaries, but he was disquieted at the "growing disposition to exalt this whole class of [secondary] motives."[29]

Brown had a right to be concerned, for some Philippine missionaries were clearly influenced by Progressive thought. Harry Farmer, for example, admired Upton Sinclair's socialist novel, *The Jungle*. Episcopalian Walter C. Clapp also admitted an attraction for socialism, though whether this affected his ministry in the Philippines is not clear. Another Episcopalian, Margaret Payson Waterman, came directly out of the Settlement House Movement, which was a central element on the altruistic side of Progressivism. Leaving a teaching position in 1890, Waterman joined the Rivington Street Settlement in New York and subsequently spent six years

as parish visitor for the Church of the Ascension. In 1897 she spent several months in London to become familiar with philanthropic organizations there, after which she accepted a position with the New York Charity Organization. She then moved to Boston, where she worked at Denison House. She became a parish worker at the Church of St. Stephen, where she met Charles Henry Brent. In the Philippines, Brent placed her in charge of the Episcopalian settlement house in Tondo.[30]

The attitudes and activities of these and other missionaries indicate the growing influence of the "secondary motivations." As a Methodist missionary put it, missionaries ought "to quicken public conscience; to nourish and stimulate moral and spiritual fiber devitalized by this Oriental atmosphere; to call men back to old ideals, and to insist that Christ shall be the pattern of the East."[31] The fact that the Methodists established a very active Committee on Public Morals, which on occasion stimulated public and political pressure to bring about moral reform, indicates that the Methodist missionaries were concerned with more than the salvation of individuals.

There was a Social Gospel commitment in other missions as well. Though the Baptists maintained one of the strongest commitments to traditional evangelism ("It is all well enough to get the good will of the people," wrote Henry W. Munger, "but our objective is to win souls, not merely to make friends"), their mission included some of the most devoted Social Gospel advocates of all. The aim of Baptist hospital work, wrote Munger himself in 1912, was "nothing less than to revolutionize the hygenic ideas and habits of the people." Edith Steinmetz and her husband also emphasized societal transformation. Cleanliness would prevent disease, education would free the mind, "and we shall rejoice that to us was given a part in the program of the world's redemption," she wrote. The Baptists also spoke out most strongly against the exploitation of the peasants.[32]

The Presbyterians excelled in educational work, and while the salvation of souls no doubt remained an important premise of such undertakings, some missionaries placed increasing emphasis on good work itself. Kenneth P. MacDonald informed students who had inquired about enrolling in a Presbyterian dormitory that he was in the Philippines "not so much to convert the Filipinos to Protestantism as to help them become the men and women that it is possible for them to be." Of course, MacDonald was attempting to attract non-Protestant Filipinos to the dorm and may have concealed from them his deeper purpose. But about the same time Charles Glunz, who was in charge of vocational training at Silliman Institute (which would later evolve into Silliman University, one of the finest private schools in the country), put intellectual and vocational training on a par with religious conversion. "We believe in combining with this that religious train-

ing which causes men to accept and follow Christ," he wrote. "But we believe also in the industrial training which will enable our students to become producers and so help themselves and their country toward economic independence."[33]

The Episcopalians, too, while never losing sight of the need for individual regeneration, established several organizations whose directly religious character was tenuous. Of these the Columbia Club, a YMCA-type social organization that provided athletic facilities for American and European men, was the most open to attack. Its purpose, which was to provide a moral alternative to the dissipation associated with the typical colonial club, fit in well with the Episcopalian hope to upgrade the character of the American community. But whether it had a truly religious character may be doubted. Mercer G. Johnston, rector of the Cathedral Parish of St. Mary and St. John in Manila, referred to the club as "respectably pagan" with little hope of becoming "really Christian" any time soon.[34]

Bishop Brent, however, always regarded humanitarian work as a legitimate part of the mission's concern. The end in view, he stated, was "to minister to the people among whom we live in soul, mind & body & to act as a nexus between the Americans & Filipinos."[35] If anything, Brent moved toward the humanitarian side of the work over the years. This was especially so with respect to the Islamic Moros, whose tenacious spirit of independence he came to admire. By the early 1910s, their conversion seems not to have been of immediate concern to him.

In sum, the stated motivations included a call from God to save souls and, to a lesser but increasing extent, to engage in good works for their own sake. But were there other factors beyond a sincere desire to save the heathen and/or better their lives that entered into the missionaries' decision to go abroad?

The evidence is admittedly sketchy, but here and there suggestive passages appear in the records. Stealy B. Rossiter, the fiery minister of the English-speaking Presbyterian church in Manila, wrote that the missionaries, who were "sweeter, richer, holier than most men," had a goal beyond the salvation of foreigners: the achievement of their own salvation by doing God's work. "It is that glimpse of the great Reward," Rossiter wrote, "that hope of seeing the king face to face, that hope of hearing the Master say, 'well done, good and faithful servant,' that keeps the spirit brave and sustained in the intolerable loneliness." One of the first women missionaries in the islands, Cornelia Chillson Moots, seems to have felt the same way. Assuming her own salvation, "Mother" Moots reflected on the joy she would experience in the afterlife in meeting those Filipinos and American soldiers whom she had brought to Christ once they were reunited in the "'Home Beautiful' in the Father's house above."[36]

Beyond the religious motivations, the missionaries, like other American colonialists, felt a sense of adventure that comes from traveling to new, reputedly dangerous and unexplored lands. Traveling to the dark places of the world was reminiscent of the American pioneer experience, and the analogy with the westward movement was not uncommon. "When his house or his chapel is stoned by men who do not understand him he gets the same thrill that came to our fathers from the war whoop off in the forest," wrote Bruce Kershner, who best expressed this element in missionary thought. "He sails stormy seas, lives on barren shores, climbs rugged mountains, swims treacherous rivers, boats over boisterous lakes, and, wet with rain and beaten by storm, finds shelter in the vermine-filled and pestilence-breeding houses. No pioneers," he concluded, "ever passed through greater dangers or displayed greater endurance." [37]

There was, then, a modest variety of motivations; there was also a potential for serious conflict between, for example, those whose entire concern was the salvation of souls and those who wanted to transform society and become involved in social and political problems. Within a very short time, in fact, the missionary movement all over the world was in disarray over these and other matters. As the Tenth Quadrennial Convention of the Student Volunteer Movement assembled in Detroit in December 1927, there was serious discussion over whether to find new terms for *mission* and *missionary*. Perhaps *Christian World Fellowship* or even just *World Fellowship* would be more appropriate to the times. Sherwood Eddy, the great advocate of missions in the past, spoke on "Can We Still Believe in Foreign Missions?" while Mordecai Johnson, president of Howard University, addressed the gathering on "Shall We Send Missionaries from Non-Christian America?" [38]

Eddy and Johnson ultimately found justification for a continuing missionary movement, and the term *missionary* was not discarded. But the speeches and discussions revealed deep-seated doubts about the very legitimacy of foreign missions. Like Eddy and Johnson, Henry T. Hodgkin, a longtime missionary in China, felt that the older justifications for missions were inadequate. They were learned long ago in Sunday School, he said, and were suited "to the age when we were about three feet high and to the mentality which we were supposed then to possess. . . . An effort is needed," he went on, "to get out of the mentality created by that type of presentation." Hodgkins suggested five new missionary motives and attitudes: world service, without any hint of racial or cultural superiority or domination; assistance in the search for freedom; a fuller life for all; patience; and, most important, "friendship" with all people. "It is friendship we need," he implored, "accepting all the risks of friendship, accepting its difficulties, working with others in a friendship inspired by Jesus Christ." [39]

Eddy, too, emphasized the need for the Social Gospel. In an earlier age, he said, "we held fervidly a personal gospel for ourselves and the world. . . . Then our chief emphasis was personal, now it is social. . . . The ethical ideals of Christianity must be applied to all aspects of human life so as to develop a civilization of brotherly sons of God, not simply to save individuals."[40] The contrast with Arthur Brown's treatise on motivation, written some nineteen years earlier, or with Henry W. Munger's assertion in 1912 that friendship was an unworthy motive, was striking.

The implications of such thought on the missionary movement were profound. The idea of personal salvation was less important than providing humanitarian service. The superiority of Occidental Christianity was no longer to be dogmatically asserted. Indeed, the association of Christian thought with Western culture was a hindrance. Missionaries were admonished to have no part in "Western imperialism or militarism." Extraterritorial privileges were to be eschewed; "indigenization" was to be encouraged, even to the extent that historical Christian creeds should not be introduced in Oriental lands. "The Chinese churches have the right to formulate their own creeds," said Eddy.[41]

Such radical ideas were almost nonexistent in the Philippines as late as 1916, but some hints of what was to come were apparent. The growing emphasis on the Social Gospel inevitably raised doubts about traditional priorities. Even more troubling were Filipino demands for ecclesiastical and political independence. Not all missionaries rejected such demands out of hand (though the majority did). As a second generation of missionaries arrived, newer ideas made some headway. Most disconcerting of all was the outbreak of World War I. How could Westerners continue to believe automatically, even smugly, in the superiority of their own culture and religion when their civilization was tearing itself apart in the bloodiest and apparently the most senseless war in recent times? World War I, Eddy recalled, "rent wide the ordered strata of our complacent world . . . [and] revealed the ghastly evils of our semi-pagan civilization."[42] All of these forces eventually combined to throw the missionary movement into confusion. But in the Philippines, as elsewhere, the consensus, and the complacency that went with it, still held by 1916, though it was under some strain.

Whatever the specific motivation, most missionaries were sufficiently convinced of their calling to accept the sacrifices that came from living in what they perceived to be a primitive, disease-ridden land with few modern conveniences. Missionaries in the field did, however, try to lessen the hardship for those who followed by providing detailed advice on health care, clothing, furniture, utensils, and travel arrangements. Prospective missionaries were admonished to have their teeth in good order, to carry extra pairs of glasses, and to make certain their trusses fit properly. Medicine and drugs, they were warned, were very expensive in the islands. It was generally agreed that satisfactory furniture could be obtained in Manila, except for metal beds, which ought to be shipped from the States, as should cookstoves and ice boxes, because they were in limited supply and expensive in the Philippines.

As for clothing, women were advised to take along washable dress skirts and white linen shirts; nothing should be lined. A raincoat and an umbrella were important items, but gloves should be left behind. Men were encouraged to do most of their shopping for clothes in Hong Kong, where Chinese craftsmen could quickly produce well-fitting "whites" very inexpensively. Shoes were cheaper in the United States.[43] If one's denomination insisted on baptism by immersion, it was also important that one's rubberized baptismal pants be in good repair. One Disciples missionary found, to his dismay, that his were full of leaks.

While advice about proper outfitting lessened the trauma of moving to an exotic land, the missionaries still anticipated and often encountered serious hardships. One thing which troubled many of them was the unexpectedly high cost of living. One Methodist missionary, for example, complained that although he and his wife lived very economically he was still forced to use uncomfortable Filipino shoes, something he thought unjust. Even more humiliating, his wife had to do her own cooking, something "no American woman ought to be compelled to do in the tropics if she had three small children to care for."[44] Such complaints reflected the smug assumptions of Western superiority, of course. Filipino pastors were always paid far less than the missionaries and presumably were expected to wear Filipino clothing and have their wives cook, regardless of the number of children they might have. Nevertheless, the missionaries often felt badly compensated for their efforts. (Not all of the missionaries were poverty stricken. Mercer Johnston inquired about the advisability of bringing with him his "negro servant girl." His board discouraged him, but Bishop Brent disagreed. "Such a servant is a treasure out here," he explained.)[45]

Missionaries also found travel problematical and perilous. Oscar Huddleston, a Methodist missionary in the Cagayan Valley of Luzon, traveled about his extensive district as best he could—by barangay, tucali, horse, carreton, carromata, banquilla, vapor, raft, and carabao, and on foot. Ella Herkert reported that on her trips to villages along the coast of Mindanao it was sometimes impossible to sleep, given the crowded quarters and the ever present and bold mosquitoes. Harry Farmer recalled that on a recent trip he had "walked about 25 miles, slept on the floor, ate what the natives do, [and] learned to undress in a room full of women."[46]

In addition to the perils of travel, missionaries sometimes had to live with persecution and humiliation; and the effects on family life could be deleterious.[47] But the most common hardship was illness from tropical diseases, climate, and, it was believed, overwork.

Some missionaries felt that women were more inclined to break down than men, which may account in part for the fact that single women were paid less than single men. Episcopalian Mercer Johnston, for example, noting the difficulties women faced in his own mission, concluded that they could never serve for more than five years. Other missions, he reported, were even worse off. The Methodist women in particular seemed to suffer. "Their Home has been little more than a hospital for some months," he wrote. "Miss Spalding's life was despaired of for a time, and Miss Parks had been up and down with amoebic." Mrs. Stuntz, he observed, "looks wretchedly" and appeared on the verge of a total collapse. As for Mrs. Rodgers, the only paid Presbyterian female missionary, "she has been doing nothing for the past six months except to try and keep body and soul together."[48]

Women were indeed among the casualties. In addition to those mentioned by Johnston, Mrs. L. V. Finster, wife of the leading Adventist missionary, had to leave the islands in 1912 on account of severe amoebic dysentery, a disease that also affected Hulda Lund of the Christian and Missionary Alliance.[49] But it is doubtful if Johnston was even statistically accurate, as male missionaries seem to have been equally affected by disease.

No mission, in fact, was untouched by serious illness. To cite a few examples, Presbyterian Leon C. Hills had to leave the islands in 1902 after contracting a tuberculosislike lung infection. Disciples missionary Bruce Kershner and Methodist Homer Stuntz were among the many victims of amoebic dysentery. The Blacks of the American Board were both in broken health when they left for home.[50] The Baptists and Episcopalians suffered serious depletions from time to time due to illness. But the Methodists— both men and women—seemed to be the most susceptible to serious illness, though this impression may be more the result of the larger number of Methodists in the islands than a truly disproportionate share of illness. In any event, many Methodists became ill. Ralph V. B. Dunlap resigned his post in 1904 on account of the ill health of his wife and son. In 1906 Willard A. Goodell's wife developed "heart lesions," and he came down with malaria. By 1907 both were invalids. "I know of no sadder case," wrote Homer Stuntz in a letter requesting that, as a humanitarian gesture, the Goodells' salary not be ended immediately. In 1908 Rex Moe had to have an operation for piles, Harry Bower went deaf in one ear, Mrs. Ernest S. Lyons caught malaria, and Lyons himself had a bad case of colitis, which developed after several years of amoebic dysentery. Lyons, wrote Bishop William F. Oldham the following year, was "nearly dead" with carbuncles, fever, and dysentery; William H. Teeter had suffered a nervous breakdown and was a near invalid; Charles Koehler was so worn out that he looked like a man of eighty; Klinefelter was "not well," and Oscar Huddleston was "miserable." Oldham blamed the situation on the lack of reinforcements, which in turn led to overwork. The following year a Methodist physician, Milton H. Schutz, contracted tuberculosis, the same disease he had been treating the people for. And so it went, year after year.[51]

Sometimes the illness ended in death. The first missionary to die seems to have been Presbyterian Leonard Davidson, who died of appendicitis on June 8, 1901. A few months later the wife of Episcopalian Walter C. Clapp succumbed to myelitis. "I shall think of her as the church's first martyr in this field," Clapp wrote sadly.[52] In 1903 John McKee of the Christian and Missionary Alliance died in Mindanao, a victim of cholera.

The most touching tragedies were the deaths of children. In 1903 Lucy Stuntz, the daughter of the Methodist missionary couple, died of spinal meningitis. In 1906 two more children of Methodist missionary parents died. In 1912 the son of Sanford B. Kurtz, a United Brethren missionary, died.[53] Both of Charles W. Briggs's sons were born in the Philippines, and both died there, one at the age of two, the other as an infant.[54]

The decision to be a missionary also meant an almost irrevocable break in relations with family and friends. Though the missionaries knew of this sacrifice in advance and accepted it as one of the prices of fulfilling their call, the reality was still difficult. "I know of no sacrifice which one makes in coming here which is harder than just that," wrote Bishop Brent. "Ties are broken which never can be replaced on earth and broken with all the space of half the world to dampen the pain." Brent should have known. Though he got home more often than most, he was in the islands when his brother died, when his mother's only surviving sister was at death's door, and when two of his best friends were critically ill as well.[55] Another tragedy of this sort involved the fiancée of Adventist Floyd Ashbaugh who succumbed to illness shortly before she was to join her husband-to-be in the islands.

It is probably true that the missionaries suffered from more illness and had a higher mortality rate than the general American population at home. Whether they were worse off than the general colonial population is doubtful. Bishop Brent, who was thoroughly familiar with missionary sufferings and who firmly believed that his own life would be shortened by accepting his position in the Philippines, sometimes made light of them. Tales of the great trials they suffered, he wrote, were "not devoid of sentimentalism." The missionaries underwent nothing that school teachers, miners, and other pioneers did not meet with. Indeed, since their cause was so much more worthy and since their work was more absorbing, missionaries should receive less, not more, consideration for their hardships, he wrote. In fact, the challenges they had to overcome put them in a better position to meet life's difficulties than those persons "at home whose lives are collapsing for the lack of knocks and jars. . . . Our compensations are greater and our pains fewer than the unexperienced are aware of all along the line."[56] Brent's critique had merit and was a needed corrective to sentimentalism; but the missionaries did undergo real hardship and tragedy.

As men and women who believed that they were doing God's work, and believed it so intensely that they were willing to sacrifice home, family, and possibly health to pursue it, the missionaries were unusually strong-willed. One result was that there existed a surprising amount of internal discord. Scarcely a mission was spared internal wrangling, sometimes of a very bitter nature.[57]

Particularly serious personnel problems developed in the Methodist, Episcopal, and Baptist missions. Some Methodists, for example, found it difficult to work with the irascible Homer C. Stuntz, the presiding elder. By one account, J. L. McLaughlin was determined not to return to his post after his furlough on account of Stuntz. Harry Farmer, who seems to have been on good terms only with McLaughlin, also attacked the mission's leadership and was censured by Stuntz. Farmer also characterized Daniel Klinefelter as a "spy," and accused Ernest Lyons of assigning another missionary, E. A. Rayner, to territory previously promised to him. "It may make it difficult for me to get along with Rayner," he wrote, "if he is disposed to look to Lyons instead of me." All in all, Farmer, while energetic, was a man of many hatreds and a bit paranoid. When Klinefelter, the mission's treasurer, refused to authorize repairs on a house in Laoag, Farmer assumed it was because he had made the request.[58]

More serious problems existed in the Episcopal mission. A major cause of dissension resulted from the existence of "Protestant" and "Catholic" wings of the church. As early as 1901, James L. Smiley, the first Episcopal missionary, objected to the appointment of Walter C. Clapp to the mission field on the grounds that Clapp was too "Catholic" in his orientation. The dispute continued to plague the mission throughout its early history. John A. Staunton, Jr., who was in charge of Episcopalian work at Sagada in the mountains of central Luzon, was so stongly Catholic in his views that, when in Manila, he refused to attend service at the Episcopal Cathedral where Mercer Johnston, a strong Protestant, was rector.[59]

Bishop Brent, who valued both the church's Protestant and Catholic heritages, never fully succeeded in reconciling the two factions, both of which considered him weak. Johnston, for example, whom Brent helped recruit in 1902 and 1903, gradually became disenchanted with the bishop's "concessions" to Catholic practices and ritual within the Church. In 1907 he described the highly ceremonial consecration of the Manila cathedral, which Brent planned, as a "semi-barbaric occasion" in which he took a minimum of interest lest his passions get out of hand. As for the bishop's behavior during the consecration, his cope "would have knocked the breath clear out of the Queen of Sheba; although she might have had good taste enough to have objected to the parti-colored picture of Christ on the back of it."[60] The next year Johnston resigned his position and returned to the United States.

Quirks of personality compounded the theological disputes within the Episcopal mission. Irving Spencer, for example, had to be removed from his post in Zamboanga, where he had been involved in land speculation and other financial transactions of a dubious nature. Reassigned to Baguio, he promptly got into trouble for injuring a neighbor's horse. Both matters involved naiveté and poor judgment rather than malicious intent, but they required extensive discussions with the bishop and the authorities, as well as correspondence with the mission board. At least three times Spencer offered to resign, and eventually he returned to the United States. "Spencer alternatively amuses & exasperates me. . . ," Brent wrote in 1908. "I am thankful that he & his wife are out of the Islands. They are such children. I was always expecting to hear of some new calamity."[61]

Mercer Johnston also caused problems for the mission. If Spencer was ever the child, Johnston was ever the moralist. A man with a rigid, even brittle, personality, Johnston found it difficult to countenance differences of style and opinion. Government toleration of social evils, such as gambling, met with his rage. But so did lapses, or perceived lapses, of his parishioners and members of the Columbia Club, which he condemned publicly and at length. On one occasion, for example, he loudly censured a tennis player at the club for being improperly dressed. When the victim complained about the manner (but not the substance) of the criticism, the minister replied in a two-and-a-half-page letter staunchly defending his actions. On another occasion one of the vestrymen threatened to resign unless Johnston withdrew a letter to a parishioner that was critical of her behavior. Since to do so "would be tantamount to a confession of the weakness of my protest—a confession that I could make only by running counter to my convictions," Johnston refused to withdraw the letter.[62] On yet another occasion Johnston publicly attacked the Atlantic Gulf and Pacific Company from the pulpit for sloppy workmanship on the cathedral. When a company spokesman, who may have been a member of the Church, protested to the bishop, Johnston responded with a nine-page letter vigorously defending his position. Actions such as these, as well as harsh words that passed between Johnston and Staunton, led the bishop to counsel the strong-willed minister to "try to soften a bit your asperity" and to be patient with the foibles of other human beings.[63] But Brent's counsel seems to have had little effect.

When Johnston resigned in 1908, a sense of relief must have percolated through the Episcopalian ranks. Such was surely the case with the vestrymen of the Cathedral Parish of St. Mary and St. John, as their response to Johnston's formal letter of resignation indicates:

> We recognize you to be a man of force and high ideals. Your sermons are forceful, original, and always aimed to arouse in your hearers a desire and inclination to lead a higher and purer christian life. You have the courage of your convictions. You are fearless and unswerving in the defense of right as you see it. You never hesitate to denounce with all the force at your command what you believe to be wrong.
>
> If at times you have seemed to us to be a little too eager for the realization of your ideals, and impatient of what may have appeared to us to be more tactful methods of righting a wrong, we have ever recognized your earnestness and singleness of purpose for the maintenance of what is highest and best in the life and the moral well being of your parishioners and the community at large.[64]

Differences within the Episcopal mission, the result of diverse theological views and personality clashes, distracted attention from more fundamental matters, much to the distress of the bishop. But in terms of sheer bitterness, no mission was so badly rent as was the Baptist one.

Charles W. Briggs, the Baptist leader, was the center of it all. A gifted writer and evangelist, a man with strong ecumenical inclinations ("my message was always ethical, not dogmatic," he once wrote),[65] Briggs was nevertheless a loner who had difficulty working closely with his associates. Given to describing his colleagues in strong and unflattering language, he also had investments in the island and lent money at interest to Filipinos, for which he was indirectly censured by the board.

Briggs's opposition in 1906 to placing Henry W. Munger in charge of a Bible school was indicative of his approach. Munger, he contended, had "plenty of pedigree" but "almost a cipher personality." Though he hoped Munger would develop into a good worker, for the present Briggs failed to see "what he is good for here." Another candidate for the position, W. O. Valentine, was also unsuited, thought Briggs. As a teacher Valentine was unequaled, but he allegedly lacked organizational and business skills. It would be "a travesty on the mission to put a man in that place that has no potency or influence at all," he concluded.[66]

Briggs's unflattering comments, which were confined neither to Munger and Valentine nor to this context, eventually led to countercharges. Charles L. Maxfield, whom Briggs once accused of lacking sympathy with the Filipinos, contended to the board that Briggs was "impulsive and dominant in name and disposition," though he also had "commendable qualities of heart."[67] Maxfield subsequently revealed that Briggs was involved, apparently, in lending money at interest to Filipinos and in making large investments in Negros. Maxfield conceded that Briggs's actions may have been legally correct, but he doubted their propriety; and he noted that Briggs did not want him to return to Negros.

Maxfield's own negative opinions of Briggs's behavior were reinforced when four letters arrived from the Philippines (Maxfield was then in the United States) which made strong allegations against the Baptist leader. One characterized him as "absolutely unscrupulous. . . . Oh! it makes me so hot when I think of his high handed actions and deplorable meanness that I can hardly write coherently. . . . And others say the same things." Another thought it might be best to expose Briggs publicly, along with his cohort, Archibald A. Forshee, though it would create a scandal of great impact. Maxfield was, in fact, willing to accuse Briggs openly of a "lack of Christian principle," though he preferred to keep the dispute private.[68]

By 1909, Briggs had very little support among the missionaries. When Maxfield returned to Iloilo, he received a vote of confidence and was reassigned to Negros, in spite of Briggs's objections. Shortly thereafter Briggs, as well as Forshee, left the mission field, doubtless to the relief of those who remained. While Briggs was on furlough, the board passed a resolution condemning the lending of money by missionaries to natives, which Briggs in turn denounced. The board, he stated, was "knifing the wrong party."[69]

A few months later Briggs resigned his missionary appointment to accept a pastorate at Ballston Spa, New York, though not without a parting shot at the board and its executive secretary, Thomas S. Barbour. Even then he remained bitter. Three months later he again attacked Barbour and termed Munger, whom the board had placed in charge of his former district, "a poor deaf, uneducated, utterly impractical fellow . . . the right one to promote misunderstanding within the mission, the friend of every man and the tool of the conscienceless. About as near a zero as could be placed at the head of that big district where so much might and should be done."[70]

The issue was not entirely closed even then, for in 1913 Briggs apparently requested reassignment to his old post. In response to inquiries from the board, Forshee strongly supported the idea of sending Briggs back, but Eric Lund implied that Briggs was insane. "Does not the field and the Board require men with [a] well balanced mind and sound judgment?" he wrote. "Unable to keep within proper limits in relation with men and things (he went beyond the rules of the Board and got into private money business) he could not be expected to remain within the 'faith which was once deliv-ered to the saints.'"[71] Briggs did not return again to the Philippines.

It would, of course, be wrong to conclude that the missions were beset by constant infighting. In their annual conventions, for example, the mis-sionaries often united in support of various programs and resolutions. Still, internal quarreling, when combined with differences between the missions (discussed in the following chapter) existed to a sufficient degree to conclude that the missions were not models of harmony.

3

Comity and Its Limits

> I pray God continually that I might ever keep upper most in mind
> the thought that we are preparing Ministers for the Church of
> Jesus Christ and not trying to make Presybterians.
>
> John H. Lamb,
Presbyterian missionary

> You are here to build up a Presbyterian constituency and are do-
> ing so whether you will openly admit it or not. . . . You are not
> here to yield a hair's breadth of Presbyterian interest in favor of
> Baptist work. You have shown that from the start, whether you
> realize it or not.
>
> Baptist missionaries
Charles W. Briggs, Eric Lund,
and Archibald A. Forshee
to the Presbyterian mission

"The Protestant missionary enterprise," writes R. Pierce Beaver, "was characterized from the very beginning by an extraordinary sense of unity across national and denominational lines." In the nineteenth century the concept of comity emerged as one expression of this sense of unity. Originally meaning "the division of territory and the assignment of spheres of occupation including the delimitation of boundaries, on the one hand, and noninterference in one another's affairs on the other," comity was often construed more broadly to include various cooperative practices. By the middle of the nineteenth century, the practice of comity (though not the word itself, which came into use in 1886) was widely accepted by missionaries and their boards, with interest in comity peaking about the turn of the century.[1]

Comity and other cooperative arrangements, therefore, appealed to many of the mission societies that were interested in entering the new territories opened to them in 1898. Indeed, since Spain had hitherto rigorously excluded Protestant missionaries from these lands, there was an opportunity for a tremendous advance in cooperative evangelization. In the past, comity arrangements tended to be verbal, applicable to relatively limited geographical areas. They were often made in the field without approval by, or even reference back to, the boards.[2] But here was a chance to apply cooperative principles, in particular the assignment of specific geographical areas among various missions, to entire countries.

The Presbyterians took the lead. Six weeks after Commodore Dewey's victory at Manila Bay, representatives of several Protestant organizations interested in entering Cuba, Puerto Rico, and the Philippines met in the offices of the Presbyterian mission board and recommended to their respective boards that, with respect to the Philippines, each organization appoint two representatives to form a committee that would consult about comity arrangements.[3]

Hopes for cooperation were not immediately realized. The proposed committee on the Philippines seems to have met only once (on November 17, 1898), at which time the Baptists and Methodists reported that for financial reasons they would not then enter the Philippines.[4] Such an explanation may have been less than candid, especially in the case of the Methodists, who within two months took steps to establish a presence in the islands.[5]

Furthermore, early Methodist activities in the islands irked the Presbyterians and called into question the Methodist commitment to comity. Arthur W. Prautch, a Methodist lay preacher and former missionary to India, for example, was a zealous worker; but according to the Presbyterian leader, James B. Rodgers, he was none too careful about whom he accepted as members. Prautch, Rodgers thought, lacked standards. Even more irksome, he allegedly stole members from the Presbyterian fold, including the talented Nicolas Zamora, who soon became the pride and joy of Philippine Methodism. He utilized poorly prepared Filipino assistants, it was said, and his veracity was open to question: Presbyterians thought he inflated membership statistics. In sum, Rodgers thought, Prautch's methods were "calculated to cheapen the Evangelical Church in the eyes of the people."[6]

The difficulties with Prautch appear to have been resolved, or at least papered over, for Rodgers was upset when the secretary of the Presbyterian board relayed his complaints about Prautch to the Methodist board. "We have settled it pleasantly or are about to do so," he wrote in July 1900. The prospects for comity, he insisted a few months later, were "better than ever."[7]

Relations with Prautch may have improved, but ecumenically inclined Presbyterians continued to be irritated at what they perceived to be the Methodists' single-minded devotion to *Methodism*. "Why can they not talk about Christianity?" lamented Rodgers. In 1900 the Presbyterian mission attempted to arrive at an informal division of territory: the Methodists would work to the north of Manila, the Presbyterians to the south. But the Methodists balked, it appears, and no agreement was reached. Thus as the time approached in 1901 for an interdenominational conference to discuss formal comity agreements, many Presbyterians doubted a favorable outcome. "To speak plainly, though I hope not uncharitably," wrote a Presbyterian missionary from India then in the Philippines, "our M[ethodist] E[piscopal] friends, as you are aware, believe in *Methodism*! To establish that is one of the fundamental considerations with the best of them." [8]

In spite of initial setbacks and skepticism, however, the missionaries managed an extraordinary advance in the history of mission comity when, in April 1901, representation of seven missionary and Bible societies established the Evangelical Union of the Philippine Islands, which in turn assigned specific geographical areas to the Methodist, Presbyterian, and United Brethren missions. The agreement meant that the Presbyterians had to abandon "some very promising work" to the Methodists, but the sacrifice was made in the larger interests of harmony. [9]

Several missionaries deserve credit for the successful conference. Jay Goodrich of the American Bible Society and a Methodist army major, Elijah J. Halford, wanted an agreement to avoid friction in the field and worked hard to make the conference a success. Rodgers, always a leader in ecumenical efforts, helped pave the way (or so he claimed) with a good dinner and reception for the delegates. [10] But ultimate credit appears to lie with a visiting Presbyterian dignitary and a Methodist bishop.

J. C. R. Ewing, president of a Presbyterian college in Lahore, India, determined to remain in Manila because "the time seems to have arrived for a decided attempt to realize something of that comity which the conditions clearly demand." Though the need was demonstrable, Ewing was not at first "very sanguine of success," given Methodist resistance to such arrangements in the immediate past. But Methodist Bishop Frank W. Warne not only cooperated but proved to be the driving force behind the eventual agreement. Ewing was frankly astonished, while Rodgers and Leonard P. Davidson wrote that Warne was "most cordial and helpful in the working out of the plans and we are very grateful." [11] A few years later Rodgers credited Warne with "crystalliz[ing] the ideas of all present into practical form." [12] Shortly, the Baptists joined the union and ratified the territorial agreements. The Christian Mission (Disciples of Christ) sent representatives to the islands in August 1901, and they too entered the union. By the time of the union's second meeting in January 1902, the two vice-presidential positions were filled with a Baptist and a Disciple. At the same meeting, the territorial divisions were revised. [13]

The formation of the Evangelical Union and the territorial divisions it imposed prompted enthusiastic comments from many missionaries. Ewing thought that "nothing better than this has ever taken place in any mission field," an evaluation in which Bishop Warne concurred. The formation of the union, he wrote, "marks a movement in the comity of missions in advance of anything ever known on any mission field. When the Union was consummated," the bishop recalled, "a holy awe and joy took possession of us, with a consciousness that a great and far-reaching work had been accomplished."[14] The dreams of ecumenically inclined churchmen, it appeared, had been realized in the Philippines.

These initial, almost ecstatic assessments were echoed in future years by other missionaries so that a tenaciously consistent interpretation of the Protestant missionary experience in the Philippines has emerged. An American Board pamphlet published in 1908 insisted that the union was "not only a most effective agency . . . but it has been a marked event in modern missionary movements, being in the line of Christian federation and the avoidance of ill-considered or divisive efforts." The territorial divisions, the account continued, were "altogether satisfactory." Similarly, in 1913 Methodist bishop William F. Oldham assured students at Syracuse University that the territorial divisions had worked "without a hitch from the beginning," while in 1919 James B. Rodgers recalled that "the greatest blessing of all has been found in the spirit of unity" on the field, a spirit "present from the beginning." Six years later Frank C. Laubach, in his standard account of the mission experience, concluded that by 1904 "the principle of division had been vindicated . . . conclusively."[15]

Scholars writing at a later date have made similar assessments. In the 1930s Donald Dean Parker concluded that "due to the Evangelical Union, unwholesome rivalry was non-existent." R. Pierce Beaver, in his important study of the history of comity, concludes that the cooperating effort in the Philippines was eminently successful, with the Episcopalian church "alone" not joining the union. Peter G. Gowing, writing in 1967, echoed the earlier evaluations. The comity arrangements, he wrote, proved to be among "the most successful in the history of Protestant missions. . . . In terms of its scope, aims, and ecumenical planning," he went on, "the Evangelical Union in the Philippines was unique in the history of the Protestant missionary endeavor up to that time."[16]

To be sure, several accounts contained an occasional reference to interdenominational conflict, but its extent and importance were minimized. Among recent observers, only Arthur L. Tuggy poses something of a challenge to the usual view by claiming that the "Evangelical Alliance . . . did not remove all sources of friction and competition. Those who had received the largest areas in which to work were the most satisfied with it." But the overwhelming consensus has been that the creation of the Evangelical Union and the assignments of specific geographical areas to the various missions succeeded in producing an extraordinary degree of Christian harmony on the mission field.[17]

To what extent does the missionary experience in the Philippines justify the accolades that normally describe it? From the perspective of 1900, there is no question that the creation of the Evangelical Union was, in itself, an event of tremendous importance. Nowhere else in the world had Protestant missionaries achieved comity arrangements as far reaching as those achieved in the Philippines. The division of territory provided the basis for efficient mission expansion. On the whole, the arrangements served the missionaries well, and to that extent the standard interpretations have validity.

Nor were other ecumenical accomplishments insignificant. The most notable achievement of the early years, aside from the formation of the Evangelical Union, was the foundation in 1907 of what became Union Theological Seminary in Manila (now in Dasmariñas, Cavite), when Presbyterian and Methodist training centers merged. The next year the United Brethren mission began sending students to the seminary. "Our relations with the Methodists and United Brethren are as cordial as ever," the seminary's Presbyterian president wrote in 1912, "and in fact the joining of the United Brethren in the seminary work has helped us in every way." Though Presbyterians and Methodists wielded the most influence in the seminary, the Congregationalists and the Disciples soon joined the United Brethren in providing students, faculty, and funds. Similarly, in the southern islands the American Board and Presbyterians cooperated in the work of a Bible school at Dumaguete, which later evolved into the school of theology of Silliman University.[18]

During these years there was considerable discussion of forming a united church. In a land where Protestantism was new, many missionaries agreed that denominational names would only confuse the people and strengthen their opponents. At the first meeting of the Evangelical Union, in fact, it was agreed that all of the member churches would adopt the name "The Evangelical Church of the Philippines," followed if necessary by the denominational affiliation in parentheses. This recommendation was never fully adhered to, and the first meaningful steps toward a united church did not occur until the 1920s. But there was a notable achievement in Manila when the American congregations of the Methodists and Presbyterians (and, in an unofficial way, the Disciples as well) united to form the Union Church of Manila. The Evangelical Union was instrumental in beginning discussion toward this end in 1912, though encouragement from the mission boards and probably also the negative pressure of a declining American population in the islands finally brought about the merger.[19]

Other examples of ecumenical concern existed. Baptists and Presbyterians joined in operating a hospital in Iloilo (though more under the pressure of circumstances than out of brotherly feelings). Common literature was sometimes used; the printing facilities of one mission served the needs of other denominations (though sometimes at inflated prices). And there was a considerable amount of personal interaction and friendship among missionaries of the various denominations.

It was fortunate for the cause of comity that the first regularly accredited Protestant missionary, Presbyterian James B. Rodgers, championed the concept. Not only was Rodgers intellectually committed to the idea of mission harmony, his life embodied the ideal. He regularly welcomed missionaries of all persuasions to the islands, literally meeting many at the boat, and even accompanied some of them to their assignments in far away stations.

Typical of Rodgers's ecumenical spirit was his relationship with Robert F. Black, the first representative of the American Board, who arrived in Manila in November 1902. Immediately upon Black's arrival Rodgers invited the missionary to stay without charge at the Presbyterian mission. Precisely one year later Black was married with Rodgers officiating. Later, Rodgers made the Blacks honorary members of the Presbyterian mission, and the Congregationalists developed a tremendous respect for Rodgers (and other Presbyterians as well; Black was, for example, close to the Jansens). The Presbyterian leader, he wrote in 1912, "is a dear venerable friend, personal and of our work." [20]

Another force for harmony was the Young Men's Christian Association. The Y not only saw itself as an ally of the missionaries, to whom it owed "a loving comradeship and sympathy," but a positive force for muting denominational rivalries. "We must be ever ready to smooth out every indication even of denominational jealousy and strife," wrote a Y official in 1901. [21]

Generally speaking, the Y served as a means of bringing together the Protestant missionaries of all denominations, except possibly the Seventh-day Adventists. Not only had the Y influenced many young people to become missionaries, but missionary comments fairly glowed with enthusiasm about the Y's work among the soldiers during the Philippine-American War. Methodist Bishop Warne, for example, thought the Y's efforts were heroic. When the missionaries began to arrive, the Y welcomed and assisted them. The first Presbyterians, for example, held English services in a YMCA tent for six months and visited marine barracks in Cavite in the company of Y officials. At the end of 1899, David Hibbard commented that the Y was "doing a good work among the men and it is appreciated." A little later, when the Y wanted to close its operations in Iloilo, Hibbard requested that it remain open. [22]

The Y was helpful to missionaries touring the islands in search of places to establish mission stations. Late in 1902, for example, Episcopalian Walter C. Clapp visited Iloilo, where, through the courtesy of Y officials, he met many of the American and British residents of the city. When Bishop Brent visited Iloilo several months later, he reported that the secretary of the Iloilo Y "showed us every courtesy. A word of commendation should be spoken for the excellent service that has been rendered by him and his associates."[23]

As the Y began to provide services for civilians, it found the missionaries among its most enthusiastic supporters. As a reporter writing about the Philippine missions put it in 1905, the YMCA was "winning warmest praise in all quarters." "The missionaries and Christian laymen rallied to the Association's support," recalled Zerah C. Collins of the Manila Y, "and the faithful untiring work of such men as McLaughlin, Hillis [*sic*], McCarl, Pierce, Halford, Stuntz, Rogers [*sic*], Colvin, Goodrich and others was the means under God of winning many a boy to a better life." Methodists A. E. Chenoweth and George A. Miller helped produce the Y's magazine, *The Graphic*, and numerous missionaries taught courses and gave lectures at the Y. Some missionaries represented the association in provincial cities.[24]

On only one important occasion was the YMCA a cause of disunity among the missionaries. In 1915 the Manila branch experimented with a series of social dances held, the officials said, to counteract the allegedly evil effects of the public dance halls, which, they contended, were little more than fronts for prostitution. Dancing, however, was then a matter of considerable controversy among the Protestant communions. The Episcopalians saw little moral problem involved and regularly hosted dances at their Columbia Club. Methodists, Disciples, and United Brethren, on the other hand, generally condemned dancing, while the Presbyterians seem to have been somewhere in the middle.

In the event, twenty-nine individual members of the Evangelical Union signed a petition of protest. The Methodist mission adopted a motion chastising the association for its action as being "out of harmony with the ideals we are seeking to raise up before the people." Methodist Daniel H. Klinefelter wrote to the Y's board in what one official described as "intemperate & violent terms," while Bishop William P. Eveland wrote directly to the Y's international secretary, the renowned John R. Mott, complaining about the dances themselves and the lack of consultation in reaching the decision to hold them. Since the Y was built with subscriptions from Christians, the bishop argued further, the use of the building for dancing came "perilously near to a breach of trust and a misappropriation of funds." The Disciples, too, officially condemned the dances, and at least one missionary, United Brethren Sanford B. Kurtz, withdrew his membership from the association. On the other hand, Presbyterian Rodgers and Methodist Bruce Wright, pastor of the Union Church, refused to sign the protest, saying that the local board was competent to decide the issue.[25]

When John R. Mott rebuked the Manila Y officials, they continued to defend their decisions, arguing in part that the judgments of Rodgers, Wright, and Brent counted "for a great deal more in this community than a large majority of the signers of the protest and writers of the letters of criticism." But Mott correctly saw the larger significance of the issue. The Y, he wrote, was not "to work apart from the Churches." Rather, the association was in the islands "to serve the Churches in such ways as they may indicate in every way in our power." By deciding to experiment with dancing, the Y threatened its position as a symbol and facilitator of cooperation.[26]

There is little question that, all in all, the Y did represent the ecumenical ideal. The fact that there was some serious disagreement with the Protestant community over a YMCA policy, however, suggests that the traditional picture of Protestant harmony in the Philippine mission experience is an incomplete one. Impressive as the very real ecumenical undertakings were, the usual accounts, by excluding or minimizing contrary trends, present a distorted view.

There was, in fact, noticeable dissent from the view that comity in the Philippines was good and/or effective. Even among the Presbyterian mission there was disagreement about the value of comity. David S. Hibbard, in charge of Presbyterian work in Dumaguete, gave it as his "private opinion" in 1902 that "the whole scheme of division of territory does not amount to anything at all and that within two years we will find the missionaries going wherever they find an opening. It is nice on paper and an interesting plan," he concluded, "but that is all."[27]

Presbyterian skepticism derived in part from a continuing suspicion of Methodist objectives. In December 1901, for example, the Methodist board apparently vetoed the proposal of one of its missionaries for a joint newspaper and a union college, a decision that led Rodgers to fear that a breakdown in comity was likely. And some Presbyterians at home continued to consider the Methodists unreliable and even treacherous.[28]

Methodist designs on some of the Visayan islands added to Presbyterian unease. The original meeting of the Evangelical Union had assigned portions of the Visayas to the Baptists and Presbyterians; the Methodists were to work in Luzon north of Manila. But they were also interested in moving into the unassigned areas of the Visayas. In October 1901 the Methodists proposed foregoing work in the Visayas in return for acquiring additional territory in Luzon, a proposal quickly backed by the Presbyterians. At the meeting of the Evangelical Union in January 1902, Methodist territory in Luzon was increased; and the previously unassigned areas of the Visayas were formally given to the Baptists and the Presbyterians, leaving a specific division to the two missions themselves. The Methodists pledged not to enter the Visayas. The issue, it would appear, had been settled amicably.[29]

Yet the very next year Homer C. Stuntz, a leading Methodist missionary, advised the union that the Methodists wanted to enter the Visayas. Presbyterians stationed in Panay, Negros, and Cebu reacted bitterly. H. W. Langheim, a Presbyterian missionary who also served as director of the provincial board of health of Negros Oriental, for example, denounced the proposal as impertinent and inconsistent with the previous agreement. "The entire question is," he wrote, "Will the Methodists do as they agreed?" And Fred Jansen reported that Presbyterians in Iloilo, Dumaguete, and Cebu "were all opposed" to allowing the Methodists a Visayan foothold.[30]

The proposed Methodist incursion had serious ramifications. In the first place it caused (or accentuated) a rift within the Presbyterian mission, for mission personnel in the Visayas felt that Presbyterians in Manila, notably Rodgers, were entirely too willing to make concessions to the Methodists. This in turn led some to denounce comity in general. "The comity problem has been a good one for all but the Presbyterians," Langheim lamented in a letter to his board. The Methodist action also caused Presbyterians in the Visayas to act hastily in establishing a Presbyterian presence at Tacloban, Leyte, where the Methodists wanted to locate.[31] This action had several unfortunate consequences as well. The missionaries acted without sufficient preliminary investigation and therefore vastly overestimated the Protestant potential on Leyte. It also widened the rift within the Presbyterian community, for Rodgers opposed the move. And most significant of all the Baptists, who had an equally valid claim to Leyte, regarded this unilateral Presbyterian expansion as a hostile act. Thus relations with the Baptists, which had been tense for other reasons, seriously deteriorated and left a legacy of ill will.

In sum, the Methodist probe, coming just over a year after that denomination had agreed to stay out of the area, was a mistake of considerable magnitude. For this, Homer C. Stuntz, an intense and somewhat insensitive man with strong opinions and strong dislikes, bears the major responsibility. But Rodgers, whose personality was in some ways the opposite of Stuntz's, was unintentionally culpable too. He failed to dissuade Stuntz from his ill-advised plan and may even have supported his efforts, as his colleagues to the south feared. He unquestionably put the Methodist action in the best possible light. And he either failed to grasp the depth of his missionaries' resentment at the Methodist proposal or else attempted to minimize it. Rodgers even failed to report the question to his board, which learned of it from other missionaries. He explained belatedly and a little lamely that "the matter was arranged so quickly that we scarcely thought of informing you of the matter." Stuntz, he went on, after an "indecisive" meeting in Manila, went to Iloilo (at Rodgers's suggestion) where, "on having his attention called to the promise made . . . not to go into the Visayas, promptly and cordially withdrew his proposition." Doubtless Stuntz was aware of his previous promise before he embarked for Iloilo. If not, Rodgers was negligent in not calling it to his attention. In any event, less than a fortnight after Stuntz "cordially withdrew his proposition," a Baptist representative reported that Stuntz "practically asserted that his mission would begin work . . . in Samar and in Leyte within a few months!" Ironically, the missionary most devoted to comity contributed to a serious disillusionment with the concept among his own missionaries.[32]

Fortunately, relations steadily improved thereafter. In spite of Stuntz's apparent inclinations, the Methodists did not pursue their plan to send missionaries to the Visayas, and by all accounts the meeting of the Evangelical Union in January 1904 was very cordial. Rodgers and Hall were delighted with the meeting, which—among other things—adopted a clearer definition of comity, endorsed again the concept of territorial division, and empowered the union's executive committee to decide territorial disputes. "As far as we personally as a mission are concerned," Rodgers and Hall reported, "we could ask for nothing better." The meeting in 1905 was equally harmonious, at least with respect to Presbyterian-Methodist relations. And, in general, relations between the two largest missions progressively improved. Territorial issues never again became a problem, and significant cooperative ministries developed in Manila.[33]

Rodgers continued to be a major force in this evolution. Presbyterian John H. Lamb also had good words from some Methodists; in particular, he liked the new union seminary. "I pray God continually," he wrote, "that I might ever keep upper most in mind the thought that we are preparing Ministers for the Church of Jesus Christ and not trying to make Presbyterians." The cause of comity was also well served by the Methodist bishop. Just as Bishop Warne had greatly facilitated the formation of the Evangelical Union, so too Bishop William F. Oldham, a man of wide vision who had episcopal responsibilities for the Philippines from 1904 to 1912, pushed hard for cooperative ventures. "Bishop Oldham is a man of great ability and is the broadest minded man we have ever had here," wrote Rodgers in 1907. Once again comity had a champion in a Methodist bishop.[34]

If relations between Methodists and Presbyterians were generally adjusted by the middle of the first decade, such was not the case with Baptist-Presbyterian relations. Despite the fact that both groups were members of the Evangelical Union and included missionaries favorable to comity arrangements, a satisfactory division of territory was not accomplished for a quarter century. In the interim there was considerable bitterness, which caused some to question the desirability of comity altogether.[35]

Some tension between the two groups was perhaps inevitable, since in 1900 representatives of both denominations established missions in the Iloilo area of Panay island (one of the Visayan group) within a three-month period. However, the initial reaction of the Presbyterians, who were first on the scene, was positive. David S. Hibbard thought his Baptist counterpart, Eric Lund, would be a "splendid co-worker" and that Lund's Visayan assistant, Braulio Manikan, appeared to be "a good and intelligent man." The following year J. Andrew Hall, a Canadian missionary physician in charge of Presbyterian medical work in Iloilo, anticipated "no trouble whatever in working with the Baptists who have always been fair." In fact, in 1900 the missionaries arrived at an informal, unwritten understanding involving a division of territory in Panay and Negros and a commitment not to baptize Filipinos living in the other's jurisdiction.[36] The following year the Evangelical Union in effect sanctioned this informal understanding by assigning the two islands to the Baptists and Presbyterians, leaving a specific division to the two missions.

Complications nevertheless developed as the two groups struggled to achieve a more permanent agreement. The disappointment of the Baptists at finding Presbyterians already in Panay when they arrived was almost certainly an underlying (albeit unvoiced) factor in this evolution. Though relations started out cordially enough (Rodgers personally accompanied the advance party of Baptists from Manila to Iloilo and helped to arrange the *modus vivendi*), the Baptists increasingly looked upon the Presbyterians as interlopers. Although the Presbyterians arrived in Panay first, the Baptists contended that they had laid claim to the area well before they had taken any interest in the island. To support their contention, the Baptists pointed out that almost from the time Commodore Dewey defeated the Spanish at Manila Bay, Manikan, a Panayan then in Spain studying in Eric Lund's Baptist mission, had been preparing Visayan translations of religious literature to take back to Iloilo. Lund, who accompanied Manikan on his return voyage, was convinced that "God wanted us there," and he privately accused the Presbyterians of occupying Iloilo hastily to head off the Baptists. Twenty years later the Baptists continued to be sensitive about the matter, and J. Andrew Hall was sympathetic. "I have felt for twenty years that we really had no right to be in Iloilo," the Presbyterian confided to his mission board.[37]

Still, the disappointment of the Baptist missionaries might not have grown to serious proportions had the respective mission boards in the United States been able to reach a compromise. Instead pride, jealousy,

and prestige combined with genuine doctrinal differences to produce failure and, in the Visayas, almost made the concept of comity a mockery.

The roots of the board's failure extended to the autumn of 1901, when
officials of both societies visited the Philippine mission field. Arthur J.
Brown of the Presbyterian board, though much more liberal in matters of
interdenominational cooperation than Frank F. Ellinwood, the board's secretary, ended his visit to the Philippines convinced that the Presbyterians
must expand their Visayan ministry.[38] In a lengthy and important report,
Brown contended that the Presbyterian claim to Panay was the stronger
one and that, though the Baptists had legitimate interests there, a Baptist
transfer to Cebu and other unoccupied Visayan islands where the Cebuano
language predominated would be in order.[39] Of course, the Baptists, whose
assigned territory was considerably smaller than that of the Presbyterians
(the latter also having an extensive field in Luzon) and who were privately
distressed at *any* Presbyterian presence in Panay, did not concur in Brown's
views. They charged that his report contained information "radically unjust" to the Baptist cause.[40]

On the other hand, Thomas S. Barbour of the American Baptist Missionary Union's executive committee was probably more responsible for
the initial difficulties than Brown. Barbour, whose trip to the islands nearly
coincided with Brown's, was convinced that the Presbyterians were indeed
intruders, and he was appalled to learn that the Baptist mission, in accor-
dance with its unofficial understanding with the Presbyterians, had not
baptized Filipino converts who lived in Presbyterian areas, having instead
referred them to the rival mission. For this dereliction, Charles W. Briggs,
the missionary in charge, was administered what Rodgers characterized as
"a bad keel hauling." By the end of 1901, the Presbyterian-Baptist cooperative arrangement in Panay and Negros was in disarray.[41]

When the Evangelical Union assigned the remaining Visayan islands to
the Presbyterians and the Baptists in January 1902, again leaving a specific
division to the two missions, success hardly seemed likely. In fact, irrita-
tions increased throughout 1902, since the Baptists no longer abided by the
previous arrangement not to baptize persons living in Presbyterian territory, and personal relations became strained. In March, for example, Hall
lauded Briggs as deeply humanitarian, "liberal, kind and considerate"; but
he now felt that Lund was excessively sectarian. Similarly, in June another
Presbyterian missionary accused Manikan of being a dogmatic zealot.[42]
Cooperation was so limited in 1902 that the missions could not even agree
on issuing joint Sunday School leaflets or a Visayan hymnal. Presbyterians
tended to place most of the blame for the breakdown in relations on
Manikan.[43]

In the United States, meanwhile, serious discussions ensued between the two governing boards. Since it was clear that the Baptists were not inclined to withdraw from Panay, the Presbyterian board proposed a division of that island and Negros—in essence, a formalization of the defunct, informal agreement of 1900 that had been reached by the missionaries themselves. Though such a division would entail "considerable sacrifice to Presbyterian interest," the board was willing to proceed "in the interest of comity and fraternal feeling."[44] When the Baptists rejected the proposal, the Presbyterians amended their plan in such a way as to give the Baptists additional territory (one-half of Negros Occidental province); but on December 27 the Baptists rejected the amended proposal and suggested instead a discontinuance of all territorial divisions.[45]

Finally, after further deliberations the two boards reached a limited agreement in April 1903 that applied only to the islands of Panay and Negros—not to the other Visayan islands. To reach the accord, the Presbyterians retreated further and gave the Baptists the entire province of Negros Occidental, and the Baptists, in turn, agreed to issue conciliatory instructions to their missionaries urging them to "respect" the views of their Presbyterian colleagues. Unwilling to deny in principle their right to go anywhere and baptize anyone, the Baptists had nevertheless implied that, in practice, they would avoid baptizing Filipinos who lived in Presbyterian areas. Given the deep Baptist feelings about the importance of immersion for salvation, the implied Baptist concession was a very significant one.[46]

The Presbyterian board, however, minimized the concession and insisted that the agreement was not "just or fair" and was accepted only when it was apparent that none other was possible. The Presbyterian missionaries agreed. "We are glad to receive even the crumbs that are granted us by their decision," Hall commented sarcastically, "and it may be after a few years more that we shall feel obliged to them for the privilege of living in Iloilo."[47]

A few months later negotiations to achieve a more satisfactory agreement began among the missionaries themselves, with serious consideration given to a Presbyterian withdrawal from Panay altogether. The main stumbling block, from the Presbyterian point of view, was doctrinal: the traditional Baptist insistence that Presbyterian converts transferring to the Baptist church would have to be rebaptized by immersion. Because of this most Presbyterians assumed the discussions would be futile, and they were very surprised indeed when the Baptist missionaries agreed to *all* of the Presbyterian conditions for a withdrawal. They would recommend to their board purchase of Presbyterian property, assumption of all the work begun by the Presbyterians, support for the Presbyterian claim to a free hand in other areas of the Visayas (the Methodists were still thought to be interested in working in the area), and acceptance of Presbyterian converts as full members without requiring immersion.[48] The Baptists had agreed, perhaps recklessly, to an astounding series of concessions. As Rodgers expressed it, their willingness to receive Presbyterians as full members "may cost them dear with their church."[49]

Within a few days of the agreement, Rodgers and Briggs urged approval by their respective superiors in the strongest terms. Rodgers pointed out, correctly, that the Baptists had "acceded to all of our demands." Briggs, who had the more difficult assignment, contended sophistically that the Baptists had made "no concessions whatever," then argued more convincingly that from such a distance the executive committee could not fully understand the problems on the field. Doctrinal squabbles, he implied, were absurd in a land where evangelical Christianity was scarcely rooted at all, and as a practical matter the question of immersion was unimportant, for when the Presbyterians withdrew, the Baptists would have a free hand.[50]

The usual, though implausible, explanation of what happened next is that "there was never a word of response from secretaries of either of the Boards."[51] In fact both boards gave careful consideration to the recommendations. The Baptists acted first, rejecting the proposal in February, largely because of the accord on accepting Presbyterians as full members. It was a bitter blow to Briggs. "I want this proposed action taken more than I can put in words," he pleaded in a lengthy response. "Now is the last chance so far as any man can see for the matter to be settled," he stated presciently. But the executive committee was unmoved. "We have no option," replied Barbour, "in respect to conformity to that which we believe clearly the will of Christ."[52]

In April the Presbyterian board also rejected the plan. It would not, the board felt, "further the real interests of missionary work in the Philippines"; neither was it an equitable arrangement, since in return for a withdrawal the Presbyterians would receive nothing except a promise that the Baptists would stay out of the Cebuano field—and the Presbyterians already had a man on Cebu.[53]

Beyond the stated reasons, the Presbyterian board was probably influenced by a division of opinion on the mission field. Though taken aback by the Baptist concessions, some Presbyterian missionaries did not fully support the recommendation of their own negotiating committee. Leon C. Hills, Lewis B. Hillis, and even J. Andrew Hall, for example, never advocated territorial division with as much enthusiasm as did Rodgers. "Dr. Hall has very different ideas," Rodgers once admitted. Hall, who had loyally joined Rodgers in recommending a withdrawal from Panay, nevertheless betrayed a sense of deep ambivalence in the ensuing weeks. "I am . . .

personally very glad to remain here where we have grown up with the work," he confessed several weeks before he could have learned of the board's decision.[54]

The most outspoken, even vitriolic, critic of the tentative accord, however, was Paul Doltz, who had arrived in Iloilo in 1902. Doltz wrote three lengthy letters on the matter in less than a week. The first, to Secretary Brown, was an extensive personal attack on Charles W. Briggs. While all other Presbyterian missionaries praised the Baptist leader, Doltz insisted that he was "the whole crux of the difficulty," that he seemed "determined to drive us out," that he was not "a man of his word," and that he was unduly influenced by Braulio Manikan, whose Christian beliefs, Doltz felt, were open to serious question. Next, in an effort to subject the tentative agreement to unusual, and probably unfriendly, scrutiny, Doltz dispatched a letter to a prominent Presbyterian in the United States asking that he "remember the Secretaries very prayerfully" as the board gathered to consider the proposal. That Doltz had the letter printed suggests that he circulated it fairly widely in order to bring pressure on the board. Finally, in another letter to Arthur Brown, Doltz contended—incredibly—that "as we expected" the recent discussions with the Baptists "yielded nothing." "We are here to stay," he commented. The fact that Doltz's correspondence was referred to in the board's minutes suggests strongly that his views were influential.[55]

Thus, an agreement that had been negotiated to bring about harmony produced instead bitterness and suspiciousness. Briggs even accused Rodgers, incorrectly, of footdragging and hypocrisy.[56]

Whether the limited agreement of April 1903 (by which the boards had agreed to divide Panay and Negros between the two missions) still remained in effect after the boards' rejection of the agreement reached in the field was another matter of dispute. Most Presbyterians claimed that it was, largely because in January 1904 the Baptists joined the majority of the Evangelical Union in voting to continue, in general, the status quo.[57] The Baptists never accepted this interpretation of their vote, although in practice they continued to observe the agreement.[58]

Even if the Presbyterians were correct in contending that the agreement concerning Panay and Negros still held, no one could successfully argue that the Presbyterian occupation of the other Visayan islands was in keeping with the policies of the Evangelical Union. The union had clearly called for mutual agreement there, and no agreement had been reached. The Baptists, therefore, not unnaturally begrudged earlier unilateral Presbyterian expansion into Cebu and Leyte. And when, in December 1904, the Presbyterians offered to withdraw from Leyte, and to give up their claims to Samar as well in exchange for Baptist concessions in Panay, the Baptists responded angrily. The Presbyterian offer was phony, they argued, and only proved that their previous expansion to Leyte was a "chess move" undertaken to better their negotiating position. The Presbyterians had blatantly disregarded the Evangelical Union's policies when they entered Leyte, as well as Cebu, the Baptists charged. "Agreements, when made and not kept, only cause friction. . . ," their representatives stated in a response to the Presbyterian offer. "We are here with the avowed intention and purpose of building a Baptist constituency among the Visayans," they went on in a letter, which was perhaps designed for Baptist consumption at home, but which nevertheless betrayed both a genuine and understandable bitterness and undue suspicion:

> You are here to build up a Presbyterian constituency, and are doing so, whether you will openly admit it or not. Any sort of agreement that blinds itself to these two facts is a waste of time. You are not here to yield a hair's breadth of Presbyterian interest in favor of Baptist work. You have shown that from the start, whether you realize it or not. We have no right to sacrifice Baptist interests, in view of our constituency that supports us from home.

The methods of the Presbyterians, they added, were "questionable." (In the original draft the Baptists characterized the Presbyterian methods as "despicable.") The Presbyterians, they charged, were "moving a pawn" in Leyte while keeping their eye on "a queen move in Iloilo province." Privately, Briggs went so far as to characterize the Presbyterians as "crafty dealers" whose ideas of comity "disgusted" him. Their practices, he wrote, were "grounds for bitterness."[59]

Thus the negotiations ended. The original informal agreement reached on the mission field in 1900 had finally been accepted in its essentials by both boards in April 1903, although not without great difficulty and some bitterness; but whether that agreement, limited to Panay and Negros, was valid after 1904 remained a matter of dispute. Efforts to agree on a pullout by one or the other mission had failed. And no agreement whatever had been reached regarding the other Visayan islands, two of which the Presbyterians had occupied unilaterally in violation of the principles of the Evangelical Union.

Happily, relations improved somewhat in future years. In 1906 the two missions agreed on joint Sunday School lessons, and the Baptists even agreed, albeit by a narrow margin, to permit the Presbyterians to build a student dormitory within Baptist territory. A little later Charles W. Briggs argued against locating a Baptist Bible school in Iloilo City, lest the students be corrupted by Presbyterian influences there. That Briggs found himself alone in opposition was perhaps symptomatic of the better relations.[60]

For a time a Baptist proposal for a jointly operated hospital threatened to upset the slowly improving relations. At first welcoming the Baptist initiative, the Presbyterian board came to suspect that the Baptists would build a competing hospital if the Presbyterians refused their proposal. Chafing under this implied threat, the Presbyterian board momentarily suggested a Presbyterian withdrawal from Panay if the Baptists would take over their work. But this time the missionaries objected, and in the end a jointly financed and staffed hospital was amicably agreed upon.[61]

The decision to form a union hospital was ultimately unhappy, however, for serious conflicts, most of them involving personality clashes, erupted over the years. At one point, Dr. Hall returned to his duties after an absence "with actual dread" and only because of his sense of "grim duty." A proposal was made to return the hospital to exclusive Presbyterian direction in exchange for giving the Baptists exclusive control of a dormitory, but this came to nothing; and in 1920 the Baptists once again suggested a complete Presbyterian removal from Panay, the Presbyterians to locate in Samar, which still had no established Protestant mission work.[62] As they had in 1903, the Presbyterian missionaries recommended, this time with enthusiasm, that the board agree. But the Presbyterian churches in the affected area resisted, and ultimately the missionaries decided to remain. The board, however, appears to have been willing to effect a withdrawal. As late as June 6, 1921, it tried to reassure the local churches that the removal of the Presbyterian missionaries would not affect their status or leave them without a Presbyterian connection.[63] Only in February 1922 did the board "acquiesce" in the missionaries' decision to remain, and even then the board members expressed the hope that Samar would soon be evangelized.[64]

Finally, in 1925 the Presbyterians agreed to withdraw from Panay and assume responsibility for Samar. By that time the work of both missions was entrenched, and the transfer was far more wrenching than it would have been if the boards had accepted a similar settlement in 1903.[65]

The Presbyterian-Baptist experience in the Philippines illustrated both the value of comity and, in contrast to traditional accounts of the early Protestant endeavors in the islands, the difficulty of fully achieving it. Although both groups belonged to the Evangelical Union, the Baptists held doctrinal views that were partially incompatible with the principle of exclusive jurisdiction. The ecumenical views of Charles W. Briggs were ahead of his time. These doctrinal differences, when combined with factors of human weakness on both sides, made a settlement of Presbyterian-Baptist problems extremely difficult. There were limits to comity.

A dispute of potentially similar proportions threatened to erupt on Mindanao, which the Evangelical Union had assigned to the American Board. The first inkling of friction emerged in 1905. The Baptists, feeling that Mindanao held better prospects for mission work than did the unoccupied portions of the Visayas, unsettled over their dispute with the Presbyterians, and feeling no longer bound by the Evangelical Union's territorial divisions, made "careful inquiries" about expansion to that island. In 1907 and 1908 Baptist missionaries made "prospecting trips" to northern Mindanao. With the Presbyterians moving into Bohol and Mindanao next on their list, thought Charles W. Briggs, the Baptists had better move at once.[66]

In almost frantic pleas to his board for immediate action, Briggs claimed that there were too many Baptist missionaries for their current Philippine field, and that when the Presbyterians went into Mindanao some of the Baptists would have to be "sent shamefacedly to China or to other fields. It is criminal," he continued in strong language, "to keep so many men piled top of each other there, without work enough." This sad situation was, he hoped, "unparalleled in the history of Baptist missions." In 1910 yet another Baptist visitation to Mindanao took place, and once again the Baptists requested approval to open a station there.[67]

Unquestionably the Baptist moves, usually taken without consulting with the representatives of the American Board, unsettled the Congregationalists. If the Baptists moved in, Robert Black, the American Board representative in Davao, foresaw "inevitable confusion." In a string of letters to his board, Black reiterated his concern. "It will be unfortunate for the future if they enter," he wrote; there would be "eventually territorial conflict"; "is it too much for us to ask the privilege of evangelizing a quarter of a million," he posited, "when others have so many, and when other fields such as Samar . . . are without any prospect of the Gospel?" "Please ask them [the Baptists] to respect our claim to North Mindanao."[68]

In the end, the Baptist board, apparently strapped for funds and possibly having discussed the matter with the Presbyterians and the American Board, declined to endorse the expansion. In 1911 the Baptists determined to evangelize Samar instead and thus in all likelihood prevented a confrontation of the sort that had marred Baptist-Presbyterian relations in the Visayas. Black was greatly relieved at the Baptist decision. "Thank God!" he wrote to his board.[69]

Yet the Baptist probe raised legitimate questions. The Evangelical Union had indeed assigned Mindanao to the American Board, but to propagate the Protestant Gospel throughout an area the size of the state of Indiana (and with a population twice as large) the American Board had provided by 1907 a single missionary and his wife. That year Charles T. Sibley and his wife joined the Blacks. The mission was situated in Davao on the southern coast, and although the missionaries made occasional visits throughout the island the Baptists (and others) were right to question the commitment of the American Board to Mindanao. As late as 1913 David S. Hibbard, the Presbyterian president of Silliman Institute, protested the lack of a meaningful American Board presence. "The Congregationalists are not caring for Mindanao," he wrote bluntly.[70]

It was a point the American Board missionaries quickly conceded, as their many impassioned pleas for reinforcements amply demonstrate. Finally in 1915 the board sent Frank C. Laubach to Mindanao, where he immediately berated the board for its negligence. The Congregationalist record in the Philippines was, he thought, "a black spot . . . a somewhat disgraceful game. . . . Everyone with whom I have talked in every denomination agrees that this is the richest, ripest, most neglected field in the Philippine Islands."[71]

If Baptist ambitions and American Board negligence threatened to undo the fragile comity arrangements in the southern islands, other aspects of the mission experience in Mindanao exemplified cooperation at its best. When the first missionary of the American Board arrived in 1902, he discovered that he was not the first Protestant representative on Mindanao. As early as 1900 John McKee had engaged in informal evangelistic work on the island and in the Sulu archipelago. After his discharge from the army, McKee had returned to Cagayan de Oro in 1902 as an official representative of the Christian and Missionary Alliance.[72]

Though miffed by reports that McKee had claimed that the Evangelical Union had assigned Mindanao to him, Black nevertheless welcomed a fellow worker. Later Black encountered the Alliance representative living with Moros not far from Iligan.[73] Whether harmonious relations would have developed between the two missions remains speculative, for in 1903 McKee died of cholera and the Alliance suspended its Philippine operations for several years. But if Black's relationship with another mission is any indication of his general posture, relations with the Alliance would have been harmonious.

In the important city of Zamboanga, the Peniel mission, based in Los Angeles, had placed two missionaries, a Scandinavian and an Apache Indian. Black found them to be uneducated but devoted Christians, fluent in the Spanish language, diligent distributors of the Scriptures, and possessed of "courage and zeal to a commendable degree."[74] He also found them cooperative. They intended to join the Evangelical Union, Black reported, and they encouraged him to establish a church in Zamboanga, a church which they would join.[75]

Following the Alliance absorption of the Peniel mission in 1908, there is no evidence of friction with the American Board representatives. Had the American Board sent large numbers of reinforcements, conflict might have developed. But given the broadly ecumenical views of Black and the cooperative approach of both the Peniel and the Alliance representatives, such an outcome seems unlikely. Indicative of the good relations, Black in 1914 invited a former Peniel missionary, Gustav Carlson, to take part in the dedication of a new church in Davao and subsequently urged his board to hire the man for school work.[76]

Another potential source of conflict arose from the fact that the Protestant Episcopal Church chose not to affiliate with the Evangelical Union. Bishop Brent thought the union's purpose admirable, but he would not join it. For one thing Brent had considerably more regard for Catholic conceptions of the priesthood, the sacraments, and ceremonies than did his Protestant brethren.[77] But the most significant obstacle was the view of many Protestants that the Roman Catholic Church in the Philippines was beyond redemption. Though Brent was well aware of the Catholic Church's shortcomings and was from time to time tempted by the prospect of work among Catholic Filipinos, he saw value in the mother church and thought it a waste of scarce resources to devote much attention to the already Christianized portion of the population.

Other Episcopalian missionaries went even further. Fr. John A. Staunton, Jr., one of the first Episcopalian missionaries, felt considerably closer to the Roman church than to the Protestant communions. Criticizing a report by Arthur J. Brown of the Presbyterian board, Staunton contended that he and Brown "could probably never agree upon the needs of this work, because we start from entirely different positions. . . . The Presbyterian Church regards herself as one of the *Protestant* sects," he explained, whereas "the Episcopalian Church regards herself as one of the historical Catholic bodies. Protestantism and Catholicism are not different phases of the same thing," he went on, "but mutual negatives of each other."[78] Had the Episcopalian mission affiliated with the union, Staunton surely would have resigned in protest.

The Episcopalian decision not to join the union disappointed many Protestants. As Homer Stuntz put it, that determination was "a matter of deep regret" to the other missions. "That the Church which so strongly emphasizes the necessity of Church unity will not unite with all others for such ends can not but disappoint our hopes," the Methodist wrote. Stuntz chided Brent for his allegedly naive views on the possibilities of the Roman Church. "The Churches of the Evangelical Union are a unit in believing that the Catholic Church in the Philippines will never lead the Filipino people out of sin into lives of righteousness," he wrote.[79]

Episcopalian assessments of missionaries from other Protestant denominations varied. Brent's initial reaction was very favorable. The churches, he wrote, were "to be congratulated on their representatives. They are strong men and true." Subsequently, though, Brent and other Episcopalians complained about the standards and behavior of various missionaries (complaints not limited, however, to Protestants). Hobart Studley, in charge of Episcopalian work among the Chinese, for example, contended that both Catholics and Protestants (the Presbyterians excepted) received Chinese converts quickly, with too little regard for real commitment, while Brent privately accused one prominent Presbyterian (the irascible Stealy B. Rossiter) and some Methodists of trying to convert Episcopalians and denying the Church's teachings. The bishop was especially irritated with Homer Stuntz. Though he acknowledged that the Methodist had hitherto been "an honorable and fair-minded man," the bishop virtually accused Stuntz of treacherous behavior when he learned that Stuntz had allegedly derided the Episcopalians. "It has been one of the sadnesses of my life," Brent wrote to Stuntz, "to find sometimes that men who did seek for outward fellowship, and who, though they could not sympathize with, at least seemingly refrained from condemning my Church, were guilty of ridiculing and attacking behind the scenes."[80]

In addition to occasional clashes of a personal and doctrinal nature, Episcopalian attempts to establish a presence in Iloilo created some friction, albeit of a relatively minor sort, with the Presbyterians and Baptists who were already located there.[81] Presbyterian J. Andrew Hall thought it best not to stand in the way of the Episcopalian undertaking, since the Episcopalians might have some impact on upper-class Filipinos whom the other Protestants had difficulty in reaching, but Paul Doltz reported misgivings in the Presbyterian fold. It is likely that the Episcopalian presence discomforted the Baptists as well, for when Episcopalian Remsen S. Ogilby visited Iloilo in 1910, he found that the Baptists were "a little suspicious of us."[82]

Another source of friction involved the Columbia Club. The club, an Episcopalian athletic and social organization for foreign men founded in Manila in 1904, overlapped the activities of the YMCA. As long as there was a growing foreign population in the city, conflicts were minor and temporary. When the rapid Filipinization of the government began in 1913 with the Democratic takeover, however, the American population declined. By one account considerably fewer than 4,000 whites of both sexes remained by 1916.[83] Competition for members now threatened to become intense.

In these circumstances Brent's decision in 1914 to approve construction of a new gymnasium angered Y officials. Elwood S. Brown, director of the Y's physical department, went so far as to report that "a small group of unchristian and, in some cases, vicious men" dominated the Columbia Club. "The gymnasium is near completion," he contended, and "the Club membership men are sniping every possible 'Y' member." A meeting with

Brent to discuss the matter proved disappointing. The bishop consistently denied competing with the Y, but he deferred to officers of the club.[84]

But if it is important to acknowledge the disagreements the Episcopalians had with other Protestant missions, such difficulties should not be blown out of proportion. On the contrary, those Protestant bodies that belonged to the Evangelical Union usually enjoyed cordial relations with the Episcopalians. Considerably more consultation and cooperation took place with the Episcopalians than with the Seventh-day Adventists, for example. It is also probably true that relations between the Disciples and the other members of the union (discussed below) were considerably worse, on balance.

One factor leading to good relations was the fact that some Episcopalians were strongly "Protestant" in their orientation. Mercer C. Johnston, rector of the Episcopal Cathedral in Manila, for example, was, according to Bishop Brent, "a rabid Protestant." His condemnations of gambling and other forms of immorality were so strong that he sorely tried the patience of his largely American congregation. He also urged Brent to proselytize more actively among Catholic Filipinos. No wonder the outspoken Methodist missionary, Harry Farmer, referred to Johnston as "a very manly preacher and brotherly friend."[85]

Brent, too, despite his reputation as being High Church, felt that the Protestant denominations had "prophetic gifts," as he put it; up to a point he had no objection to close relationships with them. "I have not the least objection . . . that our Church should be put side by side with the Protestant churches," he wrote Staunton. "I believe that we have a real bond of union with them on the side of constructive truth." Though Brent could not see his way clear to join the Evangelical Union, he welcomed the union's division of territory and pledged to avoid direct competition with all Christian bodies. "Though I cannot say that I shall never place missionaries at points where missionaries of other communions have preceded," he wrote, "I shall do so only in cases where my conception of duty leaves me no choice."[86]

Furthermore, Brent and other Episcopalians conferred regularly with churchmen of other denominations. Brent encouraged Methodist Bishop Oldham to establish Philippine Christian College (now Philippine Christian University), for example, and later contributed to the school's funding. He appeared regularly at union services, spoke at the dedication of the new YMCA complex in 1909, addressed the Evangelical Union on the occasion of its tenth anniversary, and invited Protestant representatives to participate in the consecration of the Episcopal cathedral (on which occasion he "felt just a little mischievous humor in having my friends and brethren the ministers of the Protestant churches in the choir of the Cathedral, two of them walking in procession with the vested clergy and the Bishop in cope and mitre"). A particularly noteworthy instance of a cooperative spirit involved the Presbyterian offer of the use of their church in Tondo as a center for Episcopalian work among the Chinese in that area.[87] In Mindanao, too, where the Episcopalians had a small work, relations with the missions of the American Board and the Christian and Missionary Alliance seem to have been cordial.

In sum, the Episcopalians' refusal to join the Evangelical Union and the occasional clashes with representatives of other Protestant bodies show that the Protestant missionary effort in the Philippines was marked by philosophical, practical, and personal difficulties. But in the case of Episcopalian relations with the other Protestant denominations, harmony and good will outweighed the difficulties. In good part, this was due to Bishop Brent's ecumenical inclinations and his warm assessment of Protestantism in the Philippines. For, in the final analysis, Brent, while seeing value in both Roman Catholic and Protestant persuasions and while attempting to maintain an even handed attitude, concluded that in the Philippines the Protestants had more to offer, at least in the short run. "The Protestant Churches have been of inestimable benefit to the whole religious situation," he wrote while reviewing his sixteen years in the islands. "Though numerically small, their preaching of personal religion, their insistence upon the development of Christian character, and their excellent schools, of which the Silliman Institute of the Presbyterian Church is the finest example, have had a powerful effect throughout the Islands."[88]

More disturbing to the usual view of amicable relations among Protestants in the Philippines were the relations of the Christian Church (Disciples of Christ) with the other denominations. The first Disciples arrived in 1901, and for a time relations seemed pleasant. The established missions quickly sought out the newcomers and encouraged them to join the Evangelical Union, which they did. But because the Disciples held uncompromising views on a variety of doctrinal issues, effective comity arrangements were unlikely to be instituted. Various exceptions and understandings, in fact, encumbered their membership in the Evangelical Union, of which the most significant was their refusal to accept the territorial divisions as binding.[89]

Soon the initial euphoria vanished as the Disciples began moving into territory in northern Luzon assigned to other missions. The Christians, observed Presbyterians J. Andrew Hall and James B. Rodgers in January 1904, "have done some unpleasant proselyting among the members of the Methodist Church." Later that year a Disciples evangelist moved into Presbyterian territory in Laguna Province to the south of Manila, an action that brought forth a pained protest from the Presbyterian missionary in the area.[90]

For the next several years, relations in the provinces deteriorated. Though there were occasional instances of cooperation between Disciples and other missions, and even genuine friendship with the United Brethren mission, bitterness and deep suspicion were more characteristic of the relationship. Clashes in Aparri, Cagayan, were particularly divisive. In 1906, according to the Disciples, the Methodist representative in the city attacked the Disciples on doctrinal grounds and tried to drive their representative out of the city. He further characterized Hermon P. Williams, a Disciple missionary in Vigan, as "a camp-follower, a spy, a stealer" of Methodist converts.[91] When the following spring the leading Disciple missionary, Bruce L. Kershner, learned that the Methodists intended to send another missionary to Aparri, he became enraged: "We are never going to have peace with these people until we move into their territory and teach them the gospel of Jesus Christ at the expense of their own work. . . . There can be no compromise; they intend to suppress our work. We must strike a body blow and we must strike hard." In fact, he felt that the Methodists were "more interested in crushing me and my work than in crushing Romanism and Heathenism."[92]

The Methodists reciprocated the feeling, for four months later Oscar Huddleston addressed a strong letter to the Christian mission, accusing its workers of resorting to "unmanly and unbrotherly things . . . in trying to proselyte from our church." C. L. Pickett, a Disciples missionary physician stationed at Laoag, concluded that Huddleston was out of his head and suggested that the Methodist be administered "a compound cathartic Campbellite pill" as a remedy for his insanity. He also drafted an angry reply to Huddleston in which he accused the Methodist of aggression (though whether he actually sent the letter is not clear). Two weeks later a Methodist missionary in another part of the Philippines confided to Homer Stuntz, "the only man we cannot do business with is [Disciples missionary Hermon P.] Williams and his gang." The clashes in the hinterlands were repeated in the capital city, headquarters of the Evangelical Union. The Methodists and Presbyterians, Kershner reported in November 1905, "are opposing our work strongly at every point we have in the city."[93]

These tensions were reflected in the Disciples' official relations with the Evangelical Union. In 1905 the Disciples declined to concur with the Union's understanding of comity, and Rodgers felt it would be necessary "to urge their withdrawal." Such action was not taken, but the sentiment for ousting the Disciples lingered and emerged again at the union's annual meeting in May 1906. Kershner prevented expulsion, but he began to think in terms of establishing a "passive relationship" with the union, a relationship that he defined as a "cutting loose from the thing without putting ourselves on record as opposing or hindering the organization or its work." Other Disciples demurred, however. Hermon P. Williams, for example, who thought that the union had "never been more than a tool for the M[ethodist] E[pisocpal] and Pres[byterian] Missions and is bound to break up if they don't learn to love us as we really are," preferred either a clean break or an active role. "If our name is used our vote should be heard," he wrote. Kershner remained committed to the concept of a passive relationship, and a formal statement was drafted for submission to the Evangelical Union defining the proposed relationship. But it was never presented, presumably because of dissent within the Disciples mission.[94]

By the summer of 1907 relations had improved somewhat. Kershner found the attitude of the Evangelical Union "no longer personally offensive," and though there were serious clashes in the provinces, Kershner was invited to deliver the banquet address at Union Theological Seminary.[95]

Kershner's address at the seminary was, in retrospect, an early sign of future harmony. But theological differences and deep suspicions could not be quickly set aside. Occasional periods of deep bitterness occurred. In the summer of 1909, for example, the Disciples were convinced that the Methodists had determined to drive the Disciples out of their northern strongholds, "to wipe up the north of the Island as a man wipeth a dish." "The Methodists are going ramping up and down the sea coast, like the tariff, taking everything they can get," Kershner thought, adding that they were a "horrible outfit." Such perception of Methodist activities continued into 1911, C. L. Pickett opining in February of that year that "the Methodists' whole thought is to kick us off the Island of Luzon if possible."[96]

Nevertheless, the evidence suggests that changes were in the wind. Kershner and W. H. Hanna both expressed enthusiasm about joining with other Protestants to form a union college, and Kershner even warned one of his Filipino pastors to avoid proselyting among the Presbyterians. "It is better to convert sinners and people who worship the Pope," he admonished, "than Presbyterians."[97]

By 1912 there was even some cooperation in the north. In Aparri, for example, Methodist and Disciples congregations sometimes held joint services. As might be expected, Bishop William F. Oldham seems to have had much to do with bettering relations. Early in 1912 he attended the Disciples' annual convention, where, according to a Disciples publication, he had a "very pleasant conference" with Disciples leaders regarding the relationship of the two churches in northern Luzon.[98]

In Manila, meanwhile, serious discussions ensued over the possibility of creating a union church of Methodists, Presbyterians, and Disciples. In the end, the Disciples remained out, largely over the issues of immersion and infant baptism.[99] But the very fact that such discussions took place at all was indicative of gradually improving relations.

The year 1913 resulted in serious setbacks for the cause of mission harmony, however. Recalling earlier affronts, Kershner now felt that Methodist efforts to establish a union college and a union church had been an "insidious" attempt to tie up Disciples' money, property, and personnel. Forgetting his own strong support for the college, Kershner expressed surprise that "any of our men should have been caught in such a trap," and he even suggested, at least fancifully, that the Disciples ought to put "a good strong force of our men in the very heart of their Tagalog work." The Methodists felt equally aggrieved with the actions of the Disciples, Bishop Eveland relating that the Disciples in the Vigan area "have been anything but brotherly in their dealing with our work and workers." By the end of 1913 relations in the north had deteriorated so far that C. L. Pickett pronounced the ultimate insult on the Methodists. Their "cantankerous ecclesiasticalism," he wrote on Christmas Day, was nearly as bad as that of the Roman Catholics, and "their ambitions" were perhaps equally "pernicious."[100]

Relations also deteriorated with the Presbyterians. Considerable antagonism developed between Disciples missionary J. B. Daugherty and Presbyterian Charles R. Hamilton over doctrinal differences and alleged intrusions into each other's turf. At one point the Disciples even accused Hamilton of concealing his Presbyterian affiliation in an effort to secure funds and land from Disciples in Lilio to construct a church.[101] In Mauban, on the other hand, Presbyterians charged that Disciples seriously interfered with their work and attempted, apparently with some success, to convert Presbyterians. By the end of the year, Hamilton felt compelled to report that "it has become increasingly difficult to maintain with our brethren of the Christian Mission that sweet attitude of brotherly love that becomes the saints."[102]

At the same time, however, Hamilton suggested "a frank conference between duly appointed representatives of both Missions," which, he hoped, might resolve the issues separating them. In fact, important discussions were already underway in the United States, though with the Methodists. Bishop Oldham's strong view on matters of interdenominational cooperation on the mission field led to a conference with Alexander McLean of the Disciples board about ways to end the conflicts in the islands. McLean, in turn, noting that Oldham seemed "very anxious to have peace," asked Kershner, then in the United States, to put in writing the points of conflict and to make suggestions for better relations. Kershner replied with a lengthy letter in which he isolated three major differences: the Evangelical Union's distribution of territory, to which the Disciples had never agreed; doctrinal differences about baptism and ordination; and "ungentlemanly and discourteous conduct on the part of the workers." After discussing these (and five "minor" differences) at some length, Kershner set forth nine "Suggestions in the Interest of Harmony," which called for more courteous interaction and less rigorous interpretation of the territorial divisions. On the issue of baptism, Kershner proposed three possible solutions: the adoption of immersion by all Protestant bodies, the recognition by all of immersion as "the universally accepted form of baptism," or as a last resort "the withdrawal of opposition in every form from those who believe in and practice" immersion.[103]

McLean, in turn, took Kershner's letter to Oldham. Though Oldham clearly wanted an agreement, he found "two fundamental difficulties" with Kershner's position. In the first place, he strongly defended the idea of clearly defined and accepted divisions of territory. Particularly in the Vigan area Oldham thought that "mutual concessions" looking toward a "well defined line" of division would aid both missions. Secondly, he objected to Kershner's proposal that adult baptism by immersion be made a common Protestant policy. Not only did many Protestants recognize other modes of baptism as valid, but since Filipinos were accustomed to the pedo-Baptist practices of the Roman Catholic Church, insistence on adult immersions would only hinder the Protestant cause, he felt.[104]

Since Oldham's response took issue with only two of Kershner's several observations, the Disciples missionary was encouraged. In a draft letter to McLean he acknowledged that there was something to be said for firm territorial divisions and expressed a willingness to consider "mutual concessions . . . as long as fundamental truth is not adversely affected." He held firm on the immersion question, claiming with some merit that Oldham had misunderstood his suggestions on that point. But the overall tone was conciliatory.[105]

In fact, the draft letter was too conciliatory to suit Charles T. Paul, president of the Disciples College of Missions in Indianapolis, where Kershner was temporarily residing. On Paul's advice, Kershner redrafted the letter, strengthening its tone and challenging some of Oldham's assertions more directly. But his willingness to consider "mutual concessions" on the territorial question remained intact. Clearly some movement toward a settlement had been made. Perhaps it was significant that while these discussions were taking place, the Disciples and Methodists in Vigan held a union Thanksgiving service.[106]

Shortly after this correspondence, Kershner returned to the Philippines, where he was soon engaged in negotiations with Methodist Bishop Eveland. He found himself highly gratified at the spirit shown by the bishop on questions of territorial division and immersion. Discussions between the two churches continued in the Philippines and in the United States. As was to be expected, Bishop Oldham, then assigned to his mission board in New York, more than anyone else kept the conversations going; he negotiated with Disciples officials in the United States and applied considerable pressure on Bishop Eveland to reach an agreement with the Disciples in the islands to "end the scandal of the constant friction between two evangelical bodies in a Roman Catholic land." [107]

Indicative of the progress made, an official commission of the Foreign Christian Missionary Society (Disciples) arrived in the islands in the fall of 1914 to confer on the matter, and serious and lengthy negotiations took place regarding a division of territory in northern Luzon. By now each side was willing to admit that coexistence in the same territory only created friction. For a time optimism and cooperation prevailed. Methodist missionaries in Vigan cordially assisted the official Disciples delegation, and Kershner felt that "we are on the verge of better and more progressive things in the Philippine Islands." A month later he commented on the "radical changes" of the previous two years, the most favorable of which was the changed attitude of other missions toward the Disciples. At the end of October 1914, the Evangelical Union's Committee on Union hosted a two-day conference on further union work, a meeting fully welcomed by the Disciples.[108] And in February 1915, Abe E. Cory of the Disciples board, still hoping for a settlement with the Methodists, urged Kershner to "be real liberal in dealing with the denominations over there, because the leaders here are very anxious that something really constructive be done." [109]

The Disciples commission, in fact, seems to have recommended acceptance of a comity arrangement. And yet, in spite of the considerable progress made and for reasons not entirely clear, agreement remained elusive. "I feel disappointed over the outcome of what had first promised to attain some beneficial and tangible results," Kershner confessed. Subsequent reflections led Kershner to two fundamental insights about the failure. Responding in April to Cory's request to be liberal in his attitude, Kershner defended his record but concluded that "as far as our mission is concerned the problem on the field ought to be taken up by our younger men. . . . Get some young blood on the problem." A little later he hit upon the second point. "Any real progress," he observed, ". . . will have to be made in America," where Bishop Oldham could make decisions. Bishop Eveland in the Philippines, he concluded correctly, was well intentioned but too much influenced by the missionaries in the field.[110]

Finally, in June 1918, the Disciples entered into a formal territorial agreement with the Presbyterians, the first one they had ever signed in the Philippines. But agreement with the Methodists had to wait until 1923, when it was agreed that the Disciples would withdraw from the Cagayan Valley and an area south of Vigan, and the Methodists would withdraw from the northern part of Ilocos Sur and from Abra.[111]

The pattern of relations between the Seventh-day Adventists and other Protestant bodies closely resembled that of the Disciples' relationship with the other denominations. Sharing certain common beliefs, including an antipathy toward Roman Catholicism, Adventists could at one level accord praise to the work of the other Protestant missions in the Philippines. But strongly held doctrinal beliefs, which other Protestants generally considered unessential, kept the Adventists from joining the Evangelical Union and from observing the union's territorial divisions, and led them in good conscience to convert Protestant Filipinos to their faith.

Initial contact between Adventists, who arrived in 1905, and the already established missions, were cordial enough.[112] But as time passed tension more normally characterized the relationship. Actually, given the Adventists' tenacious belief in their interpretation of Scripture, any lasting cooperation was unlikely. Indeed, the Adventists anticipated opposition and almost seemed to welcome it. As E. H. Gates put it, even while wishing the other missionaries well, "now it remains to be seen what these [other Protestant] workers will do when God's truth for these times shall be proclaimed among the millions of these islands." Nor would he tolerate territorial divisions. "God's last message must be given notwithstanding these regulations," he insisted.[113]

By 1911 Seventh-day Adventist work had advanced sufficiently to engender serious antagonism. Presbyterians reported "persistent attacks" by Adventists, while L. V. Finster, the first permanent Adventist missionary, reported "meeting bitter opposition from the other churches."[114]

Presbyterians in particular, but Methodists as well, felt that Adventists deliberately attempted to "divide or destroy" their congregations "by preaching the unessentials of doctrine." There is little evidence to support the charge that Adventists deliberately tried to destroy the congregations begun by other missions. On the other hand, it is clear that Adventist missionaries and their Filipino workers felt few qualms about converting members, and even ministers, of other denominations to their way of thinking, actions which obviously had disrupting effects. In 1911, for example, Finster was instructing two Filipino Protestant pastors: a Presbyterian and a Disciple.[115] In 1913 another Adventist missionary, Elbridge M. Adams, sent a Filipino evangelist to convert Protestants in Cavite. And the next year Finster again reported instructing Filipino Protestant pastors, this time a Baptist and a Methodist, in Adventist doctrine. The Methodist, he added, was "a minister of many years experience."[116]

There is no need to question the sincerity of the Adventists to sympathize with the charge that they were "sheep stealers." No wonder Finster reported in 1916 that, at least in Laguna, greater opposition to Adventist work arose from Protestants than from Roman Catholics.[117]

What, then, can be concluded about the nature of interdenominational relations on the Philippine mission field? The usual view that singles out the mission experience in the Philippines as a model of effective comity arrangements and harmonious relationships among the various missions needs to be modified. The formation of the Evangelical Union, the union's efforts to apply comity to an entire country, the establishment of various ecumenical institutions, the helpful role of the YMCA, and the often cordial relationships that developed among missionaries across denominational lines constitute a strong case for the traditional picture. But there was another side to the mission experience that is seldom discussed in the available literature, a side marked by bitter disagreements over territory, attempts to proselytize among members of other Protestant churches, and ad hominem attacks on missionaries of other communions. Whether resulting from sincere doctrinal differences or from such emotions as pride, considerations of prestige, or other human weaknesses, all was not sweetness and light.

Probably the two most significant qualifications to the usual picture are the bitter Baptist-Presbyterian disputes in the Visayas and the inharmonious relationship of the Disciples, on the one hand, and the other Protestants, on the other. In both of these cases all parties involved were members of the Evangelical Union. These and less important disagreements suggest that there were limits to comity in the early Protestant mission experience in the Philippines.

PART II

Missionaries and Filipinos

4

Filipino Culture and Characteristics: The Missionary Perspective

> We are not living in Boston.
> Frank C. Laubach, missionary
> of the American Board

The late nineteenth century was a period of great fascination with race and racial differences. Drawing on the insights of Charles Darwin and his popularizers, social scientists wrote learned books and articles that analyzed the various racial and ethnic groups. It was commonplace to rank the races, comparing them in terms of intelligence, culture, and possibilities for advancement. "Racist concepts pervaded Anglo-American life," wrote Bradford Perkins. Almost invariably, whites (particularly Anglo-Saxons) received the highest marks.[1]

Missionaries could scarcely escape their culture. They too found the study of racial differences fascinating, and many of them became amateur anthropologists. "We are studying the natives very carefully," wrote a missionary couple in 1906.[2] Numerous missionaries discussed the exotic "natives" at length. J. Andrew Hall completed a four-page essay on "Philippine Life and Character," while his fellow Presbyterian, David S. Hibbard, devoted an entire chapter in his book, *Making a Nation*, to "Filipino Characteristics." Methodist Homer C. Stuntz described Filipino culture at even more length in *The Philippines and the Far East*, as did Baptist Charles W. Briggs in *The Progressing Philippines*. And in an almost countless number of letters to their mission boards and in articles for their denominational journals, other missionaries commented in passing, and sometimes at length, on these curious beings. After all, unlike the typical American who could only fantasize about the exotic cultures of the mysterious East, the missionary was in daily contact with them.

With a notable exception or two, Protestant missionaries found the cultural differences between Filipinos and Americans to be substantial. "They *think* differently and *do* differently," the Reverend and Mrs. Charles Magill

65

explained to their friends back home.[3] The consequences of this perception were sometimes humorous and not particularly invidious. Officials of
the YMCA, for example, formulated different rules for American and Filipino volleyball teams. Filipino teams could hit the ball only three times on
their side of the net before passing it to their opponents, whereas there was
no limit for the Americans. The reason was "a fundamental difference in
the two races. The American does everything direct—in volley ball each
man usually tries to put the ball into the opponents' territory every time he
hits the ball," it was explained. "The Filipino does things indirectly, he likes
to tease the mouse awhile—in volley ball to pretend that he is about to put
it over the net and then does not do so." After one Filipino team hit the
ball fifty-two times on its own side before putting it over the net, the rules
were changed![4]

In speculating on the deeper significance of the perceived racial and cultural differences, some of the more literate missionaries drew inspiration
from popular intellectuals of the age. Rudyard Kipling's name and selec-
tions from his poetry flit in and out of missionary correspondence. The
famous English sociologist, Benjamin Kidd, who wrote *Social Evolution*
(1894) (which brought him instant acclaim), served to reinforce missionary
views on the justness of their presence in tropical areas.[5] Charles Edward
Woodruff's study, *The Effects of Tropical Light on White Men*, (1905), had a
direct impact on the Disciples of Christ missionaries, and perhaps on
others. This book, based on information Woodruff gathered in 1902 while
serving in the Philippines as a surgeon in the army, postulated that whites
degenerated in tropical areas. The best way to protect themselves from the
enervating effects of the tropical sun, Woodruff maintained, was to wear
red and orange clothing—a suggestion that, if widely adopted, would have
wrought a notable change in the clothing of the colonialist, which was
typically a white cotton suit. Perhaps the Disciples also read Woodruff's
subsequent book, *Expansion of Races* (1909), whose enthusiastic admirers,
according to one scholar, considered it "the most outstanding contribution to literature since Darwin's *Origin of Species.*" In *Expansion of Races*,
Woodruff acknowledged that tropical peoples were physically better
adapted to their environment than were whites. But his contempt for the
intellectual capacity of "natives" was clear. Vaccines to prevent epidemics
among domestic animals in the Philippines could be very useful, he pointed
out, "but this implies that men of much intelligence must be on the spot,
for the native has not the requisite brain."[6] Whites had to retain control.

Whether gaining insight directly from the intellectuals of the day or
merely reflecting the Darwinian milieu of the age, many missionaries enjoyed the popular pastime of making comparative racial judgments. That
there were many different cultural groups in the Philippines made the

game more complex, but also more interesting. Among lowland Christian Filipinos, missionaries generally thought the Tagalogs, who lived primarily on the large island of Luzon, the most advanced and intelligent. Bishop William F. Oldham of the Methodist Church, for example, thought them "the brightest . . . most highly cultured and most Spanishized" of the Filipinos, though he also considered them the "most superficial." Homer Stuntz thought them "the most enterprising, the most quarrelsome, the most restless race in the country," characteristics he attributed partly to circumstances but mostly to "strong racial tendencies." Similarly, a Baptist observer placed the Tagalogs first, based on "mental capacity, energy and ambition." Even the Seventh-day Adventists, who normally refrained from making racial judgments of this kind, seem to have agreed with their colleagues. The Presbyterians were perhaps in the best position to make detailed comparisons, since they had extensive work both in Tagalog regions and in the Visayan areas to the south. Written comparisons are surprisingly few, but it nevertheless seems clear that the Presbyterians shared the general perception of Tagalog superiority. For example, when Fred Jansen was assigned to Cebu, one of the Visayan islands, after having previously worked in Tagalog areas, he went with some regrets, since he felt that Tagalogs made better assistants. They were, he wrote, "much superior to the Visayan natives, and are far more reliable."[7]

Close to the Tagalogs, in the missionary mind, were the Ilocanos, who lived in northern Luzon. Stuntz attributed to the Ilocanos such positive qualities as "alertness and progressiveness . . . industry, enterprise, and trustworthiness," while another Methodist saw them as "a strong, vigorous, self-supporting people." Bishop Oldham even thought they were "much more virile and promising" than the Tagalogs, if presently less advanced. Only the Baptists (or at least the Baptist leader) disagreed, convinced that both Ilocanos and Visayans were generally too drunk to amount to much.[8]

Visayans provoked contradictory judgments. Bishop Oldham ventured the admittedly secondhand opinion that the Visayan was the "equal of the Tagalog in intelligence and is superior in staying quality and moral heft" (a judgment which Charles Briggs, the Baptist leader, would have disputed vehemently). Presbyterian James B. Rodgers probably summed up the prevailing view. Compared to Tagalogs, he wrote, the Visayans were "a weaker race intellectualy and otherwise." On the positive side, some missionaries felt the Visayans were quiet and peace-loving, even if less ambitious and intelligent.[9]

Though most missions had only limited contact with the non-Christian peoples living in the mountains of Luzon (commonly called Igorots),[10] their intriguing cultures brought forth widespread comment. All agreed that the Igorots were uncivilized, unchristian savages, many of whom engaged in such unpleasant barbarities as headhunting. Beyond that, missionary observations fell into two categories. A minority saw little of redeeming value in the Igorots and their culture. The first Methodist comment on the Igorots, for example, was disdainful. The people refused Western civilization, engaged in blood feuds, and were akin to animals, creeping into their simple huts "like quadrupeds." Stuntz admired their beautiful terraces and thought them industrious. But in his view they remained "stolid, filthy . . . savages" whose "inherited instincts" would probably stand in the way of efforts to civilize them. He even had reservations about making the attempt. "Our experience with the black man and the red man is not such as to make it entirely certain that the sudden change will bring about unmixed good," he thought.[11]

To the large majority of missionaries, however, the Igorot more closely resembled the Noble Savage. Missionaries, after all, often had mixed feelings about the value of "civilization." Modern Western society had its advantages, of course, and most missionaries hoped to make Filipinos more "progressive" and "efficient" in the Western mold. At the same time they were well aware that civilization, if introduced too quickly and without proper safeguards, could be debilitating and corrupting. One had only to look at the "half-civilized" Filipinos, as many missionaries viewed most lowlanders, to see the corrupting side of modern civilization. Some missionaries, in fact, saw it as a primary obligation to protect Filipinos (especially the mountain groups) from unhealthy and immoral outside influences, to soften the blow of Americanization. The Igorots, then, had the disadvantages of savagery, but their very remoteness from civilization had saved them from its corrupting effects. Bishop Charles Henry Brent of the Episcopal mission put it perfectly: the Igorots were "in the position of Adam and Eve—after the Fall."[12]

Thus the Igorots were seen as sturdy, industrious, intelligent, and appreciative of kindness. They were "much better . . . than the class you meet round the towns," thought a Presbyterian missionary in Legaspi. They were "very intelligent" and raised "the best corn and rice I have seen on the Islands," wrote a United Brethren missionary in 1901. The most rhapsodic expression came from Methodist Harry Farmer, who in a poem confided to the privacy of his diary, pictured the Igorots as honest, innocent, and nearly godlike: "Oh! Igorot! Dear Igorot! / Clothed with Sun and Shade / A manly man from head to foot. / For thus are all men made."[13]

The Episcopalians carried on the most active work among the Igorots. The prospect of work among the mountain people genuinely excited Bishop Brent. "If I were free to do it I would not ask a greater privilege than to give my life for these people," he wrote to his board. Not only had most mountaineers had little if any contact with Christianity (and were thus ideal subjects for a church that was reluctant to proselytize among Roman Catholic lowlanders), but they had a certain healthy independence, a sturdiness, an industriousness, and an innocence that gave them a degree of superiority over their civilized cousins. Brent wrote, on his first trip to the backcountry, that they were "wild and savage" but also good natured, "a fine race physically" with a "keen sense of humor." The Bontoc Igorots in particular appealed to him, and he immediately established mission stations in Bontoc and Baguio, the latter in the process of becoming a place for Americans and well-to-do Filipinos to escape to from the summer heat of Manila.[14]

Subsequent observations confirmed the bishop in his favorable, almost romantic, view of the Bontoc Igorots (whom he thought superior to the Benguet Igorots in the Baguio area). Though he was, of course, strongly opposed to headhunting, he rather admired the Igorots' "strong powers of resistance," even though it made change difficult to achieve. The story of Pitt-a-pit illustrated his point: "I asked Pitt-a-pit how old he was and he replied, 'Igorrotes no count how old'. He knew that he was about ten, as he afterward said; but he wished me to understand that in informing me he was but making a concession to my weakness." The Igorots, he concluded, had considerably more strength of character than did "the plastic Ilocanos."[15] Another trip to Mountain Province in 1908 reinforced his romantic view of the people. They were loyal, "simple children of nature"; he was proud the Episcopalians had taken responsibility for them and hoped to expand the work extensively.[16]

Missionaries viewed mountain people in the Visayas and in Mindanao in a light similar to the Igorots of Luzon, though there were fewer expressions of outright romanticism. Near Iloilo, Panay, for example, Baptist Eric Lund encountered a group of hill people whom the lowlanders called disparagingly "cows of the mountains." Lund thought they were undeveloped, childish, and dependent. But he thought they were stronger physically than the lowlanders and had intellectual potential. Having tested both young and old, Lund in fact concluded that they were "quite as capable of learning as any average white man."[17]

In Mindanao, such repelling practices as slavery, human sacrifice, and cannibalism made some missionaries consider the uplanders extremely crude and primitive pagans. An American Board missionary thought it almost unbelievable that as late as 1915 a human sacrifice could occur among the Bagobos "in [an] American colony under the starry flag, worse yet by people the American Board has pledged themselves to care for."[18] But if the mountain folk were "like little wild animals" with repulsive customs, they could also be viewed, like the Igorots to the north, as "little diamonds in the rough" who only needed cleaning and polishing by the missionary. As early as 1903 Robert Black concluded that the Bagobos, the mountain people with whom his mission had the most contact, were a fine, industrious, and artistic people, in spite of their attraction to the betel nut. Charles Sibley, the next American Board missionary to arrive, agreed (at least until the existence of human sacrifice became apparent to him). Before his arrival in Mindanao, Homer Stuntz had informed Sibley that the Bagobos were "a stunted pigmy race wild as rabbits." But after personal observation Sibley concluded that the Methodist had been grossly in error. Not only were they nearly as tall as other Filipinos, but they were also friendly, clever, sturdily independent, and even industrious—"that is for the P.I." [19]

As with the Igorots, there was general agreement that the mountain people of Mindanao were less corrupted than many lowlanders as a result of their isolation. In his trip across the interior of the island in 1904 with General Leonard Wood, for example, Bishop Brent learned that sexual immorality, a rare phenomenon, was punished by death. Liars could no longer reside in the community. The Bagobos in particular impressed the bishop. [20] Frank Laubach, who arrived as an American Board missionary in 1915, also praised the Bagobos. They were, he wrote, "strong, healthy, manly, clean, honest, liberty loving folk. . . . They have in them the making of a great people." The same was true of most of the mountain people who had not been corrupted by civilization, he felt, with the Bukidnons and Mandayas reputed to be "even more promising than those Bagobos whom I have learned to love and respect so soon." [21]

If the Igorots and other Malayan mountain peoples of the islands had redeeming features in spite of their savagery, the missionaries found precious little good to say about the aboriginal Negritos, who also inhabited the mountains from Mindanao to Luzon. Described by one missionary as being "about 4 ft. high, living in tiny huts, wear only G-string, use bow and poisoned arrow, do not mix with other races, hate the Filipinos, [and] kill children whose parents die," [22] the Negrito was thought to be "a savage pure and simple," [23] repulsive and stupid, animallike, and worthless. They were "near in life and habit to the monkeys," thought a Disciples missionary after an intensive interview with a Negrito informant. A Baptist missionary thought them "about as near to nature as any man can get and not be a beast," adding that one whom he encountered was "the most loathsome creature that I ever laid eyes upon." Presbyterian William B. Cooke summed up the missionary perception. Negritos were, he wrote, "at the bottom of the pile." [24]

Missionaries shared the view of anthropologists of that day that the Negritos had failed as a race in the struggle for existence and would soon disappear, conforming, as Homer Stuntz put it, "to the law which exacts obedience and labor from all who would continue to live on the face of the earth." Bishop Brent, too, characterized them as a dying race, and even the more charitable Frank Laubach thought them "hopeless" and on the verge of extinction.[25] Probably because they were thought to be incapable of civilization, the missions virtually ignored the Negrito population. Only the Methodists carried on a small work among the Negritos in Pampanga. By 1916 they seem to have had at least one Negrito worker carrying the Word to his fellows, and they hoped to increase their ministry to them. But the Negritos were still considered "very crude and benighted, almost naked and houseless dwellers in the mountain forest fastnesses."[26]

The Muslims, who inhabited large portions of Mindanao and the Sulu archipelago stretching toward Borneo, constituted another very distinctive cultural group. Called Moros by the Spanish, and subsequently by the Americans and Christian Filipinos as well, these fiercely independent people (actually several different Muslim groups) had never been fully conquered by the Spaniards. The Protestant missionary perception of the Moros was nearly unanimous. They were seen as fanatically religious and bigoted, practitioners of a degraded Islam, fierce, warlike, treacherous, and ready to plot the death of any Christian within reach. During a trip with the armed forces in Mindanao in 1903, Zerah C. Collins of the YMCA recorded an example of alleged Moro treachery. Moros hired to do road work, he stated, "may be watching for an opportunity to steal a Krag, or laying plans to cut up some unwary soldier after the day's work is over." Collins did not think the Moros were very bright, however. At the request of the army, Collins displayed a zonophone to "impress these savages with our superior skill as a people":

> One old sultan was especially interested in the machine and I asked him why the Moros did not make them. He said, "No got." I pointed to the brass and said, "Got this?" "Yes." Then to the iron; "Got this?" "Yes." Then to the wood; "Got this?" "Yes." Then to the cloth; "Got this?" "Yes." Then I tapped my forehead: "Moro got this?" The old fellow's leathery face broke into a grin and he shook his head. He saw the point.[27]

The only real question about the Moros, in fact, was whether their nature could be changed. Charles Sibley was convinced that the Moro was "naturally a bad man. . . . They have been robbers and pirates so long that it is their nature now," he thought, adding that the only hope for the Moro was the missionary who might succeed in making "a new creature." Bishop Brent was equally pessimistic initially. "I imagine but little can be done for them," he wrote to Secretary of War William Howard Taft in 1904. However, the bishop grew increasingly fond of the Moros. To be sure, they were "a repulsive looking people," largely because of their proclivity for chewing betel nuts and their susceptibility to several disfiguring diseases. They were aggressive and warlike, and practiced slavery as well. But, like the Igorots, they were independent and courageous, qualities Brent admired. "The Moro is by nature aggressive," Brent told a newspaper reporter in 1913. "His prowess, daring, mental shrewdness and manual skill put him far ahead of most men of Malay origin. He has characteristics which, when properly trained, will be an asset of civilization."[28]

Frank Laubach, who worked in Mindanao after his arrival in 1915, was equally convinced that the Moro had redeeming qualities of considerable value. Like other observers, Laubach agreed that the Moros had an unpleasant history of headhunting, piracy, murder, terror, and slavery. But that had changed notably under American rule. "The Moros are worth saving," he wrote in a plea for extended missionary work; for if the Moros were warlike, they also had enormous energy that could be harnessed for good instead of evil.[29]

Although the missionaries differentiated among the various Filipino cultural groups, many could not resist the temptation to generalize about Filipinos and to compare them as a whole with other races. As a rule, Filipinos and other Malays were ranked rather toward the bottom. A year after Charles Sibley arrived in the Philippines in 1908, he decided that the "bulk of the native people are very inferior." Disciples missionary Bruce Kershner concluded in vivid language that the only thing that kept a missionary "in sympathy with the degraded people he would otherwise despise" was his almost naive faith that there was a saintly quality in all human life.[30] Methodist Bishop James M. Thoburn, who had spent a grand total of three weeks in the islands (though he had lived for many years in India and Southeast Asia) advised the Senate Committee on the Philippines that Filipinos were a cut above North American Indians, but regrettably ranked below the Chinese and far below the Anglo-Saxons. Asked directly whether Filipinos were equal "to the American people, the Anglo-Saxons" in intellectual and moral capacity, the bishop replied without hesitation that they were not.[31]

Among the missionaries with the most consistently negative assessments of Filipino capacity and culture were three Presbyterians. Stealy B. Rossiter, pastor of the English-speaking church in Manila from 1904 to 1910, was a man of settled and fiery views. He was a strong imperialist who thought that William Howard Taft had gone much too far in turning responsibilities over to the inhabitants. More, not less, American direction was required, he argued passionately and at length. His premise was that the islands contained a "great bunch of semi-civilized human material." Filipinos were, he thought, "a simple minded people & have all the impulsiveness and prejudices of children."[32]

Paul Doltz found Filipinos downright uncongenial, at least at first. "When one has gotten over the first feelings of disgust at the filthy manner in which the natives eat it is quite interesting to watch them," he wrote in December 1906. Six months later he requested permission to begin his furlough early, citing in part the fact that he and Mrs. Doltz were "growing exceedingly irritable and impatient with the native brethren."[33]

The least charitable of the missionaries was probably Charles E. Rath, which may explain in part his inability to attract converts in Cebu and Leyte. "For four years I have been working alone here in the island of Leyte, trying to present the gospel to the people who cared little about receiving it, less about having me around," he wrote forlornly from Baybay, where he had moved after several frustrating years at Tacloban. "I seem to them, at least to a great majority of them like a useless piece of furniture does to a good housekeeper at home." If, in his intercourse with Filipinos, Rath revealed his private attitudes about them, there would have been less reason to wonder at his lack of success. The people he attempted to reach were, he thought, "poor ignorant and extremely superstitious." They also tended to get drunk. Filipino behavior irritated the missionary. "I often feel that the words used by the majority of Americans in describing the people are true," he confessed. When an American teacher was murdered in Tacloban, he reported that most Americans there felt that "the only good Filipino is a dead one." If he could not quite agree with such an extreme sentiment, he understood the attitude. "They are so very treacherous," he wrote.[34]

In other letters Rath characterized Filipinos as "in general . . . less intellectual," immoral, and especially lazy. He reported:

> In a small barrio recently the missionary was sitting by the seaside talking to a group of Filipinos. The thought came to him to find out how many of these men before him had worked that day. He asked one after the other and of the six men there was not one who had done any work. . . . And this is not an exception. One can find them sitting around in their houses and on streets, living in tumble-down shacks and subsisting on about nothing simply because they are too lazy to work.[35]

To many missionaries the most congenial way of expressing a belief in Filipino inferiority was to refer to the people as children. This was an extremely common motif, present in the correspondence of virtually all Protestant groups. Harry Farmer, for example, justified making a legal settlement out of court without consulting the Filipinos most directly affected in the case, despite their protests, because of their "child like character."[36]

Did the missionaries' references to Filipino inferiority mean that the people were more or less permanent children, incapable of further development? Or did they mean that, given the right stimulus, the people would mature into adulthood? The overall impression is a blurred one.

Some missionaries agreed with Bishop Thoburn that the Filipinos were mentally inferior beings. Bruce Kershner opined that the masses were "defective" in "thought power." A Baptist publication concluded that intellectual ability in the Philippines was "conspicuous by its absence" and that it was doubtful if the people would "ever become an intellectual people." Sanford Kurtz, a United Brethren, concluded that the failure of the Filipino to develop a good agricultural system resulted from an underdeveloped brain.[37] To such persons the defects appeared to be permanent or, at best, not remediable in the foreseeable future.

Missionary views of the sizeable Spanish and Chinese mestizo populations in the islands may also indicate a belief in permanent Filipino inferiority. Generally speaking, missionaries thought that mestizos were "gifted with stronger bodies and greater intellectual powers than the pure native."[38] When Gregorio Araneta became attorney general in 1907, for example, Bishop Brent was pleased, for Araneta, he thought, was "one of the best men . . . among the Filipinos." But he was quick to point out that this was "due to a very generous mixture of foreign blood—Spanish, I think."[39]

Logically missionaries who felt this way ought to have encouraged interracial marriages as a way of strengthening the culture and perhaps the general intelligence of the people. In fact, none did (at least where whites were concerned), in some instances revealing their innermost feelings about race. Bishop Brent is a case in point.

The issue arose when Jaime Masferre, a Spaniard living in the Igorot community of Sagada, chose to marry a local woman. Masferre had once been an officer in the Spanish army, was honorably discharged, and went to the mountains to grow coffee. Unlike many Spaniards, Masferre remained in the islands during the troubled times of the 1890s. When the Episcopalians arrived in Sagada, Masferre was the only white person nearby. He welcomed the Episcopalians, served as interpreter, and was soon hired as a fulltime staff person. The question was whether to pay Masferre on the "native" scale or not. Brent quickly concluded that Masferre's Spanish heritage saved him from the "native" classification, but the fact that he had recently married an Igorot rankled the bishop. "Perhaps his marrying an Igorot justly places him somewhat on a par with native helpers," he wrote testily. On top of Masferre's marriage, another Ameri-

can at Sagada (whether a missionary is not clear) had just married an Ilocano woman; Brent lamented, "the deed had already been done when I
reached Sagada."[40]

Brent acknowledged that rationally such marriages were much prefer-
able to the informal arrangements ("the unhallowed connection") that European and American men were prone to establish with local women.
Moreover, it was almost impossible, he thought, to lead "a continent life"
in "the sensuous tropics" unless one were married. But rational considerations could not prevail over the emotional side of the issue. "It grieves me
whenever I see one of my fellow-citizens tied for life to a Filipina," he confessed; "it seems to me unnatural, and" (a particularly telling admission)
"ordinarily I cannot get away from a sense of degradation connected with
it." Returning once again to the rational side, Brent concluded that such
marriages were "far less unnatural than any other mode of life that an un-
disciplined man can hope to live in the tropics."[41]

Thus a serious tension existed in Brent's mind. On the one hand, he
knew that interracial marriages made sense, that they could even uplift the
indigenous culture and produce a more intelligent populace. On the other
hand, he clearly preferred racial purity (at least where whites were concerned), accepting intermarriage only as a lesser evil, and feeling a con-
commitant sense of Filipino inferiority. The tension could not always be
held inside, and on occasion the bishop lashed out (usually in private
letters) in ways that revealed a contempt for Filipinos. "The Filipinos are
hundreds of years behind the Cubans," he wrote in an extreme statement in
1904. There was "conspicuous incapacity even among the so-called leaders." A little later he professed to have overestimated Filipino capabilities.
"I had no idea they were as incompetent and feeble a folk as they are," he
warned.[42]

Other missionaries, however, were more cautious in their assessment of
Filipino capacities. "There is a great mass of research work to be done on a
world scale before we can declare the ultimate law of race possibilities,"[43]
wrote a Methodist. A Baptist insisted that Filipinos were "able to think for
themselves," while a Presbyterian concluded that there were "as many
kinds of Filipinos as there are of Americans." Bishop Oldham explicitly rejected notions of racial inferiority in a speech at the Lake Mohonk Conference of 1913.[44] And the Seventh-day Adventists consistently maintained, in
published articles and private correspondence, that Filipinos were intelligent and, by implication at least, potentially as capable as any other
people.[45]

Of the more prominent missionaries, Episcopalian Walter C. Clapp
probably came the closest to transcending the racial and cultural biases of

his age. Insisting that he was utterly without racial prejudice, Clapp took issue with the commonplace judgments of Filipino inferiority. But even he admitted that it was possible to consider the people "an inferior race" (though he professed not to do so), and to "entertain reasonable doubts as to the possibilities of their becoming anything else." Such a conclusion could be based on differences in "blood," "antecedents," and the tropical climate. In spite of his inclination to disagree with such judgments, Clapp once acknowledged that the people exhibited a "childish character."[46] If the missionary most inclined to question the generally accepted wisdom of the day on racial matters displayed a certain ambivalence, then other missionaries, much less skeptical of claims of inferiority, might be expected even more readily to perceive Filipinos as deficient.

There was, in sum, no overwhelming consensus on the issue of mental inferiority. The question was in a sense left open, being—after all—ultimately unanswerable. But that Filipinos were at present inferior, at least culturally, was less open to debate among the missionaries. Even the Episcopalians, who made several convincing pleas to avoid the easy generalization, the quick judgment, the contemptuous expression,[47] could not fully avoid the temptation to do just that, the bishop being the worst offender.

Missionaries were, in fact, very specific about perceived cultural inadequacies. The most basic was lack of cleanliness. Though the Filipinos had their missionary defenders on this score,[48] observations of "dirty natives" predominate. Perhaps the most vivid statement on the matter came from Robert Black of the American Board. For more than two years Black's house also served as his chapel, but in 1905 he petitioned for funds to construct a church building. "We feel that our house is not the place for filthy, diseased natives, much as we love them," he explained. Bruce Kershner of the Disciples professed similar feelings. "Imagine them in troops of a dozen, more or less, coming to your home, some covered with sores, scrofulous, epileptic, possibly smallpox, all dirty and naked; they sit on your chairs, handle your clothes, play with your books, or any thing they can get. . . . We try to keep them from coming upstairs where we live, for they are bad enough downstairs in the chapel, vestibule, and school room," he wrote. Doubtless, Kershner, too, would have preferred to house the chapel in a separate building.[49]

Missionaries thought that poor hygienic habits accounted for their dirty state. Kershner stated that in his five years in the islands he had never seen a Filipino, except for servants and school children, wash his hands and face unless bathing the entire body. Similarly, Baptists in Iloilo hoped that the mission hospital there would "revolutionize the hygenic ideas and habits of the people," one missionary hoping that "the power of a New Ideal" would show them "the power of soap and water." Bishop Brent, not one to wait for the New Ideal to take hold, arranged for William Proctor, of Proctor and Gamble, to donate a ton of Ivory soap for the Igorots' use![50]

More central to the Protestant critique of Filipino culture were moral questions. Again, the Filipinos found a few defenders among the missionary community, one Alliance missionary insisting that morality was one of the people's strong points.[51] But their champions were so few as to be almost eccentric.

Gambling, particularly at the cockpit, attracted the most critical attention. "It is everywhere, gambling, gambling, gambling," wrote a missionary with typical Baptist emphasis. It deprived Filipinos "of the vital forces," wrote another one, and was "the curse of the Islands."[52] Its elimination was a matter of central concern for all Protestant groups.

The popularity of the cockfight was evidence of another moral deficiency, cruelty. So casual were Filipinos in the presence of suffering that some missionaries wondered if they had any conception of the meaning of cruelty. Was the cockfight cruel? one missionary inquired. "They had never thought of that." "They don't seem to have any sense of humanity," wrote another, "especially of their animals such as chickens dogs & pets." Some missionaries even seriously wondered whether the nervous system of Filipinos was as sensitive to pain as was that of Caucasians. All in all, the cockpit with its attendant vices tended "to make a nation unmoral."[53]

Bruce Kershner considered this alleged cruel streak part of the larger problem of thoughtlessness and inefficiency, criteria by which, in good Progressive fashion, he judged Filipinos. Filipino mothers loved their children passionately, he wrote by way of illustration, but they could be "thoughtless in a fit of rage" inflicting permanent injury on their offspring. They also seemed not to understand how to feed their children properly, even after repeated instruction and demonstration. Relating the story of one mother whose child was needlessly starving to death, Kershner wrote that though well-meaning the woman "afforded an instance of the common type of inefficiency so prevalent among Filipino mothers."[54]

Missionaries also condemned drinking, smoking, and chewing the betel nut, probably unaware that, in the case of the betel nut, the narcotic effect temporarily assuaged hunger. Drinking was perceived to be so widespread as to be nearly universal. "As a rule all Filipinos drink," wrote Homer Stuntz. Invariably the Protestants denounced the use of liquor, though there was some disagreement over the seriousness of the problem. Stuntz's perception, that they seldom drank to excess and that drunkenness was very unusual, was fairly common. Other missionaries, however, disagreed, especially the Baptists, who felt that drunkenness was almost the rule, not the exception. In one Panayan village, for example, a missionary reported that the people "love their tuba, not wisely but too well." Nor were the consequences minimal, as Stuntz seemed to think. On the contrary, the Baptists felt that drink more than anything else had devitalized Visayan society. Similarly a United Brethren official, presumably after discussions with the missionaries, concluded that the reason bright Filipino children faded and grew dull by about age fifteen (another common perception) was their use of tobacco and liquor.[55]

Smoking was of greatest concern to the Seventh-day Adventists. In fact, of the many social ills said to be afflicting the Philippines, the Adventists placed smoking at the top of the list. "It is no more unusual to see women smoke here than the men," wrote one Adventist. "Even little girls smoke." Upon the death of a convert who continued to smoke in secret, the missionary implied that smoking had caused her death. "It was found near the close of her life that she had not given up smoking," he wrote. "She continued to smoke until her coughing compelled her to give it up, but," he added happily, "I think she truly repented of this."[56]

Sexual immorality also exercised the missionaries considerably. As Bishop Brent explained, having become aware of the sexual customs of the Igorots, "if Christian religion fails to awaken the moral conscience in any people . . . , its failure is complete." To the missionary eye, Filipinos badly needed awakened consciences. A YMCA official, for example, wrote that immorality was "so common as hardly to be recognized as wrong at all." He was scandalized at the popularity that Manuel Quezon, the most prominent politician of the day, enjoyed among the general public, in spite of the fact that Quezon was "notorious in a land whose moral standards are none too high for the number of women he has ruined." Large numbers of Filipinos reportedly confessed to YMCA officials "terrible acts of sexual immorality" in hopes of finding ways to combat "the loathsome habits of impurity."[57]

The state of Filipino morality was brought home to Robert Black in Davao when his most stalwart members became involved in adulterous relations. "I have been almost in despair. . . ," he wrote. "Adultery seems to be nothing in their sight." The problem was not limited to Mindanao. Far to the north, a Free Methodist vividly described the *querida* system in vogue among priests and the general populace. "In some places . . . a young man is not considered in society circles unless he has several," he wrote, adding that wife swapping was equally common. Disciple Bruce Kershner combined moralistic condemnation and genuine sadness in describing the result of illicit sexual relations. Noting that many children born out of wedlock died, an apparent reference to the ravages of venereal disease, he concluded, "children of sin, they could not but garner its fruit-age, and receive its wages—death. . . . They must die, for it is impossible that they should live." [58]

Frank Laubach summed it all up in a lighter vein. "We are not living in Boston," he discovered soon after his arrival." [59]

The amount of attention the missionaries paid to alleged Filipino indo-lence at least equaled that paid to the several moral shortcomings. "They are lazy insufferably so," was a typical comment. Filipinos would work only to acquire enough money for food, some said, preferring to suffer or permit their children to suffer rather than work. They actually preferred poverty, some thought. [60] Suggestions that Filipino workers receive equal pay with Americans were scorned, since "an American will perform as much and better labor than two Filipinos at the same time." "To the Filipinos I preach, 'six days shalt thou labor,'" wrote James B. Rodgers to Secretary of War Taft. "To the Americans, 'on the seventh thou shalt rest.'" A Seventh-day Adventist was pleased that Filipinos bought his books and liked to read, but, he commented with a touch of irony, reading was "not so dis-tressing as hard work, you know." About the only debate on alleged Fili-pino indolence, in fact, was whether Filipinos or Burmans were lazier, with Methodist Harry Farmer opting for Burmans and Baptist W. O. Val-entine selecting the Filipinos. [61]

Even those Filipinos who would work lacked the sense of discipline and responsibility needed for success, it was said. Capable Filipino teachers had to be supervised with care, lest they fail to fulfill their obligations. Dr. Lucius W. Case looked forward with great anticipation to the arrival of an American nurse to assist him. His current nurse was "probably as good as the average Filipina nurse," he explained, but she was deplorably lacking in many ways and took "no responsibility about anything. You can imagine what a relief it will be to have the American nurse here," he concluded. [62]

Individual missionaries, of course, took exception to one or more of the unsavory generalizations about Filipino character. Furthermore, there were positive images of Filipinos in the missionary mind that partially off-set the negative perceptions. Not the least important was the allegedly reli-gious nature of the people. Though some missionaries disagreed, the con-sensus was that Filipinos were "an essentially religious people," whose hearts opened as "naturally and as beautifully as a rose opens to the sun-shine and the shower" in a spiritual setting. Given the limited success the missionaries had in most Asian countries, the harvest seemed abundant in the Philippines. "The Filipinos take religion so seriously that it is easy to convert them," Harry Farmer confided to his diary. "It is like Paul passing bye the Altar erected to the Unknown God—they want just what we have to give." [63]

Filipinos were also described as dignified, neat, courteous, attractive, and appreciative. John H. Lamb found them "very kind, patient and sympathetic" as he struggled to learn their language. Baptist Eric Lund conceded the ignorance of the masses but nevertheless thought the people "sensitive and . . . sensible," a judgment echoed by an Adventist who considered them "very sociable, and as sensitive as sociable." [64] They were also supposed to be talented musicians, artists, and "naturally born orators," descriptions which, if stereotypes, were intended as compliments. [65]

In addition, most missionaries acknowledged that some Filipinos at least (the "intelligent" class, as Eric Lund put it) had many good qualities. Individual Filipinos were singled out for praise, such as Candido Magno, a Methodist pastor, who gave missionary Harry Farmer and his party a very fine dinner. "It was a relief," the missionary wrote, "to sit at a table and eat like White Folks." Especially noteworthy were the martyrs of the late nineteenth century, men like Alonso Lallave, who paid with his life for translating the New Testament into Pangasinan; Paulino Zamora, who challenged ecclesiastical repression and was exiled to a Mediterranean penal colony as a result; and especially Dr. Jose Rizal, the Filipino patriot who refused to be shot in the back and instead faced his executioners. "I say that there are bright hopes for a race that can produce a man who can die like that," thought a Methodist missionary. [66] They also praised some of their own Filipino workers, though there were sharp words for others and several notable instances of revolt and backsliding, which provided evidence, to the missionaries, of weak character.

Another positive attribute of Filipino society that emerges from the missionary records is the strength of the Filipino women. One important opportunity that the missionaries had for observing and judging the women was in the mission hospital where nurses were trained. Though there were those like Lucius W. Case, who as late as 1916 disparaged the abilities of Filipino nurses, his view was not altogether typical. The Baptist experience is probably more representative.

The initial Baptist assessment in 1907 of the nurses trained in its mission hospital was generally positive. Filipinas made "fairly good" hospital nurses, they concluded. But the prevalent racial biases stood in the way of a more favorable judgment. The nurses were "remarkably efficient," went the report, "considering their natural characteristics." Among the disadvantageous "natural characteristics" was the lack of a sense of responsibility and initiative of the sort "that characterize the American nurse, or even the trained nurse of Japan." For an indeterminate number of years, the Filipino nurse would be "like a child." Soon, however, these reservations disappeared. Just a few months later, a Baptist physician contended that "the native girl is a most welcome surprise. . . . She makes a capable nurse."

Three years later, surprise had turned to respect. "The Filipino nurse has made a place for herself in the Philippine world, by virtue of hard work and persistency," he wrote, "and she ought to be honored and trusted accordingly."[67]

One of the few systematic analyses of the status of Filipino women in general came from Mary Isham of the Methodist Women's Foreign Missionary Society. In her view, Spain had done precious little for Filipinas; even so, they managed to play important roles in society. "Shut out from culture, shut in to work, but having freedom and independence unknown in any Eastern continent," Isham observed, "these women became very useful in the social fabric." Aside from everyday household chores, the women, whether Igorots or lowlanders, became deft weavers of beautiful cloth made from vegetables and pineapple fibers. Several managed careers outside of the home and controlled substantial business enterprises in Manila and elsewhere. As for their character, Isham judged them "naturally courteous and generous."[68]

Other missionaries agreed and placed even more emphasis on the influence that Filipinas maintained in the home. In fact, it was a common belief that they were "the controlling power in the home." The influential women posed certain difficulties, for it was widely assumed that if the woman was a strong Catholic (and the women were often thought to be more religious than the men), there was very little chance that Protestants could influence the family. Silliman Institute officials were disturbed that so many of their graduates married Catholic women and were thus permanently lost to Protestant persuasion.[69]

On the other hand, if the missionaries could gain any substantial following among the women, they could expect considerable gains over the long term, a point many missionaries quickly grasped. "I have no fear in overestimating the value of work for girls," wrote a missionary in Dumaguete suggesting that a school for girls be established. From Cebu Frederick Jansen pleaded for funds for a girls dormitory. "We need to reach the women of the islands very specially in order to make the work count most," he insisted, thus paying direct (if unintended) tribute to the influence of the Filipinas.[70] The result of such perceptions was that, to one degree or another, the missions began to undertake activities designed to attract Filipino women to their banners.[71] The Methodists, in fact, had done so from the very beginning of their work.[72]

But if many missionaries ascribed positive as well as negative characteristics and values to Filipinos, and even revised originally critical judgments (as in the case of the nurses, for example), negative assessments predominated. In some instances those who initially thought highly of Filipinos revised their views. Charles W. Briggs, the Baptist leader from 1900 to

1910, was such a missionary. He represents the best documented case of missionary disillusionment with Filipino character and culture over a period of several years. Unlike many Americans, Briggs apparently left the United States without preconceived negative notions about the people among whom he would soon be living. Only three weeks after his arrival, he commented that the people were "as shrewd as the Japanese," a comment running counter to the initial observations of most Americans in the islands. Briggs's favorable assessment of the Filipinos continued for another year or two. In February 1901 he wrote that the "natives are bright and full of promise," though he added that they resembled children in important respects. A year later Briggs remained optimistic, reporting that Protestant converts were "standing the test" and contributing to a new spirit. "They are glad to be told a better way, some of them at least, and glad to walk in a better way," he concluded, illustrating his point with the story of a young man who had given up chewing betel nut on the advice of an American army officer who made him feel ashamed of his "filthy habit." [73]

But the year 1902 proved to be a profoundly disillusioning one to the idealistic young missionary. He "had the painful experience . . . of coming from the romantic and ideal to the actual." Filipinos, he now felt, were deceitful and vacillating. Their "essential worthlessness" (a strong comment for a missionary) depressed him. He was discouraged to see how the "bright children become stupid as soon as becoming mature." Immorality and heathenism were rampant, he thought. The people were lazy and had "no great future before them unless their very natures can be changed." [74] And he nearly went back to the United States.

Thereafter, Briggs's comments about Filipinos were very largely critical. In 1904 he admitted that there were many good people, but even the best were "weak, weak, weak, awfull weak," a conclusion confirmed when a Filipino friend was fined for gambling in a cockpit at a time when it was supposed to be closed. In 1905 Briggs was temporarily encouraged by a religious revival among the peasants. Furthermore, his unpaid Filipino assistants were good men. But on balance the people remained ignorant, vice-ridden, and lazy. "Nature could hardly have done more for the district," he wrote in disgust, "and one hundred thousand souls could hardly have done less!" [75]

The following year the missionary had reason to suffer yet greater disillusionment, for he discovered to his horror that Braulio Manikan, the Filipino who had done more than anyone else to advance the Baptist cause in Panay and Negros, was a gambler. Manikan admitted his sin, thus dramatically confirming Briggs in his assessment of Filipino character. "Satan has possessed his [Manikan's] heart and his interest in our work has been lost,"

Briggs lamented. "He is not without genuine elements from above, but is weak. The whole people is weak, weak, weak, and trained in casuistry that makes it easy to quiet their conscience and do anything in the category of hell."[76]

Perhaps because of Manikan's backsliding, Briggs became very cynical of Filipino abilities, especially of the upper classes, whom he characterized as dishonest and vile. "They have the self-righteousness of the Pharisee that went into the temple to pray; the vices of Corinth and the Roman empire in the day of Paul; the irresponsibility of an American political boss of the grossest type; [and] all the death-breeding germs and physical diseases of India and Africa," he wrote. In the same report he noted for the first time "an appalling amount of drunkenness" among the Visayans. "They are a drunken besotted race," he concluded. In fact, by this time there was little he could find to say that was good about the people. They were ignorant, indolent, drunk, addicted to gambling, and superstitious.[77]

The following year he even became disillusioned with the peasants, who until then he had partially excepted from his negative generalizations. "Crude superstitions and heathenism" were rampant among the peasants, he now felt, a side of their culture they had hidden from him in past years. In another report he noted, probably without great surprise, that a number of Baptist Filipino preachers had succumbed to adultery and gambling. The following year he found the people of Masbate "lazy and inert . . . slow and indifferent" and, of course, intoxicated. "The impression I brought away from Masbate is that of a people sitting in the dark, but quite drowsy and willing to sit for a long time yet," he wrote.[78]

In 1910 Briggs returned to the United States, presumably glad to get away from the drunken, vice-ridden Visayans. Three years later he published a book on the Philippines. Well-written, interesting, and valuable for the insights it provides into missionary thought, *The Progressing Philippines* reveals that Briggs had a genuine affection for the Filipinos and saw many signs of progress. But his views of Filipino culture remained largely unchanged. He still felt that Filipino "indulgence in alcohol and narcotics" had undermined their "splendid mental and physical powers." Consequently, the Filipino had become "a drugged and drunken Malay, falling far short of his highest capabilities, both mental and moral, as well as physical."[79]

Many missionaries—even Briggs—were sufficiently broadminded not to place all the blame for the deplorable moral state and an indolent culture directly on the people. Spanish Catholic rule, for example, deserved considerable blame for both, thought most missionaries. For one thing, it was said that Spanish Catholicism made little if any connection between religious conviction and moral behavior; and the priests, with their concubines and children, their use of tobacco and drink, hardly provided ideal models for the people. As for alleged Spanish disdain of manual labor, it was proverbial (if not necessarily accurate) and widely mentioned in missionary correspondence and writings.

The Oriental milieu also deserved some of the responsibility for the decadent culture. "These Asiatics have never learned the Anglo-Saxon lesson of labor and thrift," Arthur J. Brown exclaimed. On more rational grounds, intolerant bosses and such partially indigenous institutions as *caciquismo* (a kind of feudal peonage system) discouraged responsible labor. So, too, it was often said, did the abundance of food that grew with little or no tending. The fact that the Igorots could seldom be induced to perform work beyond that needed to obtain food and shelter was perfectly comprehensible, thought Bishop Brent. They would probably bury any pesos they happened to earn, there being little else to do with the money, he reported. The tropical climate in the lowlands was an equally understandable barrier to industriousness. Robert Black, in fact, rather admired the custom of Filipino workers of resting from four to five hours in the mid-day heat.[80]

Yet the missionaries felt mightily that Filipino culture had to change. Immorality had to be rooted out, and the work ethic had to become as much a part of the culture as the fiesta.

Aside from the purely religious objections to immorality and indolence, missionaries felt that Filipino culture had to change for very practical reasons. If the Philippines were going to "advance," if industry was to flourish, if mines were to be dug, if roads were to be built, Filipinos would have to do the work. "It is useless to bring over white laborers," thought Arthur J. Brown. "The Americans cannot do manual labor in this climate."[81] Filipinos apparently could, but not until they acquired the discipline to work and avoided the cockpit.

Inextricably intertwined with such practical, nation-building needs were cultural biases. Though one can surely question the concept of a Protestant ethic (the non-Christian Chinese, for example, were widely perceived as hardworking capitalists), many nineteenth-century Protestants preached the gospel of hard work, thrift, and frugality, along with more fundamentally religious concepts. To encourage a more "progressive" culture—or, in more theological language, "to help men possessed of bodies to create those outward conditions which will best enable them to use their bodies as instruments of the enlarged mind and soul which are the earliest gift of Christian conversion"—the casual approach to labor had to be modified. Spanish modes of thinking were simply repulsive, in their view, aside from any detrimental effect they might have had in a practical sense. To David Hibbard, the point was brought home in 1899 shortly after his arrival in

Iloilo. His Visayan language teacher received barely enough money for his food, Hibbard reported, yet he engaged a servant to carry his one book, since "it would be a disgrace to be seen on the street carrying a package." [82] In sum, it was essential for practical, cultural, and theological reasons to instill a sense of the dignity of labor in the culture, while removing immorality.

To bring about change, the missionaries proposed three things. The first and usually foremost was conversion to the Protestant gospel. Charles R. Hamilton acknowledged that the development of a strong national character was a slow process, but he was convinced that quiet evangelism among the people would eventually produce meaningful change. "The prayer life that comes from such a consciousness will in time make any people great," he argued. [83]

In 1905 a Presbyterian missionary hit upon the second approach. "Would [to] God he [the Filipino] might exchange his contemptible cock fighting and the hell breathed spirit of gambling for the love of healthy, manly sport without which no nation has ever yet been worth the while." [84] Athletics was to be the great panacea for gambling and other forms of immoral behavior.

The first significant commitment to athletics began in Cebu, where the Reverend George W. Dunlap, a Presbyterian missionary, instituted athletic programs in Cebu High School. Dunlap, a former semiprofessional athlete from Iowa, coached the baseball team, which regularly won the scholastic league championship. He also escorted Filipino athletes to international competitions in Shanghai and Japan. In addition to his work in Cebu, Dunlap trained several teams in Dumaguete, where Silliman Institute was located, and perhaps in other towns in Negros as well. His goal, he stated, was "to kill the cock-pit." Dunlap's fame spread far and wide as the "Baseball Evangelist," and Frank Laubach hoped he would join the American Board in Mindanao to help with the Moros. [85]

Not surprisingly, athletics became a prominent feature of life at Silliman, the first Protestant school in the country. The first interscholastic athletic event in the history of the southern islands, and perhaps in all of the Philippines, took place in 1909 between Silliman and Cebu High School, a contest Silliman lost in part because the athletes' shoes were lost overboard on the voyage to Cebu. But baseball, basketball, tennis, track and field, and volleyball were enjoyed by men and women at Silliman. "Cockfighting belongs to the past cycle," President David S. Hibbard wrote a bit prematurely. "A Silliman student would feel disgraced for life if he were caught at one of the cockpits by a member of his faculty, even during the long vacations." [86]

Like Dunlap and other missionaries, officials of the Young Men's Christian Association felt certain their athletic programs could assist in over-coming the Filipinos' deficiencies. Though intended partly to counter the physical weaknesses (volleyball was introduced in part to reduce the cases of tuberculosis), the cultural goals were never far from the surface. "To combat the cockpit, low dance halls, and other evils that assail their youth," one official wrote, "wholesome substitute recreation must be provided." Similarly, Elwood S. Brown, who directed the athletic program of the Manila Y after 1909, reported that the association hoped "to put the mañana habit into the discard along with the cockpit and other gambling games."[87]

The third approach to indolence, the missionaries thought, was vocational education (or, as it was then called, industrial education). Happily, industrial education was then in vogue in the United States, and in the Philippines it became an important part of the government's approach to mass education (at least in theory).[88] It was also a part of the curriculum at the mission schools. Writing to Horace B. Silliman, who provided the funds for the institution that bore his name, Hibbard noted the twin advantages—cultural and practical—that would accrue from making industrial education a part of the school's program. "The school must be of such a character that it will attract and then instruct in the dignity of honest work," he explained, "and more than that it must only teach such trades as will give openings to the student after he has graduated."[89]

Three days after Hibbard wrote to Silliman, Charles A. Glunz, an official of the Army and Navy YMCA in Manila, made application to take charge of the proposed industrial department at Silliman. "Purely academic training will tend toward intensifying certain undesirable qualities of the native . . . ," in particular contempt for manual labor, "while industrial training will enable him to appreciate the dignity of labor, and will make him the more useful citizen," Glunz wrote. Like many other Americans interested in establishing vocational education programs in the islands, the missionary specifically recommended Hampton and Tuskegee institutes—the latter headed by the eminent Booker T. Washington—as models.[90]

Glunz was hired, and Silliman was soon offering training in such non-academic subjects as auto repairing, woodworking, printing, and building. "The dignity of labor is being realized," Hibbard wrote later, adding on the practical side that industrial education was "an important factor in the progress of the Islands."[91]

At almost precisely the same time the Baptists began to give serious consideration to a vocational education program of their own. W. O. Valentine first broached the subject in the summer of 1904 (pointing to Tuskegee as the appropriate model), and in December the mission recommended to the board that an industrial school for boys be established in Jaro, Panay. It was "urgently needed . . . ," wrote one missionary, "if this people are ever to make any headway in civilization." On October 1, 1905, the Jaro Industrial School for Boys opened with eighty students.[92]

Under Valentine's direction, the students were soon repairing buildings, digging ditches, and constructing a stable. Courses were offered in tailoring, carpentry, tinsmithing, and shoemaking. But the real goal, perhaps even more so than with the Presbyterians at Silliman, was cultural. Here was a blatant effort to transform the culture of centuries, or at least the perceived culture, and in particular to dignify common labor. The purposes of the new school, explained one missionary, were not merely to impart new skills to the natives, but "to make them industrious."[93]

Very much related to the attempt to create industrious people was the effort to bring about social democracy. This was especially so with the Baptists, who were the most sensitive of all the Protestant missionaries to the abuses of *caciquismo*, an almost feudal relationship of landlord and peasant vassal that, it was said, sapped the very personhood from the peasants. The first word the boys learned to spell at the Baptist school was *EQUALITY*, with capital letters. The school, it was hoped, would "help break down class and artificial distinctions, and spread the spirit of democracy. It should produce an intelligent industrious God-fearing middle class, which is the strength and sinews of any nation." Aristocratic young men who arrived at the school were soon taught the meaning of social democracy. When one prospective student arrived and announced that his *muchacho* would *do* the work while he would learn by watching, he was promptly put to work in the rice field "knee deep in mud and water, to learn wisdom the hard way."[94] A change in cultural thinking was clearly more important to the Baptists than the immediately practical results of such training.

In the mountains of Luzon, the Episcopalians, too, thought the casual approach to labor allegedly characteristic of Igorot society had to be modified. Here the emphasis was not on vocational schools but on practical, on-the-job training. The first element in the Episcopalian effort was the erection of a sawmill. One impetus for importing a sawmill to Sagada seems to have been to provide the missionaries with solidly constructed buildings that could withstand the periodic typhoons that swept through the area, but the possibilities of "improving" the local culture were soon apparent. Not only were the Igorots involved in all phases of the importation, assembling, and operation of the mill (and paid promptly for their labor), but a desire for better things was subtly inculcated. "The Igorot is very quick to see what is to his advantage," wrote Staunton. "The very operations for which he was paid a daily wage would enable him to live better and more successfully in his own environment."[95]

The effort to revolutionize the culture through industrial education and training met with skepticism from a good portion of the American community in the islands who found it hard to believe that Filipinos could be induced to become industrious. When in 1909, for example, Valentine attempted to place a group of students in railroad work, an American railway official told him that the students could not stand the work, would leave within three days, and would gamble away whatever they earned.[96]

But all of the missions that undertook vocational education were convinced of its success. Henry W. Munger of the Baptist mission expressed the general skepticism, along with his own optimism, in vulgar form. "'Some folks say that a nigger wont steal; and some folks say that a Filipino w*ont* work,'" he wrote, parodying a popular, if racist song of the day. "But I know he will; at least boys who have been in the Jaro Industrial School will."[97]

Munger and other missionary proponents of industrial education made poor Social Darwinists of the Sumnerian sort, since they were in the islands, in part, to assist those who seemed to have been left behind in the struggle for dominance. P. H. J. Lerrigo, a missionary physician, recorded the kind of transformation that could be expected on an individual level. A typical "heathen" youth from the mountains arrived to work in the missionary's home "shoeless, hatless, smileless and dumb; but in the genial atmosphere of the missionary home he [would] blossom." Shortly, he would smile broadly and struggle to learn some essential English words. Then shoes would appear, "announced some fine morning . . . by an ominous clomp, clomp, clomp ascending the stairs into the dining room." Then came the hat, usually "a straight-brimmed straw, with pink or blue ribbon cunningly embroidered, or, if he be of a sober turn of mind, a black Derby." Quickly, white trousers and coat appeared, "and the young man is metamorphosed."[98]

There was some disagreement over the degree of improvement to be expected in the society as a whole, though the matter was seldom the subject of systematic analysis or debate. The minimal expectation was well expressed in a poem that appeared on the cover of *Pearl of the Orient*, the publication of the Baptist mission:

> In even savage bosoms
> There are longings, strivings, yearnings
> For the good they comprehend not;
> And their feeble hands and helpless,
> Groping blindly in the darkness,
> Touch God's right hand in that darkness,
> And are lifted up and strengthened.[99]

88

To some missionaries, like R. C. Thomas, it was futile to try to "occidentalize the Orient," a sentiment with which Rudyard Kipling would have agreed. Filipinos could "never be Americans," wrote another, a belief that must have disheartened those hoping to mold little brown Americans. Yet even those holding such views, which implied permanent inferiority, expected more from Filipinos than acceptance of some basic Protestant doctrines. If they could not be totally Americanized, they could nevertheless "more nearly approximate the American spirit." If it was not possible to establish Western culture in the Orient, "enlightened nations" still had an obligation to rid the Philippines of "really gross darkness."[100]

But other missionaries saw a considerably brighter future than merely the removal of "really gross darkness." The "Oriental atmosphere" was admittedly a problem, but not an insoluble one. What was needed was sufficient outside *stimulus* (a word that appears regularly in the correspondence and literature) to change the culture, and to overcome the effects of historical tragedy, not of a mythical racial inferiority. As early as 1899 Disciple Hermon Williams wrote that the Filipinos were "capable of great things," and were "not incompetent, and hopelessly incapable of a great and honorable future." Disciples Bruce and Ethel Kershner and Presbyterian J. Andrew Hall thought the people had the potential of the much admired Japanese, while Methodist bishop Frank Warne believed that the Filipino was "no worse by nature than his white-faced conqueror."[101]

Probably the most optimistic assessment came from Frank Laubach, who arrived in 1915. Representing a new generation of missionaries that saw more value in indigenous cultures and that was less inclined to be excessively judgmental, Laubach saw no limits to Filipino development. He was not so naive or romantic as to think that the people were without faults. Filipino physicians in the constabulary did not "measure up to American doctors," he reported in 1916. But he was certain that as the educational system continued to improve, so would the doctors. The same was true of civil servants. To be sure, as Filipinos took over the major governmental positions after 1912, efficiency declined, he thought. But Laubach insisted that this was only a temporary phenomenon and "no greater than would be the case with any new untried men taking the place of those of long experience." In sum, Laubach thought Filipinos fully the equals of other people, though still needing some guidance and development.[102]

How close the missionaries ought to get to the people and their culture was a matter of debate. Missionaries ran the gamut. Laubach sympathized with a newly arrived couple who "loved to bury themselves in the life of the people and 'think Malay.'" About the same time, another American Board missionary, newly settled in Davao, wrote that he hoped to view the

Filipinos "as being real people with capacity for friendship and growth. To that end, we share some of their amusements."[103] Such sentiments were a far cry from the reluctance of Robert Black and Bruce Kershner to get close to the "filthy natives."

But the spirit of separateness lived on, in modified form, in the life of United Brethren missionary Howard W. Widdoes, who seems to have felt that genuine intimate friendship was scarcely possible across racial lines. Reflecting on the hardships the missionary wife faced, for example, he noted that for months she would be isolated without any contact at all with other American women. "She has many good friends among the native women," he wrote of his own wife, and she knew their language; "but they do not belong to her real world," he felt. And the children? They lacked playmates of their own race and therefore have "never known the exquisite pleasure that comes to the boy who has a chum or the girl who whispers secrets to her dear little friend."[104] Apparently Filipino children could not be chums or dear friends.

The issue of interracial contact also emerged in the discussions regarding whether to expand YMCA work to Filipinos. Initially the Y had served the armed forces, later extending its services to American and European civilians. In 1909 the Manila Y constructed a new facility for the use of its white constituency, a move that brought forth dire warnings that in a year of unprecedented racial tension something comparable had to be done for Filipinos. As one official, J. M. Groves, put it:

> I fear the ultimate result if we open our splendid new building, within a few score yards of the City Hall, a building at the very heart of the capital of these Islands and one which will be in some ways its finest structure, and by a week of public exercises and inspection set it apart for the use and pleasure of perhaps 500 Americans and European sojourners, or about 1/500th of Manila's approximately 250,000 people; *unless* we can at the same time prove . . . our definite intention and ability to provide at once and adequately for the Filipino young men who are our big ultimate constituency.

To meet the need, the official suggested that as the new building for Caucasians was dedicated an announcement be made of the Y's intention to open facilities for Filipinos at a specific time in the future, hopefully in 1911. He felt certain that such an announcement would end the criticism and would even be greeted with enthusiasm by Filipinos.[105]

For the first half of 1909, as the new building for Caucasians took shape, letters from influential Americans in the Philippines and other parts of the Orient poured into the YMCA's International Committee in New York recommending action along the lines Groves suggested. Justice E. Finley

Johnson of the Philippine supreme court urged John R. Mott to allocate funds for a Filipino building. The editor of the *Philippines Free Press* thought the need for a building for Filipinos was even greater than the need for the new building for Americans:

> Should such an institution be established it cannot help but exert a strong influence for good on many of the rising generation of Filipinos, those who will soon be leaders in public life here, and at the same time it would afford another striking testimonial to the benevolent and altruistic purposes actuating the American government and the American people in their relations with the Filipino people.

David Prescott Barrows, about to leave the islands after six years as director of education, wrote a lengthy letter recommending "without reservations" work among Filipinos, especially students.[106]

Indicative of the racial mentality of that era, virtually no one suggested integrated facilities. One correspondent who urged a separate Filipino plant thought that segregated facilities were "absolutely essential" to the success of the American building.[107] In fact, of those who expressed an opinion about the Y's expansion to include Filipinos, only Bishop Brent questioned the idea of segregated facilities, noting that in the atmosphere of "racial hatred" that presently existed, "the establishment of a separate building for the Filipinos side by side with that for Americans would tend to emphasize the breach." But Brent did not call for integration. On the contrary, he urged that the Y's work with whites become better established before considering a new building for Filipinos. In short, Brent suggested that nothing be done for Filipinos at all.[108] Surely, then, the Y's perception was accurate, that most Americans of all descriptions in the islands (no doubt including Y officials and missionaries) felt that "separation of the races is absolutely essential."[109]

In any event, the Y's International Committee gave its approval and in 1911 allocated substantial sums for the construction of two buildings for Filipinos, one for students, the other for business and professional men. In return, the committee required that $30,000 for equipment had to be raised locally. The goal was quickly reached. Theodore R. Yangco, a prominent businessman, pledged $10,000, allegedly "an unprecedented amount for any Filipino to subscribe toward a philanthropic enterprise." From Paris Pedro Roxas sent $7,500. Within five days of the official opening of the campaign in November 1911, over $50,000 had been subscribed. "To those on the ground," J. M. Groves reported, "the most heartening thing . . . was the unanimous reaching out of the Filipino people,—their leaders, press and rank and file—to accept the Association itself."[110]

Within a few years some progress was even made in breaching the segregated facilities. In 1915, for example, twelve teams—one of them was composed of Americans—entered a volleyball tournament. Elwood Brown thought it noteworthy enough to report that the businessmen who made up the American team (and who even employed some of their Filipino opponents) "met the Filipino young men without hesitation or embarrassment and on the common field of sport," where they eventually lost in the semifinals to the clerks from the internal revenue bureau. By the end of the next year, integration had progressed even further, as "informal group games," in which Filipinos and Americans "played indiscriminately side by side," took place over the Christmas holidays. This, one Y official thought, marked a "new departure," "and a decided step forward in the closer understanding between the two peoples." Perhaps a new era was about to begin.[111]

Robert Black, the first missionary of the American Board in the Philippines, arrived there in 1902. Photograph taken in 1902 courtesy of Houghton Library, Harvard University.

Charles T. Sibley, M.D., the second American Board missionary in the Philippines, arrived in 1908. Photograph c. 1914 by permission of Houghton Library, Harvard University.

Mrs. Robert Black, in her kindergarten in Davao, observes a greeting between an American student and a native student. Photograph by permission of Houghton Library, Harvard University.

Dr. and Mrs. Frank C. Laubach, American Board missionaries, in 1918. Photograph by permission of Houghton Library, Harvard University.

Charles W. Briggs, Baptist missionary in Panay from 1900 to 1910, with unidentified Filipino assistants. Source: Charles W. Briggs, *The Progressing Philippines* (Philadelphia: Griffith & Rowland Press, 1913).

Bruce Kershner, the leading Disciples missionary in the Philippines from 1905 to 1917. This photograph, taken seven years after he left the islands, is courtesy of the Christian Theological Seminary, Indianapolis.

Episcopalian bishop Charles Henry Brent in Baguio c. 1907. Photograph courtesy of Archives of the Episcopal Church.

Father John A. Staunton, Jr., at Sagada c. 1910, with Igorot children. Photograph courtesy of Archives of the Episcopal Church.

Episcopal priest training Sagada Igorots for the printing trade in 1914. Photograph courtesy of Archives of the Episcopal Church.

Mercer Green Johnston, minister of the Episcopal cathedral church of St. Mary and St. John in Manila from 1903 to 1908. Photograph courtesy of Archives of the Episcopal Church.

Mr. and Mrs. Herbert M. Damon, unofficial missionaries of the Free Methodist Church, school teachers in Loaog from 1906 to 1909, in a photograph taken shortly before they left for the Philippines. Courtesy of Herbert S. Damon.

Rebecca Parrish, M.D., Methodist missionary physician, before her arrival in Manila in 1906 and sometime after her departure in 1933. Photographs courtesy of United Methodist Archives.

The entire male Methodist missionary staff in the Philippines in October 1903: (first row, left to right) Marvin A. Rader, Homer C. Stuntz, Bishop H. W. Warren, Jesse L. McLaughlin, W. A. Goodell; (second row, left to right) Thomas H. Martin, F. A. McCarl, Ernest S. Lyons, W. A. Brown, A. E. Chenoweth. Source: Homer C. Stuntz, *The Philippines and the Far East* (Cincinnati: Jennings & Pye, 1904).

Nicolas Zamora, who broke with Philippine Methodism in 1909 to found the *Iglesia Evangelica Metodista en las Islas Filipinas.* Source: John B. Devins, *An Observer in the Philippines* (Boston: American Tract Society, 1905).

James B. Rodgers, dean of the Presbyterian mission, the first regularly accredited Protestant missionary to the Philippines, arrived there in 1899 and remained until 1935. Source: James B. Rodgers, *Twenty Years of Presbyterian Work in the Philippines* (n.p., n.d.); photograph courtesy of Presbyterian Historical Society.

Stealy B. Rossiter, pastor of the American Presbyterian Church in Manila from 1904 to 1910. Photograph courtesy of the Presbyterian Historical Society.

Joseph Andrew Hall, M.D., in charge of Presbyterian medical work in Iloilo from 1900 to 1919. Photograph courtesy of Presbyterian Historical Society.

Union Hospital in Iloilo, operated jointly by Baptists and Presbyterians. Source: Charles W. Briggs, *The Progressing Philippines* (Philadelphia: Griffith & Rowland Press, 1913).

Dr. and Mrs. H. W. Widdoes, United Brethren missionaries, translating the Scriptures into Ilocano. Source: Walter N. Roberts, *The Filipino Church* (Dayton, O., 1936).

Gregorio Aglipay, *Obispo Maximo* of the *Iglesia Filipina Independiente* (Philippine Independent Church). Aglipay's break with the Roman Catholic Church in 1902 evoked mixed emotions among the newly arrived Protestant missionaries. Religious News Service photograph courtesy of the Episcopal Church Archives, Austin, Texas.

5

Protestant Missionaries and Roman Catholicism

> If this is not a heathen country I know not where you will find it.
>
> Charles L. Maxfield,
> Baptist missionary

> The Roman Church has done many and commendable things for these people, a fact beyond dispute.
>
> Ernest J. Pace,
> United Brethren missionary

> It is better to plant a forest, than to cut and pile cord wood.
>
> John A. Staunton, Jr.,
> Episcopalian missionary

In 1904 an English writer, A. Henry Savage Landor, compiled a list of misfortunes that had recently befallen the Pacific Islands. Wars, insurrections, cholera, plague, rinderpests, and locusts had all taken their toll. But the worst pests of all, he wrote, were yet to come—the missionaries, who would make the people worse off than they already were. The fact that Episcopal bishop Charles Henry Brent termed the Englishman "an unmitigated liar"[1] did not lessen the fact that the missionary movement of the late nineteenth and early twentieth centuries, though widely popular, had its critics. The overseas commercial element, for example, traditionally found itself at odds with the missionaries;[2] some anthropologists regretted outside intrusions into traditional cultures;[3] and governmental officials sometimes found missionaries to be an unwanted and disturbing element among the indigenous population.

Missionaries to heathen lands had little trouble disposing of such criticism. Christ's Great Commission, after all, required believers to spread the Gospel to unbelievers. But most areas of the Philippines had long since been rescued from paganism, despite President William McKinley's famous pledge to "uplift and . . . Christianize" America's new wards. "It occurs to me that you may imagine we have savages here when I speak of missionaries," an Englishwoman wrote from the Philippines in 1906, "but that is not the case . . . for these good people [the missionaries] are here— oh such a lot of them!—to convert the Filipinos from Roman Catholicism. This is really a work of supererogation," she went on, "for . . . this religion, with its mysteries and pomp, appeals to them, and suits their dispositions perfectly."[4] One could justify sending missionaries to save the heathen, but what about to rescue Catholic Christians?

Protestant missionaries in the Philippines were well aware of this particular embarrassment. "Many Americans here and at home look upon us missionaries as intruders," Presbyterian James B. Rodgers admitted shortly after his arrival in 1899. Nor did the questions cease as the years passed. "Many Christian people look upon mission work among Roman Catholics as uncalled for," reported another Presbyterian a decade later. Even the Christian and Missionary Alliance, which had no qualms about being in the Philippines, encountered many people, "even true children of God," who questioned the need for missionaries in the islands.[5]

Though such challenges disquieted thoughtful missionaries, only the Episcopalians determined to limit their work in the Philippines to foreigners and to non-Christian groups in the islands—and even within the Episcopalian community there were some demands to proselytize among the Roman Catholic population. Other communions found sufficient justification to convert Catholic Filipinos to Protestantism. To some Protestant missionaries, such a policy was easily justified, for in their view Roman Catholicism had scarcely any connection with true Christianity. The Philippines, wrote the one semiofficial Free Methodist missionary in the islands, were "as truly a heathen land as any on the face of the earth." The Christian and Missionary Alliance denied consistently the Christian nature of Roman Catholicism, while the Seventh-day Adventists were nearly as outspoken. The "true principles of Christianity," wrote the first permanent Adventist missionary, were as foreign to Filipinos "as to the savages of New Guinea."[6]

Denials of Catholicism's claim to be Christian might be expected from the very conservative Alliance and the Adventists. However, similar sentiments existed among some missionaries affiliated with almost all Protestant groups. The leading Disciples missionary and his wife, for example, wrote that Catholicism had given the Filipinos almost nothing of value. Similarly, the American Board issued a pamphlet, based on reports from its missionaries, which concluded that Filipinos "were as ignorant of the Christian religion . . . as were the men of darkest Africa"; while Charles L. Maxfield, a Baptist, confided to his mission board, "if this is not a heathen country I know not where you will find it."[7]

For missionaries who saw no value in Roman Catholicism, the overriding deficiency, as might be expected, was the Church's alleged inability to present to the people the terms of salvation. "The atonement through the cleansing blood had been both hidden and withheld from them," wrote an Alliance missionary. Many souls, she lamented, had "returned to God without having known the way of salvation." But what fascinated them the most, and what was doubtless the most immediate reason for their conclusion that Catholicism was heathenish, was the apparent idolatry of the people. "They worship idols here," wrote Herbert Damon from Laoag, referring to the images of saints. Seventh-day Adventists repeatedly charged that the people bowed "down to wood and stone, to images they themselves have made, in the name of Christianity," while Alliance missionaries concluded that Catholic worship consisted "of adoration of wooden and stone images."[8]

Equally chilling to the missionary mind was the Catholic Church's incorporation of pagan rituals and, more generally, its failure to combat superstition. "They cook chickens and place them on the altar in front of the idols," reported Herbert Damon. Damon also described the Ilocano belief that the cure for boils was to kill a pure white chicken and carefully cook it. The prepared chicken was then placed under the sacred beleti tree, along with rice cakes, candies, and money, to propitiate the spirits living there, who had caused the boils in the first place. The appearance of Catholic-sanctioned superstition was not limited to Ilocanos, for in Zamboanga far to the south a missionary was amused to observe a Catholic funeral procession halt in front of the Alliance church long enough for a ceremony to be performed to drive away evil spirits from the place.[9]

Common as such assessments of Catholicism were, however, they were not representative of missionary opinion as a whole, which on balance conceded value in the Catholic heritage. To some missionaries, Catholicism deserved only minimal credit for introducing such basic concepts as the Christian God and for blocking the advance of Islam.[10] Others, notably the Methodists, United Brethren, Episcopalians, and some Presbyterians, praised the Church for its historic role. Many of the earliest Catholic missionaries, the editor of the Methodist *Philippine Christian Advocate* wrote, were "as sincere and devoted as any who ever went out in the name of the Master." Many Protestant missionaries conceded that the early priests Romanized the vernacular alphabet, introduced education (even on a limited scale for women), and in general raised the level of civilization. One only had to compare Filipinos with their Malay cousins in Borneo or Malaya, thought Homer Stuntz, to see the positive influences of Catholicism.[11]

More to the point, the friars introduced important religious truths. The concepts of the suffering savior and the self-sacrificing saints, love of Mary, the ideas of redemption and eternal salvation, and above all the unity of God were part of the Catholic heritage. The missionaries thought these concepts were immensely superior to the teachings of Buddha, for example, and represented an almost immeasurable advance over traditional Philippine religious beliefs. "The Roman Catholic Church has done many and commendable things for these people, a fact beyond dispute," a United Brethren representative wrote to his board.[12]

One Methodist missionary to whom this kind of analysis made especially good sense was David H. Klinefelter, who worked mostly among the non-Christian Chinese population in Manila. Whereas there were thousands of Filipino Methodists by 1907, Klinefelter could count only eight baptized Chinese. No wonder he readily concluded that Catholicism was "vastly better than no God, no Savior, and no Holy Spirit." Nor had prospects improved much four years later, when the missionary observed resignedly, "one needs only to know the conditions of a truly pagan people to know that the Filipino has been greatly helped by the system of religious teaching he has had."[13]

Nevertheless, even those Protestant missionaries who accorded the Catholic Church considerable credit felt that they were justified in entering the islands; for almost no one doubted that Catholicism, whatever its historical contributions, was a deficient form of Christianity. Central to the moderate Protestant critique of Catholicism, especially of the Latin variety, was that Church's acceptance of tradition and other elements extrinsic to the Bible as bases for faith equal to the Scriptures,[14] with the result that even as fundamental an idea as monotheism became "fogged" by the existence of multitudinous saints whose "dingy and gaudy images" were more real to Filipinos than the "persons that they were made to represent." Those who saw value in the Catholic heritage were more reluctant than their Alliance or Adventist colleagues to label such images idols; but Spanish Catholicism in the Philippines, they admitted, verged uncomfortably close to polytheism.[15]

Not only was the belief in the saints and the Virgin as intermediaries unbiblical to the Protestant mind, so too was the teaching that there was no salvation except through the priest. Protestants vehemently denied the sacerdotal character of the priesthood and the related belief that the priest had the power to forgive sins during confession. That, said the Reverend George Pentecost, was "an impertinent intrusion, . . . a blasphemous usurpation." Not only did such doctrines lack Biblical sanction, thought the missionaries, but they endowed the clergy with untoward power. "No matter how immoral the priest may be," wrote a missionary in Tacloban, "the people believe that he has the power to condemn or save." Consequently, the priests held the people in a state of virtual tyranny. "The people still believe about anything the priest tells them," the same mission-ary wrote after three fruitless years. "I believe they would believe that black was white, if he would say so."[16]

Another theological deficiency of considerable magnitude in the Protes-tant mind was the alleged failing of Catholicism, especially Spanish Catholi-cism, to relate religion to the living of a moral life. "Religion and morality had become divorced" under Catholic leadership, wrote a Baptist mission-ary.[17] The Church, for example, placed no stigma on the use of intoxicants and even accepted numerous liquor advertisements in their newspapers. "This is one way Rome has of uplifting the people," commented a Dis-ciples missionary with evident sarcasm. Neither was gambling denounced. On the contrary, the Church seemed to encourage it, for each game had its patron saint to whom the gambler prayed for success. Sometimes, in fact, gamesters took their prized fighting cocks to the church to drink holy water on the assumption that it would make them strong. Sometimes, too, communicants would feed their wafer to their roosters, believing this would make them invincible in the ring. Whatever the moral weakness—duplicity, insincerity, stealing, fornication, adultery, drunkenness, or gambling—Protestants believed, as Charles W. Briggs put it, it was "the logical fruit-age of sacerdotalism."[18]

The alleged immorality of the Catholic clergy was almost axiomatic to Protestants. Clerical corruption was "well-nigh universal," wrote a Metho-dist bishop, a corruption that included innumerable "unmentionable atrocities" (which, however, were regularly and vividly mentioned), of which the most shocking to turn-of-the-century Protestants were sexual ir-regularities. Homer Stuntz found such matters "the most unpleasant of all things I must write of," and in his early book on the Philippines he pro-vided three and a half pages of examples. "Catholics will shudder at the disclosures of this chapter," he predicted.[19]

In any event, stories of sexual immorality among the clergy abounded. A Presbyterian missionary reported that the "girls of Daet were very beau-tiful and white because the Spanish priest had done much [to] infuse white blood into the Filipino race. This you may hear on every side," he added. Similarly, a Disciples missionary in the Laoag area contended in 1914, at a time when there had been substantial reforms, that the local priest was the father of several children by different women (and was a drunkard, a gam-bler, and a smoker to boot). And yet this priest was "living a cleaner (!) life than the rest of his vile tribe. Is it necessary," the missionary concluded, "to ask if *we* are needed here?"[20]

In addition to sexual sins, the clergy, it was said, oppressed the people in a hundred ways to enrich itself and to retain its not inconsiderable political power. "Rome has its tentacles around every little barrio and every family in the Island [of Panay]," concluded Charles W. Briggs. The priests, it was constantly alleged, received excessive fees for their services and charged high rent for poorly maintained cemetery plots. (If the rent was not kept current the bones of the deceased were removed and thrown into a common pile.) The Church connived to acquire the best lands, the missionaries reported, and cheated the tenants who worked them, thus further producing indolent habits and deceitfulness. Why work if one's land would be seized on some pretext the moment it proved to be productive? Why tell the truth if one would be taken advantage of? One way or another, the Church, especially friar orders, secured the best lands and enriched itself at the expense of the people. "Her pockets seem hard to fill," stated a Baptist publication.[21]

It served the corrupt purposes of the Church to keep the masses ignorant and superstitious, thought the missionaries. "Whatever its contributions to the national uplift of the earlier day," wrote a Methodist bishop, the Church "kept the people ignorant, and imposed upon them with all manner of puerile superstitions to the enrichment of the church treasury and the mental and religious impoverishment of the people." The Church, it was alleged, plotted to keep the Philippines isolated from the winds of change. "The stream of life, economic, social and intellectual, passed them by relatively untouched," thought a Baptist missionary physician, while the "Roman Church and the Spanish Inquisition built an impregnable wall about the hearts and minds of men." Education was deliberately limited, and dissenters were thrown into jail, exiled, even killed.[22] The Church also found the Chinese to be defenseless targets for their greed, the Protestants alleged.[23]

If the most blatant ethical shortcomings were reported among the ordinary friars and priests, Protestants did not think that the Spanish-dominated hierarchy was much better. After all, the basic problem was doctrinal. Since Spanish Catholics allegedly saw no relationship between religion and moral behavior, the hierarchy could not be expected to be much concerned with the immoral behavior of the priests. Protestants quickly noticed that priestly wickedness went unrebuked. Arthur J. Brown's comparison of the Spanish Catholic bishop of Cebu, whom he interviewed, with the Protestant missionary who acted as his interpreter, speaks volumes about Protestant views of the Catholic hierarchy and illustrates the vast cultural gulf that separated Spanish Catholicism from American Protestantism. "They typified the whole wide-world difference between American Protestantism and Spanish Romanism," wrote Brown, "the missionary with his high forehead, frank blue eyes, clear cut features, whose every line and expression betokened temperate living and high thinking; and the Bishop—well, there was a noticeable difference."[24]

Roman Catholic inadequacies were further illustrated, Protestants thought, in the Church's refusal to share the Bible with the people. That, Protestants concluded, was both a symptom and a cause of Catholic theological deficiencies. Biblical truth, they felt certain, if permitted to get out would reveal to the people all the false doctrine and practices of Catholicism. To the Protestant mind withholding the Scriptures was damning evidence of the ecclesiastical conspiracy to keep the masses ignorant and dependent. No wonder the Bible was "the book the priests hate," as one missionary put it, while tramping through the wilds of Mindanao distributing the Bible. One of the more graphic elements in Protestant propaganda, in fact, were lurid stories of priests who seized Bibles from the sick and poor, or who surreptitiously purchased the available supply of Protestant Bibles and then burned them in a public ceremony.[25]

In sum, even those missionaries who saw considerable value in the record of the Catholic Church perceived gross deficiencies in theology and practice that justified without apology a Protestant presence. The Church had lost its spiritual vitality, they believed. It had become a "lumbering derelict" that had "done all she could; she has exhausted her resources and is incapable of advancing these people beyond a point reached long, long ago."[26]

But if the Church had long since lost its spiritual energy, it remained, in a temporal sense, the "most astute and skillful organization the mind of scheming man has ever devised."[27] And with the arrival of the Protestants, who threatened the status quo, the Church used much of that "scheming" power, or so the Protestants believed, to combat the new heretics.

Catholic opposition was not unanticipated, for many of the mission boards had long had representatives in Latin America and other Catholic areas, who worked under varying degrees of constraint.[28] Protestant missionaries did not invariably encounter harassment from the Catholic clergy.[29] But more often they found the opposition they expected. "The priests are opening a vigorous campaign, not against sin but against us," Presbyterian David S. Hibbard wrote in 1899.[30]

Denouncing the Protestants as "dogs and devils and the spawn of hell," Catholics allegedly harassed the missionaries and their converts in various ways. At its most elemental level, missionaries and especially their Filipino workers and converts were threatened with physical injury, stoned, beaten, and otherwise bodily abused. No missionaries were killed, but some of their followers were. A Filipino who helped the Baptist missionaries translate the Bible, for example, was assassinated, while Braulio Manikan was the target of deadly attacks on several occasions. The Baptists also reported that one Pedro Manejar, the *presidente* of Bacolod, had punished a Filipino Protestant for distributing a tract; he also allegedly encouraged persecution in a neighboring town where a man was so seriously beaten that he lost his hearing. "This is the beginning of a Diocletian reign of terror," one missionary predicted.[31]

Presbyterians also suffered. In Cebu a priest was arrested for the murder of a Protestant. "I inherited a loathing of Romanism," wrote the missionary there. "Now it is hard to keep it an abstract loathing."[32] Further to the south, in Zamboanga, a missionary reported that a priest was prepared to let an orphaned child die because the child's mother had been a Protestant. In 1912 there were hints that Catholics had brutally murdered an elder in the Disciples church in Dugo, near Aparri; and as late as 1915 in the village of San Felipe near Manila, a former village official attacked a Filipino Methodist pastor. When a parishioner intervened, the attacker nearly severed his hand with a bolo. "He held it up to me, limp and useless," reported the missionary, "to show me what a man may still suffer at the hands of the Romanists in the Philippine Islands."[33]

Beyond the threats and actual attacks, the missionaries reported a considerable amount of nonviolent intimidation. Protestant shopkeepers had to contend with boycotts, priests warned the people to have nothing to do with the missionaries, and parents of university students living in Protestant dormitories felt pressure to withdraw their children. Particularly troubling to virtually all the missionaries were attempts to thwart the missions' ability to establish new programs. Baptists found credit unavailable to them, and both they and the American Board missionaries were convinced that Catholics had attempted to block their efforts to begin a medical practice.[34] Probably the most common complaints concerned alleged Catholic efforts to prevent missionaries from renting or purchasing land. "If we try to rent a building and the friars hear of it all the machinery of the Church is set in motion to head us off," complained Homer C. Stuntz. "If we attempt to purchase land," he added, "their rage knows no bounds." In Davao, American Board missionaries had to purchase land surreptitiously when "Padre Lynch" was out of town; virtually all other missions reported similar troubles.[35]

A related form of harassment involved prejudicial ordinances and the anti-Protestant actions of town officials, both of which Protestants usually traced back to Catholic pressures. Ordinances were sometimes drawn in such a way as to interfere with Protestant street meetings, for example, and unfriendly officials took delight from time to time, or so it seemed to the Protestants, in arresting and jailing those attending Protestant functions.[36] The unwillingness of local officials to provide for public cemeteries caused considerable anguish for Protestants and was regarded as another form of persecution. For when Protestants died, there was often no legal place to bury the deceased, since Catholic cemeteries refused to accept the corpse.

"One poor man traveled through three municipalities begging for three feet of earth to bury his child," wrote a missionary on Bohol. But he found no space and finally buried the child on his own land in violation of the law. In another case, the distraught Protestants simply left the corpse in the mayor's office.[37]

Though the reports of unsound theology, immorality, and persecution appeared during the entire period of this study and beyond, over the years some missionaries concluded that their negative assessments of Catholicism in the Philippines were based on superficial impressions; or, if the early impressions reflected reality, they professed to see a gradually developing reformation in the Catholic Church that called for different attitudes. One of the first, and certainly the most prominent, to revise his views was the dean of the Presbyterian mission, James B. Rodgers, who had at first condemned the Church almost out of hand. By 1905 he concluded that much missionary criticism of the Church had been extreme and contemptuous. Those who criticized too quickly, he said, failed to recognize "the immense value of the work of the Roman Church to this people." It had, he pointed out, introduced fundamental theological truths and had raised the people "from the savagery of their sister Malay peoples." Rodgers also came to have a better appreciation of the difficulties encountered by the first Catholic missionaries. In addition, the missionary had "discovered that we must discount some of the tales that we hear about the friars and their work," one of the very few such admissions contained anywhere in the evangelical records. Rodgers still believed that Protestant missions were justified. But what is striking is how far he went in defense of the Church that numerous missionaries, some from his own denomination, considered almost sub-Christian and the dire enemy of Protestantism—and this at a very early date.[38]

To the extent that Protestants saw positive changes in the Catholic Church, they attributed it in part to the replacement of Spanish clergymen with men from northern Europe or the United States, a move they liked to think was caused by the Protestant example. Missionaries from the more mainline denominations had all along thought that Catholicism of the non-Latin variety was a considerably better sort, after all. It was not surprising, then, that a United Brethren missionary in 1909 reported that the American archbishop and most of the "parochial priests" wanted reform, though the apostolic delegate and the friars remained reactionary. The following year H. W. Widdoes observed that the six Belgian friars and four nuns stationed at Tagudin were "living clean lives and have completely renovated the church there and reformed the abuses."[39]

By 1915 the Methodist bishop concluded that there had been "a great housecleaning" in the Catholic Church, which he attributed to Protestant pressure and example. Priests were now more carefully trained, he felt. Churches, schools, and hospitals were being built. And all in all "a new and better Romanism" was emerging with the Church beginning to "behave like a true shepherd of the flock of Christ rather than like a selfish, dishonest hireling." Even in Vigan, where persecutions had been among the most troublesome in all of the Methodist territory, Oscar Huddleston noted "a marked reformation in the Roman Catholic Church." Extravagant charges for various services were no longer required, he reported; Sunday schools were operating that taught the Scriptures; and the priests were "organizing other classes for the good of the people, rather than sleep[ing] in their broken down convents and liv[ing] in vice and indolence."[40]

Such perceptions of change were by no means unanimously held, though. The Christian and Missionary Alliance, the Disciples, the Seventh-day Adventists, and the Baptists saw little if any improvement over the years.[41] Conceivably the impression of these groups resulted from circumstances peculiar to the areas in which they were located. But the more theologically conservative missions tended to view Catholicism as beyond redemption. A new American hierarchy was therefore largely irrelevant. Whatever reforms took place seemed insignificant.

Even within the more liberal missions, however, there were those who saw little change. Methodist D. H. Klinefelter, for example, though he did give the Church credit for advancing the people beyond paganism, still felt in 1915 that "Rome has not changed much since the days of the Inquisition," and if she were not stopped by the authorities, she would still be burning, flaying, and hanging Protestants in the Philippines.[42]

Catholic opposition persisted on the island of Leyte, where Presbyterian Charles E. Rath arrived in 1904. Although there were few physical attacks, Catholic Filipinos simply refused to associate with the Protestants and remained immune to missionary preaching. There was also a certain amount of psychological warfare. The people sometimes called the missionaries names; and on one occasion a putrified rat ended up in Rath's chapel, for which the missionary was quick to blame the Romanists. As late as 1914, when missionaries in many other areas were reporting the disappearance of open persecution and even friendly contacts with Catholics, a missionary in Tacloban wrote to his board:

> The opposition to Protestantism in this town is great, even greater than in other towns. The Roman priest threatens to withhold communion from any of his parishioners who enter Mr. Rath's home. We are called Judas and Nicodemus occasionally on the street. At an open air meeting a few days ago when Mr. Rath was preaching a woman excitedly stepped into the crowd and drew away her children and husband, telling them that Mr. Rath was the devil.[43]

In areas where opposition had clearly lessened, some suspicious missionaries concluded that the changes were only tactical. Roy H. Brown, for example, admitted in 1913 that the denunciation and persecution of previous
years in Albay had passed, that "the younger priests are suave and friendly
to our members," that the Catholic clergy not infrequently invited Protestants to assist in preparing for the town fiestas, and that Catholics even
allowed Protestants to teach in their schools. Yet the missionary feared that
the Catholics were no less intent than before on destroying Protestantism.
"The gentle as a dove and wise as a serpent policy is the hardest kind of
opposition to overcome," he wrote.[44] Missionaries like Brown put the
Catholics in an untenable position. If they did not reform, they were bitterly castigated. If they did change, they were thought to be even more
cunning and crafty than before.

In sum, the missionary community was not of one mind. The more conservative missions saw little reason to change their original critical assessment of Catholicism; in the larger, mainstream groups opinion was divided.
"We had a rather warm discussion [among Presbyterian missionaries] over
the general question of our attitude toward the Roman Church," Rodgers
reported in 1912.[45]

Unquestionably, Rodgers was correct when he contended that Protestants had been too quick to condemn the Spanish Church, too unsympathetic with the problems the earliest Catholic missionaries faced, too
unappreciative of the value of folk Catholicism.[46] Almost certainly the missionaries did not have a deep understanding of the dynamics of Philippine
society (at least at first) and overstated the oppression of the friars. But it is
difficult to dismiss all Protestant perceptions out of hand, the result of a
superficial grasp of the situation, figments of their imagination, or deliberate deception. There are too many reports of worldly priests, an oppressive
ecclesiastical structure, and genuine persecution to set aside easily.

Adding to the credibility of at least the broad outlines of the Protestant
critique were the experiences of the two groups that made the most serious
efforts to avoid conflict with the Roman Catholics: the Young Men's Christian Association, and the Episcopalian mission. In many respects the attitudes of the YMCA officials mirrored those of the more liberal Protestant
missionaries. They believed that the Catholic Church had performed an
important historical function in saving the Philippines for Christianity;
that, however, there had been serious clerical abuses under the Spanish regime; and that the substitution of northern European and American
priests had eliminated the worst problems and tended, as one of them put
it, "generally to redeem the situation."[47]

Though the Y was admittedly an "evangelical" association with informal
ties to the Protestant missions, it went out of its way to avoid offending the

Catholic establishment. In 1908, for example, an official of the Manila Y urged John R. Mott not to publish comments from letters and reports that discussed Protestant-Catholic conflict in the islands. Even more to the point, Y officials in the Philippines attempted to get permission from the YMCA's foreign department in the United States to allow Catholics to serve in official positions in the association, that is, to grant Catholics voting and officeholding memberships. The associate general secretary of the Manila branch discussed the matter with Sherwood Eddy, the prominent missionary statesman, and with Bishop Brent of the Episcopal Church, then wrote to Mott urging the adoption of such a policy. It would, he contended, gain the confidence of moderate Catholic Filipinos. "You will appreciate . . . the desirability first of being fair as far as possible to our Roman Catholic members. . . ," he wrote, "and second, of preventing the church from casting its great influence throughout the Islands actively against the Association movement, a thing which it naturally will do if the leaders are led to believe that the organization is entirely a pro-Protestant and anti-Catholic propaganda."[48]

The result, apparently at Mott's insistence, was a compromise. In the Philippines, the YMCA was permitted to adopt a dual standard for voting and officeholding membership. Americans in the islands were required to be members "in good standing of an evangelical church," a phrase that excluded the Catholic Church, whereas Filipinos were eligible if they were "members in good standing in the Roman Catholic Church or in any other Christian Church." The Y attempted to maintain a nonsectarian attitude, extended invitations to Catholic officials to cooperate with the association, and elected Catholics to responsible positions within the organization. In 1916, for example, the committee on management of the Manila YMCA was dominated by Catholic members.[49]

In spite of the Y's efforts to work with Catholics, the association, at least in Manila, encountered substantial resistance from the Church's hierarchy.[50] This was particularly so after 1911 when the Y began to expand its physical plant to recruit a Filipino membership. The effort immediately ran into strong opposition. "The one regrettable feature of the campaign," wrote an official, "was the attitude of the Archbishop of Manila, who made public and vigorous objections." Among other things, Archbishop Jeremias J. Harty objected when the governor general contributed $1,000 to the building fund.[51]

Opposition to YMCA work in Manila, especially among students, continued for the rest of the period. When in 1914 the vice-president of the Filipino Y, a Filipino judge, talked with Harty, for example, he found the prelate "still violently hostile." Students attending Catholic schools faced expulsion if they joined the Y and the Dominican publication, *Libertas*, brought forth abusive editorials on a regular basis. Similar observations appeared in numerous reports in 1915 and 1916 as well.[52]

In the case of the Y, then, a relatively liberal attitude and efforts to avoid antagonizing the Catholic Church did not succeed in avoiding serious resistance from the Church, or at least from its leadership.

Even more useful in evaluating Protestant reports of Catholicism in the Philippines is a study of the Episcopalian mission. The Episcopal Church has always included laypersons and clergy with widely divergent attitudes toward Roman Catholicism. This was certainly true of Episcopalianism in the late nineteenth and early twentieth centuries. To some, Episcopalianism meant Anglo-Catholicism: only the absence of a pope kept the Church from being Roman. Others felt that Roman Catholicism contained theological and doctrinal errors of more than passing significance, and that it had, in addition, become little more than an earthly power interested in temporal wealth and influence.

The Episcopalian mission in the Philippines reflected this divergence. On the one hand was Fr. John A. Staunton, Jr., founder in 1904 of the famous Sagada mission in the mountains of Luzon. Staunton worked closely with the Belgian fathers stationed in the same area, incorporated as much Roman Catholic ritual and doctrine into Episcopal services as was possible, and strongly resented "Protestant" leanings in the Episcopal hierarchy. When he was in Manila he normally attended mass in the Roman Catholic cathedral instead of worshipping in the Episcopal church. When the mission board, strapped for funds, proved unable to continue the Sagada mission on the scale Staunton thought necessary, he attempted to have it turned over altogether to the friars. After more than two decades of dedicated service, Staunton returned to the United States, where after a few years he took the vows of the Roman Catholic Church and accepted a position in the philosophy department at Notre Dame University.[53]

While Staunton was establishing the mission in the mountains, the Reverend Mercer G. Johnston, rector of the Episcopal cathedral in Manila, was trying to convince Bishop Brent that the Church should emphasize its Protestant aspects. An intense man given to moralistic outbursts, Johnston shared the views of strongly anti-Catholic missionaries in other denominations. "He is at heart a rabid Protestant," confided Bishop Brent to a fellow bishop with a touch of amusement.[54]

Never much attracted to brevity of expression, Johnston condemned Roman Catholicism in the Philippines in letter after letter, as well as in his sermons. In one twenty-two page, typewritten epistle to his father, the missionary concluded that the Roman Church was no closer to righteousness than was Buddhism. In fact, the Buddhism of Burma even had the edge, he felt. Specifically, like many Protestants he accused the Church of idolatry for encouraging the worship of wooden images of Mary and the saints. Secondly, he accused the clergy of adulterous behavior, citing chapter and verse at length. That Staunton could excuse such moral lapses on the grounds that they were so common as to be customary was incomprehensible to Johnston.[55]

The divergent attitudes toward Catholicism produced strongly varying ideas about what approach the mission ought to take toward the traditional church. Johnston preferred confrontation and open condemnation. Staunton, of course, deplored such an approach and instead wanted close and cordial relations. Only occasionally would he object to Catholic practices.

A central concern was whether or not to proselytize among Filipino Catholics. The initial Episcopalian call for missionaries contemplated work among Filipinos thought to be disenchanted with Roman Catholicism. Even Staunton himself, one of the first appointees, fully expected to find Filipinos "eagerly waiting for our ministrations."[56]

Staunton soon concluded, however, that few if any Catholic Filipinos wanted to join the Episcopal Church. On the contrary, he found that the people were, by and large, very religious and attached to their traditional church, a church that had on balance served them well. The Episcopal Church should therefore find a way to put "new roots down into the soil" instead of chopping "at the old ones," he thought. Protestant baptism of Catholic Filipinos, he determined, was too often "a sacrament of hate." "It is better to plant a forest," he concluded, "than to cut and pile cord wood." Walter C. Clapp, another of the first group of Episcopal missionaries, agreed. Like Staunton, he was initially tempted to the islands by the prospect of "native" work, but he soon came to feel that for the most part the people were devoted to their faith. If widespread infidelity developed later (a prospect Clapp did not rule out), then Episcopalians would be justified in working with the nominally Catholic population. But for the present, he concluded, "it does not seem to us right to have any part in inducing confusion or revolt."[57]

Bishop Brent, who arrived in the islands in 1902 and remained until 1918 (in spite of numerous tempting offers to return to the United States), allowed his clergy considerable freedom in doctrinal and liturgical matters. He could tolerate the extremes represented by Staunton and Johnston, for he recognized the spirit of God in both the Protestant and Roman Catholic faiths. Consequently he adopted a middle-of-the-road approach. Like Staunton, he emphasized the commonalities in theology. Though differences between the two churches existed, he wanted the mission to "lay stress on our points of contact" rather than on inessential theological distinctions.[58] "There has been altogether too much . . . abuse of Roman

Catholic theology by men who have never studied it first hand," he wrote in 1914. Much to the distress of "Protestants" like Johnston, the bishop was prone to conduct services in a Catholic manner, complete with ritual, ceremony, and brightly colored vestments. Even W. Cameron Forbes, a close friend of the bishop, was shocked (during one of his rare appearances in church) "to see the mummery indulged in by Bishop Brent." [59]

Like most Episcopalians, Brent also gave the Roman Church credit for its historical contributions to the Philippines. "That measure of Christian belief and practice which the mass of the Filipino people enjoy to-day," he wrote in 1909, "is the fruit of the labors of Spanish friars and of the Jesuits." Spain's motive, he noted with approval, was religious and not commercial. Spanish Catholicism saved the population from Islam, provided the strongest unifying force in the islands, and inculcated such virtues as domesticity, love of children, and hospitality, he thought. [60]

At the same time Brent was not blind to the Church's shortcomings. A stopover in Rome on his way to the islands in 1902 enhanced his suspicion about the moral health of the Church. Although he enjoyed cordial conversations with leading Catholic clerics at the Vatican and was deeply impressed with the "benign expression and emotion" of the pope, he came away with an uncomfortable sense of the Church's materialism, its grasping nature, and its unscrupulous methods. "Surely, surely," he wrote, "no religion can be blessed by God that tampers with truth, that schemes and plots to gain its own temporal ends, that winks at the dishonorable." And he anticipated encountering Catholicism in its "worst character" in the Philippines. [61]

What he found in the islands confirmed his fears. Citing instances where the Catholic Church had apparently engaged in criminal activities to gain its ends, Brent confessed almost complete disillusionment. "Until the last few years my mind turned toward Rome with a measure of sympathy and veneration," he wrote after eighteen months in the Philippines; "against my will that has all gone. As I see her abroad she is a world power, nothing more," he added, "unless it be that sometimes she is the enemy of Christ in morals as well as in policy." [62]

Particularly galling to the bishop was the incompetence and immorality that he perceived among the Catholic clergy, particularly the Filipino clergy. An extended trip through northern Luzon early in 1903 convinced him that the Filipino priests were "incompetent where they are not vicious," a situation he ascribed to the deliberate policy of the Spanish friars who, he thought, wanted to keep the Filipino clergy ignorant and dependent. "The *Frailes* wanted *muchacho*-priests," he wrote in a scathing indictment, "and they certainly got them." He found similar conditions on Panay. "We learned nothing encouraging about the work of the native *padres*," he wrote. By mid-1904, Brent felt forced to believe that immorality was rampant. "Inch by inch I have been forced back by the pressure of facts from the position I originally held that there was a minimum rather than a maximum of immorality," he concluded.⁶³

Thus the bishop could sympathize with Johnston's feelings. He did not, however, agree that the Roman Church was virtually non-Christian. Rome should be recognized "as an erring sister," he wrote, and the missionaries should "do what we can to reform her in kindliness of spirit & with the aid of Christ." Nor could he countenance Johnston's methods of public condemnation (though Brent's own articles in the *Spirit of Missions* sometimes contained strong language). "Denunciation & aggression as toward helpless sinners. . . ," he wrote, "is unchristian & not in accord with the example of our Lord." Instead, he preferred quiet but effective pressure and diplomacy to bring about a reformation in the Mother Church.⁶⁴

Because he valued Catholic theology and tradition and disliked confrontation, he preferred not to interfere with Catholic work in the Philippines and, where appropriate, encouraged and commended cooperative ventures. (He held the same views toward Protestant bodies.) He praised Staunton, for example, for establishing good relations with the Belgian fathers near Sagada.⁶⁵ For the same reason he established a policy of not actively proselytizing among Catholic Filipinos. Episcopalians would confine their work to the American and European communities and secondarily to the non-Christian mountain people, he insisted.⁶⁶

Yet Brent was more tempted by the prospect of working with the nominally Catholic population than he let on.⁶⁷ As early as March 1903, the bishop, angered by the poor quality of the priests he encountered in Tuguegarao, sorely wanted to open a mission station to minister to Filipinos as well as to Americans. "If I had more of a staff I should do so without delay," he wrote. Such experiences led him to charge in the *Spirit of Missions* that the Catholic Church had left the masses with a Christianity that was so nominal "that it would offer no indignity to the Roman Church were an earnest effort made to win them to religion."⁶⁸ The following year he admitted that he had been "too conservative" about providing religious instruction for Filipinos and authorized such instruction to be given in the Episcopalian settlement house, provided it was not done with a "controversial or destructive temper." Though Brent wanted thereby to make the people better Catholics, he was quite willing to accept as members any who came forward voluntarily. By the end of the year he was eyeing possible sites for a chapel for Filipinos.⁶⁹

By 1905 the Episcopalians had "a nucleus for a confirmation class," and the bishop seemed to be toying with the idea of a wider effort to seek converts. "It seems to me that if we are going to meet the attempts to proselyte. . . ," he wrote, "we must teach them in a clear way what the Church means and the value of her sacramental life."[70]

Brent, then, was more inclined to work with the Christianized Filipinos than has sometimes been believed. But even though his inclinations led him to flirt with conversion attempts, the mission in fact did very little. The settlement house, a school, and an orphanage eventually provided social services to the Filipinos in Manila, while a small chapel served the needs of the few converts. The public posture of the Episcopalians remained to avoid conflict with the Roman Church.

Unfortunately, Brent was never able to bridge successfully the philosophical gap in his mission. In spite of his efforts to mediate, he found himself the target of attack from both extremes. Staunton, in an intemperate and not entirely fair assessment made in 1920, commented that Brent's "whole career had been marked by 'wobble.'"[71] On the other hand, because not much was done in the way of working actively for Catholic converts, Johnston grew increasingly disenchanted with the bishop's leadership, even though he knew Brent's private feelings about Catholic shortcomings. As early as 1906 he considered resigning to accept a pastorate in Alabama. By the time he finally left in 1908, it was apparent that he could no longer work smoothly with the bishop, whom he considered inordinately generous in his attitude toward the Catholic Church.

Johnston was not the only Episcopalian to criticize the Catholic Church (although he felt Emily M. Elwyn and he were the only true "Protestants" in the mission).[72] At one time or another, in fact, most Episcopalian missionaries were critical of the performance of the Catholic Church in the islands. Even before Brent arrived, Staunton himself concluded that in three hundred years of contact the Church had failed to produce "love of righteousness, justice and truth in its closest adherents" because it aimed always to control rather than develop the people. Hobart E. Studley, who operated the Church's mission to the Chinese community in Manila, wrote that the priests considered him and his followers to be heretics. The same year Walter C. Clapp suggested that the detested Dean C. Worcester, who had allegedly attempted to block Episcopalian efforts to acquire land for the Bontoc mission, remained in office only because of Catholic influence.[73]

Nor was Johnston the only Episcopalian who regretted Brent's unwillingness to take a stronger stand against the Catholics. Brent's soothing words to the mission board in 1916, for example, in which he minimized difficulties with the Catholics, incensed Edward A. Sibley, an Episcopalian missionary in Bontoc. "Only blind optimism or entire ignorance could characterize [Roman Catholic opposition] as '*something* of an opposition,'" he wrote heatedly to the bishop. For the past eight years, Sibley recounted, Catholic opposition has been determined, tenacious, crafty, and unscrupulous. Though the missionaries had refrained from public criticism, in fact the situation had "tried our souls to the uttermost." Furthermore, Catholic harassment in Bontoc, Sibley thought, reflected the worldwide posture of the Church. "There is not one scintilla of evidence to show that as far as Bontoc is concerned the Roman Catholic clergy is any different in kind or intensity from what it ever has been."[74]

Although Brent had spoken softly to the mission board, he more than half agreed with Sibley's contentions. Not only are his early critical comments about the Catholic Church evidence of his disenchantment with Catholicism in the islands, but like Sibley (and other missionaries) Brent was particularly irritated at Roman Catholic efforts to thwart the mission's work. "There are indications that the Roman Church is going to use all means possible to loosen my hold on the people that we have succeeded in reaching. . . ," he wrote in 1905. "I am not a violent opponent of the Roman church as a Christian organization," he added, "but as a mode of intrigue and as a political meddler, and as an institution that uses methods unworthy of the name of Christian and hardly that of moral, I shall oppose it to the bitter end." Fearing that the Catholic Church had designs on property adjacent to his cathedral, Brent quickly purchased a thousand meters of street front property. "I am afraid I am in a very suspicious mood," he wrote to Johnston, no doubt an appreciative listener.[75] Like the missionaries from other churches, Brent found Catholics obstructing his efforts to purchase property in Manila; the Church also opposed Episcopalian efforts in Sagada, Bontoc, and Baguio, all in mountain areas inhabited by non-Christian peoples. At one point even Staunton found himself resisting the Church. "I told Staunton," Brent wrote with a touch of humor in 1905, "that it was an edifying sight to see him fighting the Roman Catholics." Two years later Brent still felt the Catholic Church was opposing the construction of an Episcopalian hospital, and in 1908 he chastised the Church for its political intrigues.[76]

Whether or not the replacement of Spaniards in the church hierarchy with Americans made any substantial difference in the conduct of the Catholic Church, as perceived by Episcopalians, is not entirely clear. Surely they anticipated better days, for they often insisted that American Catholics shared their negative assessment of the morality and competence of Latin Catholicism. But what finally emerged was a changeable and ambivalent picture.

Bishop Brent's early comments on the new hierarchy were full of hope. "I am very favorably impressed with the recent appointments of the Roman Catholic Church in the Islands," he wrote to Secretary of War William Howard Taft. The new archbishop of Manila was, he thought, "a spiritually minded man, modest and earnest," and all of the bishops had treated

Brent cordially. He saw "no reason why we should not work shoulder to shoulder in matters that relate to civic and national life, as well as in moral questions." The new clerics, he wrote for publication, would be just as shocked as any Protestant at the low state of morality among the clergy and would, he was sure, try to reform the Church—though Brent feared that the Church's celibacy requirements posed great problems in this regard.[77]

Yet, almost at the same time Brent's words were appearing in *Spirit of Missions*, the bishop was at the White House agreeing with President Theodore Roosevelt that Francis Rooker, the Catholic bishop of Jaro, was "apparently devoid of true American spirit, and would like to enforce once more the oppressive methods of the Friars." Brent had virtually echoed the words of Rooker's Baptist critics! Furthermore, Brent continued, Bishop Denis Dougherty of Nueva Segovia was "not much better." Yet a few months later Brent confided to another clergyman that "the Roman bishops are good men and I think the present Apostolic delegate, Monsgr. [Ambrose] Aguis, is a man of character as well as of ability."[78]

These contradictory statements are explained, in part, by the difference between Brent's public expressions and his private beliefs. Publicly the bishop usually avoided derogatory comments about the new hierarchy, partly, one senses, to preserve whatever influence he might have had with the archbishop. In 1906, for example, he attempted privately to secure the support of Archbishop Harty for the Moral Progress League, a non-denominational (but Methodist-inspired) organization to reform public morality.[79] Brent must have sensed that discretion in his public statements would enhance whatever influence he might have possessed with the prelate.

Persistent Catholic opposition caused Brent to lower his guard on occasion and publicly chastise the Catholics; but when he did he seems to have regretted his actions. In 1907, for example, Brent complained in private correspondence about Bishop Dougherty's decision to place Belgian and German priests in Sagada and Bontoc, where the Episcopalians had already established their work. He could, Brent felt, have located the friars in any number of areas in the province that were completely unchurched. "I wonder how the Spirit of Christ can remain in the Church that does such things," he wrote to Walter Clapp.[80] The unchristian spirit (so Brent believed) that animated Dougherty's intrusions at Bontoc and Sagada seems to have festered in Brent's mind, for the next year his sense of indignation overcame his natural caution, and in an article intended for publication the bishop lashed out at the hierarchy for forbidding social intercourse with Episcopalian missionaries and for intruding on territory already manned by Episcopalians, particularly when there were hundreds of thousands of unchurched people elsewhere in the mountains. "Oh when will Christians learn," he lamented, "that proselytizing from other Christian churches is as hateful to our Lord as the same spirit among Jews was hateful to Him when he was on earth! . . . When will we come to see that the defamation of the character of one Church by another is as despicable as the defamation of one man by another!"[81]

But Brent soon recanted, apologized personally to the archbishop, and retracted most of his views in a letter to the editor of *Outlook*:

> I have had reason to modify my judgment of several aspects of the affair. I do not think that the Archbishop of Manila had anything actively to do with it. I was hasty in my characterisation of their intrusion, and the methods employed on the occasion of the visit of the Bishop of Nueva Segovia [Dougherty] were fortunately not repeated. I told the Archbishop that I was sorry that I spoke, or rather wrote, in the terms that I used though I added that I considered that what had been done was detrimental to the highest spiritual interests.[82]

Brent's public attack on the American-dominated hierarchy in 1908 appears to have been his last. It may be that real changes in the Church eventually convinced Brent, as it did many Protestant missionaries, that a reformation was finally beginning. Perhaps, then, Brent's statements in 1916 to the Episcopal board of missions that the Belgian fathers, though needing to "present something of an opposition," really felt that "the work we are doing is part of the great work of the Catholic Church," represented his mature views. Responding to Sibley's letter that took issue with his characterization of relations between Catholics and Episcopalians, the bishop confessed, "all you say has elements of truth in it. On the other hand," he continued,

> I deprecate, as I have always deprecated, the *spirit* of rivalry. It may be that I am too optimistic in my estimate of the situation. Nevertheless, it is my fixed judgment. The main point is this: we have all the opportunity that we can possibly use. Even if from time to time we do have direct interference, the magnitude of the opportunity is not thereby seriously affected.[83]

Brent's final words on the subject suggest that after fifteen years in the islands he had reached a philosophical peace of mind. Admitting in private that there was a Catholic opposition, little would be gained by public recriminations. Such denunciations would align him too openly with his Protestant counterparts, thus alienating his High Church supporters and undercutting whatever influence he might have with the Catholic hierarchy. Furthermore, real changes had taken place, though they came slowly, under the new Catholic leadership. Besides, as he put it, "we have all the opportunity we can possibly use."

The Episcopal bishop had reached his own peace of mind, but his experiences and those of other Episcopalians lend credence to Protestant perceptions of Catholicism in the Philippines. In some respects, Episcopalian assessments of Catholic behavior were even more negative than those of other Protestants. But by the end of the period, changes were unquestionably in the works. To be sure, Presbyterian Roy H. Brown could write in 1914, "we might as well be frank . . . and say in practice and teaching we do not recognize the Catholic Church in the P. I. as the church of God or at least one that has gone far astray." Divided though the missionaries remained, it was symptomatic of a newer age that Arthur Judson Brown, who in 1902 had himself denounced the Catholic Church in the Philippines, gently rebuked the zealous missionary.[84]

Even within the Baptist community, attitudes modified, though it took a few more years. "No longer are we arrested for preaching in the public plaza, nor our Bible burnt, nor our members persecuted," wrote a long-time missionary in 1925. "In town and village, in the house of the rich and in the lowly hut of the peasant we are received with respect and our message with interest." Baptists enjoyed friendly associations with Catholics, and some Catholics even made financial contributions to Baptist medical work, dormitories, and to Central Philippine College near Iloilo, the premier Baptist institution in the islands.[85]

In a sense, both the older and the newer views of Catholicism fit in with Protestant needs. Committed to expand their work for sincerely felt religious reasons, Protestants were always in need of additional funds from supporters in the United States. Contributors to missions needed to know which evils their money would help alleviate. In pagan lands, stories of the degraded lives of the "natives" served the purpose. In the Philippines and in other Roman Catholic lands as well, accounts of an abased Christianity supplemented the tales of warped lives.

At the same time, it was comforting to the potential "investor" to know that results had been achieved. Hundreds had been converted, hospitals were serving the needy, dormitories were helping to save students from infidelity, and even Rome had cleaned its house somewhat.[86] If at first a Catholic reformation seemed threatening, as it did to some of the first missionaries, it no longer did. "One need not fear or even regret the new vigor and activity of the Catholic church in the Philippines," a Baptist wrote. Most assuring of all, victory was in sight. "If you will stand by us and invest some of the Lord's money," read one Methodist circular (appropriately divided into two sections, "The Dark Side of the Mission Field" and "A Brighter Side"), "we will by His help finish this job."[87]

6

The Protestant Missionary Response to Philippine Nationalism: The Ecclesiastical Dimension

> [Methodist missionaries are] smug young men . . . who place their national prejudices above the teachings of Jesus Christ. By word and action they have for years belittled our capabilities even to the extent of repeatedly asserting to our faces that the Filipinos are not fitted to conduct their own churches.
>
> Nicolas Zamora

The Filipino response to the entire American occupation was complex. Some Filipinos welcomed it, but the majority, while welcoming American assistance in ousting the Spanish, were reluctant to substitute American hegemony for Spanish tyranny. When it became evident early in 1899 that the United States would annex the islands, thousands of Filipinos waged a bloody war of resistance against the occupiers. Although the Americans crushed most resistance by 1902 (sporadic outbursts continued for several years), Americans in the islands, including missionaries, continued to face the reality of Filipino nationalism. Reports that Filipinos hated Americans were common. In 1903, for example, an American Board missionary traveling through Samar observed that even prostitutes were nowhere to be found, in spite of the large encampment of American soldiers on the island.[1] At least until 1916, in fact, nationalism, often with anti-American overtones, was probably the most important factor affecting relations between Filipinos and Americans. In that year the terms of the discussion changed, and tensions relaxed perceptibly, if temporarily, when for the first time the United States government affirmed that Philippine independence was the goal of American policy.[2]

Politically, Filipino nationalism was expressed in demands for complete independence, the formation of a popularly elected assembly, and Filipino participation at all levels of government. Ecclesiastically, Filipinos demanded withdrawal of the Spanish friars and a larger role in both Catholic and Protestant church affairs.

In his important study, *From Caraboa to Clipper*, Elmer K. Higdon portrays the Protestant missionaries' influence as, on balance, that of a promoter of nationalism. "The church frequently stimulated and gave impetus to the desire for independence," he writes. Some of the missionaries refrained from involvement in political matters, but "others openly declared their sympathies with the hopes and aspirations of the Filipino people."[3]

Higdon's generalization may be accurate for the missionaries of the 1920s and 1930s (though that is open to question),[4] but its validity for the first generation of missionaries is doubtful. Missionaries of Higdon's own denomination, the Disciples of Christ, demonstrated more sympathy toward independence than did some others, yet even they can only be described as ambivalent, especially when it came to giving Filipinos a voice in mission affairs. It certainly does not apply to those missionaries who were present during the Philippine-American War. Virtually all disapproved of Filipino resistance, and some gave direct support to the American authorities. A YMCA official expressed what was a common view when he sympathized with the bitter attitude of many American soldiers who had seen "their comrades cut up by treacherous natives who had passed as friends at the last halting place."[5]

Still, a sympathetic response to nationalism appeared possible in some quarters. Episcopalian Bishop Charles Henry Brent, for example, whose thinking was originally shaped by a view that "left no room for doubt . . . as to the absolute beneficence of the Western mode of dealing with Eastern life," became fascinated with the growth of various forms of Asian nationalism and hoped to guard Filipinos against "servile imitation" of their American rulers. Though foreigners had a role to play in both the political and religious life of Oriental peoples, Brent thought that salvation ultimately lay in their own hands. "Never yet was a nation Christianized except through its own prophets," he wrote.[6] Yet in practice the Episcopalian mission resisted Filipino nationalism more tenaciously than any other.

In fact, the only form of nationalism (if it can be so termed) that had the clear support of important missionaries in the earliest years was the sort represented by Felipe Buencamino, a former secretary of foreign affairs in the cabinet of Emilio Aguinaldo. While a part of the resistance, Buencamino had been a force for moderation, having at one point tried to make peace with the Americans on the basis of Philippine autonomy instead of outright independence. Due to internal discord within the insurgency, along with the capture of his brother by insurgents, Buencamino left the movement and approached Governor Taft in hopes of establishing a political party that would work with American authorities. He is, therefore, rightly considered one of "the first collaborators of the Americans." With Taft's encouragement, Buencamino helped to organize the *Partido Federalista*, which advocated statehood.[7]

If Buencamino was a collaborator, he was nevertheless a conservative nationalist, as his deep antagonism toward the Roman Catholic Church, a symbol of Spanish colonialism, made clear. He was reported to have influenced thousands to leave their historic church. To fill the religious vacuum he helped create, Buencamino approached the Protestant missionaries. Apparently he envisaged a movement on two fronts: political and religious. The Federal party would be his vehicle for direct political power, while the missionaries could be useful in his efforts to reorient the religion of the masses.

The Protestants were sorely tempted. "He promises a great landslide during the next months," wrote James B. Rodgers, the Presbyterian leader. Though Rodgers was warned of Buencamino's fickle nature, a long talk with the Filipino leader convinced the missionary to associate himself with the movement, with the understanding that he would be in charge of the religious side.[8]

In February 1901, Buencamino launched the religious side of the movement by organizing a mass rally at the Rizal Theatre in Tondo. Rodgers, Arthur Prautch (a Methodist), Nicolas Zamora, and other Filipino Protestants addressed the crowd. Though the Protestants were at pains to separate the religious aspects of the movement from the political, to the average person the distinction must have seemed contrived. In any event, the missionaries were pleased with the developments and looked "for a National movement to grow out of this."[9] Though their hopes were eventually dashed,[10] Rodgers preached in the theatre almost every Sunday for the next two years to crowds ranging from three hundred to twelve hundred. Religious nationalism that was not anti-American and that seemed to present enormous possibilities for the Protestant cause had the support of the missionary community.

A more serious form of Philippine religious nationalism in the early years was the Aglipayan schism from the Roman Catholic Church. The break resulted from a longtime Filipino resentment of Spanish ecclesiastical domination and discrimination. The oppressive practices of the friars were, in fact, major causes of the nineteenth-century rebellions against Spanish authorities, including those of 1896 and 1898. Resentment at foreign domination of Philippine religious life continued during the war against the United States, resulting in two major attempts to establish a church independent of the Spanish hierarchy but within Roman Catholicism. These efforts failed, but in the autumn of 1902 dissident clergymen proclaimed a national church separate from the Roman Church. Gregorio Aglipay soon became the *Obispo Maximo* (supreme bishop).[11]

The schism elicited extensive comment in the Protestant missionary community. Frank C. Laubach, author of an early study of Philippine religious history, contended that, among missionaries, critics of the movement were in a clear majority, a judgment echoed by some later authors as well.[12] But the missionaries were not of one mind, and Aglipay had fervent champions, as well as bitter antagonists, among the missionaries. What emerges is a picture of division and ambivalence.

On the one hand the new church's strongest American champion was Arthur W. Prautch, one of the earliest (albeit unofficial) Protestant missionaries in the islands. Granted a license as a Methodist local preacher, Prautch maintained extensive connections with church personnel of various persuasions. Just how close Prautch was to Aglipay is a matter of dispute. He once bragged to Eric Lund, the pioneer Baptist missionary, that he and his Filipina wife had, in Lund's words, "made Aglipay archbishop through the press, thrusting him, scared as he was, before the public with the mitre of cotton stuff and the crook of tinplate they had made for him."[13] If Prautch is to be believed (and his integrity was attacked at the time by none other than former governor Taft),[14] Aglipay was little more than a cipher, "a good boy floating on the top of the waves."[15] Prautch surely exaggerated his influence on the bishop, but he was of some importance. For a time he edited the church's publication, *La Verdad*, and he arranged important meetings between Aglipay and Bishop Brent.

Prautch also enjoyed considerable influence with Eric Lund, who came to Manila in 1903 expressly to meet Aglipay. Though disappointed that the bishop was out of town, he conversed at length with Prautch and became so caught up in the movement's possibilities that he spoke to large rallies of Aglipayanos in Manila and Cebu.[16]

Few missionaries were so closely attached to the movement as were Prautch and Lund, but most saw at least some advantage to their own cause from this split in Catholic ranks. "Aglipay loosens this fruit from the tree," wrote Methodist Homer C. Stuntz, "and we gather it." "This movement has aided us greatly in our work both in what it gives the people and what it fails to give them," concluded the Presbyterian mission in 1904. "It makes the original break with the past and so opens the way for us to preach the better news of the Gospel."[17] Similar sentiments existed in most missions. Consequently, it was not unusual for the missions to try and cultivate Aglipayan leaders. Homer Stuntz, for example, maintained personal contact over the years with the bishop and in 1905 invited him to address the Methodists' annual conference. The same year David S. Hibbard invited an Aglipayano bishop and his priests to attend closing exercises at Silliman Institute, an invitation quickly accepted.[18]

Whether such good relations existed away from the mission centers is more difficult to determine. But if the case of a missionary couple in Lucban, Tayabas, is at all typical, relations were cordial enough. The Aglipayanos in Lucban permitted Protestants to bury their dead in the Aglipayan cemetery, something the Catholics forbade. The local priest was very friendly, visited regularly with the missionaries, and even sent his daughter to the mission Sunday school. "This attitude is very different from that of the Roman priests who do not care to come in contact with Protestants in any way," the missionaries reported. "They are bitter, & bigots!"[19]

Few missions were more enthusiastic about the possibilities of the Independent Church than were the Baptists. Like other Protestants, the Baptists did not think that Aglipay had gone far enough in his break with Rome. But they wished him well and hoped that the American public would be sympathetic. Charles W. Briggs, the Baptist leader, was so concerned about the attitude of the public at home that he urged Baptists to read an article the bishop had written for the *Independent*. "Read and re read, and read it on their knees before God," he urged. The Baptists also had dreams of enhancing the schism's value by converting Aglipay to their faith. Sensing that the new Church was friendly to them, the missionaries sent Braulio Manikan, a Filipino Baptist leader, to meet with Aglipay when he visited Jaro, Panay, in 1903. Manikan tried to convince the bishop of the truth of Baptist beliefs. He apparently made some progress, or thought he did, for Briggs was pleased. "If Lund had been here," he wrote, "Aglipay would be a Baptist today."[20]

If Aglipay gave the Baptists the impression that he sympathized with their views, he did the same with the Seventh-day Adventists. He met with Adventist missionaries on several occasions, questioned them closely about their faith, welcomed their gifts of literature, and indicated considerable interest in their doctrines. Contacts of this sort led the Adventists to hope for extended influence and possibly even the bishop's conversion. "Pray that the seed sown with this man may not be lost," wrote one missionary. "He has a great influence and a large following."[21]

Even the most fervent Adventist must have felt inwardly that the chances of converting Aglipay were remote. But they seem to have come much closer with Aglipay's secretary, Santiago Fonacier. If Adventist information is accurate, Fonacier was studying regularly, almost daily, with Adventists in 1908. He wanted his sister to room with the missionaries and to submit to their instruction. Eventually he concluded that he could no longer accept the rationalistic doctrine of the Independent Church and would no longer teach it—or so he told the missionaries. "We believe this young man will take his stand for the truth," thought the Adventists with great optimism. "It will mean much for him to cut loose from his present church connection, especially in a country like this." At the time, Fonacier may have been sincere, or perhaps he only wanted not to offend his mentors. In any event he did not join the Adventists. Instead he remained with the Independent Church, embraced its unitarian doctrine, and became Aglipay's immediate successor as archbishop.[22]

If many missionaries welcomed the schism, established cordial relations with the Aglipayanos, and even hoped for the conversion of the leadership, others were deeply suspicious of the movement and wanted to keep it at arms length. It appears, for example, that Arthur Prautch eventually lost his license as a Methodist local preacher because of his involvement with the bishop. Even more indicative of missionary hostility was the lack of response that Eric Lund perceived among the Protestant missionary community, a perception that deeply troubled him. Like many other missionaries, including Prautch, Lund thought that the Independent Church would eventually collapse. But he doubted that the Protestants would be in a position to pick up the pieces because most of them, he thought, refused to associate themselves very closely with the movement. In spite of repeated invitations, for example, almost no missionaries came to hear Lund address Aglipayano rallies. The Presbyterian leader even gently reproved the Baptist for speaking to such gatherings.

Lund found all of this deeply disturbing. "The Aglipayanos are, as the rest of the Filipinos, sensitive and many of them are sensible people too," he wrote. "This attitude on the part of the missionaries is well observed by the Aglipayanos and it is more harmful to our protestant cause than the missionaries imagine."[23]

Missionary suspicion of Aglipay and his followers derived from several sources. For one thing, the Independent Church remained much too Catholic for many Protestants to endorse. There was really little to choose "between the Scylla of Romanism and the Charybdis of Aglipayanism," a Disciples' publication editorialized in 1909.[24] Others considered Aglipay unscrupulous and ambitious. A reporter found that many missionaries, agreeing, ironically, with the Apostolic delegate, considered the self-proclaimed bishop "a selfish schemer, an opportunist, a politician" who seemed to "stand for nothing." Similarly, a United Brethren missionary concluded in 1909 that the Church had declined mostly because of Aglipay's "vanity and inordinate ambition." The Church, he concluded, was "*not* of God."[25] But the most important reason for criticism was the alleged political character of the movement, by which missionaries meant its nationalistic thrust and its reputation for anti-Americanism. Aglipay had, after all, been a part of Emilio Aguinaldo's resistance to the American occupation. The movement's nationalism was generally, although not invariably, recognized. It "has taken so firm a hold on the people, simply because it is a Filipino movement," a Baptist wrote in 1903. To H. W. Widdoes of the United Brethren, the only missionary who described himself as an anti-imperialist, the movement's nationalism was not a cause for alarm, since he consciously sought out Filipino nationalists anyway.[26] Missions that were not much interested in politics—notably the Baptists, the Disciples, the Adventists—might approve or criticize Aglipay on doctrinal grounds, but their assessments seldom extended to the nationalistic component of the movement. The Baptist leader, interestingly, thought Aglipay pro-American, surely an idiosyncratic opinion.[27]

But suspicions of Aglipay's political orientation ran high among many Methodists, Presbyterians, and Episcopalians, even though they might see some advantages for Protestantism in the schism. Most missionaries, after all, viewed Filipinos as underdeveloped persons, even akin to children. For such a major movement to be Filipino-controlled was unnerving. Methodist bishop William F. Oldham, for example, felt that "like most Filipino leaders" Aglipay lacked "organizing ability and staying quality." Presbyterian Paul Doltz was even more suspicious of Aglipayan intentions. The Aglipayan bishop of Iloilo, Narciso Hijalda, he remarked, was "as bad as the rest of them," an apparent reference to the common belief that independent churchmen were anti-American and fomenters of insurrection. Two years later he remarked that the movement was a "purely destructive" one.[28] Doltz's views were probably not representative of the general feeling among Methodists and Presbyterians. Roy H. Brown, another Presbyterian, likely expressed the majority sentiment. The movement, he wrote, had its positive side. "They have lowered rates and are not so vindictive as the old church." But, he added, "I fear the movement is more political than religious."[29]

If ambivalence characterized the Methodist and Presbyterian evaluation of Aglipay, the Episcopalians, though immensely interested in the movement and in some ways the closest to it in terms of tradition and doctrine, were almost entirely negative in their assessments. As early as 1902, Walter C. Clapp concluded that Aglipay was a "bad man." Two years later Mercer G. Johnston accused Aglipay of adulterous behavior. "Like the padres of Rome," he wrote, ". . . he has frequently lain with the women that assembled at the door of the tabernacle of the Congregation."[30]

Bishop Brent was not more complimentary. He specifically endorsed Clapp's assessment, and a few months later characterized Aglipay as "unscrupulous and untrustworthy." Aglipay's movement, he quickly concluded, contained "no positive religious principles" but was, rather, a social and political protest "dressed in the clothes of religion" that enjoyed immediate success only because of the failings of the Roman Catholic Church in the islands.[31]

Brent's most thorough analysis of the Aglipayan church came in an address delivered before the house of bishops and delegates at the General Convention of the Episcopal Church in 1904. Written in a surprisingly objective tone, Brent presented a brief historical sketch of the Church's origins, always balancing critical commentary with Aglipay's defense. He admitted that the Church had "exhibited greater cohesion than most observers, myself among the number, expected," that Rome's irresponsibility was to blame for the separation, that like all revolutionary movements the Independent Church had its share of malcontents, but that Aglipay himself disavowed political intrigue, and that the official doctrines of the Church indicated "in the main, a sane view of ecclesiastical polity, Catholic doctrine, and moral living. Under proper leadership," he went on, "a Church that was true to the principles enunciated therein would not be far from the Kingdom of God." In view of his previous reservations about the movement, it would appear that Brent had experienced a change of heart. The change was more apparent than real, however. For what was not made public at the time were his private remarks to the bishops, in which Brent revealed that he had always thought that the movement had an insurrectionist character. Due to its political nature, the Church "was a sham," Aglipay was "fickle" and "selfishly ambitious." Consequently, it would be better that "the whole disaffected mass should be reabsorbed into the Roman communion than that it should continue its present course."[32]

Yet Brent also seemed to feel that the movement had latent possibilities. In his private addendum, Brent revealed that he had met Aglipay in the fall of 1902 and had had extensive conversations with the schismatic bishop in 1904, conversations arranged by the maverick Methodist, Arthur W. Prautch. Aglipay was clearly disturbed by the irregular way in which he had been proclaimed a bishop, admitting in fact that under Catholic canons he was not a bishop. He wondered if Brent, in conjunction with bishops from the Anglican and Old Catholic churches, might provide the necessary apostolic succession by conferring episcopal orders on him. In addition, the two men discussed the possibilities of some kind of official connection with the Episcopal Church, and Brent suggested that Aglipay petition the Episcopalian General Convention to send a commission to the islands to confer about the possibility of an official relationship. Though skeptical, Brent was drawn to the idea. He agreed to convey any message Aglipay drafted to the General Convention. In June, Aglipay responded, offering "our disinterested and enthusiastic alliance" in spreading the gospel in the Philippines.[33] In another personal letter, Aglipay said that he would welcome enthusiastically a visit to the Philippines by *"representantes"* of the Episcopal, Anglican, and Old Catholic churches, though he did not specifically say that he anticipated consecration at their hands.[34]

Since Aglipay did not mention an official commission and was vague about the proposed relationship, Brent refused to forward it and urged that it be redrafted. He even suggested specific language. In addition, he chastised the bishop for not being explicit about episcopal consecration. Although he admitted that Aglipay's second letter, when "taken in conjunction with what you have said to me in conversation . . . has a significance which it would not possess otherwise," he admonished him to "be as frank on paper as you are in conference. In matters that pertain to the church of God, honesty of motive and straightforwardness of action must go hand in hand." Brent clearly considered Aglipay unreliable and dealt with him in a patronizing manner. But the impression remains that he held out some hopes for affiliation, almost certainly feeling that American churchmen might be able to direct the movement into constructive channels. If Aglipay would redraft his letter to request an official commission to discuss the establishment of a relationship with the Episcopal Church, Brent pledged to use his "influence to secure its appointment."[35]

This proved to be the high point of Brent's relationship with Aglipay. He had momentarily replaced his strongly negative impressions with mildly skeptical ones. He was willing to listen to Aglipay's insistence that he was not an *insurrecto*, that his goals were spiritual, that the charges against him were unproved, and that the movement had greater potential than he had at first thought possible.

When Aglipay failed to answer his letter, however, Brent's original feelings returned. "I am afraid the man is too slippery to do anything with," he wrote to a constabulary officer. Later, when Aglipay told Brent that he had been in the provinces when Brent's letter arrived, thus accounting for his failure to respond, Brent dismissed his excuse out of hand.[36] By October 1905, Brent had concluded that the movement was "what it was at first—largely a political agitation." The leaders, he added, were "consciously dishonest" with their followers. He repeated his view in March 1906, in response to an inquiry from a fellow bishop. He had no reason to change his views, he stated. The movement was "so unclean that I do not see how we can ally ourselves with it."[37] Of the Aglipayan bishops, Narciso Hijalda stood out as a man of honor and integrity, Brent felt. The rest were no worse than the Roman Catholic priests, he admitted, but then they were no better either.

In later years, neither Brent nor the other Episcopalian missionaries seem to have taken a more positive attitude toward Aglipay. In fact, an incident in Sagada in 1913 brought forth vituperative assessments of Aglipay's character. When Aglipay came to the mountain village that year, he became engaged in an altercation with a man who refused to call him bishop. Jaime Masferre, the Episcopal layman, was summoned to defuse the situation. But the next day Aglipay and Masferre came to blows, allegedly because the latter, too, refused to call Aglipay bishop. Episcopal missionary Robb White witnessed the fisticuffs. Masferre then wrote to John A. Staunton, Jr., and Brent, who was then in New York, describing the affair.[38]

Brent, angered at Aglipay's actions and seeing this as a perfect demonstration of Filipino incapacity to govern at a time shortly after the Democrats had assumed office, immediately passed the correspondence along to Secretary of War Lindley M. Garrison. Aglipay, he contended, had "been an influence for evil in the life of the Filipinos ever since the American occupation, and, doubtless, for sometime prior to then." He briefly recounted his own contacts with Aglipay, saying he had told the self-proclaimed bishop that he was a "sham" and that he had led an immoral life. "His whole history is a history of trickery," he wrote, adding that he had asked Staunton and White to write as well. The next day he wrote to the president of the University of the Philippines, Murray Bartlett (an Episcopalian), about "that arch-scoundrel Aglipay." He added, "I have turned over the matter to the Secretary of War as a side light on the fitness of the Filipinos to govern themselves."[39]

In sum, Protestant missionaries were more favorable to the Aglipayan schism than some writers have suggested. At the very least, most saw advantage to the Protestant cause in the Catholic rift. But many also believed the stories of Aglipay's immorality, dishonesty, and inordinate ambition. Most of all they worried about his past association with Aguinaldo's resistance to American rule and his continuing nationalism. Many feared that he secretly still espoused insurrection. His insistence on a church manned and controlled by Filipinos disquieted foreign missionaries. How would they respond if their converts insisted on controlling the Protestant denominations? What if they broke away, even as Aglipay had done from his church?

In fact, as early as 1905 the Methodists suffered a schism when Manuel Aurora, a Methodist local preacher, rebelled and organized the *Cristianos Vivos Metodistas*. The roots of this little known schism reach back at least to the previous year, when Aurora organized the *Cristianos Vivos* as a society within the Methodist Church at Baliuag. Aurora's actions convinced the missionary in charge, A. E. Chenoweth, that the society's existence was inimical to the Church, whereupon he formally charged Aurora with "lying," "causing dissension," and "improper conduct." Ordered to appear at a church trial, Aurora instead broke away and was "ordained" a minister of the new church by a number of Filipino sympathizers, including some who had been Methodist local preachers, exhorters, and probationers.[40]

The available evidence strongly suggests that nationalistic resentment at American domination was a major factor in Aurora's action. Chenoweth reported that Aurora's followers were complaining "that they had been slaves to the Spaniards and now were slaves to the Americans." Furthermore, the previous year wages for Filipino Methodist workers had been cut without any consultation. That, Bishop Oldham wrote in retrospect, had been "a grave error," and he hoped "never to be involved in such a blunder again." The bishop reproved Homer Stuntz, the presiding elder, for being out of touch with the Filipinos. Uneasiness among them, he wrote, "was from lack of sufficient consultation and close manifest sympathy with the Filipino brethren. . . . Your men need to feel that we are *near* them." Oldham alone, however, appears to have sensed the underlying causes. Methodists more commonly concluded that the schismatics were motivated only by "spite and revenge," and that the leaders, "without convictions and without training," exhibited "the Filipino's love of office and titles." Aurora himself, they claimed, "organized the Society partly for revenge, and partly because he wanted to be a 'cabeza' or head man."[41] When nationalism struck home, Methodist ambivalence largely disappeared.

The Aurora schism produced some temporary dislocations, but by 1906 it had faded into insignificance[42]—or so it appeared. It is possible, though, that the *Cristianos Vivos Metodistas* influenced Agustin de la Rosa to break away from the Presbyterian Church in 1906, taking a few members with him. The de la Rosa break seems to have been relatively unimportant, and evidence is lacking about its motivation. But Aurora's action almost certainly lay behind more widespread discontent in the ranks of the Disciples of Christ. In 1906 Bruce Kershner concluded that some Tagalogs who wanted to form an indigenous Philippine Protestant Church were "agitators" who were "simply crazy on the subject of independence." Most of the Disciples' Filipino preachers, influenced by the Methodist schismatics, had joined "a native Evangelical Union," he added. A little later the Kershners reported that the congregation at Loreta was in danger of dividing "owing to the Independencia idea," an analysis indicating Disciples awareness of the forces of nationalism then sweeping the islands. In 1908 the Disciples suffered their first real break when the congregation in Pasay declared itself independent of the mission, professing a desire to get out from under American control. "This patriotic congregation seems to be doing quite well," Kershner reported, "for their appeal to the national desire for independence takes with the people." But he could not condone the congregation's action.[43]

Aurora's revolt, then, dislocated Methodist work, had considerable influence among the Filipino Disciples, and conceivably disrupted the Presbyterians as well. But its greatest legacy was yet to come, for it laid the groundwork for Nicolas Zamora's more famous and lasting schism from the Methodist Church in 1909.

Zamora's family was prominently identified with anti-Spanish movements in the late nineteenth century. One great uncle, Fr. Jacinto Zamora, was one of three priests executed for involvement in the Cavite Mutiny of 1872. Nicolas's father, Paulino, defied the friars and was exiled to a Spanish penal colony in the Mediterranean, returning to the Philippines only after the Treaty of Paris transferred sovereignty to the United States. Paulino and Nicolas both became Protestants, and in March 1900 Bishop James Thoburn ordained Nicolas Zamora a deacon in the Methodist Episcopal Church. He was the first ordained Filipino Protestant minister.[44]

Zamora soon became the pride and joy of Philippine Methodism. "Nicholas is a jewel," one missionary told Bishop Frank W. Warne in 1900.[45] The Aurora schism disturbed Zamora, but he did not join it.[46] The following year, 1906, the American missionaries assigned Zamora to the Tondo church, near Manila, where separatist sentiment was strong. Reluctantly Zamora went to Tondo, where he temporarily held the separatists in check. "He has shown courage, grace, good sense, kindness, wisdom and fitness for the ministry of the Methodist Episcopal Church," wrote Marvin A. Rader, the missionary in charge.[47] Three years later, however, Zamora joined the Tondo dissidents and angrily left the Methodist Church, taking with him at least 1,500 parishioners and a number of Filipino preachers. His defection was the beginning of the still extant *La Iglesia Evangelica Metodista en las Islas Filipinas* (IEMELIF).

Missionary complaints about Zamora "collecting exorbitant marriage fees" may have contributed to the break, although the immediate cause seems to have been unequal treatment accorded Filipino pastors. As an associate of Zamora told a reporter, "he objects to the American missionaries going to Baguio [the new summer capital in the mountains of Luzon] every year and getting one year's leave on full pay every five years when he is denied leave once in ten years." Such discrepancy in sabbatical arrangements was symptomatic of the deeper problem: the missionaries' stifling paternalism and their denigration of Filipino capabilities. Zamora himself made the fundamental issue clear in a newspaper interview. Methodist Church administrators in the Philippines, he said, were "smug young men . . . who place their national prejudices above the teachings of Jesus Christ. By word and action they have for years belittled our capabilities even to the extent of repeatedly asserting to our faces that the Filipinos are not fitted to conduct their own churches."[48]

The Zamora schism was the most traumatic of the Methodist encounters with Philippine nationalism in the early years, and, with the possible exception of Arthur Prautch, whose role remains unclear, the American Methodists in the Philippines condemned Zamora's apostasy. Homer C. Stuntz contended that "the spirit of insubordination" accounted for Zamora's actions, while Marvin A. Rader suggested that his "ambition to be called bishop" explained the schism. Reflecting on the matter in his annual report, Rader also admitted the nationalistic motivation. Many Filipinos wanted independence, he pointed out, and the "desire to rule" was, he thought, "insatiable among many in the Philippines." But the desire of the Filipinos to control their own destiny was not admirable, at least not yet. Filipinos were not prepared to assume positions of real responsibility. As Rader put it, a premature transfer of power would not "advance the kingdom of God in these Islands."[49]

Bishop Oldham's reaction, while generally paralleling Rader's, was more subtle and complex. Like his missionary colleagues, Oldham noted Zamora's personal ambition and alleged financial indiscretions. He also thought he saw the influence of Zamora's cousin, Dominador Gomez, whom he characterized with some truth as "a born firebrand."[50] Yet he was more sensitive to the schism's nationalistic underpinnings. Zamora had long argued for equal pay for Filipino workers, he observed, and had chafed under American supervision. Consequently, the bishop did not condemn the schism out of hand. The desire of Filipinos to assert themselves, to "show they were able to run their own affairs," he wrote, was in itself praiseworthy. He even conceded that "the appeal to Filipino prejudice and race feeling" might attract more islanders to Protestantism.[51] Still, the break was not to be condoned. If there was any doubt about God's will in the matter, subsequent conversions to American controlled Methodism in the areas most affected by the schism convinced the missionaries that Zamora's actions were ill-advised. "This is God's answer to the Zamora defection," wrote Bishop Oldham.[52]

If the Aurora schism produced uneasiness among missionaries of various denominations, the Zamora break created shock waves that reverberated through the ranks. "No one knows where the lightning will strike," wrote a Disciples missionary. The following year, in fact, at least two Disciples congregations were affected by "senseless agitation" for ecclesiastical independence.[53] Presbyterians assumed they would be similarly beset. It took three years, but Zamoristas did persuade a portion of the Presbyterian congregation at Unisan, Tayabas, to withdraw and establish their own church free from the control of American missionaries. Similar sentiments existed in the church in Sorgoson, Albay, though the dissidents were apparently persuaded not to break away. Late in the summer of 1911, moreover, a major disruption occurred when the Reverend Gil Domingo, pastor of a circuit in Cavite Province, not far from Manila, broke away from the Presbyterian mission to form the *Cristianos Filipinos*, a church free from missionary control. If missionary accounts are to be credited, Felipe Buencamino, the erstwhile supporter of the early missionaries, was the driving force behind the schism, while Manuel Quezon looked on from the sidelines. Domingo, it was said, was only "a ready tool in Don Felipe's hand."[54] Whether or not Buencamino and Quezon were involved, there is little doubt that genuine nationalistic sentiment underlay the schism. Presbyterians admitted as much when in the months after the break they made several concessions to Philippine nationalism.

The Methodist and Presbyterian schisms attracted the most attention at the time. But, as the winds of nationalism swept the islands, at least two other denominations (besides the Disciples) suffered serious disruptions, if not actual schism. There is tantalizing, but sketchy, evidence that in 1913 the Christian and Missionary Alliance in Zamboanga suffered a break of some significance. During that year one of its representatives reported such "severe trial and testing" that "there seemed nothing visible left." One of the workers, presumably a Filipino, "turned away and stirred up trouble that threatened to destroy the church here." What lay behind the revolt remains a mystery, since the Alliance destroyed the correspondence of the early years. David L. Rambo, an Alliance official and author of a study of the mission in the Philippines, contends that the revolt was really a struggle among the missionaries over personality and policy.[55] But the reports also suggest Filipino involvement. Nineteen thirteen was a year of tremendous nationalistic fervor, and it is certainly possible that resentment at perceived missionary insensibility to Filipino nationalism was one cause. In any event, the revolt appears to have ended after about eight months, most of the disaffected members reportedly returning to the Church.[56]

More significant for the future of Philippine religion were the difficulties that the Seventh-day Adventists had with Felix Manalo. On two occasions in 1913 Manalo left the Church, taking some followers with him. Within a year he had founded the *Iglesia ni Kristo*, a church that has grown to a position of power and influence in the Philippines and even has branches in the United States.

Manalo, perhaps the Adventists' best evangelist, had an interesting religious pilgrimage. He was born into a relatively poor family in the municipality of Taguig on the northwest shore of Laguna de Bay, the largest lake in the Philippines, located only a few miles from the capital. Manalo had very little formal education, though his mother, a devout Roman Catholic, provided for his religious instruction. As a teenager, Manalo flirted with the Colorum religions of Mount Banahaw. "Mysterious, secret, underground," these religions "offered immediate and reciprocal communication with the Supreme Being."[57]

Apparently not fully convinced by the Mount Banahaw sects, Manalo consorted with the newly arrived Protestants, joining the Methodists in about 1904. After his mother died, he went over to the Presbyterians, perhaps simply because they had better training facilities than did the Methodists. About 1908, after three years as a Presbyterian, he left for unknown reasons (an Adventist source says it was because of "inefficiency") and took up with the Disciples, the group that had the most influence on his theology. Three years later he left the Disciples (the Adventists later claimed because he was found to have beaten his wife), and in 1911 or 1912 L. V. Finster converted Manalo to Seventh-day Adventistism. He was soon employed as an evangelist, though he was not ordained.[58]

Early in 1913 Manalo was suspended for alleged adultery. For a time he resisted the disciplinary action and broke away, taking some church members with him. He was then reinstated but soon eloped with an Adventist girl (after his wife died of consumption), something of which the missionary in charge did not approve. Elopement was common in the islands, however, and Manalo received only a reprimand. But by this point the missionaries seem to have determined that Manalo's usefulness was at an end. The final break came at the Church's training institute in July 1913, where Manalo confessed to a number of sins, including the fact that he had been working steadily against the missionary, Elbridge M. Adams, who had replaced Finster, then on furlough. Even before Finster left, in fact, Manalo had told him that he doubted if he could work with Adams.[59]

According to Adventist sources, Manalo exhibited peculiar and erratic behavior at the meeting, confessing to various sins one day, then acting the following day as if nothing had happened. Even more bizarrely, he invited Adams to heal the breach by shaking hands, and when Adams made the attempt, Manalo withdrew his hand and said "No! No!" His behavior, Adams wrote, "made me think of a man possessed of a Devil." The missionaries then took Manalo to Malolos, where he had been preaching for some time, to have him confess his sins to the congregations there. After some partial and unconvincing confessions, he became defiant. A week later he preached against a fundamental Seventh-day Adventist belief, that the sabbath falls on Saturday. The break was now final, and Manalo left the Church. How many church members, if any, followed him is unclear, though Adams admitted that Manalo "has hindered our work."[60]

Shortly after the break, Manalo associated with atheists and freethinkers. But by the end of the year an idea he had toyed with for some time matured; he would start his own church. On July 27, 1914, Felix Manalo officially incorporated the *Iglesia ni Kristo*.[61]

As was the case with schisms in other mission churches, it is difficult to know precisely what motivated the leader and his followers. Several factors entered in. Personality clashes between Adams and Manalo may have been important; perhaps Manalo was unstable, as the Adventists suggested; perhaps also he did engage in immoral activity and was rightly accused by the missionaries. (In 1939 he was accused again of sexual misconduct.[62]) But, as with most breaks of this kind, nationalism was also a factor, perhaps the most important. According to Adams, Manalo told the Malolos congregation that "he was abused. . . . During that time he told that he wanted no more Americans over him. And that the reason that we did not want him any longer was that he did not know how to treat the Americans nice." As Arthur L. Tuggy puts it, "the answer then was to start a new church, . . . one of which he, not a foreigner, was the leader."[63]

Missionary insensitivity to Filipino nationalism may not have been the only reason for the various schisms and disruptions. But the missionaries' failure to give Filipinos more authority in mission affairs undoubtedly contributed to them. It seems significant that the two major missions that did not suffer schisms in these years—the Baptist and the United Brethren—made more genuine efforts than most to develop an indigenous church with local leadership, even though their theological and even political perspectives were quite different. The United Brethren mission, for example, was more influenced by anti-imperialist thought than any other. The mission's leader was delighted when one of his converts, Camilo Osias, soon to become a leader in Philippine education and public life, agreed to edit the mission's publication "and make the paper distinctly a Filipino factor in our progress."[64] The Baptist mission, on the other hand, was among the most apolitical.

Filipino pressure for change was undoubtedly a factor encouraging more Filipino participation. In May 1913, Howard W. Widdoes acknowledged that the "adolescent church . . . like the adolescent youth sees many defects in the plans, ideals and methods of the spiritual father."[65] But United Brethren missionaries responded positively. By 1914 even Sanford B. Kurtz, who had been something of an exception in the past in casting aspersions on Filipino leadership ability, expressed pride in the quality of Filipino pastors "and coming supervisors." "We are laying every burden that is possible for us to lay on the Filipino Church," Widdoes wrote the same year.[66] And it was only with great reluctance that in 1916 the mission requested another missionary couple due to a temporary depletion in the ranks of the Filipino leadership.[67]

The Baptists, too, were quick to turn responsibilities over to the Filipinos.

"Our one central aim is to raise up self-supporting, self-propagating native churches, composed of baptized and regenerated believers in Jesus Christ," read one of their statements of purpose. The Baptist commitment to Filipino-controlled churches came less from a commitment to nationalism than from a traditional emphasis on local control of churches. There were, furthermore, practical reasons for a Filipino ministry. "The white man . . . knows he is powerless among so many," wrote Charles Maxfield, "unless he is developing a native force of workers."[68] Most other missions would have agreed with Maxfield in principle, but the Baptists seem to have carried out the mandate with more success.

Like other Americans, Baptists did not think Filipinos were equal in ability to Americans. Within this mind-set, however, they thought highly of their own Filipino workers. Even Charles W. Briggs, who had become increasingly disillusioned with Filipinos, was pleased with the work of Filipino pastors in the rural churches. The city congregation, directed by foreign missionaries, was somehow artificial, he thought. "But up in the barrios where they own their land and churches and have their own pastor and support him themselves there is a ring to the very atmosphere that satisfies my soul. These native pastors are all hardworking fellows, too, preaching in all the surrounding towns within a radius of thirty miles—and that is quite a distance to go afoot to preach. Give me the country work and the country people every time," he concluded. "Christ and John the Baptist belong to that class, too."[69]

Thus the United Brethren and the Baptists, different in many ways, seem to have succeeded in Filipinizing their churches more effectively than other missions. Even more important, they apparently managed to convey to their converts a sense that their destiny was in their own hands. That neither mission experienced schismatic movements may have been the result of good fortune, or, more plausibly, the remoteness of each mission from Manila. But their strong commitment to a Filipino church should not be underestimated. As a Baptist statement of principles put it, the missionaries studiously avoided "any appearance of trying to run things for the Filipinos."[70]

Most other missions shared at least some commitment to a Filipino ministry. As F. V. Stipp put it in his study of the Disciples mission, "in all this work of evangelism, the nationals have borne the chief burden and to them should be given the chief glory. . . . The officers of the local churches have always been Filipino from the beginning. . . . Only in rare instances have missionaries served as pastors of churches."[71] But in fact few of the missions found it easy to relinquish real power to the Filipinos. When some modicum of power was transferred, it usually came after considerable pressure from Filipinos. Sometimes such transfers were more apparent than real and were insufficient to prevent divisions. Sometimes concessions to nationalism came only in the wake of schism.

Methodist missionaries, for example, resisted efforts to administer the Philippine Islands Missionary Conference as a "home" conference, a move they realized the Filipinos would interpret as "inimical to the cause of independence, which is dear to the heart of every Filipino."[72] Yet they regularly deprecated attempts to achieve political independence and significant influence within the mission. Such limited concessions as they made could not prevent the Zamora schism.

The Presbyterians were even slower to react. Though they virtually assumed that the Zamora schism would have serious effects on their own work, Presbyterian missionaries took no meaningful steps to meet Philippine nationalism until they suffered their own schism in 1913, at which time they made concessions to nationalist sentiment that appeared to be significant.

The Presbyterian synod in the Philippines was under the control of the General Assembly of the Presbyterian Church in the USA. At the synod meeting in October 1913, however, the missionaries supported efforts by Filipinos to petition the General Assembly to release it from control and establish a fully independent Presbyterian Church in the Philippines. A part of the plan also stated that ministers were to derive their authority from the presbytery, not from the missionaries. The mission board concurred, and the following June the General Assembly voted unanimously to establish an independent church in the Philippines.[73]

The missionaries had made a strategic, self-conscious retreat in the face of determined nationalism within the Church. It was not something they would have chosen to do on their own. As J. Andrew Hall put it, "I should have preferred as I think we all should to have let it go a while yet had it not been for the spirit of independence in the air, and the separation of one church not far from Manila." In fact, to many missionaries the action was little more than a public relations gesture, something to assuage Filipino opinion for the moment. "Do not speak of it as tho the church were really independent or self supporting to any great extent," Rodgers wrote to Brown. ". . . . There will probably be no change at all in the management of affairs."[74]

The establishment of a theoretically independent church may have prevented further schisms, but it was insufficient to win back the dissidents. By 1919 the *Cristianos Filipinos* still existed, though they were thought to be weaker than before. The new church later joined forces with several other independent congregations to form the *Iglesia Evangelica Unida de Cristo*, "a strong organization," according to none other than James B. Rodgers.[75]

Equally significant was the Disciples' experience. Like the Baptists the

Disciples had a very loose organizational structure that emphasized the local church, and like the Baptists they were in theory committed to the establishment of a strong native ministry. Perhaps for these reasons they were less critical of ecclesiastical schisms, even within their own denomination, than were other missionaries (though they never condoned them). When Zamora died in 1914, for example, the *Philippine Christian* found considerable value in his ministry, particularly in "the impetus it has given to individual thinking along religious lines."[76]

Still, the Disciples mission was slow to respond to Filipino demands for more influence in the affairs of the mission. In part this seems to have resulted from a certain disillusionment with their own workers. In 1906, for example, Bruce Kershner, noting the lack of training and moral sense among his Filipino evangelists, confessed that his "original intention of turning our work of evangelization rather largely to our natives is being rapidly shaken. . . . All their work will have to have personal oversight and supervision."[77]

The Disciples missionaries attempted to keep the affairs of the mission distinct from the affairs of the local churches and in theory viewed the latter as autonomous. The Filipinos, however, saw little distinction and at least as early as 1910 demanded representation at the mission conventions. In response to such pressure, the mission organized a separate convention for Filipino pastors, which was, at least in theory, under local control (though a substantial amount of indirect missionary influence was apparent).[78] But reservations about transferring much responsibility to the Filipinos remained. W. N. Lemmon, for example, confessed that it was difficult for him "to trust the native against our own," and six months later Kershner urged great caution in substituting Filipinos for Americans. "Prudence sees many actual and possible dangers in the effort," he concluded. As late as 1913 he admitted that the mission had not yet developed "a working native ministry."[79]

The issue came to a head in 1917, when Filipino evangelists from the provinces of Abra, Cagayan, and Ilocos Sur addressed a letter to the missionary society headquarters in Cincinnati pleading for representation at the Philippine mission's conventions. Filipinos were present at such gatherings of Methodists, Catholics, Presbyterians, and other denominations, they pointed out, but in spite of repeated requests the Disciples had denied them the privilege. "If the missionaries are to discuss plans for the interest of the Filipino people," the evangelists wrote, "why [are] not those who are concerned allowed to have a part in the planning for uplifting the spiritual health of the Filipinos?" At the same time, workers in Ilocos Norte sent a lengthy letter to the society requesting higher salaries.[80]

Bruce Kershner, by then retired from the mission field and living in Mt.

Vernon, Illinois, expressed sympathy with the request for higher salaries but demurred on the question of representation. "The Filipino does not think as the American thinks and he does not have either the background or the preparation to take an equal place in the decision of important questions such as arise in the Mission field," he explained. Kershner preferred to keep the Church and the mission distinct. Each should be fully autonomous, he felt.[81]

The laymen's secretary of the missionary society, however, had already written to the mission urging a change in policy. Though not willing to dictate the specifics, the official noted that the issue of native involvement in mission affairs was "becoming more and more acute in every field where we have work." "We cannot indefinitely in any field withhold from the native Christian any part in decisions that must be made which concern them," he wrote.[82]

The result was a modest change in policy. By January 1918, Filipino representatives were present in the mission convention, though only in an advisory capacity without vote, and the future was not clear. The Ilocanos were much more insistent on getting a share of mission management than were the Tagalogs, Leslie Wolfe reported. "We will have to feel our way."[83]

Philippine nationalism in its ecclesiastical expression had brought about meaningful change. But the attitudes of the missionaries remained ambivalent about Filipino direction of church affairs.

The Protestant Missionary Response to Philippine Nationalism: The Political Dimension

> If we have erred at all, it has been in placing in the hands
> of the Filipino governmental duties and responsibilities far
> beyond his capacity to exercise them.
>
> *Philippine Christian Advocate*

Just as Filipino Protestants pressured the missionaries for a larger role in church and mission affairs, so too the people as a whole pushed for a larger role in governmental affairs, with independence their ultimate goal. Indeed, insistence on control of their political institutions clearly influenced Filipino demands for a larger role in ecclesiastical affairs and vice versa.

Although a few missionaries either supported Filipino desires for a larger voice in political affairs or were simply uninterested in political matters, a sizable majority, it appears, were uneasy about the prospect of Filipino political control. A number of influential missionaries were more than disquieted: they were strongly opposed and tried to prevent it.

Even as the Philippine-American War went on, Americans debated the future of the islands. No one in the administration suggested independence in the near future, but the civil governor, William Howard Taft, determined to try to prepare the people for some form of self-government. Whether full independence would result was left open.[1] An important ingredient in Taft's plan was an elected assembly, which would become the lower house of the Philippine legislature. The debate over the assembly proposal was long and bitter and divided the imperialist community. Such important imperialists as Henry Cabot Lodge, Albert Beveridge, John C. Spooner, and William B. Allison strongly opposed it. But Taft battled fiercely for its establishment, and he finally succeeded in securing a provision for an assembly in the Philippine Government Act of 1902, popularly known as the Organic Act. The act provided that two years after the publication of a census an election would be called for an assembly, provided the country was peaceful.[2]

Had the missionaries been consulted, they probably would have advised against the early establishment of a popular assembly, despite their general admiration for Taft. Methodist Homer C. Stuntz, in fact, wrote to Henry Cabot Lodge supporting the senator's antiassembly posture, and Lodge in turn passed Stuntz's letter on to President Theodore Roosevelt.[3] In 1904 Episcopal bishop Charles Henry Brent confessed that he, too, was apprehensive about the anticipated assembly. The idea of a popular assembly seems, in fact, to have greatly distressed the bishop, for during the next three years, until the assembly was elected in 1907, Brent made increasingly derogatory statements about Filipino capacity for self-rule. He thought Taft's hope to control the assembly from within was fatuous, and three months before the elections (held on July 30, 1907) he predicted disaster within a year after the assembly convened.[4]

Brent left the Philippines for a visit to the United States just prior to the elections, but before leaving he preached what President Roosevelt termed "a very foolish sermon" that lambasted the government for allowing the elections. In a letter to Silas McBee, best remembered for its description of the Philippines as "our heel of Achilles," the president presented a lengthy and, at points, perceptive analysis of the sermon in which he questioned the bishop's veracity, suggested that his knowledge of history was sadly deficient, and complained that his analogies were inept and his arguments absurd, and that he had unwittingly given aid and comfort to the anti-imperialists.[5]

Brent's anger was not quickly cooled. Apparently spurred on by an inflammatory letter from Leonard Wood about the nature of the election, the quality of the delegates selected, and the likelihood of renewed insurrection, Brent lashed out at Filipino demands and American capitulation, as he viewed it, to these pressures. In an address to his fellow bishops only two weeks before the new assembly convened in October, Brent asserted that Filipinos were "at least 100 years behind the Cubans, and . . . they will never be able to govern themselves if the government continues its present policy."[6]

Sensational as Brent's remarks were, the most celebrated antiassembly and antinationalistic feeling existed within the Presbyterian mission in the person of Stealy B. Rossiter, pastor of the English-speaking Church in Manila. For some time Rossiter had felt that the American government was making entirely too many concessions to Philippine nationalism. In 1905 he was temporarily reassured when Secretary of War Taft took a hard line on the question of independence. "The Filipinos will have to have this hammered out of them," Taft wrote to the Presbyterian leader, James B. Rodgers. "The people here are getting used to the idea that it will take a generation or two before we can think of granting more power than they now have." And when the secretary of war visited the islands a few months later, he indicated that the Americans would stay as long as was necessary to prepare the people for self-government. "He spoke so plainly that he disappointed & hurt the Filipinos present," Rossiter wrote.[7] But the Presbyterian was encouraged.

Rossiter's euphoria was short-lived, however. Taft's tough words did not dampen Philippine nationalism. In fact, that same year the conservative *Federalista* party, which had close ties to the Presbyterian leaders, dropped its advocacy of statehood in favor of eventual independence. Other political groups urged immediate independence. In April 1907 the two most important proindependence factions merged to form the *Partido Nacionalista*, which officially demanded immediate independence.[8] Anti-American feeling seemed to be growing apace. Then, on top of these developments, President Roosevelt ordered elections for the assembly, declaring that the conditions established in the Philippine Government Act had been met. Against the judgment of important segments of the missionary community, the elections were held, and the assembly convened in October.

The decision to hold the elections greatly exercised those who, like Rossiter, took what Rodgers termed "the ultra American" or "military point of view." Adding to their disquiet was Secretary Taft who was now speaking of "the Philippines for the Filipinos." The former governor did not, thereby, mean that the Philippines should be given independence. As before, he preferred not to define the future relationship with the United States; he probably hoped that in the long run the Filipinos would opt to stay with the United States. All he meant to convey was that the Americans were pledged to develop the islands in the interests of the islanders, not the Americans. He expressed well the altruistic side of "the white man's burden."

Nevertheless, it was easy to misconstrue Taft's desires, and some "ultra Americans" even disagreed with Taft's actual intentions, feeling that the Americans should benefit first from the colony. All in all, Rossiter and people like him had lost confidence in Taft's leadership, especially since unfounded, even absurd, rumors were about that Taft intended to sell the islands. The result was a meeting of Americans in the islands in October 1907 to consider forming a league to lobby for American interests.[9]

Those present at the meeting elected Rossiter to chair a committee to draw up a constitution and bylaws. The minister used the occasion to deprecate Washington's policy of the Philippines for the Filipinos as a "false cry." In the end the group decided to hear Taft out (he was coming to the

Philippines to open the new assembly) before creating a league of Americans, and the secretary was invited to address the Quill Club of which Rossiter was president. After several postponements, Taft met with the Quill Club on October 31. Rossiter took advantage of his position to deliver an opening address critical of American policy. Among other things, Rossiter said that the islands could not be sold; and he was ready, it appeared, "to duck in the Pasig [River]" a noisy anti-imperialist then speaking in the islands. But the heart of the address was Rossiter's contention that Americans in the islands should have "a free rein" and that "the prosperity of the Americans must come first and that of the Filipinos would follow."[10]

According to the *Manila Times*, Taft's address, in turn, was dispassionate, until he met the issues raised by Rossiter. "It was when he took up for argument the statement of Dr. Rossiter that the prosperity of the Filipinos would follow that of the Americans," the *Times* went on, "that the vibration of his great frame and the quivering timbre of his voice gave warning of the 'heart to heart talk' which followed." There were eight million Filipinos, Taft said, and American prosperity rested ultimately with their prosperity and not vice versa. "The real development of the islands both politically and financially must rest finally and ultimately with the Filipino people," he insisted.[11]

The Rossiter-Taft confrontation was a genuine cause célèbre. The supporters of the respective sides engaged in "attack and counter-attack [that] went on for months," a Presbyterian missionary recalled nearly two years later.[12] In the three weeks following the Quill Club incident, the *Manila Times* ran no less than four editorials on the matter, reprinted Taft's address (which the secretary had personally proofread), and printed in full a patriotic sermon preached by Rossiter at the dedication of the new Presbyterian church in Manila, in which the fiery pastor reiterated his positions. God put the Americans in the islands, he insisted, and in doing so He benefited not "America alone, but . . . Spain and the Philippines, and China, and Japan, and India, and the rest of the world." In particular, he thought, Americans brought "initiative" to the islands, something the Filipinos allegedly lacked. The *Times*, siding with Taft throughout, thought Rossiter's comments at the Quill Club had trampled "the mild and benevolent reign of the Man of Galilee under foot"; and the sermon, the paper contended, was virtually blasphemous.[13]

Rossiter's identification with the anti-Filipino partisans "greatly troubled" Rodgers, who was notably lukewarm in recommending that Rossiter be reappointed to the Manila church. "It took a great deal of care on my part to keep the matter from being fanned into a flame," he complained. Rodgers's concerns were legitimate, for it was this kind of insensitivity (during the controversy Rossiter wrote that the islands would be under American rule for hundreds of years) that created bitterness and was, at least in part, responsible for the schisms.[14]

In some ways Rossiter was not fully representative of the missionary community, as Rodgers's remarks suggested. His rhetoric was extreme; his belief that Americans should benefit first from the colonial relationship was unusual in the missionary community; his methods were impolitic. But the major objection to Rossiter concerned his tactics rather than his position. In the two or three years before the assembly opened, many other missionaries were nearly as worried as he was about manifestations of Philippine nationalism. In 1904, for example, an American Board missionary hoped that Theodore Roosevelt's election would cause Filipinos to accept their fate and be reconciled to the new order. In 1906 the Disciples leader complained of anti-American demagogues; and as the elections approached, he observed that political activities were interfering with evangelistic work.[15]

Missionaries from Rossiter's own denomination were among the most concerned. In 1905, for example, Rodgers wrote in worried tones to Secretary Taft about the increasing talk of independene. In the minds of the younger generation, he reported with evident concern, the only debate was "whether independence will come now or in five years." Silliman Institute's president, David S. Hibbard, brooded over the deterioration of relations between Filipinos and Americans, a situation he ascribed in good part to the idea of independence that seemed to have captured the public imagination.[16]

More outspoken was Charles E. Rath, then stationed in Leyte, who was "strongly convinced that our government has made a big mistake in the Philippines by being too lenient." He thought the Filipinos were prone to take advantage of American concessions, did not respect authority, and even refused to learn English. The thought of such persons in positions of political influence appalled him. "If they get their Assembly," he warned, "then they can pass a law after their own heart." It was not a prospect he wished to contemplate. Charles N. Magill put the matter somewhat more moderately a few days before the elections. The people's cry for independence was an honest expression of opinion, he admitted, "but we believe they now enjoy many more privileges and much more liberty and protection and safety than if they had their own independence."[17]

In sum, though Stealy B. Rossiter expressed the "ultra American" point of view, most missionaries seem to have agreed with him that Philippine nationalism was to be regretted and that the assembly was premature. In fact, only Baptist leader Charles W. Briggs found much comfort in the coming elections. He rather liked the thought that in Baptist areas the Protestant electorate held the balance of power, causing politicians to court the Protestant vote. "That is something to have seen grow up in seven years," he wrote with a touch of amusement and pride. Yet given Briggs's increasingly critical assessment of Filipino character he could hardly have been a strong champion of Philippine nationalism.[18]

In the months and years following the inauguration of the assembly in October 1907, there is little to indicate that missionary sentiment about political independence changed. A month after the assembly began its work, Bishop Brent admitted he was "filled with fears" regarding its existence; and its subsequent deliberations did not convince him to modify his views. On the contrary, he wrote the following May, "government affairs fully justify all my criticisms. . . . The Assembly looks well at a distance and seems to be an advance in our democratic scheme for the people, but it is not what it pretends to be."[19] Similarly, the Methodist publication in the islands contended in 1908 that if the Americans "erred at all, it has been in placing in the hands of the Filipino governmental duties and responsibilities far beyond his capacity to exercise them." Filipinos were ungrateful, the publication's editor thought, and failed "to discern the unparalleled benefit acruing from the American Occupation." The editorial concluded with a plea to persevere in "the white man's burden."[20]

During these years many missionaries reported a sharp deterioration in race relations, with Filipinos keeping their distance from Americans. As a result the missions suffered. A Disciples missionary reported in 1908 that the movement for independence had hurt the mission. "There seems to be a feeling that the Americano is only the fifth wheel to the wagon anyhow," he observed. When an American Board missionary traveled to Cagayan de Oro in 1911, he found the people "very much anti-American," though also "intelligent and courteous."[21] By 1912 J. Andrew Hall, the Presbyterian physician in Iloilo, felt that anti-American opinion was growing. Filipinos increasingly patronized Filipino physicians instead of coming to the mission hospital, and in general the ties between the missionaries and the people seemed to be much weakened. Nationalism even took its toll on the United Brethren mission. Growth slowed, and predictions were that it might well come to a standstill.[22]

Instead of making concessions to the public mood, missionaries more typically resisted it and often belittled Filipino capacity for self-rule, to say nothing of independence. Paul Doltz, for example, thought it was idle to talk of independence until the masses were fully prepared to defend their rights, a process, he observed, that had taken Europeans some fifteen hundred years. Fellow Presbyterian Charles Magill shared Doltz's opinion and added that, by the time Filipinos were ready for independence, they would "not want it," since by then they would "realize what an honor it is to be a part of the greatest nation in the world."[23]

As the American elections of 1912 approached, some missionaries actively tried to influence opinion away from independence. Early in 1912, for example, Bishop Brent turned down the provostship at Trinity University in Canada, partly so that he could remain in the Philippines to fight attempts to grant the Philippines independence. In August he told an audience in Zamboanga that American tutelage was still required, though at "some distant date" the Filipinos might be expected to handle their own affairs constructively—and even then he did not mention independence explicitly.[24]

Then, shortly before the election, James B. Rodgers delivered an address of some significance at the Lake Mohonk Conference in New York, in which he discussed "Some Remnants of Pagan Belief among the Christianized Filipinos." Though Rodgers insisted he spoke not to demean Filipinos, his description of customs that must have struck Americans as degraded if not barbaric almost certainly had that effect and lent comfort to those opposed to independence. His final words, in fact, strongly implied that he opposed the granting of independence: "the question is not whether the Filipinos are ready for independence—any nation can be independent—but whether by being independent they can have a greater measure of that liberty that makes for the happiness of all mankind than if they remain longer under American guidance." The irrepressible Stealy B. Rossiter was even more blunt. To great applause, Rossiter attacked Congressman William A. Jones's bill providing for Philippine independence as disastrous and shameful. Independence was impossible, he insisted, because Filipinos lacked initiative, a quality he alleged was "constitutional" with Filipinos and other Malays and thus inalterable by education. "I think within ten years' time, if this bill . . . were passed," he went on, "grass would be growing in the streets of Manila and hogs would be in the front yards."[25]

Such activities could not prevent the victory of the Democrats, whose party was officially anti-imperialist. The election of Woodrow Wilson was not, therefore, a cheerful moment for most missionaries. Despite Wilson's deep religious convictions, the missionaries were "greatly disturbed" by his victory, according to a prominent Methodist. Given alleged Filipino unreadiness for independence, he wrote, it was the "unanimous opinion among the missionaries" that any "radical change . . . now or in the near future" would be a mistake. Consequently he urged Bishop William F. Oldham, who had recently returned to the United States to serve on the mission board, to express the missionaries' fears directly to President-elect Wilson.[26]

Oldham, however, had always been more sensitive to Filipino aspirations than many missionaries. In the past he had sometimes criticized his colleagues for not being close enough to their Filipino brethren and had urged a wider role for Filipinos within the Church. "We must give them more rope, even at the risk of seeing them hang themselves," he wrote to the new bishop, William P. Eveland. "There must be more Filipino and less American in the administration of the Church, as there surely will be in the administration of the State." A year later he urged the missionaries to "learn the high virtue of St. John the Baptist, the willingness to decrease while the Filipino increases."[27] He did not write to the new president.

Yet ironically Oldham, along with some former Methodist missionaries, joined Presbyterians Rodgers and Arthur J. Brown, the latter of the Presbyterian Board of Missions, and Bishop Brent in taking action to thwart an early grant of independence under the Democratic administration. The most sensational action was the affiliation of Oldham, Rodgers, Brown, and Brent with the Philippine Society, an ostensibly nonpolitical organization founded in 1913 "to diffuse among the American people a more accurate knowledge of the Philippine Islands" and to promote social and cultural ties between the two countries. In actuality, however, the organization was, as Manuel Quezon understated it in his public letter of resignation, not "impartial on the subject of Philippine independence." On the contrary, it was strongly retentionist, as a quick glance at its officers might suggest. William Howard Taft was honorary president, former governor general Luke F. Wright was president, and the honorary vice-president was William Cameron Forbes, the current governor general. Yet Oldham, Rodgers, and Brown agreed to serve on the society's executive committee. Brown in particular took an active role in the organization's affairs, writing at one point to the members of the Presbyterian board of missions and the board's executive council urging them to join the society, which he thought "will probably have a large influence in public opinion"— this only six weeks after he had written to the new secretary of war advising him that the missionaries would not align themselves against independence![28]

Bishop Brent seems to have taken a less active part in the Philippine Society. He considered the society's initial banquet "ghastly" and sympathized with Quezon's assertion that the society had used him unfairly.[29] As criticism mounted, Rodgers apparently resigned from the executive committee. But Oldham, the least "imperialist" in his thinking of them all, unaccountably remained on the committee. Oldham also publicly spoke out on two occasions that year. In the spring of 1913 he told students at Syracuse University that, although the Filipinos had progressed admirably, their society was not sufficiently democratic to consider immediate independence. He contended that too few Filipinos understood "even the elements of popular liberty" to permit the Americans to leave the islands for at least "two or three more decades."[30] More important because of the publicity it evoked was Oldham's address at the Lake Mohonk conference in October. There was much in this speech that Filipino nationalists could applaud. The bishop rejected notions of racial inferiority, applauded President Wilson's efforts to bring more Filipinos into decision-making positions, and, in clear contrast to Bishop Brent and the Republican establishment, urged that a definite date be established for a final Filipino determination about independence. But he continued to argue against immediate independence.[31]

Of the missionaries who actively attempted to prevent any meaningful change under the Democrats, Charles Henry Brent was the most persistent and influential, in spite of his relative disregard for the Philippine Society. Brent hoped that President-elect Wilson would be conservative and not alter the course of Philippine affairs in a drastic way. But he was not content merely to hope. Believing that to bring to fruition the desires of anti-imperialists would be "disastrous in its consequences," he took an active part in the independence debate, as he put it, "to save it from the political flummery of men like [William A.] Jones and from the rash optimism of [Manuel] Quezon and the group of Mestizos whom he represents."[32]

Brent's first significant action while still in the Philippines was to write a lengthy story for the New York *Tribune* published on April 21, 1913. In this front-page article, which featured a two-column photograph of the bishop, Brent decried efforts to reduce America's paternalism. Though professing not to oppose ultimate independence (he felt the use of the terms *imperialist* and *anti-imperialist* only fogged the issue, since the only question was one of timing), Brent urged "slow speed" on the government. The clamor for independence was not sufficient reason to grant it, he insisted. What had to be determined was Filipino capacity to govern; that, he wrote, would "not be revealed until the school-boys of to-day are in active public life." The United States did not have the luxury of withdrawing and leaving the islands "to go to perdition in their own way. . . . We are in the Philippines because we are required there," he concluded.[33]

After conferring at length with Governor General Forbes,[34] Brent embarked for the United States, where he hoped to confer with officials of the Bureau of Insular Affairs, the secretary of war, and even the president. In June he secured appointments with President Wilson and Secretary of War

Lindley M. Garrison. In his discussions he seems to have moderated his previous opposition to Filipinization to the extent of advocating an elective senate. Garrison pointed out that this would require congressional legislation. Appointment of a Filipino majority to the Executive Council (the Philippine Commission), which served as the upper house, would accomplish the same objective without requiring legislation he pointed out (something he had previously suggested to the president).[35] Brent quickly agreed that new legislation was inexpedient, probably because it would inevitably bring the independence question to a head. Indeed, he soon came to see the advantages of Garrison's approach, since an executive order could easily be rescinded if the experiment proved unwise.[36] He conferred with Quezon, came away with the impression that the Filipino leader would agree to such a step, and then once again discussed the question with Garrison.[37]

The interviews reassured Brent for the moment. "The President and Secretary of War seemed to me very reasonable in all they said to me," he wrote to the archbishop of Canterbury. "I feel further satisfied now that there will be no headlong action." Quezon would urge a conservative course on his people, he added. The next week he commented that he thought the president and the secretary of war "wish to play the game fair." He thought his interviews "were of great value."[38]

Brent correctly considered his efforts with the administration successful (Garrison, at least, was impressed with Brent's presentation); but the bishop's doubts deepened when he learned of certain prospective appointments to the islands. (He would have been even more disturbed, indeed outraged, had he known that Quezon had already received firm assurances that both Forbes, the governor general, and Dean C. Worcester, the secretary of the interior, would be replaced.[39]) While Brent still hoped that the new administration would pursue a moderate policy, he feared Wilson would make "purely political" appointments in the islands. Like other colonials who had grown up with the Republican administrations, Brent held to the fiction that the Republican appointees, even the governor general, were nonpartisan civil servants and that the goals they pursued were nonpolitical. Brent's concern about the rumored appointments, therefore, was based on two considerations. His surface fear was that inexperienced men would now be in positions of leadership. But his deeper fear was that the new administration would pursue policies more sympathetic to Philippine nationalism, perhaps even supporting complete independence.[40]

In this context Brent wrote to James Bryce, the influential British observer of America and ambassador to the United States, urging him to visit the Philippines and make a study of conditions there with a view to informally influencing legislation concerning the islands' future. Though professing a desire that Bryce should not go to the islands with any preconceived ideas, Brent expressed confidence that the Englishman's conclusions "would be those at which I myself have arrived," and he specifically accused Wilson of making "purely political" appointments in the islands. Brent's confidence in the administration's intention was doubtlessly not increased when he received a cable from Forbes asking him to block the appointment of W. Morgan Shuster (who had been Forbes's bête noir in past years) to the commission.[41]

Brent may have had a role in derailing Shuster's ambitions, but Wilson's ultimate choice for governor general, Francis Burton Harrison, would not have had the bishop's endorsement. Though Brent might have agreed with Harrison's strong views on the dangers of trusts and on other domestic issues, the congressman's lack of experience in colonial administration and his strongly anti-imperialist views could only have confirmed Brent's suspicion that Wilson's appointments were based on political considerations. Brent must have thrown up his hands in despair when Harrison stepped off the boat in Manila and delivered President Wilson's emotional message to the Filipinos that declared, "every step we take will be taken with a view to the ultimate independence of the Islands and as a preparation for that independence."[42]

The deed had been done, however, and only a few days later in an address at the annual Lake Mohonk conference, Brent found it expedient to say that he believed "heartily in the coming Filipino independence." But having shifted his ground once again to keep up with developments, he took back most of what he had conceded by insisting that independence could not "be now or in the very near future." When Christian influence permeated to much deeper levels of society and produced a strong Christian character among the people, then and only then could independence be considered. "When those who are now school boys are old enough and experienced enough to take the lead in the public life of the people, it will be time enough to discuss independence," he said, and concluded, "Impatience is to be expected, but we must meet it with muffled patience."[43]

The anti-independence statements and activities of missionary spokesmen like Rodgers, Oldham, Brown and Brent, coming at a time of general joy among Filipinos at the election results, caused profound reverberations for their brethren in the Philippines. In January 1914 a Disciples missionary reported that Brent was "pretty cordially disliked" by Filipino nationalists. About the same time a YMCA official observed that "several of the Protestant missions have been embarrassed and their work interfered with, by popular resentment at actual or supposed anti-independence activities of

missionaries or board officers in America." Several months later the same
official elaborated at some length:

> The least appearance of activity or partisanship in the political discussion
> on the part of people connected with the missions and other returned Ameri-
> cans who have important relations with things here is cabled or otherwise
> sent out here from America and immediately published broadcast in all the
> Filipino papers. For example, good Dr. Rodgers, the senior missionary of the
> Presbyterian Church, who is as discreet and non-controversial a man as you
> could find, was present at the Lake Mohonk Conference on the Indians and
> Other Dependent Peoples and gave a perfectly inoffensive talk on an odd
> remanent of a pagan sect which exists in the Cavite hills in his territory. The
> cabled comment included him, however, with the most pronounced anti-
> Filipino retentionist speakers without discrimination; and the missionaries
> have been trying ever since to convince their Filipino churches and the public
> that he made no speech on a subject which involves the aspiration for nation-
> ality and independence, which is to them sacred. As a result a schism has oc-
> curred, in which some of the strongest churches which they had were in-
> volved. The Methodists similarly have been greatly hampered and their work
> cut down by the unguarded utterances of Dr. Stuntz, the prominent part
> taken by Bishop Oldham in the Philippine Society which is looked upon here
> as an "Imperialist" affair, and others.[44]

The official's observations were perceptive. So concerned were Methodist missionaries that at their annual conference in 1914 they passed a resolution asking American churchmen to refrain from commenting on the independence question, and Bishop Eveland tactfully counseled Oldham to
be careful in his public statements.[45] Presbyterian missionaries felt the
same way, one of them warning Brown that his and Rodgers's identification with the Philippine Society gave the unfortunate impression that they
were imperialists out to destroy the dream of the Filipinos.[46] And virtually
all Presbyterian mission stations reported deep misgivings about the public statements and actions of prominent Presbyterians.

One Presbyterian missionary theorized that Manuel Quezon and Felipe
Buencamino were deliberately making an issue of Presbyterian statements.
Quezon's reasons were blatantly political, it was thought, while Buencamino was acting out of spite because the Presbyterians had failed to secure a decent appointment for him.[47] In any event, the situation became so
serious that the mission issued a lengthy statement in Tagalog, English,
and Spanish that countered allegations that the Church and its mission
board had been "active in working against Philippine Independence and
using their position and influence to prove the unfitness of Filipino people
to govern themselves."

Although the statement contended that missionaries were strongly advised not to take part in political matters, it did not specifically refute the charges. Rodgers's remarks at the Lake Mohonk conference had been misunderstood and contained no references "to political conditions." He was not "working against the political aspirations of the Filipino people or in any way . . . a party to political discussion." As for the Philippine Society, Brown and Rodgers had not "knowingly" joined to oppose independence; if they discerned that the society had political objectives, they would withdraw, as Quezon had done. As for another accusation, that Stealy B. Rossiter had spoken openly against independence, there was little the mission could say, except that Rossiter spoke only for himself.[48]

The Presbyterian statement may or may not have had the desired effect on Filipino opinion, but as an historical document it is not a convincing defense of the Presbyterian position (except that it was doubtless correct in pointing out that the mission and the board had taken no official position on the matter of independence). It is clear that most missionaries opposed independence, something not at all evident from the statement. On precisely the same day that Brown wrote to Secretary of War Garrison stating that the missionaries would not oppose independence, another missionary wrote to Brown that it would "not be a good day for our work if the islands are granted independence—it would be a blow to us." Another missionary hoped in vain that the desire for independence was passing. Yet another feared that Governor General Harrison was going to go too fast in the direction of independence. "Let us hope the work of the past fifteen years is not to be undone in the next five," he wrote. Another confessed that even as the sentiment for independence grew, "I sometimes feel as though the capacity was growing less."[49] In fact, not a single Presbyterian missionary supported independence, though some were edging toward the view that they could continue their work even if that unhappy event came to pass.

Most Methodists also feared the possibility of independence. Like other Americans, they believed that the character of the populace was immature and that, on the whole, the American government had done a good job of carrying out the white man's burden. They were naturally fearful of seeing this experiment in nation-building collapse out of a theoretical concern for democratic participation. Some missionaries feared independence because they were concerned about possible hostile Japanese designs on the islands. "It is exceedingly hazardous to play with fire on a windy day," wrote one, cautioning advocates of independence.[50]

Yet the Methodist mission was more willing than the Presbyterian to make some accommodation with national feeling. By the time word of Oldham's activities reached the islands, independence was in the air. The new Democratic governor general was moving quickly to bring more Filipinos into the government, and the missionaries were subjected to intense pressure to back the popular will. The independence issue "absorbed the minds of the people to the exclusion of all things else," Marvin Rader reported in January 1914. Unprepared to advocate independence, yet needing the support of their Filipino workers and the people, the missionaries preferred to lapse into silence, arguing that evangelism was more important than politics. "Our people are considerably distressed over some of your utterances," one prominent missionary advised Oldham. "They do not say you are wrong," he added significantly, "but that every utterance of this kind is as powder in the hands of the enemy to afflict the preachers who remain true to us."[51] Thus ironically Oldham, the foremost Methodist advocate of Filipino self-determination, found that the same missionaries who had resisted his efforts to increase Filipino participation were now upset because he counseled patience. Advocates of immediate independence, they felt, would use Oldham's words to discredit the missionary enterprise. More precisely, they wanted Oldham to say nothing at all. It was a delicate and embarrassing balance.

The years 1915 and 1916 saw a relaxation of tension and a partial change of heart among the Methodist missionaries. In 1916, for example, Rader, in a remarkable volte-face, termed the Jones Bill, which promised the Filipinos eventual independence, "splendid legislation." Many missionaries were comforted with the belief, at best partially correct, that Filipinization and the movement toward independence derived naturally from the objectives of the previous Republican administrations. Their fears were assuaged, too, because the material and educational accomplishments of previous years continued, in spite of the Democrats. Furthermore, the quality of the new officials, both Filipinos and Americans, eventually impressed them. Even Governor General Harrison, initially disliked, won them over. Though subjected to occasional criticism as late as 1915, Harrison eventually found himself commended for his efforts to better interracial feeling. "Do not be misled by the exaggerated statements of prejudiced politicians," the *Philippine Observer* warned in 1916.[52] Doubtless Harrison's decision a few months later to express personally to the Methodist missionaries his deep distress over the tragic, accidental death of Bishop Eveland helped confirm their new view.[53]

To the Methodists, furthermore, a growing acceptance of Filipinization and even independence did not mean that American influence would decrease. "Even though the Filipinos win their coveted independence," Bishop Eveland wrote in 1915, "they will still remain the wards of Uncle Sam. It was his strong hand that . . . lifted these people out of the tyranny, superstition, and ignorance of medieval times." The physical presence of Americans might decrease, but their ideas would survive. By 1916 the missionaries were cautiously optimistic that the Filipinos had absorbed enough of Anglo-American culture to succeed. Indeed, by late 1916 Marvin Rader was convinced that Filipinization had succeeded in demonstrating the capabilities of the people, judged by the extent to which they imitated Americans. "I believe that they will make good," Rader observed, "and that the Filipinos will rapidly adopt our type of civilization."[54]

Bishop Brent, too, shifted his position, marginally, so that he managed to get along tolerably well with the new governor general. He had already advocated giving the Filipinos more power through a Filipino-dominated upper house and had for a time even advocated an elected senate. At Lake Mohonk he professed to favor eventual independence. Finally he even came to support moderate Filipinization of the government. Bringing more Filipinos into the government was, he wrote Harrison, "both logical and inevitable" and, he contended, was in line with Taft's policy as evident in his establishment of the assembly in 1907. (Brent did not point out that he had opposed establishment of the assembly.) "My fear about Filipinization," he added, "is in its rapidity, and the danger for Filipinos' sake. While recognizing that men learn by doing, and this, I suppose is peculiarly true in public affairs, there is need of long technical training to prepare them to handle the higher positions in as specialized a form of government as ours is. . . . I am of the opinion that our chief danger lies in the direction of undue speed."[55] Brent's shift of positions was, therefore, more apparent than real. By pointing out the dangers of rapid Filipinization, he was, in effect, urging a return to the politics of the Republicans.

Other Episcopalians were even more strongly opposed to Filipinization than was Brent. Remsen B. Ogilby, for example, opposed the appointment of even one Filipino to the five-member city council of Baguio, contending (according to Harrison) that Filipinos "had not in the premises sufficient interest to make such an appointment advisable"—this in spite of the fact, as Harrison pointed out, that Filipinos owned more than one-third of the real estate in Baguio and paid most of the taxes. Consequently, Harrison did not accede to Brent's suggestion that Ogilby replace the bishop on the council.[56]

The bishop managed to keep on relatively cordial terms with the new governor general, though, Harrison at one time writing to him, "sometime, if we can arrange it and you feel I will not be a burden upon you, I should like to go off with you on one of those lonesome cruises you are taking. I can think of nothing more satisfying than to sail in the southern seas from place to place, without a schedule to adhere to, and limited in our stay at any one point only by lack of people to be given aid and assistance." But his relationship with the Democratic governor was never as intimate as it was with Taft or Forbes. And the election campaign of 1916 saw Brent back in the United States urging the election of the Republican candidate, Charles Evans Hughes. In October 1916 he declined Forbes's request to write something on behalf of Hughes, but only because it would "do as much damage as good," given the bias against clergymen taking a role in partisan politics. Still, he regularly delivered addresses to groups of businessmen, telling "them frankly what my position was and gave my reasons for desiring a change of administration." His reasons, in good part, concerned the Philippines. When the electorate returned Wilson, Brent was depressed. He particularly regretted the probable effects in the islands, though he hoped that the Jones Bill, which he had long thought had possibilities, would prevent political unrest for the next four years. Though unhappy, Brent determined to return to the islands after an absence of some sixteen months "to play my own part and do well the work for which I am responsible." [57]

About a year later, however, Brent left the islands permanently to serve with the YMCA on the European front. He might have left in any event. "It did not need a moment's consideration to reach a decision," he recalled, "and I cabled my readiness to go." [58] At the same time, he had long insisted he would leave if independence threatened. Wilson had promised independence, the Jones Bill committed the government to independence (though without specifying a date); and Harrison was carrying out Filipinization much too quickly to suit the bishop, having in fact virtually abdicated his authority to the Filipinos. Discouraged over Hughes's defeat, discontented with Democratic policies and practices, the time had come to go.

If some missionary spokesmen openly opposed Philippine nationalism during and after the election campaign of 1912, and if many others made only a reluctant accommodation to Filipino attitudes, several others concluded within a year or two of Wilson's inauguration that increased Filipino participation in the government, and even independence, were not to be feared. By September 1914 the Disciples leader Bruce L. Kershner was prepared to see the United States pull out, even if it meant a Japanese takeover. "Personally, I confess that manifest destiny seems to me to assign this little bunch of islands to the realm of the mikado," he wrote in direct contrast to Methodist Marvin Rader, who thought the Japanese threat demanded an American presence. "I don't see why Uncle Sam should stay over here." The mission was religious, not political, Kershner concluded, and could be carried out under any regime. By the end of the year, he felt that "the present political condition is working well for us. Our plea appeals to the instinct of freedom and independence." [59]

Equally favorable statements about Philippine nationalism and political independence emerged from the United Brethren and the American Board missions. At about the same time that Bishop Brent was doing what he could to move Wilson's policy in a more conservative direction, the secretary of the United Brethren mission board visited the Philippines. Upon his return he passed along to President Wilson a comment from Howard W. Widdoes, the mission's leader, commending the administration's Philippine policy. "I have had other similar expressions from other missionaries," he added, "and I believe it is part of my Christian duty to pass on this note of encouragement and the assurance of our prayers to you in your great work."[60]

The American Board was divided. C. T. Sibley deplored Philippine nationalism, but other missionaries disagreed. Sibley reported, for example, that Robert Black "thinks it may even be advantageous to our mission should the Flag be withdrawn." Frank C. Laubach, who arrived in 1915 and who may be said to epitomize the thought of the second generation of missionaries, had little objection to independence. "To my mind the ability of a certain portion of the Filipinos to rule their country is quite as great as that of Americans, and their understanding of the problems and of the Malay mind is much greater than that of any American," he wrote, though he was still not fully sure that there were enough educated Filipinos "to make control of the ignorant classes certain." The desire for freedom was "sound at the center," he insisted, "and it is essentially the same passion as that which we eulogize so highly in the forefathers of our own country." By the end of 1917, virtually all doubts had been erased. Commenting on the policy of rapid Filipinization, Laubach observed that "the way in which the positions have been filled proves that the Filipinos are equal to the tasks of government." Though the departments were not run quite as efficiently as before, "the difference is not nearly so great as the calamity howlers had expected."[61]

In sum, many missionaries' attitudes about Philippine nationalism had changed significantly by 1916. To be sure, not all had. The Presbyterians in particular continued to fear independence.[62] But others actually looked forward to the approach of independence with gratification. A larger number was at least willing to avoid opposing independence, while at the same time making significant concessions to nationalistic sentiments within their own churches. Even Bishop Brent, who had repeatedly vowed he would leave the islands the moment independence was declared, moderated his views under the pressure of events. The changes in missionary thought were, then, real. But paternalism and ambivalence still characterized the missionary community.

PART III

Protestant Missionaries and American Colonialism

8

Protestant Missionaries and American Governance of the Philippines

We treated Manila as we had treated Havana—
found it a pesthole, and made it a health resort.
                    Methodist Bishop Henry W. Warren

The ministers are after me on the cockfighting in the
Carnival. Lord keep and save me from ministers!
                    W. Cameron Forbes

Missionary expansion to the Philippines was part of a religious crusade that sent missionaries all over the world. Therefore, those who went to the Philippines were not ipso facto agents of the national purpose. For many applicants, the Philippines was only one of several locations they were willing to be sent to. On the other hand, many missionaries in the Philippines shared the belief, accepted by most Protestants since at least the Civil War, that the survival and expansion of the United States was part of the divine plan. "God cannot afford to do without America," a Methodist Episcopal bishop told a large crowd in 1864.[1] Increasingly, Protestants believed that American-style democracy required an evangelical base. "The August Ruler of all the nations," said the president of Wesleyan University in 1876, "designed the United States of America as the grand repository and evangelist of civil liberty and of pure religious faith. And," he added, "the two are one."[2] Such sentiments were commonplace. As a group of Methodists advised President William McKinley a quarter of a century later, "civil liberty is really found only under the shadow of the evangelistic gospel."[3]

Ideological compatibility between church and state found practical expression in the missionary efforts to further the national purpose and in the close relations many of the missions enjoyed with the government. As early as the 1830s, missionaries in the Oregon country served the nation as well as the Church, a fact that caused William A. Slacum, an emissary from the president, to do what he could to fortify the Oregon missions. Perhaps the closest ties between the missions and the state occurred in 1872 when

President Ulysses S. Grant, in a move designed to eliminate corruption and provide more efficient management, entrusted administration of the Indian reservations to various mission boards.[4] A little later, Mrs. Rutherford B. Hayes, wife of Grant's successor as president, accepted the presidency of the Methodist Women's Home Missionary Society.[5]

Given the ideological ties between American Protestantism and the national government, it was scarcely surprising to find that most Protestant clergymen and many laypersons viewed American territorial expansion in 1898 as divinely inspired, even as they had given enthusiastic support to the war to liberate Cuba. "God has given into our hands, that is, into the hands of American Christians, the Philippine Islands," the Presbyterian General Assembly affirmed only two weeks after Commodore Dewey's victory at Manila Bay. "By the very guns of our battleships," the statement continued, God "summoned us to go up and possess the land." One Methodist bishop was so carried away by the excitement of the hour that he summarily appointed the Reverend Charles A. Owen to "First Church, Manila." That the Philippines were not within the bishop's area of ecclesiastical authority (thus making Owen's appointment illegal under church law), that the bishop acted without consulting the Church's mission board, and that "First Church, Manila" was nonexistent, seems not to have mattered.[6]

The large majority of first generation missionaries in the Philippines accepted the providential viewpoint. The Seventh-day Adventists, who believed that America's expansion was foretold in the book of Revelation, were the most theologically committed to the providential perspective.[7] Few other missionaries were willing to cite specific scriptural references, but the belief that the American occupation of the Philippine Islands was divinely inspired was the prevailing one. "God . . . put us" in the islands, Methodist Bishop James M. Thoburn told the Senate Committee on the Philippines in 1902. Subjected to a withering challenge by Senator Thomas M. Patterson, the bishop, with considerable assistance from imperialist senators on the committee, held firm.[8]

Counterbalancing those missionary applicants who listed the Philippines as only one of several choices were those who chose to go to the archipelago precisely because here was an unprecedented opportunity for the purest religion (evangelical Protestantism) to join hands with the most Christian of states (the United States) in carrying out the plan of Providence. One missionary, for example, was thrilled when her ship dropped anchor in Manila Bay, "not because it was my first touch with eastern life, for I had been in many other eastern cities, but because it was my first experience of this kind of life under the Stars and Stripes. I had lived many years in Burma under the British flag," she explained, "and now I was to learn what American rule would do for this branch of the Malaysian race in the Philippines."[9]

There were some dissenters. W. H. Lingle, sent by the Presbyterian board to investigate the prospects for mission work in the Philippines, reported back only days before the Philippine-American War erupted that hostilities were likely. Rather than fight, he wrote, the United States should withdraw. Howard W. Widdoes of the United Brethren mission considered himself an anti-imperialist.[10] Others, though not precisely anti-imperialist, were either oblivious or indifferent to the national purpose and felt uncomfortable with those who were so confident of God's intentions, particularly when the deity was invoked to defend the nation's actions. Methodist J. L. McLaughlin, for example, complained in 1902 that American institutions had been forced upon the people "at the muzzle of the Krag rifle." The following year he placed even more distance between himself and the idea of a national mission. "We have not sought to superimpose any preconceived American ideas or religious priorities," he wrote. Even Bishop Brent, who was as strong an imperialist and supporter of the state as any missionary in the islands, sometimes doubted that American actions conformed to the divine will. In 1908, for example, when Brent returned from a visit to Spain (which he found in a "pathetic" condition), he felt "as though in the War we in our strapping manhood had struck a decrepit old woman,—it is about as bad as that."[11]

Far more common, though, were expressions of strong support for the national purpose. There was in fact an almost incestuous quality to the thought of several prominent missionaries on this point. Presbyterian James B. Rodgers joined Methodist bishop William F. Oldham in appealing for funds "to serve God and the fatherland."[12] Brent wrote that his only motive in going to the Philippines was "to serve the nation and the kingdom of righteousness." He even insisted that Episcopalians build dignified edifices and use good equipment because Filipinos "estimated the value of the State through the Church."[13] Homer C. Stuntz, a prominent Methodist, thought that the interdenominational college he was attempting to found would "be a desirable ally of the Government," while Bruce Kershner cautioned his fellow Disciples missionaries to measure carefully the ramifications before criticizing the government, lest they foster revolution.[14] From such perspectives, not only was the national role to be a Christian one, but the mission's role was to be national in orientation. Few would have contested the chairman of the Presbyterian Church's standing committee on foreign missions, when he reminded missionaries in the Philippines that "patriotic loyalty is a cardinal tenet of American Protestantism."[15]

In supporting the government, of course, the missionaries expected it to pursue goals worthy of a Christian nation. To many this meant the infusion of American cultural and spiritual values, as well as Western political and economic concepts and arrangements. Methodist commentators, for example, wanted the United States to introduce "Western civilization of the Anglo-Saxon type" to the East, to "transform the Filipinos into a modern and free people," to bring "a new and brighter day" to the islands, and to "spread the idea of DEMOCRACY around the world."[16] There was a strong cautionary note, however. Some missionaries felt that an unselective and rapid infusion of Western culture could overwhelm and demoralize Philippine society. This was especially true where the mountain people were concerned. But the question was one of timing and method, rather than one of deep resistance to the spread of American ideas. Furthermore, it was the responsibility of the missions to help prepare the people for the coming changes.

Given their belief in the many deficiencies of Filipino society, the missionaries also expected the new government to be strongly paternalistic, to carry out the white man's burden, even when that meant conflict with the majority of the people. Like other humanitarian imperialists, the missionaries were sometimes overly sanguine about the possibilities of effecting meaningful societal transformation and blind to the consequences. But, like Rudyard Kipling, few expected the people to be grateful, at least in the short run. The United States should not expect "to enjoy the sweets of appreciated service," wrote a Methodist missionary. But it should "courageously bear the 'white man's burden,'" come what might.[17]

One of the difficulties the United States encountered from "unappreciative" Filipinos was armed resistance. Believers in the white man's burden were thus confronted with an immediate and bloody challenge. Yet those missionaries who welcomed America's assumption of sovereignty, particularly those who believed that it was part of a providential design, could not logically object to the use of force, if necessary, to confirm that sovereignty.

There was, in fact, virtually no missionary opposition to the military purpose. A few extremists thought that God himself directed American operations during the conflict; others argued that America's wars had always been humanely inspired and the Philippine campaign was no different.[18] It was also comforting to think, as most missionaries did, that the resistance was composed of disorganized, marauding bands of common bandits.[19] Insurgent leaders, it was commonly said, were motivated chiefly by "personal ambitions for place and power" and did not enjoy much popular support. Emilio Aguinaldo might be intelligent, wrote the secretary of the Presbyterian board after an extended visit to the islands in 1901, but he was an "Oriental despot" whose rule, if allowed, would be as bloody as that of the sultan of Turkey.[20]

Some missionaries, along with some civil and military officials, acknowledged that the resistance had widespread support and that the Filipino forces fought bravely and capably.[21] This view revealed that missionaries were not of one mind and embarrassed the government, which took great pains to deny the popular base of resistance. But varying assessments of the nature of the resistance did not produce differing recommendations, for the missionaries spoke with virtually one voice in saying that the resistance was misguided and must be crushed, regardless of the degree of popular support it enjoyed, so that American beneficence could proceed. "All that the governor, the commission, the school master, the civil judge, and the missionary are attempting," Homer Stuntz wrote in a widely read account, "would have been impossible without the work of the soldier."[22]

The propensity of most Americans (including missionaries) to characterize the armed conflict as an "insurrection" served further to disguise the nature of the Filipino resistance. The term *insurrection* implied an uprising against an already established American regime, which was correct, if at all, only in the Manila area. For the most part, the conflict was objectively an American war of conquest. Whether most missionaries who used the term *insurrection* consciously intended to misconstrue the nature of the resistance may be doubted. But Bishop Brent, at least, understood that *insurrection* had certain important connotations favorable to the American cause, for he once chastised the English writer, John Foreman, for referring to the *war* in the Philippines rather than to the *insurrection*.[23]

Occasionally, the issue of American atrocities during the war troubled the missionaries. Early in 1902 a Baptist in Panay complained, without results, to military authorities that American soldiers had killed a number of innocent people.[24] But that was exceptional. The more common view was that isolated acts of cruelty were unfortunate but inevitable and should not distract attention from the generally praiseworthy conduct of the military. Few missionaries criticized the American version of the Spanish tactic of *reconcentracion*, the herding of civilians into secure enclosures to make the elimination of guerrillas easier. In 1905, in fact, Bishop Brent and another Episcopalian missionary (and registered nurse), Ellen T. Hicks, visited the reconcentration camp at Bacoor and exonerated the government. Brent's visit convinced him that the policy was defensible in areas where resistance remained strong. Neither he nor Hicks thought the camp inhumane. "There was nothing reprehensible in the treatment of the *reconcentrados*," the bishop reported.[25] Zerah C. Collins of the YMCA even defended the infamous General Jacob Smith, who ordered Samar turned into a "howling wilderness." When President Roosevelt retired the general, Collins surmised that he had been punished undeservedly for political reasons.[26]

Missionary refusal to take seriously the atrocity issue resulted, in part, from the fact that anti-imperialists, whom most missionaries cordially distrusted, made it a central theme in their critique of American imperialism. Reluctant to give aid and comfort to enemies of the American administration, missionaries refused to condemn the army. Homer Stuntz observed that critics who publicized the atrocities, possessed minds that "forever miss currents, and get caught in eddies."[27]

What criticism there was of military policy tended to be that the army was not aggressive enough. Even those who rejected the optimistic picture painted by American authorities, instead of urging negotiation or withdrawal, hoped for new and "vigorous measures." All looked forward to the election of 1900, assuming that McKinley had restrained the military to benefit his candidacy. Once William Jennings Bryan, the anti-imperialist candidate, was defeated, Presbyterian J. Andrew Hall reasoned, "we look forward for all this to change." The authorities, Hall wrote approvingly, would no longer "be so lenient with those they catch as heretofore."[28] When in fact the president ordered a more vigorous policy after the election, the missionaries were pleased. The new policy "seems to be working like a charm," wrote one, "and the country is coming to its right mind."[29]

For similar reasons, the earliest missionaries deplored the so-called Bates Agreement (or Treaty) of 1899. That agreement, negotiated by General John C. Bates on behalf of the United States with the sultan of Sulu, was irregular, but apparently legal. Though the agreement served the immediate purpose of neutralizing Muslim areas during the Philippine-American War,[30] it was widely condemned. James B. Rodgers found it "irritating to see the Sultan treated with so much deference for he is a villain," and he considered the agreement another example of the doubtful policy of conciliation. Even more opposed was John McKee of the Christian and Missionary Alliance who, ignoring provisions of the agreement that restricted the movement of Americans and, by implication, forbade proselyting among the Muslims, preached in Sulu and other Muslim areas in 1900 and again in 1902. "God has laughed at such diplomacy," McKee concluded.[31]

Though the military must have considered missionaries like McKee a nuisance, good relations more normally prevailed.[32] Missionary reports and letters, for example, regularly included accounts of assistance from the military in such matters as housing, transportation, and communication. The YMCA enjoyed the closest of relationships with military personnel since it was a semiofficial arm of the government. If Y materials are to be credited, in fact, military officers were unanimous in their enthusiastic support of the organization. But the missionaries of other agencies also received encouragement, as well as favors, from the military and in some instances accepted military advice on when and where to begin work. Some missionaries, in turn, offered suggestions on ways to increase the army's efficiency. In 1899, for example, Bishop James M. Thoburn, who was

in Manila when the war commenced, urged the United States to follow the English colonial practice of enlisting indigenous people into the
ranks. The Filipinos, after all, knew the terrain and local conditions better
than the newcomers. And there was an added benefit: "three natives . . .
will cost no more as soldiers than one American," he pointed out. James B.
Rodgers, who arrived a few weeks later, interviewed and evaluated prisoners of war. It is difficult to disagree with one scholar's recent assessment, that "Rodgers was clearly working with the United States occupation forces; he would have been termed by Marxists an instrument
of imperialism."[33]

Just as the missionaries supported the military during the Philippine-
American War, those with responsibilities in Mindanao applauded initial
attempts to exert military control over the Muslims. For centuries the various Muslim groups of the South had fiercely maintained a practical independence of Spain, and they were no more inclined to acknowledge
American hegemony without a struggle. But as the fighting became pro-
tracted and brutal (it lasted for more than a decade after the official end of
the Philippine-American War), Bishop Brent, who had admired the re-
pressive policy of military governor Leonard Wood, at first demurred, and
then openly attacked the American use of arms. "The Moro is still unsub-
dued," he said in October 1913, "and I say more honor to the Moro! We can
go on with our oppressive measures to the end of time," he added, "but all
we can effect is annihilation." Brent's opposition, which was late in developing, was the only significant exception to missionary support of the
military's combatant role.[34]

Outside of Muslim areas, overt resistance to American arms had largely
ended by the time President Roosevelt declared the "insurrection" at an
end on July 4, 1902, and the civil government took over the bulk of the
white man's burden. The missionaries applauded much that the government undertook. Improvement in public health and public works attracted
especially widespread favorable comment. The missionaries repeatedly remarked on the transformation of Manila under American rule. Under the
Spanish, wrote a Seventh-day Adventist, the capital city "was indescribably
filthy."[35] The change was apparent by 1904. When Fred Jansen, a Presbyterian, returned to the city that year after an extended absence, he could
scarcely recognize it.[36] By 1909, one missionary insisted, Manila "was fast
becoming one of the most attractive cities of the Orient," and two years
later another claimed it was "one of the nicest and cleanest cities of the
East." Perhaps Methodist bishop Henry Warren summed it up most color-
fully; the Americans, he wrote, found Manila "a pesthole, and made it a
health resort."[37]

There were occasional discordant notes. A YMCA official admitted that "in a city where scores of thousands live in wretched nipa shacks on low, undrained land," there was too much truth in the observation that "many if not most of the splendid improvements that are being made in the Islands, are chiefly for the pleasure or advantage of the Americans and foreigners generally." But such criticisms were rare and confined to an occasional private letter—especially in the case of Y officials.[38] Most would unhesitatingly have agreed with a United Brethren spokesman, that "the American Government is here doing a real missionary work on a very large scale."[39]

Although the missionaries thought the government's purpose deserved support, they sometimes encountered indifference, even hostility, from government officials who did not share their view that the interests of church and state were intermingled. Homer Stuntz recalled that American officials in Dagupan initially "cursed us, and expressed the wish that we would go away and never return." A Presbyterian found that civil employees feared to identify themselves with the Protestant cause for fear it would "hurt their prospects of promotion," while as late as 1911 the leading Baptist missionary felt that government officials still considered missionaries "a pernicious element in the Philippines."[40] And there were numerous complaints that officials catered too much to the Roman Catholic hierarchy, which was by definition opposed to Protestant missions.[41]

Among the important officials whom the Protestants viewed with suspicion was James F. Smith, a Catholic who served on the Philippine Commission from 1903 to 1909, including over two years as governor general (1906–9). His appointment was a blow to Protestant hopes and diminished the missionaries' regard for Secretary Taft and President Roosevelt. People "ought to revise much of their thought with reference to our strenuous president," a Baptist commented.[42] The missionaries also found W. Cameron Forbes, who succeeded Smith as governor general (1909–13), less than cordial. Though Forbes respected Bishop Brent, served on the boards of some Episcopalian organizations, and contributed to the YMCA, he was contemptuous of most clergymen. Missionaries, he once wrote, were "usually the most grossly incompetent people that live."[43]

The official against whom the missionaries voiced their strongest objections was the outspoken and arrogant secretary of the interior, Dean C. Worcester. When the commissioner attempted to block Episcopalian efforts to purchase land in Bontoc for a mission station, missionary Walter C. Clapp could not contain his anger. Worcester, he wrote, was "a despot as merciless and malicious as one would expect to find in the Middle Ages," while Bishop Brent, agreeing with his subordinate, prepared a letter (left unsent) to his friend Theodore Roosevelt asking that the official be deposed. If the missionaries disliked Worcester passionately, they could take comfort in the fact that they were not alone. An official of the Manila

YMCA wrote that the secretary was "most cordially hated by his subordinates and Americans generally and . . . is almost universally execrated by Filipinos."[44]

On the other hand, government officials who encouraged mission work more than counterbalanced those who were critical. Expressions of encouragement ranged all the way from polite but meaningless gestures (Governor General Luke Wright once granted an interview to Seventh-day Adventists and flattered them by suggesting that, inasmuch as they took seriously the biblical admonition to labor six days and rest on the seventh, they could do good service by teaching the Filipinos how to work) to monetary contributions and active involvement in mission work. Especially in Mindanao government officials were solicitous. Peter G. Gowing's statement, that "beyond the extension of a few courtesies, American governmental officials [in Mindanao] did not actively aid any Christian missionary activities,"[45] underestimates the encouragement and assistance rendered by the officials. Robert F. Black, the first Congregationalist to venture to the islands, found officials in Mindanao eager to assist him. Black was permitted, for example, to travel on government ships after that privilege had been withdrawn from other civilians. "I hardly think I am going to compromise myself by accepting these favors," he wrote uneasily to his board. "What do you think?"[46]

Government assistance to Black was not merely a matter of courtesy, for officials saw value in his missionary activity. They encouraged Black and other American Board missionaries to expand their work. By 1911 Governor Henry Gilheuser of the Davao district stated publicly that "the church is one of the strongest governmental agents that we have." The new Congregational chapel that the governor was helping to dedicate, he said floridly, constituted "another stone in the wall of Americanism which is slowly but surely being built up around these Islands." In 1915 Frank Carpenter, the popular governor of the Department of Mindanao and Sulu (1914–20), urged the Congregational missionaries to take charge of a government school in Mumungan (now Baloi), and a few days later he asked Frank C. Laubach to introduce athletics—"base-ball evangelism" Laubach termed it—to the Moros.[47]

Episcopalians, too, found officials on Mindanao eager for them to begin work. Both Leonard Wood, the provincial governor, and General George W. Davis, the supreme military commander in the Philippines, agreed that there was "great opportunity" for the Episcopalians on the island. From Zamboanga, a little later, the Episcopalian missionary in charge reported that Wood was "in thorough accord with & will back us in every way." Brent in fact was concerned that criticism would develop if it were generally known how candid governmental officials had been in their expressions of support. "This is not for publication or notice at all in print," he once cautioned his mission board, while relaying Wood's words of encouragement.[48]

Those officials who encouraged the establishment of Protestant missions were surely shrewder than those who were indifferent or hostile, for the missionaries were, at least in the short run, a force for reconciliation and conservatism.[49] No one understood better the value of the missions to the government than William Howard Taft. As the first civil governor of the islands (1901–3) Taft established lasting relationships with several Protestant missions. He traveled to the islands in 1902 with Bishop Brent and later that year sought the bishop's counsel when President Roosevelt offered him a seat on the supreme court.[50] The following year, shortly before he returned to the United States to become secretary of war, Taft spent an hour with the Methodist leader Homer C. Stuntz, who had admired the governor ever since his inaugural address, and hammered out an agreement whereby missionaries could submit names to fill vacancies in the Philippine-American government. In future years the missionaries did not hesitate to communicate with Taft, and some became his staunch political supporters as well.[51]

If it is true that in India the British government did its best to inhibit the spread of Christianity and that "never at any time or in any way" did it "identify itself with the missionary cause,"[52] the same was demonstrably not so with the American government in the Philippines.

Of all the government's undertakings, none was so missionarylike as the massive educational effort. In other lands, in fact, a major portion of the missionary's time and resources was devoted to establishing and operating schools. Because the government undertook the task of education in the Philippines, the missionaries there were left free to engage in other pursuits. This alone might well have predisposed them to praise the schools. But to the missionary mind, the schools also had important cultural dimensions favorable to their cause. American Protestants had long viewed the public school in the United States "as part of the strategy for a Christian America." They could help in the same way in the Philippines by helping to create a new Philippine society, free from superstition and outmoded styles of life. The New Filipino would be democratic in inclination, questioning in mind, strong in body, and in general capable of contributing to the new society. His value structure would be American. The schools, wrote a Presbyterian, inculcated "American ideas" and were creating "a practical American spirit." Finally, the New Filipino would be pro-American and would reject emotional calls for independence.[53]

To the missionary mind one very important result of the school's effort to recast Philippine society was the liberation of the people from Roman

Catholic authority, in their view a goal of both religious and national importance. Frank C. Laubach stood quite literally alone in arguing that the public schools provided no opening at all for the Protestant message. The rest insisted fervently and often openly that, as a Baptist missionary expressed it, "every public school can be counted an evangelical force in a Roman Catholic country." By 1911 Methodist missionary Marvin Rader insisted that the public schools had "broken the hold Romanism has upon these students."[54] So frank were the missionaries about the value of the schools in the fight with Rome that government officials, had they read the missionary press, would have been sorely discomforted.

At the same time, the missionaries always feared that Catholics had or threatened to have too much influence in the educational system at all levels. As early as March 1899, James B. Rodgers observed that the Catholics would "make desperate efforts to hold the schools in their power and try to perpetuate the old system," and throughout the period the missionaries remained ever vigilant. They often found evidence of Catholic efforts to influence educational policy; too often, they felt, the "Romanists" were succeeding. In 1903 Presbyterian missionaries noted the arrival of two Catholic teachers in Dumaguete and assumed that their appointment indicated increasing Catholic influence in high places.[55] The following year a Baptist missionary in Panay felt that the government was pandering to the "Romanist party," while Methodist Harry Farmer, in Pangasinan Province, reported that Catholic teachers and principals taught Catholic doctrines in the schoolroom, required students to attend mass, and warned them not to listen to Protestants.[56] In 1907 Homer Stuntz complained directly to President Roosevelt about the "rapid promotion of Roman Catholic teachers."[57] In 1908 a Disciples missionary felt that the department of education exhibited "a spirit of fear and subserviency to Roman Catholic opinion," while the following year an Alliance missionary reported that Jesuits had infiltrated the schools of Zamboanga. Complaints of this sort never outweighed the positive aspects of the educational system, in the missionary mind; but as late as 1915, when Frank Laubach dismissed the schools as essentially without value to the Protestant cause, he pointed to Catholic influence to support his argument.[58]

Missionaries sometimes misconstrued the efforts of educational administrators to remain absolutely neutral in religious affairs as evidence of hostility and/or Catholic influence. Protests of this nature were especially evident during the years 1901–3 when Fred W. Atkinson was secretary of education. During the Atkinson period, missionaries complained that Protestant teachers and administrators were flatly forbidden to express their religious views, even outside the classroom.[59] If one Presbyterian report is to be credited, teachers could not even entertain a missionary in their homes, "even when there was no other place in the village where he might obtain boiled water and food free from cholera germs."[60] Reports of this sort led one missionary to refer to the "terrors of the Atkinson period" in one of his annual reports.[61]

The missionaries were gratified when David Prescott Barrows, a devout Protestant, succeeded Atkinson as superintendent in 1903. But in 1904 James F. Smith, a Catholic, became secretary of public instruction. As Barrows's superior, Smith had ultimate responsibility for the islands' educational system. A report that the Catholic Church in the United States had condemned the unfortunate Smith's supervision of the department of education did little to lessen Protestant suspicions. "When dealing with tricky people it is well to be cautious," a Baptist publication advised, adding that few Protestants in the Philippines took the denunciation seriously.[62]

In any event, the basic policy requiring teachers to remain neutral in religious matters and to refrain from influencing the religious views of their students remained unchanged, and some missionaries continued to feel that the policy represented an unconstitutional infringement; furthermore, they complained, the policy was enforced only on Protestant teachers. Observing cases of drunkenness among some teachers, one missionary mused that it would be better for the government to order "its employees to abstain from alcohol rather than from religion."[63]

In fact, however, the policy of maintaining a religiously neutral school divided the missionary community deeply. Even during the Atkinson period some missionary spokesmen, notably Arthur J. Brown, argued that the policy was essential to minimize Catholic influence.[64] A few years later Brown received sharply differing opinions when he asked the Presbyterian missionaries to comment on the government's policy.[65] But probably a majority of missionaries agreed with the government. In 1910, for example, the Presbyterian committee on religious liberty concluded that the policy was reasonable, and the mission as a whole concurred.[66]

While most missionaries viewed the public schools as allies in the effort to reshape Philippine society and battle Catholicism, they also agreed that, left to themselves, the schools would produce skeptics, not evangelical Christians. As early as 1902 Arthur J. Brown observed that by calling into question the old verities, the schools would be preparing the soil for the "noisome seeds of infidelity and atheism." To the missionary, this presented grave dangers, for it was from the schools that the leaders of the new society would come. Educated pagans (to use Laubach's phrase) in leadership positions presented a spectacle too horrible to contemplate.[67]

The mission, therefore, had an important responsibility. The establishment of parochial schools was one response to the dangers of free thinking.[68] But instead of erecting competing institutions, the missionaries more usually attempted to create a Protestant presence near the public schools in the form of kindergartens, dispensaries, social clubs, and above all dormitories. If the government was going to provide the schools, an undertaking most missionaries strongly approved, and if religion could not be taught in the schools, something the majority probably accepted, then the missions felt a deep obligation to reach the students—the future leaders—as best they could. A portion, at least, might be saved from secularism, and they in turn would help ensure the success of the American-created new society.[69]

Protestant worry about the direction of public education was connected with the larger issue of religious liberty. The freedom of religious expression, in fact, was to the missionaries the most important advantage of American rule. But especially in the early years, the missionaries questioned whether the government took seriously enough its role as the guarantor of religious freedom. Time after time the missionaries complained that local officials (usually Filipinos) failed to investigate instances of interference with their religious meetings and of persecution of their adherents. If a case was brought before a justice of the peace, it was too often dismissed on a pretext or technicality.[70] Though appeals to higher authorities (often Americans) might achieve better results, the situation would never be truly satisfactory, the missionaries believed, as long as the government at the highest levels remained inordinately sensitive to Catholic interests.

The Philippine Commission's decision in 1904 to proclaim a holiday in honor of Nuestra Señora de Rosario, the virgin of Antipolo, was an early example, the missionaries thought, of the insular government caving in to "Romish pressure," as Homer Stuntz put it in a long letter to Theodore Roosevelt. Three years later Protestant sensitivities were even more deeply bruised when the commission deigned to be present while Nuestra Señora was crowned patron saint of the Philippines.[71]

Significantly, the latter action occurred when James F. Smith was governor general, a period when complaints alleging religious persecution and governmental unconcern seem to have multiplied. Baptist Charles W. Briggs wrote that "all who have been watching the course of events have noted the decided increase in religious preferment and in persecutions since our present Catholic Governor-General came into office," while a Presbyterian in Cebu went so far as to claim that "religious liberty is a myth."[72] The most celebrated allegations of religious persecution during Smith's tenure, and of the government's ineffectual response, were brought to public attention by the Reverend Harry Farmer, a prominent Methodist missionary. Convinced that affairs in the islands were "very much in the hands of the Roman Catholics, and to all indications and purposes, Church and State are one,"[73] Farmer filed at least four complaints with the authorities in 1908 alleging persecution in Navotas, Meycauayan, and Vigan. When Farmer concluded that government officials had failed to investigate his complaints adequately, he published the details in a Methodist publication, after which religious magazines in the United States picked up the story. It created a minor sensation for a time and threatened to embarrass William Howard Taft, the Republican candidate for the presidency.[74]

Complaints of religious persecution diminished notably under Smith's successor, an irony given Cameron Forbes's contempt for missionaries. The Presbyterian committee on religious liberty received no complaints at all in 1909 and only one the following year. In 1911 missionaries in Bohol reported "a good deal of persecution," but they added that it occurred in "a quiet way." The same year mission personnel in Camarines observed that persecution occurred only in out-of-the-way places.[75]

Just as the missionaries were willing to criticize the government for allegedly failing to uphold religious freedom, so, too, they were not silent when the government pursued policies or sanctioned activities that departed from American Protestant moral norms. They were, in this sense, the conscience of the American experiment.

Even while the Philippine American War was in progress, some missionaries engaged in sustained attacks on the army's policy that permitted soldiers to purchase intoxicants on military bases. Dismissing as insubstantial the argument that it was better to provide a regulated environment for soldiers who drank than to force them to patronize the "vile vino shops" off the base, Methodist bishop Frank W. Warne adduced seven reasons why the army canteen should be abolished.[76] The missionaries were apparently successful in closing the canteens, though whether this increased temperance among the soldiers may be doubted.

The missionaries also insisted, especially in the early years, that public officials set a good example by regular attendance at religious services. So vocal did criticism become of members of the Taft Commission for alleged nonattendance that each commissioner felt obligated to file a written statement denying that there was a government policy discouraging church attendance.[77] Bishop Brent dismissed most of these allegations (some brought by his own Episcopalian missionaries) as unjustified. (Taft did not attend at first, apparently because no chair could comfortably accommodate his ample frame, whereupon Brent ordered a suitable chair constructed.) But like other missionaries, the bishop believed that public officials had an obligation to maintain high standards of conduct, including church attendance. When Judge Adolph Wislizenus objected to being treated as "a potted palm that can be carried around to decorate a religious festival," Brent shot back, "attendance on public worship is a public duty."[78]

Another moral issue that attracted missionary attention in the early years was the sale of opium. In particular, the Protestants were outraged when in 1903 the Philippine Commission proposed to regulate the sale of the drug by granting a monopolistic franchise to the highest bidder. The missionaries regarded this proposal as unbecoming for an American government and feared that under the plan the opium concessionaire would not, as he was supposed to do, limit his sales to persons already addicted. Because of strong missionary pressure (Methodist Bishop James M. Thoburn told Secretary of War Elihu Root to his face that the monopoly idea was "bad, and only bad, and bad continually"),[79] the government backed down. President Roosevelt personally ordered Governor Taft not to pass an opium bill until he, Roosevelt, had approved it.[80] In the end Taft shelved the plan and appointed a three-man commission, which included Bishop Brent (at Brent's request), to review the matter. After a serious investigation, the special commission suggested a solution that met with the approval of all concerned: a gradual phaseout of the opium trade without a government-sponsored franchise. "Our gratitude to God for this termination of the opium debate should be very real and very great," concluded the Methodist committee on public morals.[81]

The missionaries regularly urged the elimination of a host of other evils including prostitution, dance halls, intemperance, work and recreation on the Sabbath, uncensored films, inadequate laws relating to marriage and divorce (Mercer Johnston wanted the government to force unmarried persons living together to marry),[82] usury, and obscene postcards. But the moral issue that most persistently attracted their attention was gambling, something they fervently tried to eliminate or at least place under the most stringent regulation.

The issue came to a head in 1906, apparently because an American, W. W. Brown, was deeply involved in promoting gambling at the cockpit. Filipino gambling was bad enough, but an American promoting the evil was more than right-thinking Protestants would stand for. To tolerate it would be to sacrifice the obligations of the white man's burden. "I do not see how any American, in or out of office, can henceforth speak of the benevolent intentions of our Government towards the people of these islands," Mercer Johnston wrote to Governor General Ide.[83] The commission, he said, ought to take action.

Ide sympathized with Johnston but suggested that the matter be deferred until the Philippine Assembly met the following year. Were the American-dominated commission to place severe restrictions on gambling, he pointed out, "there would be a great outcry against the interference with the long established customs of the people." It would be better to let the representatives of the people pass the necessary laws.[84] To Johnston and others, the governor general's response was pusillanimous at best. How could the obligations of the white man's burden be carried out if the government was unwilling to take strong action against immorality? That the majority of the Filipinos might disagree was no excuse for inaction. The government was shirking its responsibility.

Instead of assenting to the governor's suggestion, Johnston joined with the Methodist mission in forming the Moral Progress League to arouse the public and put pressure on the commission. For those involved it was a moment of high drama:

> Surely, this battle in which we are about to engage is the Lord's [wrote Johnston]. Let's put on our head-pieces, and keep them on, and gird up our loins, and keep them girded up, and win it for Him. All morning I have been sniffing the battle. My nostrils are full of the odor of powder—black, dank, foul-smelling powder, and [the] smoke of which rises up to heaven. . . . Red Blood Corpuscles have been marching through my veins arousing the martial spirit of every molecule in my make-up. Let's take as our inward motto in this fight, "so fight I, not as one that beateth the air," and stay in until death.[85]

League activists worked feverishly to gain widespread support. The Methodists cancelled their usual midweek prayer meetings to attend strategy meetings. Scores of postcards went to influential citizens urging support. By mid-June the league was powerful enough to organize a mass rally in the Zorrilla Theater. Eventually they lined up Emilio Aguinaldo, the Filipino Academy of Social Sciences, eight daily Manila newspapers, high government officials, and even the Roman Catholic archbishop, Jeremias Harty. The league had become a formidable pressure group. "Never before in the history of *the American* government of the Philippines or at any previous period have all parties and classes been able to agree upon any subject whatsoever," the Methodist *Christian Advocate* observed, "and that this longed-for harmony has come over a gigantic protest against a national wrong is taken to be the beginning of an era of better feeling and effective cooperation."[86]

In the face of intense pressure, the commission began to give way. By the end of June the government had requested that the league submit to it a draft law concerning race-track gambling, and the governor general himself had drafted a law concerning gambling in the cockpit. Still, the commission held back. On July 2 it appointed a fact-finding committee to ascertain opinion about the control of gambling, particularly in the provinces. League officials considered this action evidence of timidity, but they were glad the commission had come as far as it had. League officials wrote letters to missionaries in the provinces asking them to gather opinion there and to write the commission.[87]

Then on July 15 the league received the tremendously important endorsement of Bishop Brent. The league had its weakness, Brent admitted. It tended to be overly emotional and did not provide sufficient alternatives for those who would be deprived of gambling. But in a biting sermon that received front-page coverage in the Manila papers, the bishop charged that the commission had failed miserably to come to grips with the problem, and to the extent that the league could bring pressure on the government, he gave it his blessing. "The Spirit of Good is in it," he proclaimed.[88]

Things now moved quickly. Two days after Brent's sermon the league's lawyers had ready a draft law that limited gambling at horse races to only ten days per year.[89] Within a month the commission had given the proposed law three separate readings, as was required by law, and enacted it with minor modifications. The Moral Progress League had achieved a major victory in an amazingly short period of time. The missionaries had demonstrated that on occasion they were a political force to be reckoned with.

The league's success did not end disputes over gambling, however, and less than two years later governmental authorities raised missionary hackles by allowing a large cockpit to operate at the semiofficial Manila carnival. Late in 1907 or early in 1908, the Philippines Carnival Association let a concession for the cockpit and then sought the necessary license from the Municipal Board of Manila. The license was quickly granted.[90]

When the Evangelical Union caught wind of the cockpit (and other undesirable aspects of the carnival, notably the proposed sale of intoxicants), it appointed a committee, chaired by Johnston, to investigate. Although the matter was essentially local, the missionaries directed protests not only to the Carnival Association and the Municipal Board, but to the Philippine Commission (particularly to Commissioner Forbes who had become president of the Carnival Association after the arrangements for the cockpit had been made), as well as to Governor General Smith. In fact, they suspected that Smith was secretly responsible for the entire matter and berated him and the commission as much as the Manila authorities.[91]

The missionaries' anger seems misdirected. Not only was the matter not legally in the commission's hands, but those commissioners who angered the missionaries most, Forbes and Smith, agreed, as Smith put it, that "it would have been very much better if no concession had been granted for a cockpit and no permit issued by the city of Manila." Forbes privately thought the Municipal Board consisted of "fools," and he fancifully suggested that it be abolished.[92]

Unfortunately, the contract had been legally let, and the concessionaire had presumably invested a substantial sum in preparation for the carnival. The only way out, Governor General Smith thought, was to buy up the contract, which he estimated to be worth about 8,000 pesos, or possibly more.[93] For his part, Smith was willing to put up 1,000 pesos from his personal funds, as was Forbes; some other officials agreed to subscribe lesser amounts.

The Evangelical Union agreed to cooperate with the effort to buy up the contract and promised to match the governor general's subscription of 1,000 pesos. But the missionaries continued to feel that the government was doing a miserable job of carrying out the white man's burden. To allow the cockpit, Johnston wrote to Smith, would be "a crime against the natives of these islands and a burning shame to our American administration here." He suggested that the Municipal Board buy up the contract with funds to be called the "Municipal Board sin-offering," and he threatened to raise a public protest of the sort generated by the Moral Progress League if results were not forthcoming soon.[94] (Unknown to Smith, Johnston that same day asked several Filipino newspapers to publish a protest about the cockpit.)[95]

Three days later Forbes, in his capacity as president of the Carnival Association, wrote the Evangelical Union that 8,000 pesos was inadequate to purchase the contract, that instead it would take "several times this sum." Forbes's almost insulting letter ("I cannot see why you have fixed the sum of eight thousand pesos in this matter") no doubt irritated the missionaries, since only a week earlier the governor general himself had provided the figure of 8,000. It was only then that the missionaries moved into high gear. Three days after Forbes's letter was received, Johnston denounced the government in a colorful sermon entitled "A Covenant with Death, an Agreement with Hell."[96] A rally of six hundred students protested the cockpit decision, and Johnston sent a cable to President Roosevelt begging him to intervene. The Evangelical Union followed with its second cable to the president.[97]

The increasingly militant attitude of the missionaries irked Forbes, who, although he agreed that the cockpit contract was a mistake, considered it a violation of "common business morality" to cancel the contract without adequate compensation as the missionaries seemed to be demanding. "I tell my co-workers," he wrote, "that if these propositions of the ministers were made to me as a business man at home the least that could happen to them would be to be taken by the seat of the breeches and back of the neck to the top of the stairs and then to be kicked down." He even thought of attending the cockpit the following Sunday out of spite. "Lord keep and save me from ministers!" he exclaimed. He was delighted, of course, to learn that a number of parishioners had resigned from Johnston's church in protest over his fiery sermon.[98]

This time Protestant efforts to purify the American government proved unavailing. The authorities in Washington refused to intervene,[99] and those attending the carnival that year found the cockpit operating as planned.

A common thread runs through missionary criticism of the government. Whether the missionaries chastised the government for pursuing a too lenient military policy, for being too susceptible to Catholic pressure, for not encouraging church attendance, or for failing to deal effectively with moral issues, the government stood charged with lacking leadership ability, with suffering from a failure of nerve. This was most apparent to the missionaries when they evaluated the government's overall performance as upholder of the white man's burden, of carrying out its moral obligations to the Filipinos. Thus when the authorities proved ineffective in preventing the carnival cockpit, for example, Johnston denounced the "astounding moral torpidity of many of my own countrymen, especially of those into whose callous hands the fate of this island people has been committed." So enraged was Johnston over this and other ethical failings of government officials that he was almost willing to say a kind word for the anti-imperialists. "I have said some pretty hard things about those gentlemen, and I meant exactly what I said," he wrote, "but I will not stand for the morally low-grade government that Taft is fostering here the while he makes the welkin ring in the states with altruistic yelling."[100]

The Baptists, too, wondered if the government was carrying out its responsibilities to the people. More than any other mission group the Baptists wanted to eliminate the system of *caciquismo* (rural bossism), which they perceived as exploitative and degrading, something that sapped the very personhood from the peasants. The American regime, they were sure, would root out the prevailing practice: "the conditions . . . exist today in an atmosphere where they can no longer thrive. The government system . . . is going to undermine the whole social structure that has so long been dominant." But within a few years doubts developed about whether the government really wanted to carry through the kind of social revolution required to dislodge an institution as deep-seated as caciquismo.[101]

The government's failure to lead manifested itself in the granting of too many concessions to Filipinos who were as yet ill-suited, most missionaries thought, to carry out important responsibilities, especially if they involved the making of policy. This attitude was evident in the skepticism with which they greeted the establishment of the Philippine Assembly in 1907 and in the efforts of important missionaries to prevent the Democrats from making even more concessions, including possibly independence, following their election victory in 1912. To be sure, missionary opinion was not monolithic by this time, but the majority still felt that the American government had been too prone to accede to Filipino demands.

To these missionaries, the government needed to rule with a steady hand. The government must have "the whip over the door," as one Episcopalian missionary put it bluntly, "for the Malay Willie will not be a good boy nor learn his lessons unless it is in sight." Missionaries of this persuasion were "running scared," genuinely fearful that the American experiment would fail. The Filipinos would "never be able to govern themselves if the government continues its present policy," Brent stated publicly in 1907. To educate and elevate the Filipinos to the desired level was not the work of a day or even of a few years. It required a dedicated, imaginative, career-oriented colonial civil service working for at least a generation. "If a man like General [Leonard] Wood could be undisturbed as governor for twenty years and be surrounded by men of the same type," another Episcopalian wrote, "the thing to all appearance would be done."[102]

Unfortunately, the missionaries felt that the American colonial service did not measure up. Politics infested it. Administrators, including the governor general, were replaced all too often. Too many colonial officials despised their surroundings and longed to return home. Too often they remained aloof from Filipino society, exploited the people, and addressed them contemptuously. American *policy* in the Philippines would "never be accussed of a lack of imagination. . . ," wrote a Baptist medical missionary in a sensitive essay, "but I fear that many who endeavor to execute that policy may be accussed of a lack of *heart*." He explained:

> The building of roads, the opening up of the interior, the establishing of new avenues of communication, new and better governmental methods and the maintaining of a splendid school system all accomplished by determination and indomitable energy, will not avail to win the hearts of the people and lead them to a higher life, so long as it is done in a deliberate, calculating way with none or very little heart-felt sympathy. . . . The Islands need men and women who are willing to admit that the spiritual and temporal welfare of the humblest peasant is worth as much as ours or mine. How unfortunate it is to find that the majority of minor governmental officials and some other Americans find it impossible to speak a good word for the Filipino people.[103]

In their efforts to save the government from its own mistakes, a number of missionaries, though by no means all, held out the example of European colonial administrations, notably the British in India. Methodist Bishop Thoburn, who had lived for many years in India, alluded to the British model on occasion, as did Bishop Brent, who read and traveled widely in an effort to familiarize himself with non-American colonialism. Though Brent did not entirely approve of British administration, sensing the Brit-

ish colonialists were too self-serving and overly pessimistic about the prospects of eventual native rule, at least the British experience was not characterized by the "instability, superficiality, feverish haste, and unreality" that,
he felt, infected the American effort.[104] On the contrary, the English, Brent
thought, possessed a steadfastness of purpose, good government, a sense
of duty, a dedicated colonial civil service, and policymakers who, through
long experience, had acquired perceptive insights into the "Oriental mind."

This is not to say that the missionaries were completely disillusioned.
Few of the first generation, after all, supported Filipino demands for independence, though that was beginning to change. Most would have insisted
that the government had pursued an enlightened colonial policy, all things
considered, that deserved support. Much as some of them admired the
British, they contended that the American vision was more humane, more
democratic, perhaps even more Christian. If only America would slow
down a bit and professionalize its colonial service, if it would pursue its
goals at a "steady jog trot" instead of a "gallop," as Brent put it, American
colonialism might yet become the best in the world.[105]

Were, then, the missionaries agents of American imperialism? They defined their task in theological terms: to carry the Protestant Gospel to a
land that had hitherto excluded it. Those who could clearly differentiate
between Protestantism and Americanism cannot properly be called imperial agents. But an important segment of the missionary community, including the leading missionaries of most churches, consciously sought to
infuse American concepts and values along with Protestantism, just as they
often did in other lands.[106] And probably most missionaries could not escape, did not even want to attempt to escape, the bounds of their culture.
They, too, served the interests of the state, if not always consciously. They
viewed the American occupation as providential or at least as an expression
of American benevolence that deserved their support. They accepted the
necessity for the military conquest of the islands. During the war they deferred to military opinion, and a few gave advice and even direct support
to the authorities. In the main they applauded the civil government's
attempts to remake Philippine society, physically and culturally, along
American lines. They served as a force to reconcile Filipinos to their new
fate. As one high-ranking officer told the Reverend George F. Pentecost,
"the presence of a Protestant missionary in any part of the islands was
worth more than a battalion of soldiers for all purposes of pacification."[107]
Their sometimes heated, sometimes telling criticisms of the government
were intended to purify American colonialism and make it more effective;
almost none of them questioned the American presence.

9

American Colonialists:
The Missionary Assessment

One of the hard things to explain to the Filipinos is why
so many Americans are so bad and have no religion.
Leon C. Hills,
Presbyterian missionary

Most missionaries welcomed the American decision to acquire the Philippines, supported the military effort to subdue the resistance, thought most government policies benefited the populace, and considered the nation's mission generally a civilizing, uplifting one. But what did they think of the American personnel who came to the Philippines as representatives of a supposedly enlightened culture?

Even before the missionaries arrived, some of them foresaw that large numbers of unprincipled, disreputable Americans would set foot on these newly won American shores. Bishop James M. Thoburn, the first official Methodist representative, predicted in 1899 that "adventurers of all classes will soon be flocking there . . . in order that they might enter upon schemes of various kinds for exploiting the islands." Episcopalian Walter C. Clapp, nearing Hong Kong on his way to Manila, predicted that the immediate impact of Americans on the Philippines would be a secularizing, demoralizing, and disintegrating one. Similarly, Presbyterian David S. Hibbard wrote that he feared the end of the Philippine-American War would "turn loose upon us a vast horde of the moral scum of America, coming in search of money at any price."[1]

The missionaries' pessimistic predictions were borne out. In letter after letter, report after report, missionaries found the American community in the Philippines sadly wanting. In 1902, for example, a Presbyterian missionary complained to his board that it was difficult to explain to Filipinos "why so many Americans are so bad and have no religion." The following year the Methodist committee on public morals deplored "the presence of so many dissipated and vicious Americans in all parts of the Provinces, who by their vices drag down the standards which this nation is endeavoring to set up." In 1904 Stealy B. Rossiter felt "very much ashamed of the bulk of American Protestants" in the islands.[2]

The missionaries accused the Americans of a variety of lapses. Perhaps the most common was their alleged addiction to strong drink. They also charged them with failure to attend church, gambling, immoral sexual liaisons, greed, general irreligiosity, and with displaying a condescending, even bitter, demeanor toward Filipinos. There were, of course, exceptions, and not all missionaries wrote so critically. But overall the missionary portrait of the American community, especially in the first four or five years of the American occupation, was very negative.

Reports of immoral Americans were received from all parts of the archipelago; but if Presbyterian Charles E. Rath is to be believed, the American presence was at its worst in Tacloban, Leyte. Shortly after his arrival in 1904, Rath reported that the moral conditions of this town were "very bad," a situation he blamed on the Americans, who, in turn, resented his presence. The postmaster told him bluntly that missionary influence was detrimental around the world. Hardly anyone came to his meetings. Even written invitations elicited only a modest audience, mostly of soldiers. "The civilians did not turn out," he lamented. Eight months later he reported that only two Americans had bothered to attend a recent service.[3]

Missionaries described the morals of the American more often than they accounted for them. Some, however, blamed the "sensuous tropics" and the "oriental atmosphere" for the degradation. Bishop Brent, for example, felt it was difficult for unmarried men to lead "a continent life" in the islands. Others compared conditions in the Philippines to a frontier setting with its disorganization, rough and ready character, and lack of a settled family life.[4]

Just as the American West became more settled and civilized over time, missionaries could look forward to improvement in the Philippines. As the war ended and the civilian government extended its authority, a better element of Americans arrived, often in family groups. As early as 1904 a Presbyterian noted that the vagrants were departing.[5] By 1905 change was apparent. That year the Methodist committee on public morals felt able to report "steady improvement in the morals of the American residents in the Islands." Early the following year, a Disciples missionary wrote that the quality of the American community was much improved. And by 1912 a YMCA official stated that the islands were "happily rid now of most of that numerous class of unprincipled adventurers and hangers-on who drifted here in the early days of the American occupation."[6]

The change was by no means dramatic, however, for reports of ungodly behavior continued. The Methodist committee, for example, continued to find many faults with Americans, in particular with their propensity to gamble, a perception shared by an Episcopalian who suggested that his church establish a presence in Iloilo because the Americans there, especially the younger ones, drank and gambled to excess. The Baptists, who had been in Iloilo for a decade, could easily substantiate his observation. As late as 1914 one Baptist, perhaps expressing an extreme view, claimed that a good majority of Americans were degenerate. "Our own countrymen need the Gospel quite as much as the natives," he concluded.[7]

Church attendance seemed to improve somewhat over the years, but irreligiosity was still a problem. A Disciples missionary estimated that of the 5,000 Americans in Manila in 1910 less than 20 percent were churchgoers. Whether racial prejudice lessened is doubtful. Even those who saw a general improvement in manners and morals often noted that Americans still treated Filipinos with disdain. In Zamboanga, for example, the Episcopalian missionary reported that Americans refused to attend religious services with the local people, and as late as 1914 a Baptist insisted that many Americans retained "fossilized racial prejudices."[8]

Racial exclusiveness, gambling, excessive luxury and leisure came together in the numerous private clubs that catered to Americans. Bishop Brent, who thought many Americans in Manila were "riff-raff," condemned the "vicious features of club life in the Far East." The clubs, he stated, had "buried more young men and blasted more fair promise than climate or disease," while a YMCA official contended that club life was detrimental to the "exercise, study and religious life" of those who joined.[9]

To counteract such dissipation, the missions founded or supported institutions they hoped would provide Christian alternatives. The YMCA, of course, turned its primary attention to Americans with a variety of programs and put itself in explicit and direct competition with the secular clubs. Similarly, in November 1905, the Episcopalians opened the Columbia Club to give American "young men such opportunities for pleasant intercourse and wholesome amusement as will enable them, amidst all the temptations of Oriental life, to maintain the high standards of personal and national duty with which they left home." Their club, Episcopalians felt, complemented the work of the YMCA.[10]

The Y and the Columbia Club were the most well-known and successful of such undertakings. Eventually, in fact, they became occasional rivals, particularly when the American population began to decline after 1912. But other missions attempted to provide similar alternatives for Americans. In Nuevas Caceres, for example, a Presbyterian established a library club, which seems to have succeeded; and in Camarines, missionaries founded a social club that prohibited gambling and liquor, though it failed.[11]

How much influence these and other efforts had on the morals of the

American community is difficult to judge. The consensus among the missionaries seems to have been that significant changes took place. But the battle was never permanently won. "Elemental passions run wild in a land of easy virtue and low standards," a YMCA official explained in 1917. "Men are like reeds in the wind. Young fellows who were staunch and steadfast at home find that in some subtle way their ideas have undergone a change and almost before they realize it they are fighting the battle of their lives to keep clean and true, to stand up straight."[12]

In general, then, missionaries found the American community wanting; indeed, they sometimes feared for the success of America's humanitarian mission because of the character of Americans. Still, when the missionaries commented on specific groups of Americans, a more complex picture emerges.

One group of Americans that elicited considerable comment from the missionaries was the business community. Relations in the nineteenth century between missionaries and the foreign business community have usually been portrayed as antagonistic. Businessmen, it is said, considered the missionaries impractical zealots who might inadvertently create antiforeign feeling. The missionaries in turn thought the businessmen behaved in unchristian ways and exploited the people.[13] This ill feeling was well expressed by Mark Twain. Writing with reference to the white community (largely commercial) in Hawaii, Twain wrote, "the missionaries are sorry the most of the other whites are there, and these latter are sorry the missionaries don't migrate."[14]

An analysis of the thought of missionaries in the Philippines generally supports the traditional picture of missionary-businessmen tension. Yet the missionaries also held theological and ideological views that, in theory, caused them to welcome the extension of American enterprise to the Orient. For those who held strongly to the providential view, the hand of God was to be seen in the establishment of large business concerns, in particular the new steamship and railroad lines, that sprang up in the wake of Western expansion. "Here again is seen the guiding hand of God in providing rapid and comfortable traveling facilities for his messengers of peace and good will to men," explained a Seventh-day Adventist appeal for a more concerted effort in the East. A belief in the white man's burden, held by virtually all missionaries, also inclined them to feel that, among other things, Filipinos needed new economic skills. New products, organizational expertise, and methods of production were vital elements in their uplift. "An important factor in teaching the native planter," a Presbyterian missionary thought, "will be the introduction of thoroughly modern methods on large American plantations."[15]

But the theory seemed exploded when missionaries encountered businessmen directly. The sleazy side of American commercial interests was evident from the beginning. "All the varied missionary work of the Devil is very much at hand," a missionary wrote in 1899. Among the works of the devil was the American saloon, which catered primarily to American soldiers and presented the worst side of the American character to the Filipinos. After the army eliminated liquor from the posts, the saloon became nearly ubiquitous, many of them owned by discharged soldiers.[16]

Missionaries also complained that the commercial people seldom observed the Sabbath. Not only did businessmen not attend church, but they required employees to work on Sunday. For Protestants of that age, keeping Sunday free of commercial transactions was a matter of grave import. "Protestants hold this day as sacred to the worship of God, as did Jesus hold the ancient Jewish Temple sacred as God's house of prayer," the Reverend George F. Pentecost explained. "That in these Islands where God has so strangely brought us this holy day is so entirely disregarded and desecrated by the vast majority of Americans," he continued, ". . . is a matter not only of profound sorrow . . . but the ground of a profound apprehension for the welfare of our own country and the well-being of the people among whom we have come, professing a desire and purpose to teach and give to them the blessings of a higher and better Christian civilization. God cannot and will not bless any people or country that profanes His Sanctuary day and abandons His worship," he warned. So sensitive were the missionaries on this point that Dr. J. Andrew Hall, the Presbyterian medical missionary in Iloilo, canceled a contract with J. G. White Company, which constructed railroads, because the company required Sunday work.[17]

In addition to being irreligious, the missionaries feared that most businessmen lacked sympathy with the Filipinos. Scarcely interested in the demands of the white man's burden, they acquired their profits with an air of superiority and blatant racial prejudice. An agent of the American firm of Smith, Bell, and Company, for example, forbade a Methodist missionary to conduct religious meetings in one of the company's storerooms primarily because the missionary was allegedly "spoiling the Filipinos by treating them as white men, and he wanted it understood that he could not treat them as such, as he was their superior and he would cuff any Filipinos who presumed to be his equal." There were, no doubt, businessmen who held other views. But a condescending, unsympathetic attitude toward Filipinos was said to be typical "of the average commercial American" and contrasted sharply with the "far more lovable" attitude of the Church.[18]

To the south, in Mindanao particularly, the commercial elements with which the missionaries had the most meaningful contact were American owners of hemp plantations, many of whom were former soldiers. Then as now, Mindanao was a frontier area. Many of the planters were, in the view of one missionary, "quite similar to the Western Cowboy." The planters attracted considerable missionary interest largely because they employed mountain people who lived near or even on the plantations. If the missionaries wished to reach these people (as did the missionaries of the American Board, the Episcopal Church, and the Christian and Missionary Alliance), they had to have the cooperation of the planters. "A good influence upon the planters themselves goes much farther than the planters," explained the C. T. Sibleys, a missionary couple with the American Board.[19]

The missionary perception of the planter was generally a positive one. The Sibleys thought them "splendid men, excellent representatives of our country." Many of the planters welcomed the missionaries. Charles Sibley, in fact, had agreements from several planters to build schoolhouses for the people and to provide room, board, and protection for the teachers, if the mission board would provide the teachers. He also had the active support of General Pershing and other government officials, Pershing once agreeing to do his best to provide financial assistance.[20]

Though American Board missionaries felt that the majority of the planters welcomed them, it is evident that a sizable number considered them intruders. Some openly feared that educated and Christianized people would lose much of their value as laborers. Others disliked missionary criticism of their morality, in particular of their practice of taking *queridas* or mistresses. "They know it is wrong," the Sibleys explained, "and a missionary is a reminder of their wrong doing, hence unwelcome." Robert Black spoke out so strenuously against various forms of immorality in Davao that a fellow missionary reported that "American feeling in general here is against Mr. Black." Several years later, when Frank Laubach wrote some disparaging accounts of planter morality near Davao, he found it expedient not to locate in that part of the island, since "the favor and assistance of the planters . . . is the sine qua non of effective work in that district."[21]

Missionaries in many countries encountered American merchants, but what was unusual about the Philippines was that, being an American colony, sizable numbers of Americans other than those involved in commercial ventures were also present. Until at least 1902, in fact, the most numerous group of Americans was the soldiers. After the war, the military presence continued to be significant, especially in Mindanao. The missionaries, by and large, supported military undertakings; but what did they think of the men who executed the policies they approved?

During the Philippine-American War missionaries occasionally accused officers of scorning their efforts or of at least considering them to be disruptive. There were also some imputations about the officers' bad treatment of Filipinos. Methodist Bishop James Thoburn, for example, found General Robert P. Hughes, the provost marshal, "very bitter against Filipinos," while Baptists complained that military officials in Panay ignored their reports of atrocities committed by American soldiers.[22]

Such complaints, a minor theme during the war in any event, largely disappeared once the war ended, though Baptist W. O. Valentine contended in 1904 that military medical doctors were "far less considerate of missionaries than were the English physicians and surgeons in Burma." The Episcopalians felt a particular attachment to the military. They had quickly abandoned hopes for a large work among the Christianized Filipinos and concentrated their efforts among the American residents. The army proved to be the mainstay of their ministry in Manila and, later, in Zamboanga. "It is from the officers of the Army that the Church here has had the most loyal support from the very first until now," Brent wrote in 1902. Brent, in fact, received favored and courteous treatment from military officials, particularly when he undertook his numerous trips through the more remote regions of Luzon and Mindanao. During his sixteen years in the islands, the bishop never changed his mind about the military. His correspondence and published articles are replete with praise for military officialdom (though he later grew disenchanted with military policy in Mindanao) and amply support Alexander Zabriskie's judgment that "Brent was more attracted to the Army and Navy personnel than to any other Anglo-Saxons in the Philippines."[23]

None of the other missions was as dependent on the officers as was the Episcopalian, but often they too enjoyed close ties with the military. Robert F. Black, the first American Board representative, received special treatment from the military in Mindanao and was forever grateful to the military doctor who saved the life of his wife during childbirth.[24] Many of the missionaries commented with admiration on the character of individual army officers. Methodist Marvin Rader, for example, admired General Pershing's "Job-like patience" in dealing with Moros in Jolo, and he thought General J. Franklin Bell "a gentleman in every particular" who had the welfare of the Filipinos at heart. "He has been open, frank, and courteous to all classes of people," Rader wrote. At Malolos, Captain L. W. Cook spent the better part of one day showing Alliance representatives about Aguinaldo's former capital.[25] Presbyterian David S. Hibbard thought Admiral John C. Watson, who had succeeded George Dewey as commander of the Asiatic squadron, "a noble man and worthy of all the honor that his position can give him." A decade later George W. Wright, another Presbyterian, commented appreciatively on the cordiality of the commandant and other military officers he encountered in Albay.[26]

Missionaries, then, generally perceived the officers in a highly favorable light. Their attitude toward the common soldier, in marked contrast, was mixed, with unfavorable comments outweighing positive ones. As might be expected, the most favorable evaluation of the character of the common soldier came from Bishop Brent. Taking advantage of an opportunity in 1904 to walk "shoulder to shoulder with the common soldier" in Mindanao, the bishop found nothing to complain of except bad language. "Good order, respect for the property of others, cheerfulness reigned," he reported. "I found the men ready to receive frank language, and to respond to a moral appeal." He bitterly castigated the English writer John Foreman for writing in the *Atlantic Monthly* that "drunken brawls, indiscriminate revolver firings, indecent assaults on women, kicks and cuffs to any Filipino, burglary in broad day-light and thefts from shops and street vendors" were common soldierly occurrences.[27]

YMCA officials who worked closely with the soldiers inclined toward a favorable assessment as well, though they acknowledged the mixed character of the army and the enormous temptations that confronted young soldiers. As one Y official put it, "we are acquainted with the fact that the army is composed of all classes of men—men who have come from the lowest stations in life, placed on an equality with men possessing the dignity that God has endowed them with. The clean, honest life, cast into a low, filthy, degraded life, will become smerged and blighted unless a hard and continual effort is put forth to keep clean."[28]

Most missionaries thought the average soldier succumbed to temptation more often than not, especially to drink. Methodist J. L. McLaughlin recalled that when he arrived in Manila in 1900, the Escolta, a major commercial area, "was so full of tipsy soldiers we could scarcely get through." An Alliance representative estimated that only about ten percent of the soldiers were total abstainers, though he found less drunkenness than he expected. Methodist bishop Frank W. Warne was more pessimistic, estimating the number of teetotalers in the army at no more than five percent, a situation he ascribed primarily to the deleterious influence of the post canteen.[29] Though the missionaries were apparently successful in getting the canteen abolished, the results were problematical, since the soldiers simply purchased their drink at off-post establishments, many of them run by former servicemen. A YMCA official admitted that appeals for temperance had "borne less fruit in the Army and Navy especially in the Philippines than any where else on earth." As late as 1912 the Methodist committee on public morals complained that some intoxicated soldiers made "beasts of themselves."[30]

Beastly behavior manifested itself in ways other than excessive drinking. Several reports indicated cruel treatment of Filipinos. David S. Hibbard characterized the soldiers' treatment of the people as "brutal." In Manila,

Filipino coachmen reportedly preferred to haul Spaniards and their own countrymen, having learned from experience that American soldiers treated them and their ponies badly.[31] Prostitution was a problem with the army in the Philippines, as it must be with any army. Though American Board missionaries usually had high praise for the army's officialdom, they found that most soldiers in Davao had little use for missionaries, apparently because they had thwarted efforts to import Japanese prostitutes from Zamboanga. Soldiers also reportedly took advantage of Filipino women. "There has undoubtedly been wanton cruelty practiced on native women by enlisted soldiers, who married them, hiding in their hearts the cowardly intent to desert them whenever their regiments left the islands," reported Edwin S. Eby, a United Brethren missionary.[32] The plight of the children who resulted from such arrangements was pitiable. "These little ones have been left to a life that is worse than that of the natives," a Methodist missionary reported in 1909. Moved by their circumstances, he founded a small orphanage for mestizo children. Similarly, in Zamboanga, the strong-willed Hulda Lund of the Alliance mission devoted her considerable energies to establishing and operating a primary school for such children.[33]

In the missionary literature drunkenness, whoring, abusive language, cruelty toward Filipinos, and irreligiosity in general[34] come through strongly as common, if not altogether typical, traits of American soldiers. Bishop Brent might rail against John Foreman's depiction of the soldiers, yet the Englishman's description more accurately captured the usual missionary perception than did the bishop's apologia. To missionaries who considered native life degraded and wanted to help bring about a higher civilization, it was demoralizing to have the most numerous representatives of American culture living at a level akin to, if not below, that of the Filipinos. How could the white man's burden be carried out when some soldiers set "a fearful example . . . before the natives in drunkenness?" they asked. "Since I have lived in such close proximity to the boys in Khaki," wrote Charles F. Rath in Tacloban, "I am losing that pride in the men who represent the strength of the American Government. They are immoral, reckless, vulgar, and libertines, preying upon the people wherever they happen to be," he added. "The natives seeing the Government through the soldiers and some of the men in civil life certainly cannot form a very good opinion of the American people as a whole. As I look and see the flag of my country floating in the breeze which is the emblem of a christian government, and then look around me and see the men sent over here to represent us, I feel ashamed."[35]

As the military made American sovereignty effective, civilian rule increasingly replaced martial law. Soon civilians appeared in governmental posts across most of the archipelago. Just as missionaries generally stood behind military policy, they supported the purposes of the civilian government and wished the officials well. But how did they view the Americans who implemented and administered the programs?

In 1905 James B. Rodgers stated that most government officials worked "as hard and with motives as lofty and purposes as true as the best of our missionaries."[36] Rodgers, the dean of the Presbyterian mission and one of the earliest regularly accredited missionaries in the islands, had extensive contacts with all denominations in the Philippines. His views were respected, and no doubt his comments on the character of government officials reflected a widely held belief in the missionary community. The arrival of William Howard Taft, the first civil governor, was crucial in this respect, for Taft was a man of great probity who attracted respect. Had it been otherwise, the missionary attitude might have been different. As it was, the governor received accolades from the representatives of all denominations. A United Brethren missionary referred to him as "our honored Governor." A Baptist leader thought he could trust Taft to be "fair and right." Methodist Homer C. Stuntz was so attracted to Taft that he became an ardent political supporter.[37]

Taft was especially close to Bishop Brent. The two men first met in 1902 at St. John's Church in Washington shortly before Brent was to sail for the Philippines. "I like Governor Taft immensely," he wrote, and he made arrangements to travel with the governor to the islands. Once in the Philippines, Brent conversed often with the governor, counseled him personally, and sought his advice and assistance on a variety of matters. He was appalled at the thought that Taft might resign and return to the United States.[38]

After Taft left the Philippines in 1903 to become secretary of war, Brent corresponded regularly with him, a correspondence reflecting their mutual admiration. Brent sometimes expressed dissatisfaction with Taft's policies and more particularly with his administrative style,[39] but unlike some missionaries he never lost faith in Taft's personal qualities or questioned his integrity. "I believe heartily in Taft's sincerity," he wrote in November 1907, at a time when he was questioning some of Taft's policies, "more so than ever since his last visit to the Islands." He hoped that Taft would be the next president. "I should like to see the next President a man of poise who would not keep the country at too high a temperature," he wrote. "Taft I believe in and like. He has extraordinary personal influence, and I am sure would make a good chief executive."[40]

The governors who followed Taft were lesser men. But with the exception of James F. Smith, a Catholic who served from 1906 to 1909 and against whom the Protestants were unquestionably prejudiced, the missionaries commented favorably on all of them. The fact that Luke Wright,

Taft's successor, had a Catholic wife put the missionaries on their guard. But the Baptist leader thought him "a fair man," while the Seventh-day Adventists found him to be cordial and graceful, as would befit a Southern gentleman.[41] Wright's successor, Henry C. Ide, was said to be "an executive of the first order" who had "won the confidence of Americans and Filipinos alike of all parties and creeds." William Cameron Forbes, governor general from 1909 to 1913, disliked missionaries as a class and alienated many of them over the issue of gambling prior to his elevation to the governor generalship. But during the years he served as chief executive the missionary correspondence is remarkably free of negative comments about Forbes's character. For his part, the governor general maintained reasonably close relations with the YMCA and especially with Bishop Brent, with Brent, one senses, being the dominant figure in the relationship. "I believe he is going to leave his mark on the Islands for good," wrote Brent. "He has his own ideas, clean ideals & a firm hand."[42]

Francis Burton Harrison, who served as governor general from 1913 to 1921, arrived with two strikes against him, for he was a Democrat and an anti-imperialist with no colonial experience. His efforts to Filipinize the civil service with all deliberate speed increased missionary apprehensions, and there were occasional expressions of personal dislike as well. But Harrison tried hard to win over the missionaries. When in 1914 he learned that the Evangelical Union was about to meet in Manila, for example, he "very graciously" invited the delegates to attend a reception in Malacañan Palace, his official residence. The same year the governor general laid the cornerstone of the new YMCA building.[43] He communicated regularly with Bishop Brent; and when Methodist bishop William P. Eveland was accidentally killed, he expressed personally his deep sense of loss to the missionaries. Thus, in spite of disagreements over policy, Harrison succeeded in evoking a sympathetic personal response. Presbyterian J. Andrew Hall perhaps captured the missionary feeling toward Harrison best when he observed that he was "pleased with him as a man but I fear he is going to go too fast."[44]

The missionaries seem to have equally favorable opinions about most of the commissioners, provincial governors, and bureau chiefs. The reports of Bishop Brent and other Episcopalians, for example, provide substantial evidence. A trip in 1903 to Mountain Province led Brent to praise Lieutenant Governor T. M. Hunt, a physician, as a man who had "done untold good." On the same trip Brent found William Dinwiddie, governor of neighboring Lepanto Province, to be very hospitable.[45] Irving Spencer, who was for a time in charge of Episcopalian work in Mindanao, wrote that Governor E. C. Bolton of Davao possessed a good deal of "wisdom and energy" in carrying out his duties, especially with regard to the moun-

tain peoples, in whom the Episcopalians were particularly interested. Similarly, at the end of the period, Brent praised the governor of Kalinga, W. G.
Hale, for his "habit of industry, practical ability and common sense." Hale
was, he thought, "one of many Americans in the Philippines whose labors
will never be widely known in history but who belong to that sturdy, pioneer, uncompromising type of man, who by hidden service in rough conditions make the history of a country progressive."[46]

The provincial governor who evoked the most numerous compliments
was the very able Frank W. Carpenter, who was the chief executive of
Mindanao and Sulu from 1914 to 1920. Frank C. Laubach, the talented
American Board missionary in Mindanao, had great respect for Carpenter
as a man and as an administrator. Laubach thought that Carpenter was a
"strong friend" of the mission, but was in no sense partisan, and that he
would work just as quickly with Catholics "if they proved better instruments of civilization than we." Bishop Brent was even more effusive, paying the governor the supreme compliment of comparing him to the great
British colonial administrators in the Orient: Sir Stamford Raffles, Rajah
Brooke, and Sir Frank Swettenham. "His understanding of and sympathy
with the native give him a power which is never the fruit of mere policy,"
Brent wrote in 1918.[47]

Of the many bureau chiefs, the missionaries particularly praised David
Prescott Barrows, who served as director of education from 1903 to 1909.
The pastor of the American Presbyterian Church in Manila, who lived
across the street from Barrows, described him as "an earnest Christian
gentleman." A Baptist publication termed him "a gentleman of high character and scholarship," while Bishop Brent thought of him as "first-rate"
and "level headed."[48]

Government physicians were also the object of praise for their skill and
dedication. As early as 1903, for example, a Baptist missionary praised the
Insular Board of Health for its support of the mission's medical work (in
contrast to the unhelpful provincial board headed by a Filipino). A Presbyterian was "specially impressed by the high standards of those in control
of the medical affairs of the Islands." Government doctors were, he thought,
"of a far higher quality both professionally and morally than is the case in
similar positions in most American cities."[49]

Perhaps the best known of the government medical doctors was Najeeb M.
Saleeby. Saleeby was born in Syria in 1870, received a medical education in
the United States, served as an army surgeon during the Spanish-American
War, and was appointed assistant chief of the Bureau of Non-Christian
Tribes in the Philippines then headed by David Prescott Barrows. Soon he
was appointed director of education for Moro Province. Bishop Brent was
immediately attracted to Saleeby, who he found was sympathetic to the

Moros, a skilled surgeon, and an indefatigable worker. In 1905 he convinced Saleeby to take over Episcopalian work in Manila, and in 1907 Saleeby joined the Church. "I do not believe there is any doubt that he is the man we have been waiting for," wrote Brent; "indeed, I never hoped to secure a man of his calibre and standing."[50]

In sum, the missionaries accorded high praise to most governors and other officials of high rank. But there was another side of their attitude. In stark contrast to James B. Rodgers's contention that officials were missionary-like in their motives and personal conduct, a prominent YMCA official, J. M. Groves, wrote that "a large number of the Government servants in the Philippines . . . seem to be here chiefly, if not solely, to make all the money they can in a short time, and while they are making it they have very little use for the 'Little Brown Brother.'" Written at a time when the Y served Americans exclusively, Groves's opinion deserves respect equal to Rodgers's. Nor was his perception unique. Methodist Bishop Oldham, for example, contended that some government servants "think of themselves above the people; we [missionaries] must be of them." Ernest Lyons found a similar attitude among government officials in northern Luzon, officials who claimed, he wrote, that "there are no sincerely righteous people among the Filipinos," a claim Lyons thought foolish.[51]

In addition to racial arrogance, missionaries also found that many government officials led immoral lives. H. W. Widdoes recalled that officials in the area he served drank and organized dances. In Davao, Robert Black's outspoken opposition to the importation of Japanese prostitutes seems to have angered civilian officials, as well as the soldiers.[52] Frank Laubach complained that the moral lives of American officials (and other Americans) were worse than those of the Philippine hill people, whom he admired. He was especially critical of officials who cohabited with Filipino women. A Baptist missionary summed it up best. "The lives of our American official class," he wrote, "are not always what we would like."[53]

There was, then, a mixed judgment on the character of American officialdom. To some extent these contradictory assessments no doubt resulted from the personal qualities of the various officials. They may also reflect the missionaries' attitude toward the Catholic officials who, they tended to believe, were almost by nature immoral. More often the higher level officials evoked missionary praise for their private character, their moral uprightness. Even the detested Dean C. Worcester was disliked more for the policies he pursued than for defects of character; and he eventually inspired respect. On the other hand, accounts that reflected poorly on the private lives of government officials seldom named individuals, suggesting that the unflattering observations applied mostly to lower level officers.

One group of American civil servants, the teachers, deserves more extended analysis, since the missionaries were greatly interested in the American educational experiment. Americans had traditionally placed great stock in education. This sense was reflected, perhaps even enhanced, among missionaries. This was partly due to the missionaries' view of the intrinsic value of education in developing the individual, partly due also to the need for literacy to read and understand the Scriptures, partly due (especially in the Philippines) to the desire to undercut the traditional Roman Catholicism of the populace, and partly due to a burning desire among most missionaries to impart the best of American traditions and culture to the new wards. Consequently, the missionaries viewed the teachers as the most important group of Americans in the islands, outside of themselves. Fanning out across the archipelago, placed in towns and barrios, as well as in major cities, the teachers were "in a position to do more for the immediate social condition than the missionary." More than anyone else, teachers could be "the white civilizers, moralizers and demoralizers of their respective towns."[54] The teacher, then, was a person of great importance who could do great good or irreparable harm.

Indicative of their belief in the importance of the teachers, some missionaries actually served in the public schools. Hulda Lund of the Alliance mission taught in the Zamboanga schools. Episcopalian John A. Staunton, Jr., served as deputy superintendent of the schools in Cebu in 1902. Herbert M. Damon and his wife, semi-official representatives of the Free Methodist mission board (and soon to be assigned as official missionaries to India), taught in Laoag.

Of all definable groups of Americans in the islands, the teachers elicited the warmest comments from the missionaries. "Hundreds of devoted American school teachers are enduring hardships and privations, giving the best part of their lives and the best part of themselves to the Filipino youth and children," a YMCA official wrote; he added, "And the results are truly marvelous." Methodist Bishop Eveland thought that by 1915 the accomplishments of the teachers were "remarkable."[55] A Baptist thought the teachers "a fine lot of people and . . . the best representatives of true Americanism" in the Philippines. Bishop Brent was deeply impressed by teachers he met in Mindanao and in the central highlands of Luzon. "I have met but one whom I distrusted," he wrote.[56] A Presbyterian missionary couple wrote that "all the American teachers are excellent people and are doing a great work," while a Seventh-day Adventist thought many of the teachers were "among the brightest young people America produces."[57]

Missionaries were perforce thrown into contact with teachers. On their rounds, especially in the rural areas, missionaries regularly lodged with them. "What would the missionary do in many instances out in distant place[s], were it not for the friendly American school teacher . . . ?" asked

Presbyterian Charles R. Hamilton. "It is not sufficiently recognized," he added, ". . . how much of a missionary the American teacher in the Philippines is, going, as he often does, to the remote regions, the only white man in the locality, amid conditions sufficiently lonely, and providing a place where the wayfarer may find a hearty American welcome, while carrying perhaps more than his share of the 'White Man's Burden' in his duty toward the 'little brown brothers.'"[58] Out of such experiences, close relationships often developed.[59]

An important reason for the positive image teachers evoked in the missionary mind was the fact that most of them were Protestants.[60] Teachers who took part in Protestant activities naturally received high praise. In 1901, for example, a Presbyterian missionary reported favorably on the participation of teachers in the Thanksgiving service. One teacher was so overcome by the beauty of the event that he nearly wept; another sent an account of the service to the *Outlook*.[61] Teachers who distributed Bibles to their students, held Bible study sessions in their homes, or attempted to proselytize in other ways received the highest plaudits. Those missionaries who resented the government's insistence on religious neutrality in the schools particularly admired those teachers who resisted or even sabotaged the policy.[62]

Indicative of the importance missionaries attributed to teachers of high character, several attempted to recruit suitable Protestants for vacancies in the school system. While on leave in the United States, for example, United Brethren Ernest J. Pace "endeavored everywhere to line up Christian young men for the school department in the P.I. as indispensable factors in the success of our national project there." Eric Lund pleaded with American Baptists to send teachers. "The influence of the Christian teacher is incalculable," he wrote. "We Baptists have hundreds of them, nay thousands. Why should we not as a denomination do all in our power to fill the Islands with worthy Christian teachers?"[63]

Once in the islands some missionaries actively worked to convert the teachers. The Seventh-day Adventists made the most vigorous efforts. Soon after their arrival in the islands, they began sending *Signs of the Times* and other Adventist publications to all American teachers.[64] The results were less than overwhelming. "Continually we received postal notices giving information that the papers laid at the P.O. and were refused," an Adventist reported; and "Some personal letters were sent refusing the paper." Consequently the Adventists discontinued mailing literature to all teachers and concentrated their efforts on Filipinos, who seemed more receptive.[65] Still they continued to work with American teachers whenever possible. Ironically, when the occasional conversion occurred, the convert was placed in a difficult position, since teachers were expected to work a half-day on Saturday. The true Adventist was thus forced to end his teaching career, since he could not in good conscience work on the Adventist Sabbath.[66]

Though missionaries generally praised the teachers, they also made critical assessments. As Eric Lund put it, "the medal has its reverse." Since the missionaries almost invariably defined Americanism as Protestant, Roman Catholic teachers were usually perceived as a threat. Arthur W. Prautch complained that an American teacher at Villasis taught Catholicism in the classroom, tried to force other teachers to do so as well, and insisted that all students attend mass. Harry Farmer complained of precisely the same thing at Manaog. In Cebu the Presbyterians complained that the American teachers hobnobbed "with the padres a good deal." And Frank Laubach, one of the very few who questioned the value of the public school system, did so largely because of the Catholic teachers, "who fear us, and do what they can to keep the children away from our influence."[67]

Aside from the Catholicism of some teachers, missionaries sometimes complained about what Eric Lund termed "unclean" behavior. "I was once a newspaper boy in the States and heard the language of the saloons," one American told Lund, "but I never heard such filthy language as at a gathering of school teachers at H., Philippines." Such teachers, Lund thought, were "vile and a disgrace to themselves and to the nation they represent." Similarly, in Paniqui, Harry Farmer encountered a teacher who had gained the ill will of his colleagues when he refused to join them in orgies. Robert W. Carter reported in 1909 that the last three teachers assigned to Maasin were heavy drinkers, while the Disciples publication complained that too often teachers had followed and not led when it came to social activities. In particular, they had often "fostered the dance with its questionable accompaniments and downward pull."[68]

The missionaries thought that immoral activity of this sort resulted from at least three causes. Given the allegedly loose moral climate of the tropical Philippines, it was easy to succumb to the manifold temptations. Some missionaries also blamed the religiously neutral posture of the government. They thought such a policy tended to drive dedicated Christian teachers out of the system and, in any event, discouraged moral and religious instruction.[69] Finally, missionaries commonly ascribed immorality among teachers to the influence of their Catholic colleagues and supervisors. Admitting that the Bureau of Education had the lowest percentage of dismissals for immorality of all government agencies in the islands, Lewis B. Hilles pointed out that most of those dismissed on such grounds were part of "a lot of R.C. teachers sent over a few years ago." Similarly, a Disciples missionary complained that a Catholic supervisor prohibited

Protestant teachers from carrying on Bible study in their own homes while at the same time tolerating "drunkenness, gambling and whoremongering in other teachers."[70]

In sum, the missionary assessment of Americans living in the Philippines was mixed at best. The first missionaries fully expected to find a substantial contingent of disreputable Americans, and they were not disappointed. The adventurers withdrew after a time or settled down. But the missionaries continued to turn a skeptical eye toward members of the business community. Military officers and high-level civilian officials were praised, while common soldiers and lower-level bureaucrats were often disparaged. Teachers were thought to lead lives of a higher moral quality than other groups of Americans in the islands, but Roman Catholics and the irreligious and immoral minority among them evoked only scorn.

At first glance such an assessment is paradoxical, for the missionaries were disposed to applaud the larger objectives of the American military and civil government that followed. The government, they assumed, was bringing to the people a new and superior civilization. Yet the representatives of the superior culture often seemed to belie the altruistic rhetoric.

To be sure, the missionaries were well aware that evil existed even in the United States, despite the views of committed Protestants that the country, more than any other, embodied values consonant with the divine will. Drunks, gamblers, and atheists were not foreign to America's shores. But the disreputable element seemed to arrive in the Philippines in disproportionate numbers; and the consequences, the missionaries thought, were potentially tragic. Their very presence called into question American claims of cultural superiority, and their existence threatened to corrupt totally a culture which the missionaries considered already in a deplorable state. How could the United States preach the white man's burden in good faith and succeed in lifting up the people under these conditions? How could the missionaries transform a benighted culture with far too many equally benighted Americans at hand? For the committed missionary of that age, it was a challenge of the first order.

10

Conclusion

The first generation of Protestant missionaries in the Philippines reflected the certainty of nineteenth-century American Protestantism. Drawn to missionary service through the Moody revivals, the YMCA, the Student Volunteer Movement, or other missionary support organizations, most believed intensely in the righteousness of their calling. Doubt and skepticism were alien to their character. As strong-willed individuals, they found it difficult to welcome opposing views. Given these realities, the comity arrangements that emerged were little short of miraculous. But these came about mostly due to the generous nature of a few important mission leaders. The rank and file was less enthusiastic, and in any event there were internal conflicts in several of the missions, as well as acrimonious disputes among different missions.

Cultural relativism was an equally foreign concept to most missionaries; Filipino society, with its Malay and Spanish roots, therefore seemed backward and debased. Most Filipinos were Roman Catholic Christians, to be sure, but Protestant missionaries of that age viewed Catholicism, particularly the Hispanic variety, as at best a corrupted form of the faith. Consequently Filipinos could not expect their Church to be of much assistance in upgrading the society. On the contrary, missionaries believed (especially at first) that the Catholic Church in the Philippines, whatever its contributions in previous centuries, was very much a cause of the weak and degraded culture they perceived when they arrived in the islands.

But the missionaries believed implicitly in the possibilities of spiritual and cultural regeneration, and they were confident of their own ability to transform individual Filipinos and the society as a whole. Conversion to their faith was the first step. Finding many of the people only nominal Catholics and others alienated from the Church, the missionaries anticipated great results. "The fields are white for the harvest" was a common refrain. They also applauded the work of the American military and civilian authorities who, at their best, were also intent on bringing the Filipinos into the modern age by introducing efficient, secular government, mass education, new cultural norms, and economic development.

Most missionaries felt that the transformation of society would require a considerable period of time, and consequently they resisted calls for political independence. The culture was too immature and unchristian, they surmised, to sustain a viable and just government without close supervision. Decades of dedicated work by missionaries and American colonial officials would be necessary before such an experiment should be contemplated. But together they could uplift the people so that at some undefined point in the future Filipinos could assume more responsibility for their own destiny.

Although the missionaries considered themselves allies of the government in the difficult task of encouraging cultural change, they often judged themselves truer believers in the white man's burden than government officials. The colonial administration, they often felt, was too prone to make unwise concessions to the demands of Filipino politicians. Thus, for example, the missionaries regretted the creation of the Philippine Assembly in 1907. The government also occasionally pursued policies that conflicted with Protestant norms. When the army established canteens or when the Philippine commissioners appeared to sanction gambling, the wrath of the missionaries knew no bounds. Such decisions not only contravened Protestant ideals but, more important, set a poor example for the country's new wards and set back the day of cultural transformation. The white man's burden was a heavy responsibility, and when the government was tempted to lay it down, the missionaries stood forth as the conscience of the American community (just as the friars had been in the early years of the Spanish occupation). American colonialism, they insisted, must be steadfast to bring about a transformed society, to create a New Filipino.

Did American colonialism create a New Filipino? There is no clear consensus among scholars concerning how substantial the American impact was on Philippine society and culture. Peter W. Stanley argues that the Philippine-American encounter "has been a major determinant of [Filipino] political, social, cultural, and economic development."[1] But others have minimized the American impact. Preexisting patterns of political and social leadership, for example, survived American rule largely intact, despite the institutional innovations the Americans brought. The forms changed, but the substance remained unaffected. Even the much heralded, American-designed system of public education, it has been argued, produced only superficial change, in spite of the fact that it was undeniably staffed and directed by idealistic Americans who almost desperately wanted to transform the culture along American lines. "In the long run," writes

Glenn May, "American attempts at social engineering did not produce fundamental change."[2]

A thorough analysis of the American impact on Philippine society and culture is an extraordinarily complex task and is well beyond the scope of this study. It does seem clear, however, that the Americans produced some lasting changes, superficial though they may be. Today, even the casual visitor to the Philippines is aware that, despite nearly four decades of national independence, American popular culture remains important in Philippine life. Santa Claus is a part of the Christmas celebration. *I'm Dreaming of a White Christmas* is a favorite holiday song in the snowless islands. Sounds of the latest American pop recordings compete noisily with Tagalog hits in the colorful Jeepneys of Manila. Prestige is more often associated with the ownership of American produced goods than with identical items manufactured in the Philippines.

At a deeper level, English remains the language of the schools, universities, courts, and the larger newspapers. English is used, to be sure, with various Filipino nuances that distinguish it from American English. Nevertheless, the continuing pervasiveness of the English language surely carries with it important cultural baggage that, to some degree, has been absorbed by the general populace.

Democracy is another case in point. Filipino attachment to democratic values—something that was apparent to all observers until President Ferdinand Marcos's declaration of martial law in 1972—is not entirely the result of American rule. The pre-Hispanic Philippines may have been proto-democratic, and the liberal reformers of the late nineteenth century urged Spain to move in a more democratic direction. Nevertheless, the Americans imposed a democratic political system (albeit with limitations and within the context of a colonial system) and made some gestures toward making the society more socially democratic as well. The interest of Filipinos in democracy certainly owes something to their American past.

None of these American inheritances has gone unchallenged. There are constant criticisms of the Filipino "colonial mentality," with nationalistically minded Filipinos urging their countrymen to reject American culture. A new national language has been introduced. The public school system has been attacked as uniquely incompatible with Filipino culture.[3] Finally, President Marcos destroyed the political system that was inherited from the Americans, arguing in part that American democracy was unsuited to Philippine conditions, and he replaced it with an authoritarian form of parliamentarianism.

The very fact that Filipino cultural nationalists have attacked their countrymen's attachment to these various Americanisms, however, suggests that many of them have been deeply absorbed into the culture. As for the political change, many segments of the society, anxious about the society's stability and cohesiveness, initially welcomed martial law. But as conditions worsened, many Filipinos began to call for a return to American-style democracy; and exiles, calling for American pressure on the Marcos regime, were fond of reminding Americans that they had taught the Filipinos democracy in the first place.

What, then, was the impact of the missionaries? As is the case with American colonialism in general, it is extremely difficult to make definitive judgments. Some things can be said, however. Compared with the meager results Christian missionaries usually achieved in Asian countries, the number of converts was striking. By 1925 there were approximately 105,000 members of churches begun by the missionaries.[4]

Impressive as the number of conversions was, however, it fell far short of the initial euphoric anticipations. In 1904, for example, Homer Stuntz predicted that there would be 500,000 Filipino Methodists alone within twenty years.[5] In part the results were not greater because of the inability of the boards to send more missionaries than they did. Thus, for example, the American Board had one missionary family on the entire island of Mindanao. Their work was supplemented by the small Peniel mission in Zamboanga and a token Episcopalian presence in the same city. Large results could hardly be expected under such circumstances. In addition, in some areas at least, the people proved to be surprisingly loyal to their historic church. Presbyterians on Leyte, for example, might as well have been in China, considering the few converts they made in the early years. Also damaging to the Protestant cause was the failure of the schismatic Philippine Independent Church to make deeper inroads than it did among the Roman Catholic population. Though the Independent Church at one time had as much as one-third of the nation behind it, it faded rapidly, particularly after a Supreme Court decision in 1906 allowed the Roman Church to regain control of property seized by the schismatics. Another factor in the inability of Protestants to attract a larger percentage of the people to their banner was the fact that the Roman Catholic Church instituted reforms in a quiet way which remedied some of the abuses that had alienated segments of the populace.

In addition, most missionaries, reflecting the intellectual milieu of the late nineteenth century, displayed condescending, paternalistic, and sometimes racist attitudes toward Filipinos. Though their attitudes in this regard were no worse (and perhaps were more enlightened) than those of other American colonialists, their openly expressed skepticism of Filipino capacity may well have hindered their efforts to convert the people. Such attitudes were especially noticeable in the missionary response to expressions of Filipino nationalism. Although most missionaries hoped eventually to produce self-governing and self-supporting churches, they could, at first, scarcely imagine Filipinos in leadership positions anytime soon. Thus they deplored Filipino-led schisms, which they blamed on ambitious, immature, and corrupt men. The Aglipayano schism from the Roman Church evoked a more complex reaction, since it weakened their historic antagonist. But many were suspicious of a Filipino-controlled church of any description and considered the self-proclaimed bishop of the Independent Church a radical nationalist and something of a charlatan.

In any event, only about three percent of the present-day population traces its religious roots directly to Protestant missionaries. That is, however, well over a million Filipinos, a number nearly as large as that of the Muslims; and it is a commonplace belief that Protestants have exerted a disproportionate influence at many levels of society.[6] Some impressionistic observers credit Protestantism with raising the moral tenor of society, with fostering a respect for law and education, and for inculcating such "Protestant values" as frugality and social equality. It has even been claimed that Protestantism increased respect for women, the family, and the elderly. But objective studies are scarce, and further investigation may show that the missionaries had only a limited impact on the larger society.[7]

The Episcopalian effort in Luzon's Mountain Province in the four decades prior to World War II is a case in point. At Sagada, Bontoc, Baguio, and later at Besao and Balbalasang, the Episcopalians converted thousands of mountaineers to their faith. Other thousands sought treatment in Episcopalian dispensaries, while hundreds matriculated through their schools. As a result of the Episcopalian presence, many individual lives were significantly changed. It also appears that a certain amount of cultural change in the larger context took place, such as, for example, the new converts' challenge to traditional superstitions and customs in matters like marriage and burial that they felt conflicted with Christian values.

Yet, doubts about the missionaries' effectiveness remained. In 1920 the new bishop wrote to his board that "we have to record more failure than success."[8] And those working directly in the mountain areas increasingly complained about the deep-rooted paganism of the Igorots that seemed impervious to significant outside influence. Reports of backsliding also increased. Countless Igorots, they reported, were only nominal Christians who continued their pagan ways behind the backs of the missionaries.[9]

Of course the Episcopal experience was not altogether typical, because the missionaries were working with the small non-Christian minority. Other missions working among the lowlanders may have had a greater impact in certain respects. Throughout the colonial period, the Protestant churches in the Philippines were organically tied to their American counterparts. American churchmen visited the islands regularly. The most promising Filipino pastors and educators studied at institutions of higher learning in the United States. Only after national independence arrived did the major Protestant churches achieve an independent status, notably with the merger of several missionary-founded churches to establish the United Church of Christ in the Philippines (UCCP) in 1948. Even today, however, the UCCP retains close ties with American church-related organizations, and the United Methodist Church in the Philippines is still officially connected with the American branch. As late as 1973–74, in fact, an American United Methodist bishop exercised temporary ecclesiastical authority over the crisis-torn Philippine Church.

Nationalistic resentments did sometimes erupt against American missionaries, resulting in important schisms. But the bulk of the congregations remained loyal, and a fascination with America was a notable attribute of prominent Filipino Protestant clergymen.[10] Although many church leaders today are concerned about the Filipino "colonial mentality," Filipino clergymen continue, at times, to express themselves in language resembling that of the early missionaries. Three United Methodist bishops, for example, all active in the 1970s, have written that the American occupation of the Philippines was providential. President McKinley, the distinguished clergyman D. D. Alejandro writes, brought "a new day for religious liberty and freedom of conscience in the Philippine Islands, a country long enslaved by a so-called Christian church, utterly selfish, intolerant and unscriptural in its practices."[11] If Filipino Protestants can accept missionary-inspired notions of providential history, is it not reasonable to assume that they also absorbed important American values championed by missionaries?

The influence of the missionaries may, in the long run, have reinforced the larger American effort to make Philippine society more democratic, politically and socially. The missionaries hoped, for example, that the public schools would release the masses from an allegedly enslaving caciquismo and outmoded patterns of thought. They disliked Hispanic Catholicism in part because they thought it exploited the people and kept them dependent.

To be sure, the missionaries were paternalistic and resisted calls for Filipino control of governmental and other institutions, including their own missions. Nevertheless, they quickly trained Filipino pastors and church workers who, in turn, increasingly insisted on being included in policy-making bodies. Within a few years most of the missions had given in, at least to some extent. Furthermore, Protestant churches, with their sessions or administrative boards, involved members in running the affairs of the local churches. Such involvement provided some degree of practical experience in democracy, surely more so than had been possible in the Catholic Church. In sum, the efforts of the missionaries tended toward the breaking down of social stratification and the development of individual potential.

The Filipino Protestant response to President Marcos's martial-law regime is instructive with respect to the possible impact of the missionaries. In ending the democratic system that had been in place since 1946 (in important respects since 1935), Marcos promised to reduce crime and corruption, to institute land reform, and to speed economic development. The two largest Protestant churches—the United Church of Christ in the Philippines and the United Methodist Church—joined many other Filipinos in greeting the declaration of martial law with at least cautious enthusiasm. But as the promises failed to result in meaningful reform, while civil liberties remained in abeyance, support for the administration eroded, especially within the UCCP. In 1978 its quadrennial assembly condemned martial law and called for a restoration of democratic liberties. Since the assassination of Senator Benigno Aquino in August 1983, human rights activists within the Church have openly called for the president's resignation.[12]

The United Methodist Church was slower to take issue with the Marcos regime, but in 1979 a Methodist bishop introduced a motion at the assembly of the National Council of Churches in the Philippines that called for the lifting of martial rule. The motion passed. With the assassination of Aquino the Methodists put even more distance between themselves and President Marcos. Perhaps the missionaries were more effective agents of American democratic principles than either they or the government ever imagined.[13]

Notes

KEY TO ABBREVIATIONS IN NOTES

American Board Mission Records
Philippines Mission Correspondence and Reports, American Board of Commissioners for Foreign Missions, Houghton Library, Harvard University.

Baptist Mission Records (followed by appropriate microfilm reel number)
Correspondence and Reports, American Baptist Missionary Union, American Baptist Historical Society, Rochester, New York.

B.I.A. Records (followed by appropriate file number)
Records of the Bureau of Insular Affairs Relating to the Philippine Islands 1898–1935, National Archives, Washington, D.C.

Brent Papers
Papers of Charles Henry Brent, Manuscript Division, Library of Congress, Washington, D.C.

Doltz Papers
Papers of Paul Doltz, Presbyterian Historical Society, Philadelphia, Pennsylvania.

Episcopal Mission Records
Philippine Mission Correspondence and Reports, Episcopal Church, Archives and Historical Collections of the Episcopal Church, Austin, Texas.

Ferrer Papers
Papers of Cornelio M. Ferrer, United Methodist Archives, Lake Junaluska, North Carolina.

Forbes Papers
Papers of William Cameron Forbes, Houghton Library, Harvard University.

Free Methodist Mission Records
Records of the General Missionary Board, free Methodist Church, Free Methodist World Headquarters, Winona Lake, Indiana.

Mrs. Harry Farmer Materials
Mrs. Harry Farmer Materials, Record Group 43, box 339, United Methodist Archives, Lake Junaluska, North Carolina.

Johnston Papers
Papers of Mercer Green Johnston, Manuscript Division, Library of Congress, Washington, D.C.

Kershner Papers
Papers of Bruce L. Kershner, Disciples of Christ Historical Society, Nashville, Tennessee.

Methodist Mission Records

Philippine Mission Correspondence and Reports, Methodist-Episcopal Church, United Methodist Archives, Lake Junaluska, North Carolina.

Parrish Papers

Papers of Rebecca Parrish, in the possession of United Methodist Bishop Paul Locke A. Granadosin, Baguio, Philippine Islands.

Presbyterian Mission Records (followed by the appropriate microfilm reel number)

Presbyterian Church, U.S.A. Board of Foreign Missions. Record Group 85. Secretaries' file, Philippine Mission Correspondence and Reports, 1898–1910. Microfilm series, reels 287–89. Presbyterian Historical Society, Philadelphia, Pennsylvania.

Presbyterian Mission Records 1911–21 (followed by the appropriate box and file number)

Presbyterian Church, U.S.A. Board of Foreign Missions. Record Group 85. Philippine Mission Correspondence and Reports, 1911–21. Presbyterian Historical Society, Philadelphia, Pennsylvania.

Seventh-day Adventist Records

Archives of the General Conference of Seventh-day Adventists, Washington, D.C.

Taft Papers (followed by the appropriate microfilm reel number)

Papers of William Howard Taft, Manuscript Division, Library of Congress, Washington, D.C.

United Brethren Mission Records

United Brethren Board of Missions. Philippine Islands, 1907–22. Correspondence and Reports, File 10-VI. United Methodist Archives, Lake Junaluska, North Carolina.

YMCA Records

Records of the Young Men's Christian Association, Historical Library of the YMCA, New York.

CHAPTER I

1. Benito Legarda, Jr., "American Enterprise in the Nineteenth-century Philippines," *Explorations in Entrepreneurial History* 9 (February 1957): 156. For another discussion of early American contacts with the Philippines, see William H. Gray, "First Constitution of the Philippines," *Pacific Historical Review* 26 (November 1957): 341–51.

2. There was some scientific interest in the islands. See Dean C. Worcester, *The Philippine Islands and Their People* (New York: Macmillan, 1898), and Martha C. Bray, "The Minnesota Academy of Natural Sciences," *Minnesota History* 39 (1964): 111–22.

3. Quoted in Bradford Perkins, *The Great Rapprochement: England and the United States, 1895–1914* (New York: Atheneum, 1968), pp. 70–71. See also Richard Hofstadter, "Manifest Destiny and the Philippines," in *America in Crisis*, ed. Daniel Aaron (New York: Alfred A. Knopf, 1952).

4. John A. S. Grenville and George B. Young, *Politics, Strategy, and American Diplomacy: Studies in Foreign Policy, 1873–1917* (New Haven: Yale University Press, 1966), pp. 267–96.

5. Charles S. Olcott, *The Life of William McKinley*, 2 vols. (Boston: Houghton Mifflin Company, 1916), 2:111.

6. Julius W. Pratt, *Expansionists of 1898: The Acquisition of Hawaii and the Spanish Islands* (Baltimore: Johns Hopkins Press, 1936), pp. 279–316.

7. See, for example, Horacio de la Costa, *The Jesuits in the Philippines 1581–1768* (Cambridge: Harvard University Press, 1967), pp. 15–36; and J. Gayo Aragon, "The Controversy over Justification of Spanish Rule in the Philippines," in *Studies in Philippine Church History*, ed. Gerald H. Anderson (Ithaca: Cornell University Press, 1969), pp. 3–21.

8. Horacio de la Costa, "The Development of the Native Clergy in the Philippines," in *Studies in Philippine Church History*, ed. Anderson, pp. 65–104.

9. Cesar Adib Majul, "Anticlericalism during the Reform Movement and the Philippine Revolution," ibid., p. 166.

10. Conrad Myrick, "Some Aspects of the British Occupation of Manila," ibid., pp. 113–30.

11. T. Valentino Sitoy, Jr., "Nineteenth Century Evangelical Beginnings in the Philippines," *South East Asia Journal of Theology* 9 (October 1967): 45.

12. T. Valentino Sitoy, Jr., "An Aborted Spanish Protestant Mission to the Philippines," *Silliman Journal* 15 (1968): 243–80.

13. John Marvin Dean, *The Cross of Christ in Bolo-land* (Chicago and New York: Fleming H. Revell Co., 1902), p. 44.

14. Jay C. Goodrich, *Bible Work in the Philippine Islands* ([New York]: American Bible Society, 1901), p. 11; copy in Harry N. Cole Papers, Michigan Historical Collections, Ann Arbor.

15. Dorothy U. Compagno, "Distribution in the Philippine Islands, 1898–1932," American Bible Society Historical Essay #15, part VI-J, 1967, American Bible Society Archives, New York.

16. James M. Thoburn, *India and Malaysia* (Cincinnati: Cranston & Curts, 1892), pp. 502–4.

17. Cornelia Chillson Moots, *Pioneer "Americanas"; or, First Methodist Missionaries in the Philippines* (n.p.: By the author, 1903), p. 12; Homer C. Stuntz, *The Philippines and the Far East* (Cincinnati: Jennings & Pye, 1904), p. 434.

18. Frank C. Laubach, *The People of the Philippines: Their Religious Progress and Preparation for Spiritual Leadership in the Far East* (New York: George H. Doran Co., 1925), pp. 183, 482.

19. William H. Lingle to Frank F. Ellinwood, January 17, 1899, Presbyterian Mission Records, reel 287. James B. Rodgers, *Forty Years in the Philippines: A History of the Philippine Mission of the Presbyterian Church in the United States of America, 1899–1939* (New York: Board of Foreign Mission of the Presbyterian Church in the United States of America, 1940), p. 2.

20. Laubach, *People of the Philippines*, p. 482; Rodgers, *Forty Years in the Philippines*, pp. 201–2.

21. Stuntz, *Philippines and the Far East*, p. 465.

22. Henry W. Munger, "The Beginning of Baptist Work in the Philippines: Fore-runners of the Missionaries," *The Chronicle* 19 (October 1956): 169–72.

23. The best evidence as to the Peniel mission's beginning in Zamboanga comes from McKee, who wrote in 1903 that the mission opened "last summer." John McKee, "Alliance Missions," *Christian and Missionary Alliance* 31 (October 31, 1903): 307. See also Robert F. Black to Judson Smith, December 27, 1902, American Board Mission Records. On the independent missionaries, see David L. Rambo, "The Christian and Missionary Alliance in the Philippines, 1901–70" (Ph.D. diss., New York University, 1974), pp. 58–61, which is based in part on interviews with the son of one of the first missionaries to affiliate with the Peniel group.

24. Laubach, *People of the Philippines*, p. 193.

25. Ibid., p. 483.

26. Ibid., p. 484.

27. For a brief account of the Damons' experience in the Philippines, see Woman's Missionary Society, Free Methodist Church, *Lighting the Philippine Frontier* (Winona Lake, Ind.: Light & Life Press, 1956), pp. 23–24. According to this publication, the Damons were officially recognized as Free Methodist missionaries in the Philippines in 1907. In 1908 they returned to the United States. The following year they went to India under the Free Methodist Board.

28. Frank P. Thornton to O. L. Ingalls (copy), January 18, 1907, Johnston Papers, box 38. Charles W. Briggs, *The Progressing Philippines* (Philadelphia: Griffith & Rowland Press, 1913), p. 135.

CHAPTER 2

1. See, for example, Robert T. Handy, *A Christian America: Protestant Hopes and Historical Realities* (New York: Oxford University Press, 1971), passim.

2. The classic statement of the influence of humanitarian sentiment on American policy of the 1890s is in Pratt, *Expansionists of 1898*.

3. Gerald H. Anderson, "Providence and Politics behind Protestant Missionary Beginnings in the Philippines," in *Studies in Philippine Church History*, ed. Anderson, pp. 279–300.

4. James B. Rodgers, "One Score Years," in *Twenty Years of Presbyterian Work in the Philippines* (n.p., n.d.), p. 9 (an address Rodgers delivered before the Presbyterian Mission Board in New York on October 29, 1919).

5. Valentin H. Rabe, *The Home Base of American China Missions 1880–1920* (Cambridge: Council on East Asian Studies, Harvard University, 1978), pp. 87–93; Paul A. Varg, *Missionaries, Chinese, and Diplomats: The American Protestant Missionary Movement in China, 1890–1952* (Princeton: Princeton University Press, 1958), pp. 52–61.

6. Rabe, *Home Base*, pp. 92–93.

7. For example, Milton H. Schutz to the corresponding secretary of the Methodist Episcopal Board of Foreign Missions, May 1, 1907, Methodist Mission Records; William A. Guerry, "From Western Texas to the Philippines," *Spirit of Missions* 68 (August 1903): 567; B. O. Peterson, "My Christian Experience," manuscript accom-

panying his application of August 27, 1903, Methodist Mission Records; Harry Farmer to the Missionary Board of the Methodist Episcopal Church, December 29, 1903, Methodist Mission Records.

8. Guerry, "From Western Texas to the Philippines," p. 567; application of C. F. Hartzell, Methodist Mission Records; Daniel H. Klinefelter to Adna B. Leonard, September 1, 1904, ibid.; Marvin A. Rader to Homer C. Stuntz, December 15, 1902, ibid.; Grace Myrtle Edmonson to Leonard, ibid. (A. L. Snyder folder); Herbert M. Damon to B. Winget, August 8, 1908, Free Methodist Mission Records.

9. "A Call to the Philippine Islands," *Christian and Missionary Alliance* 36 (June 3, 1911): 151, 155, 158.

10. Arthur J. Brown, *The Why and How of Foreign Missions*, 3d ed. (New York: Laymen's Missionary Movement, 1908), pp. 6–11; *Spirit of Missions* 44 (August 1929): 529.

11. Brown, *Why and How of Foreign Missions*, pp. 13–14; Rabe, *Home Base*, pp. 102–103.

12. Damon to Winget, August 8, 1908, Free Methodist Mission Records.

13. Bessie White, "God's Providence in the Entering of the Philippines," *Christian and Missionary Alliance* 25 (September 1, 1900): 118; McKee, "Alliance Missions," p. 303; Hulda C. Lund, "Southern Philippines," *Alliance Weekly* 37 (December 30, 1911): 200.

14. A declining concern with saving the "perishing heathen" was also apparent among English missionaries in the late nineteenth century. See Stuart Piggin, "Assessing Nineteenth-Century Missionary Motivation: Some Considerations of Theory and Method," in *Religious Motivation: Biographical and Sociological Problems for the Church Historian*, ed. Derek Baker (Oxford: Basil Blackwell for the Ecclesiastical History Society, 1978), pp. 330–31.

15. [Bruce L. Kershner], "Convention Address," Manila, December 1909, Kershner Papers.

16. Hulda Frykman Lund, "The Philippines as a Mission Field," *Christian and Missionary Alliance* 34 (September 10, 1910): [378]; J. L. McElhany, "Philippine Mission," *Union Conference Record* 10 (October 1, 1906): 62.

17. W. O. Valentine to Thomas S. Barbour, March 28, 1904, Baptist Mission Records, reel 211; Charles W. Briggs to Barbour, November 29, 1903, ibid., reel 181.

18. See, for example, John McKee, "Mindanao, Our New Mission Field," *Christian and Missionary Alliance* 33 (April 19, 1902): 215.

19. Charles Henry Brent, "A Study of Missions among a Primitive People," pp. 1, 4, Episcopal Mission Records.

20. Mercer G. Johnston to John W. Wood, March 23, 1905, ibid.; Charles Henry Brent, "World Missionary Conference, 1910: Answers to Questions," filed July 1909, Brent Papers; Irving Spencer, "Bagobo Land," *Spirit of Missions* 70 (May 1905): 387.

21. Johnston to Mrs. C. W. Richmond (letterbook copy), August 13, 1904, Johnston Papers, box 39; Charles Henry Brent, "Address," in *Missionary District of the Philippine Islands 1904* (n.p., n.d.). A copy of this pamphlet is in B.I.A. 3319. This address was perhaps Brent's most eloquent statement on the need to minister first

Protestant Missionaries in the Philippines

to Americans, but similar statements abound in his published and private writings, as well as in the writings of other Episcopal missionaries. Walter C. Clapp, "On the Way to the Philippines," *Spirit of Missions* 67 (March 1902): 179.

22. Frank C. Laubach, *The Crucial Spot—Mindanao* (pamphlet), p. 7, American Board Mission Records.

23. Hermon P. Williams, "The Word of God for the Philippines," *Christian Standard* 45 (February 9, 1909): 251. Frank C. Laubach of the American Board, as well as Bishop Brent, thought in similar terms.

24. Bruce L. Kershner, "President's Address" delivered to the Convention of the Philippine Mission (F.C.M.S.), December 28, 1908, Kershner Papers.

25. For example, W. N. Lemmon to Stephen J. Corey, August 26, 1913, ibid.

26. Charles L. Maxfield to Barbour, August 27, 1906, Baptist Mission Records, reel 198; Brent to Wood, January 11, 1907, Episcopal Mission Records. See also Briggs to Henry C. Mabie, September 11, 1901, Baptist Mission Records, reel 181.

27. Rebecca Parrish, *A Tribute to Dr. Hawthorne Darby* (pamphlet), p. [5], Parrish Papers; Rebecca Parrish, "Scattering Gospel Seed," ibid; Rebecca Parrish, "Tell Us about Jesus," ibid.

28. Rodgers, "One Score Years," pp. 7–8.

29. Brown, *Why and How of Foreign Missions*, pp. 18–20.

30. Harry Farmer, "Private Journal of Harry Farmer: Beginnings of Methodism in the Agno Valley Area, the Philippines, 1904–1907," January 24, 1907, p. 250, United Methodist Headquarters, Manila; Walter C. Clapp to Brent, October 14, 1914, Brent Papers; untitled manuscript, Episcopal Mission Records; Charles Henry Brent, "With God in the Philippine Islands," *Spirit of Missions* 68 (February 1903): 81.

31. Isaac B. Harper, in *Official Journal of the Fourth Annual Session of the Philippine Islands Mission Conference of the Methodist Episcopal Church* (1908), p. 69.

32. Henry W. Munger, "After Twenty-Five Years," *Missions* 16 (December 1925): 658; id., "In the Hospital," *Pearl of the Orient* 9 (July 1912): 14; Edith Steinmetz, letter to the editor, ibid., 4 (July 1907): 7–8; see also H. H. Steinmetz, "Iloilo Station," ibid., 9 (October 1912): 4–8.

33. Kenneth P. MacDonald to Buster Bustamente, April 26, 1912 (a form letter), Presbyterian Mission Records, 1911–21, box 1, file 6; Charles A. Glunz, "Industrial Department," *Philippine Presbyterian* 4 (March 1913): 10.

34. Johnston to Walter Mitchell (letterbook copy), May 7, 1906, Johnston Papers, box 39.

35. Brent to Margaret P. Waterman, draft accompanying Brent to Johnston, September 20, 1904, ibid., box 38.

36. Letter from Rev. S. B. Rossiter, D.D., Manila, P.I. (copy), August 15, 1907, Presbyterian Mission Records, reel 289; Moots, *Pioneer "Americanas,"* p. 60.

37. Bruce L. Kershner, "Missionary Inspiration," n.d. (probably 1911), Kershner Papers. Stuart Piggin has observed a similar sense of adventure among English missionaries of the same period, though he adds that romanticism faded quickly in light of the many hardships of living in less developed areas. Piggin, "Assessing Missionary Motivation," p. 336.

38. Gordon Poteat, ed., *Students and the Future of Christian Missions: Report of the Tenth Quadrennial Convention of the Student Volunteer Movement for Foreign Missions* (New York: Student Volunteer Movement for Foreign Missions, 1928), pp. 75–107.

39. Ibid., pp. 65–74.

40. Ibid., pp. 78–79.

41. Ibid., pp. 89–91.

42. Ibid., p. 75.

43. Presbyterian Mission, "Suggestions for Missionary Outfit and Journey" (mimeographed), Johnston Papers, box 38; H. R. Talbot, "Philippine Outfit," ibid.

44. Klinefelter to Board of Foreign Missions, Methodist Episcopal Church, January 1, 1916, Methodist Mission Records; see also Marvin A. Rader to Leonard, August 17, 1904, ibid.

45. Wood to Johnston, April 24, 1903, Johnston Papers, box 38; Brent to Johnston, May 15, 1903, ibid.

46. "Early Days of Methodism in the Cagayan Valley," Ferrer Papers; Ella Herkert, "A Message from the Philippines," *Alliance Weekly* 39 (November 30, 1912): 136; Farmer, journal, April 13, 1904, p. 5.

47. See Charles T. Sibley to Enoch F. Bell, January 24, 1914, American Board Mission Records; and "Biography of H. W. Widdoes" (typescript), pp. 261–62, United Brethren Mission Records.

48. Johnston to Brent (letterbook copy), October 14, 1904, Johnston Papers, box 39.

49. I. H. Evans to T. E. Bowen, April 16, 1912, R.G. 21 (Secretariat), Incoming Letters, 1912-E, Seventh-day Adventist Mission Records.

50. J. Andrew Hall to Frank F. Ellinwood, June 28, August 26, 1902, Presbyterian Mission Records, reel 288; Laubach, *The Crucial Spot*, p. 3.

51. Ralph V. B. Dunlap to Stuntz, December 10, 1904, Methodist Mission Records; Williard A. Goodell to Leonard, July 5, 1906, ibid.; Stuntz to E. K. Carroll, April 15, 1907, ibid.; Ernest S. Lyons to Leonard, August 12, 1908, ibid; William F. Oldham to Leonard, September 7, 1909, ibid.; Rader to Leonard, August 12, 1909, ibid.; Ernest S. Lyons to Leonard, May 15, 1910, ibid.

52. Clapp to Wood, May 12, 1902, Episcopal Mission Records.

53. Fred A. McCarl to Leonard, April 9, 1903, Methodist Mission Records; Klinefelter to Leonard, January 3, 1906, ibid.; B. O. Peterson to Leonard, September 21, 1906, ibid.; Sanford B. Kurtz to Samuel S. Hough, March 28, 1912, United Brethren Records.

54. Briggs to Barbour, October 12, 1905, October 26, 1909, Baptist Mission Records, reel 181. Briggs dedicated his book, *The Progressing Philippines*, to the memory of his sons.

55. Brent to Johnston, September 17, 1903, Johnston Papers, box 38.

56. Brent to William Howard Taft, January 11, 1903, Taft Papers; Brent to Wood, April 17, 1904, Episcopal Mission Records.

57. Thus, in the tiny American Board mission, the Sibleys, the second missionary couple to be sent to the islands, could not get along with their predecessors, the Blacks. In the Alliance Mission, Hulda Lund proved so domineering that she ap-

pears to have been partially responsible for disrupting the congregation in Zamboanga. By one account the M. W. Mummas, a United Brethren missionary couple, felt like outcasts in their own mission. See David L. Rambo to author, November 4, 1980; Farmer, journal, February 13, 1907, pp. 263–64. Of the larger missions, the Presbyterian seems to have been the most congenial, surely due in good part to the gentle ways of their longtime leader, James B. Rodgers. But Presbyterians in the Visayas at times distrusted those in Manila. And there were occasionally clashes among Presbyterian missionaries in the provinces. Rodgers to Brown, April 12, 1913, Presbyterian Mission Records, 1911–21, box 1, file 5.

58. Farmer, journal, September 3, October 19, 1905; July 14, 15, 20, 1906, pp. 150, 202, 203.

59. James L. Smiley to Joshua Kimber, June 3, 1901, Episcopal Mission Records; William Henry Scott, "Staunton of Sagada: Christian Civilizer," in *Hollow Ships on a Wine-Dark Sea and Other Essays*, ed. William Henry Scott (Quezon City: New Day Publishers, 1976), p. 97. This essay first appeared in *The Historical Magazine of the Protestant Episcopal Church* 31 (December 1962): 305–39.

60. Johnston to Dr. Correll (letterbook copy), July 10, 1907, Johnston Papers, box 39.

61. Brent to Johnston, January 2, 1908, Johnston Papers, box 38. For an example of Spencer's offer to resign, see his ten-page letter to Kimber, February 5, 1906, Episcopal Mission Correspondence.

62. Charles E. Brunner to Johnston, August 25, 1906, ibid.; Johnston to Brunner (copy), September 1, 1906, ibid; Johnston to F.(?) Bennett, December 17, no year, ibid.

63. Johnston to Wickham Quinan (letterbook copy), August 2, 1907, ibid., box 39; Quinan to Johnston, August 15, 1907, ibid., box 38; Brent to Johnston, n.d., ibid., box 38.

64. The vestrymen of the Cathedral Parish of St. Mary and St. John to Johnston, August 20, 1908, ibid.

65. Briggs to J. H. Franklin, September 11, 1913, Baptist Mission Records, reel 181.

66. Briggs to Barbour, October 2, 1906, ibid. Valentine appears to have assumed the position, at least for a time. See Henry W. Munger, *Christ and the Filipino Soul: A History of the Philippine Baptists* (n.p.: privately published, 1967), p. 38; American Baptist Historical Society, Rochester, New York. Briggs's harsh comments may have been designed to delay the opening of the Bible school, which he opposed. Drawing on rural Baptist traditions, Briggs was skeptical of a highly educated ministry. He may also have preferred a relatively ignorant force of pastors because he could more easily control them. "I want to make my work and personality result in building up a corps of men that can preach and shepherd the flocks in my district," he wrote. "I want them under my own supervision and training. I want to work with them. . . . I want to be the one to guard them against the dangers I see in my district better a hundred times than a teacher can see shut up in class-room or study." Briggs to Barbour, December 10, 1907, ibid; see also Briggs to Barbour, September 2, 1909, ibid.

67. Charles L. Maxfield to Barbour, February 11, 13, 1909, Baptist Mission Records, reel 198.

68. Quoted in Maxfield to Barbour, March 30, 1909, ibid; Maxfield to Barbour, April 2, 1909, ibid.
69. George B. Huntington to Briggs, January 20, 1911, ibid., reel 181; Briggs to Huntington, January 22, 1911, ibid.
70. Briggs to Barbour, June 22, September 8, 1911, ibid.
71. Lund to Franklin, August 27, 1913, ibid., reel 197.

CHAPTER 3

1. R. Pierce Beaver, *Ecumenical Beginnings in the Protestant World Missions: A History of Comity* (New York: Thomas Nelson & Sons, 1962), pp. 15–80, quotations at pp. 15, 18
2. Ibid., p. 44.
3. Arthur Judson Brown, *One Hundred Years: A History of the Foreign Missionary Work of the Presbyterian Church in the U.S.A.* (Chicago and New York: Fleming H. Revell Co., 1936), pp. 861–65; Beaver, *Ecumenical Beginnings*, pp. 135–36.
4. Brown, *One Hundred Years*, p. 864.
5. Stuntz, *Philippines and the Far East*, pp. 420, 434.
6. For quotation, see James B. Rodgers to Frank F. Ellinwood, October 4, 1899, Presbyterian Mission Records, reel 287; see also ibid.: Rodgers to Ellinwood, March 6, March 15, 1900; Leonard P. Davidson to Ellinwood, September 11, 1900.
7. Rodgers to Ellinwood, July 9, September 11, 1900, ibid. Indicative of improved relations, Rodgers served as Prautch's translator at a mass rally, organized by Felipe Buencamino, in the Rizal Theater in Tondo. See Davidson to Ellinwood, February 16, 1901, ibid., reel 288.
8. Rodgers to Ellinwood, March 6, 1900, reel 287; Rodgers, *Forty Years in the Philippines*, p. 163; J. C. R. Ewing to Ellinwood and Robert E. Speer, April 18, 1901, Presbyterian Mission Records, reel 288.
9. Brown, *One Hundred Years*, p. 867. The original members of the Evangelical Union included the Presbyterians, Methodists, United Brethren in Christ, YMCA, British and Foreign Bible Society, and American Bible Society. A representative of the Christian and Missionary Alliance was also present, but it is not clear that the Alliance formally joined the union.
10. Ewing to Ellinwood and Speer, April 18, 1901; Rodgers, *Forty Years in the Philippines*, p. 163; Rodgers to Ellinwood, April 29, 1901, Presbyterian Mission Records, reel 288.
11. Ewing to Ellinwood, April 26, 1901, ibid.; Rodgers and Davidson to Ellinwood, April 29, 1901.
12. James B. Rodgers, "Lessons from Five Years of Protestant Work in the Philippine Islands," March 15, 1905, ibid. Portions of this manuscript were read at the meeting of the Evangelical Union in Manila on March 16, 1905.
13. *A Statement of the Plan and Purpose of the Evangelical Union of the Philippines Islands* (Manila: n.p., 1902).
14. Ewing to Ellinwood, April 26, 1901; Warne's comments, dated May 1, 1901, are in his "Prefatory Note" to Alice Byram Condict, *Old Glory and the Gospel in the*

Philippines: Notes Gathered During Professional and Missionary Work (Chicago and New York: Fleming H. Revell Co., 1902), p. 6.

15. American Board of Commissioners for Foreign Missions, *Missions in the Philippines: Ten Years in the Islands* (Boston: American Board, 1908), p. 8; William F. Oldham, *India, Malaysia, and the Philippines: A Practical Study in Missions* (New York: Eaton & Mains, 1914), p. 278; Rodgers, "One Score Years," p. 16; Laubach, *People of the Philippines*, p. 205.

16. Donald Dean Parker, "Church and State in the Philippines, 1896–1906" (Ph.D. diss., Divinity School, University of Chicago, 1936), p. 265n; Beaver, *Ecumenical Beginnings*, pp. 136, 140; Peter G. Gowing, *Islands under the Cross: The Story of the Church in the Philippines* (Manila: National Council of Churches in the Philippines, 1967), p. 128.

17. Arthur Leonard Tuggy, *Iglesia ni Cristo: A Study in Independent Church Dynamics* (Quezon City: Conservative Baptist Publishing, 1976), p. 6. Other works that reflect the usual interpretation include Richard L. Deats, *Nationalism and Christianity in the Philippines* (Dallas: Southern Methodist University Press, 1967), p. 95; Dwight E. Stevenson, *Christianity in the Philippines: A Report on the Only Christian Nation in the Orient* (Lexington, Ky: College of the Bible, 1955), p. 20; Walter N. Roberts, *The Filipino Church: The Story of the Development of an Indigenous Evangelical Church in the Philippine Islands . . .* (Dayton, O.: Foreign Missionary Society of the Women's Missionary Association, United Brethren in Christ, 1936), p. 3; Peter G. Gowing, "Christianity in the Philippines Yesterday and Today," *Silliman Journal* 20 (1965): 137–38; and Camilo Osias and Avelina Lorenzana, *Evangelical Christianity in the Philippines* (Dayton: United Brethren Publishing House, 1931), pp. 90–91.

18. George W. Wright to Arthur J. Brown, June 25, 1912, Presbyterian Mission Records, RG 85, box 1, file 5; Rodgers, *Forty Years in the Philippines*, pp. 166–69.

19. Rodgers, *Forty Years in the Philippines*, pp. 130–36.

20. Robert F. Black to Judson Smith, November 20, 1902, November 21, 1903, American Board Mission Records; Rodgers, *Forty Years in the Philippines*, p. 156; Black to Enoch F. Bell, June 24, 1912, American Board Mission Records.

21. E. W. Hearne, "Field and Prospects," included in "Second Conference of the Secretaries of the . . . Y.M.C.A.," p. 8, YMCA Records.

22. Frank W. Warne, "Protestantism in the Philippines," *Christian Advocate* 75 (November 15, 1900): 1844; Rodgers, *Forty Years in the Philippines*, p. 4; David S. Hibbard to Ellinwood, December 29, 1899, Presbyterian Mission Records, reel 287; Hibbard to Ellinwood, July 24, 1900, ibid., reel 288.

23. Walter C. Clapp, "Some Notes of Matters Philippines," *Spirit of Missions* 68 (May 1903): 327; Charles Henry Brent, "From Iloilo to Capiz," ibid., 69 (July 1904): 507.

24. William T. Ellis, "On the Trail of the American Missionary," unidentified clipping, Mrs. Harry Farmer materials; Zerah C. Collins, "With the Army Y.M.C.A.," pp. 24–25, YMCA Records; J. M. Groves, "Annual Report for the Year Ending September 30, 1911," ibid.

25. Information on the dancing question comes from Board of Directors of the

Young Men's Christian Association of Manila to John R. Mott, November 27, 1915, YMCA Records; William P. Eveland to Mott, November 29, 1915, ibid.; J. M. Groves to Mott, January 4, 1916, ibid.; *Official Journal of the Ninth Annual Session of the Philippine Islands Conference* (1916), p. 23; "Minutes of the Fifteenth Annual Conference of the Philippine Mission of the Foreign Christian Missionary Society [1916]," Kershner Papers.

26. H. C. Fraser to Mott, February 28, 1916, YMCA Records; Mott to Fraser, January 13, 1916, ibid.

27. Hibbard to Ellinwood, July 18, 1902, Presbyterian Mission Records, reel 188. Hibbard found a receptive reader in Frank F. Ellinwood, a longtime secretary of the Presbyterian board. Rodgers, in fact, literally begged Ellinwood at one point (in vain as it developed) "not to put anything disparaging in the annual report about the question of comity." Rodgers to Ellinwood, January 30, 1902, ibid. Ellinwood retired in 1907.

28. Rodgers to Ellinwood, December 5, 1901, ibid; J. M. Twydewood (?) to Ellinwood, December 26, 1901, ibid.

29. "Minutes of an extraordinary meeting of the Philippine [Presbyterian] Mission," October 17, 1901, ibid; *Statement of the Plan and Purpose of the Evangelical Union.*

30. H. W. Langheim to Lewis B. Hilles, July 1, 1903, Presbyterian Mission Records, reel 288; Fred Jansen to Brown, July 28, 1903, ibid.

31. Jansen to Brown, July 28, 1903, ibid; Langheim to Brown, July 25, 1903, ibid.

32. Rodgers to Brown, October 30, 1903, ibid; Charles W. Briggs to Thomas S. Barbour, November 11, 1903, Baptist Mission Records, reel 181.

33. J. Andrew Hall and Rodgers to Brown, January 14, 1904, Presbyterian Mission Records, reel 288; Rodgers to Brown, March 18, 1905, ibid.

34. John H. Lamb to Brown, July 13, 1907, ibid., reel 289; Rodgers to Brown, April 13, 1907, ibid. Other Methodists also supported union projects. Harry Farmer and Homer Stuntz, for example, worked hard to make Union Seminary a success. But each disliked several colleagues in other missions. On one occasion, for example, Farmer wrote disparagingly of "weak-kneed, society flatterers" in the Presbyterian fold. Farmer to William F. Oldham, December 2, 1908, Mrs. Harry Farmer Materials.

35. The only work to discuss Presbyterian-Baptist relations at any length is Rodgers's significant book, *Forty Years in the Philippines*, pp. 68–72, 150–51, 164–65; important as Rodgers's account is, it scarcely reveals the intensity of the early disputes. Arthur J. Brown, in his equally important and massive study, *One Hundred Years*, acknowledges that "a temporary embarrassment developed on the Island of Panay" (p. 867), but he limits his discussion to one paragraph. Brown's earlier work, *The New Era in the Philippines* (Chicago and New York: Fleming H. Revell, 1903) includes little on Presbyterian-Baptist relations. Another Presbyterian missionary, David S. Hibbard, makes no reference to relations between the two missions in his account, *Making a Nation: The Changing Philippines* (New York: Board of Foreign Missions of the Presbyterian Church in the United States of America, 1926). On the Baptist side, Charles W. Briggs, who was at the center of the disputes, gives no

hint of difficulties in his book, *The Progressing Philippines*; neither does Henry W. Munger in *Christ and the Filipino Soul*. Munger's study is the best on Baptist beginnings in the islands.

36. Hibbard to Ellinwood, May 16, 1900, Presbyterian Mission Records, reel 288; Hall to Ellinwood, May 2, 1901, ibid.; Eric Lund to Barbour, August 9, 1902, Baptist Mission Records, reel 197; Rodgers, *Forty Years in the Philippines*, pp. 150–51, 68.

37. Munger, "Beginnings of Baptist Work in the Philippines," pp. 172–73; Briggs to Barbour, April 9, 1903, Baptist Mission Records, reel 181; Lund to Barbour, August 9, 1902, ibid., reel 197; Charles R. Hamilton to Brown, November 9, 1920, Presbyterian Mission Records, RG 85, box 11, file 7 (Iloilo 1903–27); Hall to Brown, October 28, 1920, Presbyterian Mission Records, 1911–21, box 11, file 7.

38. Hall to Ellinwood, November 14, 1901, Presbyterian Mission Records, reel 288; Barbour to Lund, July 25, 1902, Baptist Mission Records, reel 197.

39. Arthur J. Brown, *Report of a Visitation of the Philippine Mission of the Board of Foreign Missions of the Presbyterian Church in the United States of America* (New York: Board of Foreign Missions of the Presbyterian Church in the United States of America, 1902), pp. 17–23.

40. Hall to Ellinwood, November 14, 1901; Board of Foreign Missions of the Presbyterian Church in the USA, Minutes 20 (1902–3), April 6, 1903, p. 264. (Hereafter cited as Presbyterian Board Minutes.)

41. See Hall to Brown, November 19, 1901, Presbyterian Mission Records, reel 288; Leon C. Hills to Ellinwood, January 13, February 3, 1902, ibid.; "Philippine Mission [Presbyterian] Minutes" (January 1902), p. 7, ibid., reel 289; the quotation is from Rodgers to Brown, July 30, 1902, ibid., reel 288. In 1903 Briggs angrily denied that Barbour had censured him. Nevertheless his own account indicates that, at the very least, a change in policy took place following Barbour's visit. One is led to speculate that Briggs was more angered at the fact that Barbour learned of Presbyterian accounts of his "censure" than at any distortion of the facts. See Briggs to Barbour, March 6, 1903, Baptist Mission Records, reel 181.

42. Hall to Ellinwood, March 3, 1902, Presbyterian Mission Records, reel 288; Hills to Ellinwood, June 5, 1902, ibid. Both groups feared the zealous nature of new Filipino converts.

43. "Philippine Mission [Presbyterian] Minutes" (December 1902), p. 8, ibid., reel 289; Hall to Ellinwood, June 2, 1903, ibid., reel 288.

44. Presbyterian Board Minutes 20, June 16, 1902, pp. 44–45. Brown's report had, in fact, suggested such a division if a withdrawal could not be effected.

45. Ibid., July 28, 1902, p. 69; November 3, 1903, pp. 122–23; February 2, 1903, p. 210.

46. Ibid., April 6, 1903, pp. 263–65; Barbour to Briggs, April 22, 1903, Baptist Mission Records, reel 181; Rodgers, *Forty Years in the Philippines*, 68–69; Hall to Ellinwood, June 2, 1903, Presbyterian Mission Records, reel 288. Conceivably the Baptists made concessions under the pressure of unilateral Presbyterian expansion to Cebu and threats of additional expansions to other areas of the Visayas, moves that violated the Evangelical Union's comity agreements. But there is no firm evidence to support such an hypothesis.

47. Presbyterian Board Minutes 20, April 6, 1903, p. 264; Hall to Ellinwood, June 2, 1903. See also Rodgers, *Forty Years in the Philippines*, pp. 68–69.

48. Rodgers and Hall to Brown, December 29, 1903, Presbyterian Mission Records, reel 288; included with the letter were copies of relevant correspondence with the Baptists. Briggs to Barbour, December 21, 1903, Baptist Mission Records, reel 181, includes copies of relevant position papers and is more complete than the Presbyterian records at this point. Rodgers, *Forty Years in the Philippines*, p. 69.

49. Rodgers to Brown, January 4, 1904, Presbyterian Mission Records, reel 288. The Baptists hoped, understandably, that the final point could be kept confidential.

50. Hall and Rodgers to Brown, December 29, 1903, ibid.; Briggs to Barbour, December 21, 1903. Briggs's ideas are elaborated in Briggs to Barbour, April 3, 1904, Baptist Mission Records, reel 181.

51. Rodgers, *Forty Years in the Philippines*, p. 164.

52. Briggs to Barbour, April 3, 1904, Baptist Mission Records, reel 181; Barbour to Briggs, July 13, 1904, ibid. Years later another Baptist missionary echoed Briggs's views. "We face a condition and not a theory. . . ," wrote Henry W. Munger. "If it is objected that open membership is inconsistent with our interpretation of the meaning of baptism, granted. But I will sacrifice consistency everytime rather than spiritual values." Munger, *Christ and the Filipino Soul*, pp. 120–21.

53. Presbyterian Board Minutes 21 (1903–4), April 18, 1904, pp. 321–22.

54. Rodgers to Brown, October 30, 1903, Presbyterian Mission Records, reel 288; Hall to Brown, April 4, 1904, ibid.

55. Paul Doltz to Brown, December 28, 1903, ibid; id. to Dr. Hamlin, December 30, 1903, ibid; id. to Brown, January 3, 1904, ibid.

56. Briggs to Barbour, April 3, 1904.

57. Hall and Rodgers to Brown, January 14, 1904. Briggs thought this vote influenced the Presbyterian board's decision to reject the agreement reached in the field. See Briggs to Barbour, April 3, 1904.

58. Barbour to Briggs, July 13, 1904; Lund, Briggs, and Archibald A. Forshee to the Presbyterian Mission, February 1, 1905 [misdated 1904], Presbyterian Mission Records, reel 288 (copy in Baptist Mission Records, reel 181).

59. Briggs, Lund, and Forshee to the Presbyterian Mission, December 14, 1904, Presbyterian Mission Records, reel 288 (copy in Baptist Mission Records, reel 181); Charles E. Rath to Brown, January 11, 1905, Presbyterian Mission Records, reel 288; Lund, Briggs, Forshee to the Presbyterian Mission, February 1, 1905; Briggs to Barbour, February 16, 1905, Baptist Mission Records, reel 181.

60. Doltz to Brown, August 10, 1906, Presbyterian Mission Records, reel 289; Briggs to Barbour, January 24, 1907, Baptist Mission Records, reel 181.

61. See actions of the Presbyterian board of foreign missions of March 18, December 2, December 16, 1907, and March 16, 1908, in "Board Actions Adopted Regarding Iloilo Station," Presbyterian Mission Records, 1911–21, box 11, file 7. Presbyterian fears of a competing hospital were probably unwarranted, for although there was talk along such lines among the Baptist missionaries, Briggs argued convincingly that costly duplication would result. Briggs to Barbour, December 12, 1906, Baptist Mission Records, reel 181.

62. Charles R. Hamilton to Brown, November 9, 1920, Presbyterian Mission Records, 1911–21, box 11, file 7. See actions of the Presbyterian board of foreign missions of June 30, 1920, in "Board Actions Adopted Regarding Iloilo Station," ibid. In 1910 the two groups had designated Samar as Baptist territory.

63. Hamilton to Brown, October 23, November 9, 1920, ibid.; Hall to Brown, October 28, 1920, ibid.; George W. Wright to George T. Scott, February 26, 1921, ibid.; Hall to Scott, September 20, 1921, ibid. See actions of the Presbyterian board of foreign missions of June 6, 1921, in "Board Actions Regarding Iloilo Station," ibid.

64. See actions of the Presbyterian board of foreign missions of February 6, 1922, ibid. Rodgers, *Forty Years in the Philippines*, pp. 69–70, correctly identifies the problems that blocked withdrawal, but he does not note the favorable attitude of the Presbyterian board toward the proposal.

65. Rodgers, *Forty Years in the Philippines*, p. 70.

66. Black to Smith, September 21, 1905, American Board Mission Records; Black to James Barton, March 25, 1907, ibid.; notes by Charles W. Briggs, September 21, 1910, Baptist Mission Records, reel 181; Briggs to Barbour, February 21, 1908, ibid.

67. Briggs to Barbour, September 7, 1909, Baptist Mission Records, reel 181; notes by Charles W. Briggs, September 28, 1910, ibid.

68. Black to Barton, March 25, 1907, November 12, 1909; Black to Cornelius H. Patton, August 5, 1907, American Board Mission Records; Black and Charles T. Sibley, "Recommendations of the Philippine Mission," June 20, 1908, ibid.; Black to Bell, November 5, 1909, ibid.

69. Black to Barton, June 2, 1911, ibid. The Baptists did not, however, go to Samar.

70. Hibbard to Brown, May 18, 1913, Presbyterian Mission Records, 1911–21, box 1, file 7.

71. Frank C. Laubach to Barton, March 4, 1915, American Board Mission Records.

72. McKee, "Alliance Missions," pp. 303–4.

73. Black to Smith, February 4, May 27, 1903, American Board Mission Records.

74. Black to Smith, December 27, 1902, ibid.; see also Black to Smith, February 4, February 28, April 29, 1903, ibid.

75. Black to Smith, February 28, 1903. A few years later Black urged his board to incorporate two of the Peniel missionaries (Mr. and Mrs. David O. Lund, who had arrived in 1904), but his recommendation was not followed, and in 1908 the Lunds and the other Peniel missionaries affiliated with the Christian and Missionary Alliance, which had found the means to revive its Philippine work. Hulda F. Lund, "The Philippines as a Mission Field" (September 10, 1910): [377]–78; *Twelfth Annual Report of the Christian and Missionary Alliance (reorganized)*, (n.p., n.d. [1909]), pp. 27–29; Rambo, "Christian and Missionary Alliance in the Philippines," p. 62.

76. Black to Barton, April 21, November 24, 1914, American Board Mission Records.

77. Charles Henry Brent to John W. Wood, September 20, 1902, Episcopal Mission Records; Brent to Arthur Seldon Lloyd, October 4, 1902, ibid.; Brent to John A. Staunton, Jr., December 10, 1906, Brent Papers.

78. Staunton to Wood, November 15, 1902, Episcopal Mission Records.
79. Stuntz, *Philippines and the Far East*, pp. 472, 471.
80. Brent to Wood, September 20, 1902; Hobart F. Studley to Joshua Kimber, March 23, 1904, Episcopal Mission Records; Brent to Arthur C. A. Hall (copy), December 19, 1906, Brent Papers; Brent to Stuntz (copy), May 27, 1907, ibid.
81. Clapp, "Some Notes of Matters Philippine," pp. 327–28; Hall to Ellinwood, May 4, 1903, Presbyterian Mission Records, reel 288; Doltz to Ellinwood, June 29, 1903, ibid.
82. Hall to Ellinwood, May 4, 1903; Doltz to Ellinwood, June 29, 1903; Remsen S. Ogilby to Brent, September 5, 1910, Brent Papers.
83. See, for example, J. M. Groves, "Annual Report, October 1, 1910–September 30, 1911," p. 9, YMCA Records, for references to "a temporary difficulty" between the Y and the Columbia Club, a difficulty Brent solved by removing the man who had caused it; J. M. Groves to Mott, January 15, 1916, ibid.
84. Elwood S. Brown, "Annual Report. October 1, 1914–October 1, 1915," pp. 20–21, ibid. YMCA officials placed direct responsibility for the friction on the club's members, but they thought Brent naive. The bishop, wrote the director of the Y to John R. Mott, "is a man who lives in a world of ideals and generous enthusiasms. He has always been friendly to the Association and apparently has no idea that this program [expansion of the Columbia Club] will be disastrous to our American Work." Groves to Mott, January 15, 1916.
85. Farmer, journal, May 3, 1905, p. 127.
86. Brent to Staunton, December 10, 1906, Brent Papers; Charles Henry Brent, "The Church in the Philippine Islands," *Spirit of Missions* 68 (September 1903): 637. Not all Episcopalians agreed, however. Irving Spencer reportedly thought that the division of territory was "entirely unnecessary." Black to Smith, October 19, 1904, American Board Mission Records.
87. Oldham to Brent, May 23, 1908, Brent Papers; Brent to Silas McBee (copy), February 27, 1907, ibid.; Studley to Lloyd, January 13, 1908, Episcopal Mission Records.
88. Charles Henry Brent, "Sixteen Years in the Philippines," *Spirit of Missions* 83 (March 1918): 167. For a tribute to Brent's ecumenical attitude, see E. K. Higdon and I. W. Higdon, *From Caraboa to Clipper* (New York: Friendship Press, 1941), p. 46.
89. Rodgers to Ellinwood, August 5, 1901, Presbyterian Mission Records, reel 288; James B. Rodgers's report on the Evangelical Union's conference of January 1902 dated January 15, 1902, ibid.; Hermon P. Williams, "The Philippines Experiment," *Christian Standard* 43 (December 14, 1907): 27; Rodgers to Brown, October 30, 1903, Presbyterian Mission Records, reel 288.
90. Rodgers and Hall to Brown, January 14, 1904; J. Eugene Snook to Brown, December 27, 1904, ibid.
91. W. H. Hanna to Kershner, June 28, July 23, 1906, Kershner Papers. The quotation is from the latter.
92. Kershner to Hanna, March 23, 1907, ibid.

93. Oscar Huddleston to the Missionaries of the Christian Mission, July 20, 1907, ibid.; C. L. Pickett to Kershner, July 28, 1907, ibid.; Harry Farmer to Stuntz, August 14, 1907, Mrs. Harry Farmer Materials; Kershner to Abe McLean, November 24, 1905, Kershner Papers. Kershner did achieve some success in establishing social relationships with other missionaries. But his perceptions of the Presbyterians and Methodists seemed to vary considerably over time. At times he thought one or the other mission very friendly, but on other occasions he was extremely suspicious of them.

94. Rodgers to Brown, March 18, 1905, Presbyterian Mission Records, reel 288; Kershner to McLean, May 7, 1906, Kershner Papers; id. to Hermon P. Williams, July 31, 1906, ibid.; Williams to Kershner, July 2, 1906, ibid.

95. Kershner to Corey, July 23, 1907, Kershner Papers; Hanna to Kershner, August 13, 1907, ibid.

96. [Kershner ?] to Hanna, July 16, 1909, ibid.; Kershner to Pickett, August 11, 1909, ibid; Pickett to Kershner, February 27, 1911, ibid.

97. [Kershner] to Hanna, April 13, 1911, ibid; Hanna to Kershner, June 19, 1911, ibid.; Kershner to Tomas Revuelta, May 6, 1911, ibid.

98. "Aparri Station," *Philippine Christian* 7 (January 10, 1912): [3–4]; "Our Annual Convention," ibid. (February 1912): [3].

99. "A Union Christian Church in Manila," ibid. (September 10, 1912): [3–4]; W. N. Lemmon to Kershner, November 9, 1912, Kershner Papers.

100. Kershner to D. C. McCallum, April 26, 1913, Kershner Papers; William P. Eveland to Oldham, April 25, 1913, Methodist Mission Records; Pickett to Kershner, December 25, 1913, Kershner Papers.

101. J. B. Daugherty to Charles R. Hamilton [April, 1913], Kershner Papers; W. N. Lemmon to Kershner, September 29, 1913, ibid. When Hamilton's denominational ties became known, the Disciples' people withdrew their funds and support.

102. [Charles N. Magill] to Leslie Wolfe, July 13, 1913, ibid.; Charles R. Hamilton, "Laguna Station Report, 1913," Presbyterian Mission Records, RG 85, box 1, file 6.

103. Hamilton, "Laguna Station Report"; Kershner to McLean, August 12, 1913, Kershner Papers.

104. Oldham to McLean, November 5, 1913, Kershner Papers.

105. Kershner to McLean (draft), December 20, 1913, ibid.

106. Kershner to McLean, December 26, 1913, ibid.; "Thanksgiving Day in Vigan," *Philippine Christian* 7 (December 10, 1913): [2].

107. Kershner to Hanna, January 18, 1914, Kershner Papers; Corey to Kershner, February 12, 1914, ibid.; Oldham to Eveland (copy), May 9, 1914, Methodist Mission Records.

108. D. C. McCallum, "Commission of the F.C.M.S. among the Ilocanos," *Philippine Christian* 9 (September 10, 1914): [3–4]; Kershner to Abe F. Corey, September 2, 1914, Kershner Papers; Kershner to Corey, October 5, 1914, ibid.; W. H. Hanna, "Looking Towards Unity," *Philippine Christian* 9 (November 10, 1914): [2]. However, a poll revealed that missionaries of various churches were not yet united

on the question of unity. See Kershner to Corey, December 24, 1915, Kershner Papers.

109. Corey to Kershner, February 8, 1914, Kershner Papers.

110. F. V. Stipp, "The Disciples of Christ in the Philippines" (D.D. thesis, Yale University Divinity School, 1927), p. 39; Kershner to Corey, February 5, April 30, May 6, 1915, Kershner Papers.

111. See Leslie Wolfe to Kershner, July 3, 1918, Kershner Papers; Stipp, "Disciples of Christ in the Philippines," p. 29; "Comity in the Philippines," *World Call* 7 (September 1925): 36–37. Apparently there was no written agreement in the latter case; instead each mission took the necessary action on its own.

112. When Adventist G. A. Irwin reached Manila in 1905 he had "two to three pleasant talks" with Rodgers and was invited to speak in the Presbyterian church. The following year another Adventist official, E. H. Gates, praised the work of the Bible societies in the Philippines, wrote that the Protestant churches had "taken a noble stand in their determination to flood the Philippines with the written Word of God," and wished them "Godspeed" in their efforts. G. A. Irwin, "En Route to the General Conference," *Union Conference Record* 9 (July 15, 1905): 3; E. H. Gates, "The Philippine Islands," *Advent Review and Sabbath Herald* 83 (March 25, 1906): 15; id., "The Philippine Islands," ibid. (May 24, 1906): 13.

113. Gates, "The Philippine Islands" (May 24, 1906), p. 13.

114. "Station Report of Manila Station," received December 29, 1911, Presbyterian Mission Records, 1911–21, box 1, file 2; L. V. Finster to A. G. Daniells, August 23, 1911, RG 11 (Presidential), Incoming Letters, 1911-F, Seventh-day Adventist Records.

115. Edward I. Campbell, "Station Report of Manila Station [1912?]," Presbyterian Mission Records, RG 85, box 1, file 4; Finster to Brother Spicer, February 6, 1911, RG 21 (Secretariat), Incoming Letters, 1911-F, Seventh-day Adventist Records.

116. "Philippine Islands," *News Letter for the Asiatic Division* (Seventh-day Adventist) 2 (May 1, 1913): 5; L. V. Finster, "Week of Prayer in Manila," *Asiatic Division Mission News* (Seventh-day Adventist) 3 (November 1, 1914): 5. See also L. V. Finster, "Experiences in the Philippines," ibid. (October, 1914): 3.

117. L. V. Finster, "A Filipino Tent Meeting," *Asiatic Division Mission News* 5 (July 15, 1916): 1.

CHAPTER 4

1. Perkins, *The Great Rapprochement*, p. 75; see also Thomas F. Gossett, *Race: The History of an Idea in America* (Dallas: Southern Methodist University Press, 1963); Richard Hofstadter, *Social Darwinism in American Thought*, rev. ed. (Boston: Beacon Press, 1955).

2. Mr. and Mrs. Charles N. Magill to "friends," March 5, 1906, Presbyterian Mission Records, reel 289.

3. Ibid. One notable exception was J. M. Groves, an official of the Manila YMCA, who felt that the differences were only superficial. "In his make-up and what appeals to him the Easterner is not so very different from the Westerner at all," he

wrote. J. M. Groves, "Annual Report for the Year Ending September 30, 1912," YMCA Records.

4. Elwood S. Brown, "Volley Ball in the Philippines," in *When Volleyball Began: An Olympic Sport* (n.p.: Spalding Athletic Library, 1966), pp. 87–88.

5. Arthur Judson Brown, *Report of a Visitation*, p. 87; Elijah W. Halford, "The Question of the Philippines," *Christian Advocate* 88 (April 3, 1913): 464.

6. Bruce L. Kershner to C. L. Pickett, January 11, 1910, Kershner Papers; John M. Poor, "Charles Edward Woodruff," *Dictionary of American Biography*, 10: 496–97; Charles Edward Woodruff, *Expansion of Races* (New York: Rebman Co., 1909), p. 25.

7. William F. Oldham, "The Philippine Situation," *Christian Advocate* 84 (May 6, 1909): 701; Stuntz, *Philippines and the Far East*, pp. 40–41; "The Travelogist in the Philippines," *Missions* 7 (April 1916): 267; E. H. Gates, "In the Philippine Islands," *Advent Review and Sabbath Herald* 83 (February 22, 1906): 13; Fred Jansen to Frank F. Ellinwood, December 23, 1902, Presbyterian Mission Records, reel 288.

8. Stuntz, *Philippines and Far East*, p. 41; Ernest S. Lyons to Adna B. Leonard, July 28, 1908, Methodist Mission Records; Oldham, "The Philippine Situation," p. 701; "Report of Charles W. Briggs," January 16, 1907, Baptist Mission Records, reel 181. Another Baptist observer, however, thought the Ilocanos "the most industrious, openhearted and tractable" of the Filipinos. "The Travelogist in the Philippines," p. 267.

9. Oldham, "The Philippine Situation," p. 701; James B. Rodgers to Ellinwood, January 31, 1903, Presbyterian Mission correspondence, reel 288; Stuntz, *Philippines and Far East*, p. 41.

10. The term *Igorot* is an indigenous one meaning simply people of the mountains or mountaineers. From time to time it has acquired derogatory connotations and its use has been resisted. At other times the people of the mountains have used it with pride. See William Henry Scott, *On the Cordillera: A Look at the Peoples and Cultures of Mountain Province* (Manila: MCS Enterprises, 1969), pp. 154–74. As used in this book the term is merely descriptive, meaning people of the mountains.

11. Frank W. Warne, "The People of the Philippine Islands," *Christian Advocate* 76 (January 17, 1901): 94; Stuntz, *Philippines and Far East*, p. 35.

12. Brent, "Study of Missions among a Primitive People," p. 1.

13. Roy H. Brown to Arthur Judson Brown, November 13, 1905, Presbyterian Mission Records, reel 289; Edwin S. Eby to editor, September 20, 1901, *Woman's Evangel* 21 (January 1902): 8; Harry Farmer, journal, following p. 253; see also Ernest J. Pace to Samuel S. Hough, November 5, 1909, United Brethren Mission Records. James B. Rodgers, the Presbyterian leader, was not as sanguine as some about the Igorot's future, but he could "not help but admire their sturdiness and industry both as farmers and as workers." James B. Rodgers, "A Christmas among the Pines," *Attica Daily Press*, February 17, 1912, Presbyterian Mission Records, 1911–21, box 1, file 4.

14. Charles Henry Brent to John W. Wood, February 12, 1903, Episcopal Mission Records; id. to Mrs. George Monks (copy), February 16, 1903, Brent Papers; id., "The Church in the Philippines: A Trip through Northern Luzon," *Spirit of Missions* 68 (November 1903): 788–95; id., "The Church in the Philippine Islands" (September 1903): p. 635.

15. Brent to Wood, April 17, 1904, Episcopal Mission Records; id. to Arthur C. A. Hall (copy), Maundy Thursday, 1904 (1906?), Brent Papers. Internal evidence suggests the latter may have been misdated.

16. Charles Henry Brent, "Among the Mountain Tops," manuscript accompanying Brent to Wood, November 21, 1908, Episcopal Mission Records; published as id., "Among the Philippine Mountain Tops," *Spirit of Missions* 74 (February 1909): 88–94. Other Episcopalian missionaries generally agreed with Brent that the Igorots had a good future, though Walter C. Clapp thought the adults hopeless. Robb White, Jr., was even more optimistic. The Igorot was already "far superior to many of the more civilized Filipinos, to our Negroes, and in some ways so far as I can see we have but little in our vaunted Anglo-Saxon civilization to lend him to his profit," he wrote. Walter C. Clapp, "The Hope of the Philippines," ibid., 79 (February 1914): 110; Robb White, Jr., to Wood, July 29, 1909, Episcopal Mission Records.

17. Eric Lund to Henry C. Mabie, October 4, 1900, Baptist Mission Records, reel 80.

18. Charles T. Sibley to James L. Barton, January 12, 1915, American Board Mission Records. For other negative assessments of the people, see Sibley and Annie E. Sibley to Barton, April 14, May 8, 1908, ibid.; Irving Spencer to Joshua Kimber, n.d., received May 7, 1904, Episcopal Mission Records.

19. Annie E. Sibley to Barton, March 15, 1910, American Board Mission Records; Charles T. Sibley to Barton, April 22, 1910, ibid; Robert E. Black, "Travels in Mindanao," September 1903, ibid.; Sibley and Sibley to Barton, May 1, 1908, ibid; Charles T. Sibley to Barton, October 13, 1909, ibid.

20. Brent to Wood, July 15, 1904, Episcopal Mission Records; Charles Henry Brent, "Religious Conditions in the Philippine Islands," *Spirit of Missions* 69 (September 1904): 660. (Others, such as the Calaagans, were "not prepossessing and stood low in the human scale," Brent thought.) See also Robert F. Black, "Otao Po: A Salutation from Mindanao," August 1905, American Board Mission Records.

21. Frank C. Laubach to Barton, May 6, July 5, 1915, American Board Mission Records, in the latter of which Laubach states that the morals of the mountain people surpass those of the lowlanders.

22. Farmer, journal, September 19, 1904, p. 70.

23. This phrase was used by both Methodist Homer Stuntz, *Philippines and Far East*, p. 32, and by Seventh-day Adventist L. V. Finster, "Who are the Filipinos?" *Union Conference Record* 13 (November 29, 1909): 2. Finster, in fact, appears to have plagiarized Stuntz's book.

24. "The Negritos," *Philippine Christian* 6 (April 1911): [4]; Archibald A. Forshee to "fellow workers," October 7, 1909, Baptist Mission Records, reel 188; William B. Cooke, "Building Church and State in the Philippines," *Philippine Presbyterian* 4 (August 1913): 1.

25. Stuntz, *Philippines and Far East*, p. 33; "World Missionary Conference, 1910: Answers to Questions, by Bishop Charles Henry Brent," n.d., Brent Papers; Laubach to Barton, March 27, 1916, American Board Mission Records.

26. Edwin L. Housley, in *Journal of the Tenth Annual Session of the Philippine Islands Annual Conference* (1917), p. 81. For a discussion of the scientific perception of

Negritos at this time, see Renato Rosaldo, "Utter Savages of Scientific Value," paper delivered at the First International Philippine Studies Conference, Western Michigan University, Kalamazoo, Michigan, May 1980.

27. News Release, October 31, 1903, News Service of Massachusetts and Rhode Island, YMCA, YMCA Records. For other comments on the warlike, treacherous, and fierce Moro, see Stuntz, *Philippines and Far East*, pp. 36–38; J. L. McElhany and Cora McElhany, "Sydney to Manila," *Union Conference Record* 10 (May 28, 1906); J. Lamar McElhany, "Entering the Philippine Islands," *Advent Review and Sabbath Herald* 83 (July 12, 1906): 14.

28. Charles T. Sibley to Barton, July 29, 1908, American Board Mission Records; Brent to William Howard Taft, February 6, 1904, Taft Papers, reel 42; Ralph M. Whiteside, "Bishop Brent's Solution to the Philippine Problem," *New York Tribune*, October 20, 1913, p. 4.

29. Laubach, *The Crucial Spot*, p. 2.

30. Charles T. Sibley to Barton, August 11, 1909, American Board Mission Records; Bruce L. Kershner, *The Head Hunter and Other Stories of the Philippines* (Cincinnati: Powell & White, 1921), p. 8; see also Brown, *Report of a Visitation*, p. 1.

31. Senate Committee on the Philippines, *Hearings: Affairs in the Philippine Islands*, 57th Cong., 1st sess., 1902, S. Doc. 331, pp. 2670, 2675.

32. Stealy B. Rossiter, "Report for the Month of September [1905]," Presbyterian Mission Records, reel 289; Rossiter to Brown, July 1, 1905, ibid.

33. Paul Doltz to "Charley," December 11, 1906, Doltz Papers; Doltz to Brown, June 18, 1907, Presbyterian Mission Records, reel 289. Doltz apparently overcame his aversion to Filipinos, for he remained in the Philippines until 1936. To this day there is a Paul Doltz dormitory at Silliman University.

34. Charles E. Rath to Brown, November 19, 1908, ibid., reel 288; July 10, July 24/August 1, December 11, 1905, reel 289.

35. [Charles E. Rath,] "Station Report of Leyte Station," n.d., received December 29, 1911, Presbyterian Mission Records, 1911–21, box 1, file 2.

36. Farmer, journal, May 31, 1904, p. 31.

37. Kershner, *Head Hunter*, p. 8; "Travelogist in the Philippines," p. 267; Sanford B. Kurtz, "What of Philippine Self-Support?" *Philippine Informant* 1 (October 1909): 7.

38. Warne, "The People of the Philippine Islands," p. 94. For similar assessments, see Leon C. Hills to Ellinwood, March 18, 1902, Presbyterian Mission Records, reel 288; W. H. Hanna, "Mixed Marriages," *Philippine Christian* 5 (July 10, 1910): [2]; William F. Oldham, "News from the Philippines," unidentified clipping, Mrs. Harry Farmer Materials; *Missions in the Philippines* (Boston: American Baptist Missionary Union, 1906), p. 8; Brown, *Report of a Visitation*, p. 7.

39. Brent to Anson Phelps Stokes, Jr. (copy), July 12, 1907, Brent Papers. For Brent's views on Chinese mestizos, see "National Awakening in the Philippines," *Report of the Thirtieth Annual Lake Mohonk Conference*, October 23–25, 1912 (1912), p. 146.

40. Brent to Arthur Seldon Lloyd, May 28, 1907, Episcopal Mission Records.

41. Ibid.

42. Brent to Wood, April 27, 1904, ibid; Brent to Hall, Maundy Thursday, 1904.
43. Ernest A. Raynor, "Uplifting Tropical Peoples," *Christian Advocate* 87 (November 7, 1912): 1586.
44. F. H. Rose, "Industrial School," *Pearl of the Orient* 10 (June 1913): 20; L. B. Hilles, manuscript article, n.d., received May 11, 1903, Presbyterian Mission Records, reel 288; William F. Oldham, "The Profits and Peril of Philippine Autonomy—At This Time," *Report of the Thirty-First Annual Lake Mohonk Conference*, October 22–24, 1913 (1913), p. 123.
45. For example, Finster, "Who Are the Filipinos?" p. 3; id. to T. E. Bowen, February 5, 1913, RG 21 (Secretariat), Incoming Letters, 1913-F, Seventh-day Adventist Records; J. E. Fulton, "A Missionary Tour of the Far East: No. 1, The Philippines," *Advent Review and Sabbath Herald* 92 (July 8, 1915): 13.
46. Clapp to Lloyd, August 21, 1902, Episcopal Mission Records; Clapp to Wood, November 3, 1902, ibid. Presbyterian Lewis B. Hilles perhaps rivaled Clapp's liberalism.
47. John A. Staunton, Jr., "Some first impressions which remain after a week's residence in Manila," Episcopal Mission Records; Clapp to Lloyd, August 21, 1902; Brent to Wood, September 20, 1902, ibid.; Brent to Major E. C. Carter (copy), May 30, 1907, Brent Papers.
48. Charles Magill and his wife were impressed with the cleanliness of Lucban, Tayabas, and its inhabitants, for example, and Frank Laubach reported that the Bagobos were clean. Mr. and Mrs. Charles N. Magill to "Friends," January 1, 1906, Presbyterian Mission Records, reel 289; Laubach to Barton, May 6, 1915, American Board Mission Records.
49. Black to Judson Smith, February 1, 1905, American Board Mission Records; Kershner to Mrs. Harry N. Torrey, May 8, 1911, Kershner Papers.
50. Kershner to Torrey, May 8, 1911, Kershner Papers; Henry Watson Munger, "In the Hospital," *Pearl of the Orient* 8 (July 1912): 14; Edith M. Steinmetz to editor, ibid., 4 (July 1907): 7–8; Brent to Wood, July 16, November 23, 1903, Episcopal Mission Records.
51. Bessie White, "The Philippines from a Missionary Standpoint," *Christian and Missionary Alliance* 29 (March 24, 1900): 1; Sanford B. Kurtz to Hough, December 8, 1909, United Brethren Mission Records; George W. Dunlap to Brown, May 31, 1910, Presbyterian Mission Records, reel 289.
52. Forshee to "Friends," March 9, 1909, Baptist Mission Records, reel 177; Kurtz to Hough, December 8, 1909; George W. Dunlap to Brown, May 31, 1910, Presbyterian Mission Records, reel 289.
53. Black, "Otao Po," p. 5; Charles T. Sibley and Annie E. Sibley to Barton, May 1, 1908, American Board Mission Records; Kershner, *Head Hunter*, pp. 72–73; Hibbard, *Making a Nation*, p. 34.
54. Kershner, *Head Hunter*, pp. 73, 76.
55. Homer C. Stuntz, in *Annual Report of the Missionary Society of the Methodist Episcopal Church for 1903* (1904), p. 315; Henry Weston Munger, "Watchman: What of the Night?" *Pearl of the Orient* 6 (July 1909): 24; Mrs. B. F. Witt, "The Filipinos," *Woman's Evangel* 22 (March 1903): 37.

56. Elbridge M. Adams, "Some Things about the Philippine Islands," *Advent Review and Sabbath Herald* 89 (May 30, 1912): 13; "The Philippine Islands," *News Letter for the Asiatic Division* 1 (November 1, 1912): 6.

57. Brent, "Study of Missions among a Primitive People," p. 6; J. M. Groves, "Annual Report for the Year Ending September 30, 1912," p. 6, YMCA Records; id., "Annual Report for the Year Ending September 30, 1911," p. 2, ibid.; E. S. Turner, "Annual Report for the Year Ending September 30, 1917," p. 4, ibid.

58. Black to Enoch F. Bell, November 21, 1913, American Board Mission Records; Herbert M. Damon to Rev. B. Winget, August 22, 1908, Free Methodist Mission Records; Kershner, *Head Hunter*, p. 72.

59. Laubach to Bell, July 26, 1916, American Board Mission Records.

60. Forshee to "Friends," March 11, 1903, Baptist Mission Records, reel 188; Black, "Otao Po"; Charles A. Glunz, "Dumaguete: Industrial Education," *Philippine Presbyterian* 1 (August 1910): 4.

61. J. L. McLaughlin to editor, *Christian Advocate* 77 (August 28, 1902): 1381; Rodgers to Taft, March 25, 1905, Taft Papers, reel 39; R. A. Caldwell to "Brother," July 1910, RG 21 (Secretariat) Incoming Letters, Seventh-day Adventist Records; Farmer, journal, January 17, 1907, p. 247; W. O. Valentine to Thomas S. Barbour, May 23, 1904, Baptist Mission Records, reel 182.

62. Charles L. Maxfield to Barbour, August 14, 1906, Baptist Mission Records, reel 198; Lucius W. Case to Bell, July 24, 1916, American Board Mission Records.

63. William P. Eveland, in *Annual Report of the Board of Foreign Missions . . . for 1912* (1913), p. 208; Farmer, journal, June 12, 1905, p. 137.

64. Lund to Barbour, March 29, 1905, Baptist Mission Records, reel 197; Adams, "Some Things about the Philippine Islands," p. 13.

65. For example, Homer C. Stuntz, in *Annual Report of the Missionary Society . . . for 1905* (1906), p. 278; Ella Finster, "Good Friday in Manila," *Union Conference Record* 13 (November 15, 1909): 4.

66. Lund to Barbour, March 29, 1905, Baptist Mission Records, reel 197; Farmer, journal, June 11, 1904, p. 38; Jay C. Goodrich, "Methodism in the Philippines," *Christian Advocate* 75 (April 19, 1900): 614; Rayner, "Uplifting Tropical Peoples," p. 1586.

67. "Central Field Iloilo, and Medical Field of Iloilo and Southern Negros," *Pearl of the Orient* 4 (April 1907): 3; R. C. Thomas, "Jaro Station: The Iloilo Hospital Project," ibid., 4 (July 1907): 17; id., "Nurses' Graduation," ibid., 7 (October 1910): 9.

68. Mary Isham, "Our Little Brown Sister in the Philippines," unidentified clipping, Mrs. Harry Farmer Materials.

69. H. W. Langheim to Brown, February 25, 1905, Presbyterian Mission Records, reel 288; Paul Doltz to Brown, February 2, 1907, ibid., reel 289; "Report of Dumaguete Station, 1915," ibid., 1911–21, box 1, file 10. See also Leslie Wolfe, "Light Is Breaking," *Philippine Christian* 7 (October 10, 1912): [3].

70. Langheim to Brown, February 25, 1905, Presbyterian Mission Records, reel 288; Frederick Jansen to Brown, December 10, 1910, ibid., reel 289.

71. In the case of the Presbyterian requests cited above, a dormitory for girls was

opened in Cebu in 1913, and girls were enrolled at Silliman, a step that "strengthened the school in many ways," according to the president. See Rodgers, *Forty Years in the Philippines*, p. 85; Hibbard, *Making a Nation*, p. 76.

72. Mary Isham, *Valorous Ventures: A Record of Sixty and Six Years of the Woman's Foreign Missionary Society of the Methodist Episcopal Church* (Boston: Woman's Foreign Missionary Society Methodist Episcopal Church, 1936), p. 378. See pp. 378–90 for a summary of Methodist women's work in the islands.

73. Briggs to Barbour, December 21, 1900, February 18, 1901, Baptist Mission Records, reel 80; id. to [ ], March 7, 1902, ibid.

74. Charles W. Briggs, "Report . . . 1902," pp. 5–6, ibid.

75. Briggs to Barbour, March 8, 1904, ibid.; id., "Report . . . 1905," pp. 1–2, ibid.

76. Briggs to Barbour, October 2, 1906, ibid.

77. Briggs, "Report . . . January 16, 1907," ibid.

78. Briggs, "Report . . . January 9, 1908," ibid.; id., "Report of 1908" (specific date obscured), ibid.; Briggs to Barbour, March 30, 1909, ibid.

79. Briggs, *Progressing Philippines*, pp. 35–36.

80. Brown, *Report of a Visitation*, p. 4; Charles Henry Brent, "A Missionary Sawmill," *Spirit of Missions* 71 (October 1906): 837; Black, "Otao Po."

81. Brown, *Report of a Visitation*, p. 4.

82. Brent, "Study of Missions among a Primitive People," p. 3; Hibbard, *Making a Nation*, p. 59.

83. Charles R. Hamilton, "Laguna: At the Throne of Power," *Philippine Presbyterian* 1 (April 1910): 3.

84. *Bethlehem Letters* 2 (June 30, 1905): 4.

85. Rodgers, *Forty Years in the Philippines*, p. 95; Dunlap to Brown, May 31, 1910, Presbyterian Mission Records, reel 289; Laubach to Bell, January 6, 1915, American Board Mission Records.

86. Hibbard, *Making a Nation*, pp. 76–77. See also Arthur Judson Brown, "The Philippine Problem Not Political," *Report of the Thirtieth Annual Lake Mohonk Conference*, p. 173.

87. Brown, "Volley Ball in the Philippine Islands," p. 87; Groves, "Report for Year Ending September 30, 1912"; Elwood S. Brown, "Annual Report for the Year Ending September 30, 1917," YMCA Records.

88. Glenn A. May, *Social Engineering in the Philippines: The Aims, Execution, and Impact of American Colonial Policy, 1900–1913* (Westport, Conn.: Greenwood Press, 1980), pp. 89–93, 104–5, 113–23; Peter W. Stanley, *A Nation in the Making: The Philippines and the United States, 1899–1921* (Cambridge: Harvard University Press, 1974), p. 85.

89. Hibbard to Horace B. Silliman (copy), January 5, 1904, Presbyterian Mission Records, reel 288.

90. Rodgers, *Forty Years in the Philippines*, pp. 76–77; Charles A. Glunz to A. W. Halsey, January 8, 1904, Presbyterian Mission Records, reel 288. On the general popularity of the Hampton and Tuskegee models for the Philippines, see May, *Social Engineering*, pp. 89–93.

91. Hibbard, *Making a Nation*, pp. 58–65, quotations are on pp. 59, 64.

92. Valentine to Barbour, July 19, 1904, Baptist Mission Records, reel 211; For-shee to Barbour, June 16, 1905, ibid., reel 188; Munger, *Christ and the Filipino Soul*, p. 39.

93. Munger, *Christ and the Filipino Soul*, p. 40; Henry W. Munger, "Jaro Industrial School Republic," *Pearl of the Orient* 3 (October 1906): 21–23.

94. Munger, *Christ and the Filipino Soul*, p. 40; id., "Jaro Industrial School Republic," pp. 22–25; see also Briggs, *Progressing Philippines*, p. 55.

95. Brent, "A Missionary Sawmill," pp. 837–39; John A. Staunton, Jr., "Winning the Igorots," *Spirit of Missions* 76 (April 1911): 322–24. The Episcopalians understandably felt a sense of pride when the government adopted similar methods among the Kalingas. The Belgian friars, too, imitated Episcopalian methods in their own work with the Igorots. Charles Henry Brent, "Kalinga," ibid., 80 (October 1915): 675–76; id., "Study of Missions among a Primitive People," p. 4.

96. [W. O. Valentine], untitled manuscript article [1909], Baptist Mission Records, reel 211.

97. Henry W. Munger, "The Last Word: Jaro, Panay, P.I.," *Pearl of the Orient* 7 (April 1910): 29–30.

98. P. H. J. Lerrigo, "Some By-Products of Missionary Work," ibid., 4 (October 1907): 18–19.

99. Ibid., 14 (April 1916): cover.

100. R. C. Thomas, "Too Late," ibid., 7 (April 10, 1910): 4; A. E. Bigelow, "Some Incongruities," ibid., 5 (October 1908): 10. Missionaries with minimal expectations might have believed in inherent racial inferiority. Elwood Brown reported that his Filipino assistant at the YMCA in Manila had developed "far beyond our expectations." Given another year and close supervision by an American, he would "rank with native men anywhere," Brown stated, strongly suggesting a belief in absolute limits to development for "natives." Brown, "Report for Year Ending September 30, 1917."

101. Hermon P. Williams to editor, *Christian Standard* 35 (May 13, 1899): 597; Bruce Kershner and Ethel Kershner to Nell B. Ford, February 26, 1906, Kershner Papers; J. Andrew Hall, "Philippine Life and Character," p. 4, Presbyterian Historical Society; Warne, "People of the Philippine Islands," p. 94.

102. Laubach to Barton, October 30, 1916, American Board Mission Records; Frank C. Laubach, "Report . . . for 1917," ibid.

103. Laubach, "Report . . . for 1917," ibid.; Julius S. Augur to Mr. Lord, February 5, 1917, ibid.

104. "Biography of Widdoes," p. 261, United Brethren Mission Records. Also suggestive of Widdoes's need for racial companionship was his decision to sell a lot in Baguio on which the mission intended to build a rest house. The public explanation for the sale was the "brewers and wealthy foreigners built all about us so that we would not have the neighbors and society that we wanted." In private the brewers and foreigners were not mentioned. Instead "Rich Filipinos" had purchased the land, making it advisable to seek a more "congenial atmosphere" for the rest house. Howard W. Widdoes, "Christmas in Baguio," *Woman's Evangel* 23 (March 1913): 106; id. to Hough, April 14, 1912, United Brethren Mission Records.

105. J. M. Groves to W. D. Murray, June 30, 1909, YMCA Records.

106. E. Finley Johnson to John R. Mott, April 22, 1909, ibid; E. McCulloch Dick to W. A. Tener, April 24, 1919, ibid; David Prescott Barrows to Mott, June 14, 1909, ibid.

107. John Humpstone to Frederick B. Pratt, March 27, 1909, ibid.

108. Brent to Mott, April 30, 1909, ibid. A few years previous, Brent had made it clear that there would be no interracial contacts in Episcopalian schools in Baguio. See Brent to Johnston, May 4, 1906, Johnston Papers, box 38.

109. "Buildings for the Philippines," manuscript received October 24, 1910, YMCA Records.

110. J. M. Groves, "Annual Report. October 1, 1910–September 30, 1911," ibid.; id., "Report . . . Year Ending September 30, 1912."

111. Elwood S. Brown, "Annual Report: October 1, 1914–October 1, 1915," ibid.; Alfred T. Morrill, "Report to the International Committee of the Young Men's Christian Association . . . by the City Department, Manila Young Men's Christian Association of the Philippine Islands [for the year 1916]," ibid.

CHAPTER 5

1. A. Henry Savage Landor, *The Gems of the East: Sixteen Thousand Miles of Research Travel among Wild and Tame Tribes of Enchanting Islands* (New York: Harper & Brothers, 1904), p. 545; Charles Henry Brent to William Howard Taft, October 17, 1904, Taft Papers, reel 46.

2. Varg, *Missionaries, Chinese, and Diplomats*, p. 84; Stephen Neill, *Colonialism and Christian Missions* (New York: McGraw-Hill Book Co., 1966), p. 128.

3. Frederick W. Starr is one example. See Kenton J. Clymer, "Humanitarian Imperialism: David Prescott Barrows and the White Man's Burden in the Philippines," *Pacific Historical Review* 45 (November 1976): 504.

4. Mrs. Campbell Dauncey, *An Englishwoman in the Philippines* (New York: F. P. Dutton & Co., 1906), pp. 107–8.

5. James B. Rodgers, untitled sermon written in Manila for delivery in the Central Presbyterian Church, Rochester, New York, November 18, 1899, Presbyterian Mission Records, reel 287; J. Andrew Hall, "Explanations to accompany the Iloilo estimates for 1909–1910," February 1909, ibid., reel 289; Hulda Frykman Lund, "The Philippines as a Mission Field" (September 3, 1910): [361]. See also Charles Hamilton, "Laguna: 'The Heathen in his Blindness Bows Down to Wood and Stone,'" *Philippine Presbyterian* 1 (September 1910): 4.

6. Herbert M. Damon to Reverend B. Winget, August 22, 1908, Free Methodist Records; J. Lamar McElhany, "Philippine Mission," *Union Conference Record* 10 (October 1, 1906): 62. The reports of the first Adventist visitor to the islands, E. H. Gates, were, on the other hand, notable for their objectivity and restraint. E. H. Gates, "En Route to the General Conference," *Union Conference Record* 9 (July 1, 1905): 3; id., "In the Philippine Islands," *Advent Review and Sabbath Herald* 83 (February 22, 1906): 14; and id., "Philippine Islands," ibid., (May 10, 1906): 11. McElhany's successor, L. V. Finster, however, was strongly anti-Catholic. See L. V. Finster, "Philippine Islands," ibid., 88 (August 17, 1911): 12.

7. Bruce L. and Ethel S. Kershner to Nell B. Ford, February 28, 1906, Kershner

Papers; American Board of Commissioners for Foreign Missions, *Missions in the Philippines*, p. 6; Charles L. Maxfield to Thomas S. Barbour, May 6, 1905, Baptist Mission Records, reel 198. For similar sentiments, see Charles T. and Annie E. Sibley to James L. Barton, May 1, 1908, American Board Mission Records.

8. Bessie White, "The Philippines," *Christian and Missionary Alliance* 23 (September 9, 1899): 226; Damon to Winget, August 8, 1908, Free Methodist Mission Records; L. V. Finster, "Philippine Islands," p. 12; McKee, "Alliance Missions," p. 304.

9. Damon to Winget, August 8, August 22, 1908, Free Methodist Mission Records; Earl R. Harvey, "Philippine Islands," *Alliance Weekly* 42 (September 26, 1914): 426.

10. The task facing the Protestant missionaries, the Baptists acknowledged, was "not exactly the laying of foundations." S. S. Huse, Jr., stated a common view when he wrote that the Catholic Church was Christian, but "of the lowest form." S. S. Huse, Jr., *Missions in the Philippines* (Boston: American Baptist Missionary Union, 1906), pp. 10–11. This pamphlet was based on information supplied by missionaries Charles W. Briggs, Archibald A. Forshee, and P. H. J. Lerrigo. S. S. Huse, Jr., to Haggard, April 21, 1902, Baptist Mission Records, reel 194.

11. J. L. McLaughlin, "The Philippine Problem," *Christian Advocate* 80 (November 9, 1905): 1787; Stuntz, *Philippines and the Far East*, p. 319. See also Mary Isham, "Our Little Brown Sisters in the Philippines," unidentified clipping, Mrs. Harry Farmer Materials.

12. Stuntz, *Philippines and the Far East*, pp. 89–97; William F. Oldham, "Hopeful Signs in the Philippines," *Christian Advocate* 85 (June 9, 1910): 814; Ernest J. Pace to Samuel S. Hough, September 12, 1909, United Brethren Mission Records.

13. *Journal of the 3rd Annual Session of the Philippine Islands Mission Conference of the Methodist Episcopal Church* (1907), p. 60; *Journal of the 4th Annual Session of the Philippine Islands Mission Conference* (1911), p. 35.

14. See, for example, George F. Pentecost, "Protestantism in the Philippines," sermon preached in Manila, December 21, 1902, p. 10, Presbyterian Historical Society.

15. Huse, *Missions in the Philippines*, p. 10; Forshee to "friend," September 6, 1905, Baptist Mission Records, reel 188.

16. Pentecost, "Protestantism in the Philippine Islands," p. 10; Charles E. Rath to Arthur J. Brown, April 18, 1904, Presbyterian Mission Records, reel 288; Rath to Brown, October 7, 1907, ibid., reel 289.

17. Forshee to "fellow workers," June 9, 1909, Baptist Mission Records, reel 188; see also Huse to Haggard, April 21, 1902, ibid., reel 194. "Morality and religion," wrote Huse, "may not unjustly be said to be divorced."

18. John Lord to Bruce L. Kershner, July 22, 1908, Kershner Papers; Kershner to Alexander McLean, May 30, 1910, ibid. "Sacerdotalism logically needs no morality," Briggs wrote in "Visayan Barrios," December 17, 1904, Baptist Mission Records, reel 181; Charles W. Briggs, Report of January 22, 1904, Baptist Mission Records, reel 181.

19. William F. Oldham, "The Philippines: The Duty of the House, II," unidentified clipping, Mrs. Harry Farmer Materials; J. C. Goodrich, "Methodism in the

Philippines," *Christian Advocate* 75 (April 19, 1900): 614; Stuntz, *Philippines and the Far East*, pp. 109, 113.

20. Roy H. Brown, "On the Firing Line in Albay," *Philippine Presbyterian* 4 (January 13, 1913): 6; A. G. Saunder, "Laoag Report—May 1914," *Philippine Christian* 9 (June 10, 1914): [3].

21. Briggs to Barbour, June 9, 1902, Baptist Mission Records, reel 181; Warne, "People of the Philippines," p. 94; "Philippine Events of Note," *Pearl of the Orient* 3 (October 1906): 37–38.

22. William F. Oldham, "The Latest Word from Manila," *Christian Advocate* (April 28, 1910): 604; P. H. J. Lerrigo, "Thirty Years of American Occupation Reviewed," *The Baptist* 12 (August 29, 1931): 1020.

23. For example, Charles W. Briggs, "Chinese Filipinos," *Pearl of the Orient* 6 (October 1909): 26.

24. Brown, *Report of a Visitation*, p. 73.

25. For example, E. White Jansen, "Toiling and Reaping in the Philippines," *Christian and Missionary Alliance* 30 (May 30, 1908): 138; W. H. Hanna, "Bible Now, Heretics Formerly," *Philippine Christian* 9 (January 10, 1914): [4].

26. Pace to Hough, September 12, 1909, United Brethren Mission Records.

27. William F. Oldham, "The Philippines, III," unidentified clipping, Mrs. Harry Farmer Materials.

28. Rodgers to F. F. Ellinwood, March 5, 1899, Presbyterian Mission Records, reel 287. Rodgers left a post in Brazil to go to the Philippines, and he expected "violent opposition by the Romanists." Likewise, Eric Lund spent twenty years in Spain as a Swedish Baptist missionary. Presumably he also expected opposition.

29. For an example of a cordial reception by Catholic padres, see W. H. Hanna, "A Prospecting Tour in the Philippines," *Christian Evangelist* 39 (August 2, 1902): 552.

30. David S. Hibbard to Ellinwood, August 7, 1899, Presbyterian Mission Records, reel 287.

31. *Minutes of the 4th Session of the District Conference of the Philippine Islands of the Methodist Episcopal Church* (1903), p. 25; Briggs to E. R. Merriam, April 11, 1901, Baptist Mission Records, reel 181; Munger, "After Twenty-Five Years," p. 657; Briggs to Merriam, April 11, 1901, Baptist Mission Records, reel 181.

32. Lillian H. Graham to Brown, December 16–17, 1907, Presbyterian Mission Records, reel 289. The killing of a Presbyterian worker by a mob, allegedly directed by a priest, is also reported in "Religious Strife in the Philippines," identified as a clipping from the *New York Herald*, January 4, 1908, enclosed in W. A. Kissam to "Colonel," B.I.A. file 1158. This likely refers to the same incident.

33. E. White Jansen, "A Visit to Zamboanga, Philippines," *Christian and Missionary Alliance* 32 (May 8, 1909): 90; "Aparri Station," *Philippine Christian* 7 (October 10, 1912): 1; D. H. Klinefelter, in *Journal of the 8th Annual Session of the Philippine Islands Annual Conference of the Methodist Episcopal Church* (1915), p. 73.

34. Briggs to H. C. Mabie, July 8, September 11, 1901, Baptist Mission Records, reel 181; Lerrigo to Barbour, September 26, 1903, ibid., reel 196; Sibley to Barton, August 24, 1908, May 24, 1909, American Board Mission Records.

35. Homer C. Stuntz, "Protestantism in the Philippines," *Christian Advocate* 76 (August 1, 1901): 1222; Sibley to Barton, September 1, 1908, American Board Mission Records.

36. For example, *Annual Report of the Board of Foreign Missions of the Methodist Episcopal Church for 1910* (1911), p. 347.

37. "Report of Bohol Station," received December 29, 1911, Presbyterian Mission Records, 1911–21, box 1, file 5; Kershner, *Head Hunter*, pp. 91–96.

38. Rodgers, "Five Years of Protestant Work in the Philippines."

39. Pace to Hough, September 12, 1909, United Brethren Mission Records; H. W. Widdoes to Hough, August 30, September 4, 1910, ibid.

40. William Perry Eveland, in *Annual Report of the Board of Foreign Missions . . . for 1915* (1916), p. 168. *Official Journal of the 9th Annual Session of the Philippine Islands Annual Conference* (1916), p. 79. For similar assessments, see William B. Cooke, "Building Church and State in the Philippines," *Philippine Presbyterian* 4 (August 1913): 2–3; Paul Doltz, "Romanist Priests," ibid., 5 (September 1914): 7.

41. Hulda C. Lund, "Zamboanga, Philippines," *Alliance Weekly* 40 (July 26, 1913): 267; W. H. Hanna, "Bibles Now, Heretic Formerly," p. [4]; Finster to W. A. Spicer, February 5, 1914, RG 21 (Secretariat), Incoming Letters, file 1914-F, Seventh-day Adventist Records; Briggs to Mabie, December 13, 1909, Baptist Mission Records, reel 181; Munger, "After Twenty-Five Years," p. 657; Charles L. Maxfield, "Southern Negros," *Pearl of the Orient* 8 (January 1911): 90.

42. *Official Journal of the 8th Annual Session of the Philippine Islands Annual Conference*, p. 73.

43. Rath to Brown, May 27, 1907, Presbyterian Mission Records, reel 289; Warren J. Miller to Brown, June 5, 1914, Presbyterian Mission Records, 1911–21, box 1, file 9.

44. Roy H. Brown, "Albay Station Report, 1913," Presbyterian Mission Records, 1911–21, box 1, file 6.

45. Rodgers to Brown, April 12, 1912, ibid., file 5.

46. For an interesting discussion of the renewed interest in syncretic Catholicism in the Philippines, see Vincente Marasigan, S.J., "Rituals in Manila's Catacombs," *Philippine Studies* 27 (1979): 74–81.

47. J. M. Groves, "Annual Report for the Year Ending September 30, 1911," pp. 2–3, YMCA Records; see also Groves to John R. Mott, June 28, 1911, ibid.

48. W. A Tener to Mott, September 1, 1908, ibid; Groves to Mott, June 28, 1911, ibid.

49. J. M. Groves, "The Basis for Membership in the Young Men's Christian Association in the Philippine Islands," ibid.; E. S. Turner, "Young Men's Christian Association," February 19, 1916, ibid.

50. There was apparently considerably less opposition in the provinces. See Groves to Mott, February 12, 1912, ibid.

51. Groves to "friends at home," May 1, 1912, ibid.; W. Cameron Forbes, Journal, October 31, 1911, 5:61, Forbes Papers.

52. J. M. Groves, untitled report [1914?], YMCA Records. In 1916, for example, Alfred T. Morrill noted that the opposition from the Catholic Church was an "ever-present" problem. "Whenever the Association enters upon any special ac-

tivity which attracts wide attention," he wrote, it could expect "bitter" and some-times "libelous editorials" in Catholic publications. (Alfred T. Morrill, "Report of the International Committee of the Young Men's Christian Association . . . by the City Department, Manila Young Men's Christian Association of the Philippine Is-lands" for the year 1916, p. 20, ibid.) The Y's usual response to such attacks was silence, and the organization took comfort in the fact that many prominent Fili-pinos and even some Catholic publications defended the association. For a Catho-lic assessment of the Y that defends the Church's policy toward the organization, see Leo A. Cullum, "The Religion of the Y.M.C.A.," *Philippine Studies* 1 (December 1953): 249–69.

53. Charles Henry Brent, "Opportunity and the Orient," *Spirit of Missions* 81 (June 1916): 410–11; Scott, "Staunton of Sagada," in *Hollow Ships on a Wine Dark Sea*, pp. 69–102.

54. Brent to Arthur C. A. Hall (copy), December 19, 1906, Brent Papers.

55. Mercer G. Johnston to his father (letterbook copy), August 27, 1904, Johnston Papers, box 39.

56. Scott, "Staunton of Sagada," pp. 74–75; John A. Staunton to George C. Thomas, December 10, 1901, Episcopal Mission Records.

57. John A. Staunton, Jr., "Some First Impressions Which Remain after a Week's Residence in Manila," especially pp. 6–7, ibid.; Walter C. Clapp to Arthur Seldon Lloyd, August 21, 1902, ibid.; see also Staunton to Thomas, December 10, 1901, ibid.

58. Brent, "Study of Missions among a Primitive People," p. 5; see also Brent, "Religious Conditions in the Philippine Islands," pp. 666–67.

59. Charles Henry Brent, "The Years That Are Past: III, The Uttermost Parts of the Earth," clipping identified as from *The Churchman*, February 28, 1914, B.I.A. file 12848; Forbes, journal, June 23, 1911, 4:399.

60. Brent, "Religious Conditions in the Philippine Islands," pp. 662–63.

61. Brent to Hall, June 7, July 23, 1902, Brent Papers.

62. Brent to Hall (copy), November 13, 1903, ibid.

63. Brent to Johnston, March 30, 1903, Johnston Papers, box 38; Brent, "The Church in the Philippine Islands" (November 1903): 793; id., "From Iloilo to Capiz," *Spirit of Missions* 69 (July 1904): 507; id., "Religious Conditions in the Philippine Islands," p. 664. The following year he informed a prominent Swiss clergyman, "I am not exaggerating when I say that it is difficult to find a decent Filipino priest." Brent to Edouard Herzog (copy), July 28, 1905, Brent Papers.

64. Brent to Johnston, September 20, 1904, Johnston Papers, box 38.

65. Brent, "Opportunity and the Orient," pp. 410–11. This is the published ver-sion of an address Brent delivered to the board of missions on May 10, 1916.

66. Alexander C. Zabriskie, *Bishop Brent: Crusader for Christian Unity* (Phila-delphia: Westminster Press, 1948), pp. 64–65.

67. Historians, including myself, have underestimated Brent's inclination to work with Catholic Filipinos. See ibid., and Kenton J. Clymer, "The Episcopalian Missionary Encounter with Roman Catholicism in the Philippines, 1901–1916," *Philippine Studies* 28 (1980): 89–90.

68. Brent to Johnston, March 30, 1903, Johnston Papers, box 38; Brent, quoted in

"The Church in the Philippines," *Spirit of Missions* 68 (September 1903): 636–38.

69. Brent to Miss Waterman, draft accompanying Brent to Johnston, September 20, 1904, Johnston Papers, box 38; Brent to Johnston, December 20, 1904, ibid.

70. Brent to Johnston, May 11, 1905, ibid.

71. Quoted in Scott, "Staunton of Sagada," p. 98.

72. Johnston to his father (letterbook copy), August 27, 1904, Johnston Papers, box 39.

73. Staunton, quoted in "Philippine Problems and Possibilities," *Spirit of Missions* 47 (March 1902): 166; Hobart F. Studley to Lloyd, January 13, 1908, Episcopal Mission Records; Clapp to John W. Wood, July 9, 1908, ibid.

74. Edward A. Sibley to Brent, August 25, 1916, Brent Papers.

75. Brent to William Lawrence, April 26, 1905, ibid; Brent to Johnston, May 19, 1905, Johnston Papers, box 38.

76. Brent to Lawrence, April 26, 1905; Brent to Wood, April 13, 1907, May 2, 1908, Episcopal Mission Records.

77. Brent to Taft, February 6, 1904, Taft Papers, reel 42; Brent, "Religious Conditions in the Philippines," p. 665.

78. Brent to Henry T. Allen (copy), October 12, 1904, Brent Papers; Brent to Herzog (copy), July 28, 1905, ibid.

79. Brent to Wood, July 18, 1906, ibid.

80. Brent to Clapp (copy), May 22, 1907, ibid.; see also Brent to Wood, May 20, 1907, Episcopal Mission Records.

81. Brent, "Among the Mountain Tops," essay enclosed in Brent to Wood, November 21, 1908, Episcopal Mission Records.

82. Brent to Ernest H. Abbott (copy), July 2, 1909, Brent Papers.

83. Brent, "Opportunity and the Orient," p. 411; Brent to Sibley (copy), October 16, 1916, Brent Papers.

84. Roy H. Brown to Arthur J. Brown, November 27, 1914, February 25, 1915, Presbyterian Mission Records, RG 85, box 6.

85. Munger, "After Twenty-Five Years," p. 658.

86. For a fine study of the "home base" of the missionary movement and of the problems and techniques of fund raising, see Rabe, *Home Base.*

87. Lerrigo, "Thirty Years," p. 1022; J. F. Cottingham, printed appeal, n.d. but after 1913, Methodist Mission Records.

CHAPTER 6

1. Robert F. Black to Judson Smith, May 27, 1903, American Board Mission Records. See also Walter C. Clapp to Arthur S. Lloyd, August 21, 1902, Episcopalian Mission Records.

2. Among the best discussions of the Filipino reaction to American rule are Bonifacio Salamanca, *The Philippine Reaction to American Rule 1901–1913* (Hamden, Conn.: Shoe String Press, 1968); Glenn A. May, "Filipino Resistance to American Occupation: Batangas, 1899–1902," *Pacific Historical Review* 48 (November 1979): 531–56; Norman G. Owen, "Introduction: Philippine Society and American Colonialism," in *Compadre Colonialism: Studies on the Philippines under American Rule,*

ed. Norman G. Owen (Ann Arbor: University of Michigan Center for South and Southeast Asian Studies, 1971), pp. 1–12; Teodoro A. Agoncillo, *Malolos: The Crisis of the Republic* (Quezon City: University of the Philippines Press, 1960); and John A. Larkin, *The Pampangans: Colonial Society in a Philippines Province* (Berkeley: University of California Press, 1972).

3. Higdon and Higdon, *From Carabao to Clipper*, pp. 77–78.

4. Mariano C. Apilado, "Revolution, Colonialism, and Mission: A Study of the Role of the Protestant Churches in the United States' Rule of the Philippines, 1898–1928" (Ph.D. diss., Vanderbilt University, 1976), pp. 389–409. Deats, *Nationalism and Christianity*, generally agrees with Higdon. See pp. 95–141.

5. Zerah C. Collins, "With the Army Y.M.C.A.," n.d., pp. 23, 40, YMCA Records.

6. Brent to Randall Thomas Davidson (copy), May 28(?), 1907, Brent Papers. (Davidson was archbishop of Canterbury.) Brent to F. C. Carter (copy), May 30, 1907, Brent Papers; see also Charles Henry Brent, "Address," in *Missionary District of the Philippines*, January 27–29, 1904 (n.p., n.d.), copy in B.I.A. file 3319.

7. Stanley, *Nation in the Making*, p. 96; Agoncillo, *Malolos*, p. 645.

8. James B. Rodgers to Frank F. Ellinwood, January 31, 1901, Presbyterian Mission Records, reel 288; Brown, *Report of a Visitation*, p. 38.

9. Leonard R. Davidson to Ellinwood, February 16, 1901, Presbyterian Mission Records, reel 288.

10. By the end of the year 1901, the Presbyterian mission reported that the movement had not "fulfilled the hopes of it's originators." "Philippine Minutes, December, 1902," ibid., reel 290.

11. The standard, if often conflicting, accounts of the Aglipayan church are Pedro S. de Achutegni and Miguel A. Bernad, *Religious Revolution in the Philippines: The Life and Church of Gregorio Aglipay 1860–1960*, 2d ed. rev., 2 vols. (Manila: Ateneo de Manila Press, 1961–66); and Lewis Bliss Whittmore, *Struggle for Freedom: History of the Philippine Independent Church* (Greenwich, Conn.: Seabury Press, 1961). See also Norman S. Binsted, "The Philippine Independent Church (Iglesia Filipina Independiente)," *Historical Magazine of the Protestant Episcopal Church* 7 (1958): 213–15; and Sister Mary Dorita Clifford, B.V.M., "Iglesia Filipina Independiente: The Revolutionary Church," in *Studies in Philippine Church History*, ed. Anderson, pp. 223–55.

12. Laubach, *People of the Philippines*; Deats, *Nationalism and Christianity*, p. 69.

13. Eric Lund to Thomas S. Barbour, March 29, 1905, Baptist Mission Records, reel 197.

14. Taft described him as "a man utterly unscrupulous, utterly lacking in any reputation for veracity. . . . There is hardly a man in the islands, Filipino or American, less credible than he." William Howard Taft to Horace White, November 21, 1906, in Achutegui and Bernad, *Religious Revolution*, 1:251n, 385.

15. Lund to Barbour, March 29, 1905.

16. Ibid.

17. Stuntz, *Philippines and the Far East*, p. 495; *Report of the Philippine Mission of the Presbyterian Church in the U.S.A. 1904* (1905), p. 18; see also Homer C. Stuntz, "The Philippine Independent Church," *Christian Advocate* 78 (April 16, 1903): 623–24.

18. Homer C. Stuntz to W. H. Warren, January 5, 1905, Methodist Mission Records, file 74–11; *Official Journal of the First Annual Session of the Philippine Islands Mission Conference* (1905), p. 12; *Christian Advocate* 80 (July 13, 1905): 1102; David S. Hibbard to Arthur Judson Brown, March 7, 1905, Presbyterian Mission Records, reel 288.

19. Rev. and Mrs. C. N. Magill to "friends" (mimeograph), December 12, 1908, Presbyterian Mission Records, reel 289.

20. C. W. Briggs, Report of January 22, 1904, p. 6, Baptist Mission Records, reel 181; Briggs to Barbour, November 29, 1903, ibid.

21. J. L. McElhany, "Philippine Mission," *Union Conference Record* 11 (April 1, 1907): 3; see also O. A. Olsen, "Report of the Australasian Union Conference," *Advent Review and Sabbath Herald* 86 (July 1, 1909): 11.

22. J. L. McElhany, "The Philippine Islands," *Advent Review and Sabbath Herald* 85 (July 16, 1908): 14; Achutegui and Bernad, *Religious Revolution in the Philippines*, 1 : 444.

23. Lund to Barbour, March 29, 1905, Baptist Mission Records, reel 197.

24. W. H. Hanna to Bruce L. Kershner, March 19, 1905, Kershner Papers; see also "Religious Notes," *Philippine Christian* 4 (September 10, 1909): [4]. The Disciples did, however, recognize that the schism presented a golden opportunity for the Protestants, especially after the Supreme Court in 1906 ordered the Aglipayans to relinquish Roman Catholic churches and church property they had occupied. Urging new funds for evangelism, one Disciple explained "the responsibility for this opportunity is simply overwhelming every time I stop to think of it." C. L. Pickett to Kershner, May 17, 1908, Kershner Papers.

25. William T. Ellis, "On the Trail of the American Missionary," unidentified clipping, Mrs. Harry Farmer Materials; Ernest J. Pace to Samuel S. Hough, September 12, 1909, United Brethren Mission Records. Whether Pace's opinions were typical of his mission is debatable, for in previous years, at least, other United Brethren missionaries had found reasons to support the movement.

26. Archibald A. Forshee to Barbour, April 13, 1903, Baptist Mission Records, reel 188; "Biography of Widdoes," pp. 25, 86.

27. C. W. Briggs, Report for 1903, Baptist Mission Records, reel 181. Briggs paints a warm picture of the independent church in his subsequently published book, *The Progressing Philippines*, but he does not term it pro-American (pp. 113–19).

28. William F. Oldham, "The Philippines: The Duty of the Hour, II," unidentified clipping, Mrs. Harry Farmer Materials; Paul Doltz to Brown, December 30, 1905, February 19, 1907, Presbyterian Mission Records, reel 289.

29. Roy H. Brown to Mr. Comstock, April 8, 1907, Presbyterian Mission Records, reel 289.

30. Clapp to John W. Wood, November 3, 1902, Episcopal Mission Records; Mercer G. Johnston to Charles Henry Brent, June 30, 1904, Brent Papers.

31. Brent to Arthur C. A. Hall (copy), March 16, 1903, Brent Papers; Brent, "The Church in the Philippine Islands" (September 1903): 637.

32. Charles Henry Brent, "Religious Conditions in the Philippines," Episcopal Mission Records. This was later published in the *Spirit of Missions* 69 (September

1904): 658–69; Brent, "Private Addendum to Report on Religious Conditions in the Philippine Islands," Brent Papers.

33. In Achutegui and Bernad, *Religious Revolution*, 1:389.

34. Gregorio Aglipay to Brent, June 17, 1904, Episcopal Mission Records. I am indebted to Mr. Mark Norbeck for bringing this letter to my attention. It has been referred to before (see Achutegui and Bernad, *Religious Revolution*, 1:389–90), but the letter itself has hitherto not been seen by historians.

35. Brent to Aglipay, July 10, 1904, in Achutegui and Bernad, *Religious Revolution*, 1:390–91.

36. Brent to Henry T. Allen (copy), October 12, 1904, Brent Papers; Brent to William Lawrence (copy), April 26, 1905, ibid.

37. Charles Henry Brent, "Various Notes on Philippine Matters," October 24, 1905, Episcopal Mission Records, published in *Spirit of Missions* 71 (May 1906): 372–77; Brent to David H. Greer, March 5, 1906, Brent Papers.

38. Masferre's letters are printed in Achutegui and Bernad, *Religious Revolution*, 1:525–28.

39. Brent to Lindley M. Garrison, July 22, 1913, B.I.A. file 7552; Brent to Murray Bartlett (copy), July 23, 1913, Brent Papers. If Staunton wrote to Garrison, the letter has not been preserved. White did write, however, giving a very bleak picture of the Filipino bishop. Including a statement from an unidentified source in the constabulary that testified to Aglipay's cruelty during the Philippine-American War and to his bad moral character, White held Aglipay up as an example of "the kind of cruel intimidation and reckless outcast that gets the ascendancy over the people." Robb White, Jr., to Garrison, September 27, 1913, B.I.A. file 7552

40. A. E. Chenoweth sent a detailed report to Homer C. Stuntz, a copy of which is attached to a letter from Stuntz to Adna B. Leonard, February 15, 1905, Methodist Mission Records, file 74–11 (Stuntz folder), hereafter cited as Chenoweth Report. The Aurora schism is discussed in J. Tremayne Copplestone, *History of Methodist Missions: Twentieth-Century Perspectives* (*The Methodist Episcopal Church, 1896–1939*) (New York: Board of Global Ministries, United Methodist Church, 1973), pp. 223–25.

41. Chenoweth Report; William F. Oldham to Stuntz (copy), May 23, 1905, Mrs. Harry Farmer Materials; Stuntz, in *Official Journal of the First Annual Session of the Philippine Islands Mission Conference* (1905), p. 26.

42. *Official Journal of the Second Annual Session of the Philippine Islands Mission Conference* (1906), p. 24.

43. Rodgers to Brown, September 17, 1906, Presbyterian Mission Records, reel 289; Bruce Kershner to F. M. Rains, June 21, 1906, Kershner Papers; Bruce L. and Ethel S. Kershner to Nell B. Ford, n.d. [1906–8], ibid.; Bruce L. Kershner, "Evangelistic Report Submitted to the Convention of the Philippine Mission, F.C.M.S. for the year 1908," ibid.

44. Richard L. Deats, "Nicolas Zamora: Religious Nationalist," in *Studies in Philippine Church History*, ed. Anderson, pp. 325–26, 329–30; Laubach, *People of the Philippines*, p. 164; John B. Devins, *An Observer in the Philippines* (Boston: American Tract Society, 1905), pp. 305–6.

45. *Eighty-Second Annual Report . . . of the Year 1900* (New York: Missionary Society of the Methodist Episcopal Church, 1901), p. 238; see also Deats, "Nicolas Zamora," pp. 332–33.

46. Oldham to Stuntz (copy), May 23, 1905, Mrs. Harry Farmer Materials.

47. *Official Journal of the Third Annual Session of the Philippine Islands Mission Conference* (1907), p. 33.

48. Oldham to Leonard, February 23, 1909, Methodist Mission Records, file 74–11. Zamora's associate is quoted in a clipping, "Filipino Methodists Secede from Church," *Cablenews-American*, March 4, 1909, Forbes Papers, Philippine Data Political, 6:1584. Zamora is quoted in another clipping, "Bishop Says Move Is Much Needed Reformation," ibid., March 6, 1909, p. 1585. I am indebted to Mr. Michael Cullinane for calling these clippings to my attention

49. Stuntz to Harry Farmer, April 30, 1909, Mrs. Harry Farmer Materials; Marvin Rader to Leonard, March 12, 1909, Methodist Mission Records, file 74–11 (Rader file); *Annual Report . . . for the Year 1909* (New York: Board of Foreign Missions of Methodist Episcopal Church, 1910), p. 349.

50. Oldham to Leonard, February 25, 1909, Methodist Mission Records, file 74–11.

51. "The Defection in the Philippines," *Christian Advocate* 84 (April 29, 1909): 647, which quotes Oldham's letter of March 6, 1909; Oldham, "The Philippine Situation," p. 701.

52. Oldham to Leonard, September 7, 1909, Methodist Mission Records, file 74–11 (Oldham folder). Zamora died in 1914 at the age of thirty-nine, a victim of cholera. "I sincerely regret the death of Nicholas Zamora," Oldham wrote at the time. "I liked the man in spite of all his weakness and he always did me personally the high honor of believing that in my treatment of him I was both sincere and kind." Oldham to Farmer, November 4, 1914, Mrs. Harry Farmer Materials.

53. [Kershner] to John Lord, March 3, 1909, Kershner Papers; Kershner to Mrs. Harry N. Torrey, October 14, 1910, ibid.

54. Stealy B. Rossiter to Brown, March 3, 1909, Presbyterian Mission Records, reel 289; Charles N. Magill, "Station Report of Tayabas Station, 1912," Presbyterian Mission Records, 1911–21, box 1, file 4; Roy H. Brown, "Report of Albay Station, 1913," ibid., file 6; John H. Lamb to Brown, September 30, 1913, ibid., file 7.

55. David L. Rambo to the author, November 4, 1980.

56. Hulda C. Lund, "From the Philippine Islands," *Alliance Weekly* 40 (July 12, 1913): 232; *Seventeenth Annual Report of the Christian and Missionary Alliance (Reorganized)* (n.p., n.d.), p. 16.

57. Tuggy, *Iglesia ni Cristo*, pp. 17–35, quotation at p. 22.

58. Ibid., pp. 17–35.

59. I. H. Evans to W. A. Spicer, January 19, 1913, RG 21 (Secretariat), Incoming Letters, 1913-E, Seventh-day Adventist Mission Records; "Statement of Elbridge M. Adams in the case of Felix Manalo," accompanying Adams to Spicer, September 18, 1913, ibid., 1913-A; Tuggy, *Iglesia ni Cristo*, p. 33.

60. Elbridge M. Adams, "Statement"; Adams to Spicer, September 18, 1913, RG 21 (Secretariat), Incoming Letters, 1913-A, Seventh-day Adventist Mission Records.

61. Tuggy, *Iglesia ni Cristo*, pp. 34–48.

62. See Joseph J. Kavanah, S.J., "The 'Iglesia ni Cristo,'" *Philippine Studies* 3 (March 1955): 21–26.

63. Adams, "Statement"; Tuggy, *Iglesia ni Cristo*, p. 35.

64. Howard W. Widdoes to Samuel S. Hough, December 18, 1912, United Brethren Mission Records.

65. "Council Minutes," May 28, 1913, ibid.

66. Sanford B. Kurtz to Widdoes, June 15, 1914, ibid.; Widdoes to Hough, July 3, 1914, ibid.

67. This is not to say that the United Brethren mission was free of paternalism. "The need for 'big brother' missionary's advice will remain for some years to come," wrote Widdoes. Widdoes to Hough, May 18, 1916, ibid.

68. [Archibald A. Forshee], "A General Statement of the Work Being Done on the Bacolod Station of the American Baptist Missionary Union," received April 30, 1909, Baptist Mission Records, reel 188; Charles L. Maxfield to editor, *Pearl of the Orient* (October 1905): p. 3.

69. Briggs to Barbour, September 2, 1909, Baptist Mission Records, reel 181; see also Charles L. Maxfield, "Harvesting upon the Mountain Side" [1908], ibid., reel 198.

70. [Forshee], "Statement of Work Being Done on the Bacolod Station."

71. Stipp, "Disciples of Christ in the Philippines," pp. 25, 41–42.

72. *Official Journal of the Fourth Annual Session of the Philippine Islands Mission Conference* (1908), p. 27.

73. "Resolution Adopted by the Synod of the Philippines at its Meeting in Manila, Beginning the 6th of October, 1913," Presbyterian Records, 1911–21, box 1, file 6; Board of Foreign Missions, Presbyterian Church, to the Philippine Mission, June 11, 1914, ibid., file 8.

74. J. Andrew Hall to A. W. Halsey, October 16, 1913, ibid., file 7; Rodgers to Brown, September 12, 1914, ibid., file 9.

75. James B. Rodgers, "Personal Report . . . , 1915," ibid., file 10; id., "One Score Years," p. 17; id., *Forty Years in the Philippines*, pp. 177–79, quotation at p. 177.

76. "Manila Notes," *Philippine Christian* 9 (October 10, 1914): [4].

77. Kershner to F. M. Rains, March 21, 1906, Kershner Papers.

78. Kershner to Mrs. Harry N. Torrey, October 14, 1910, ibid.

79. W. N. Lemmon to Kershner and W. H. Hanna, June 6, 1910, ibid.; [Kershner], Do We Need a Revised Plan of Work?" speech given in January 1911 at the Vigan convention, ibid.; Kershner to Leslie Wolfe, July 19, 1913, ibid.

80. S. P. Anunciacion et al. to the Foreign Christian Missionary Society, August 15, 1917, ibid.; Narciso Umandap et al. to the Foreign Christian Missionary Society, [August, 1917,] ibid.

81. Kershner to R. A. Doan, October 31, 1917, ibid.

82. Doan to Wolfe, October 19, 1917, ibid.

83. Wolfe to Kershner, April 9, 1918, ibid; see also Karl Border to Kershner, January 14, 1918, ibid.

CHAPTER 7

1. Stanley, *Nation in the Making*, pp. 51–80.

2. For a good discussion of the debate, see Oscar M. Alfonso, *Theodore Roosevelt and the Philippines 1897–1909* (New York: Oriole Editions, 1974), pp. 85–94.

3. Ibid., pp. 89–90.

4. Brent to Hall, Maundy Thursday, 1904, Brent Papers; Brent to Mrs. George Monks (copy), April 27, 1907, ibid.

5. Theodore Roosevelt to William Howard Taft, September 3, 1907, in *The Letters of Theodore Roosevelt*, ed. Elting E. Morison, 8 vols. (Cambridge: Harvard University Press, 1951–54), 5:782; Roosevelt to Silas McBee, August 27, 1907, ibid., pp. 772–75. Brent first met Roosevelt in 1902, shortly after his consecration as bishop. In subsequent years, the two men carried on an occasional correspondence, and their friendship survived Roosevelt's displeasure with Brent's action in 1907.

6. Leonard Wood to Brent, August 23, 1907, Brent Papers; *Manila Times*, November 16, 1907, p. 2, quoting *Washington Post*, October 9, 1907.

7. Taft to James B. Rodgers (copy), April 25, 1905, B.I.A. file 12662; Stealy B. Rossiter to Arthur J. Brown, August 14, 1905, Presbyterian Mission Records, reel 289.

8. Stanley, *Nation in the Making*, pp. 127–29.

9. *Manila Times*, October 7, 1907, p. 1.

10. Ibid., October 8, p. 1; October 10, p. 2; November 1, p. 3.

11. Ibid., November 1, p. 3.

12. Charles R. Hamilton to Brown, August 14, 1909, Presbyterian Mission Records, reel 289.

13. *Manila Times*, November 21, 1907, pp. 1, 2, 4, 6; November 2, 1907, p. 4.

14. Rodgers to Brown, February 25, 1908, Presbyterian Mission Records, reel 289; Rossiter to Brown, November 18, 1907, ibid.

15. Robert Black to Judson Smith, November 11, 1904, American Board Mission Records; Bruce L. Kershner to Nell B. Ford, June 27, 1906, Kershner Papers; Kershner to Abe McLean, July 31, 1907, ibid.

16. Rodgers to Taft, March 22, 1905, B.I.A. Records, file 1266; David S. Hibbard to Brown, December 12, 1905, Presbyterian Mission Records, reel 289.

17. Charles E. Rath to Brown, July 23, 1906, Presbyterian Mission Records, reel 289; Charles N. Magill to Brown, July 4, 1907, ibid.

18. Charles W. Briggs to Thomas S. Barbour, August 26, 1907, Baptist Mission Records, reel 181. For Briggs's assessment of Filipino character, see ch. 3 above.

19. Brent to W. C. Rivers (copy), November 25, 1907, Brent Papers; Brent to John W. Wood, May 2, 1908, Episcopal Mission Records.

20. *Philippine Christian Advocate* 7 (November 1908): [3]. Such heavy-handed paternalism caused Nicolas Zamora to exclaim at one point, "we only want to be independent." Richard L. Deats, *The Story of Methodism in the Philippines* (Manila: National Council of Churches in the Philippines for Union Theological Seminary, 1964), p. 44.

21. Kershner to C. L. Pickett, October 20, 1908, Kershner Papers; Black to James L.

Barton, March 14, 1911, American Board Mission Records; see also Black to Enoch F. Bell, May 31, 1912, ibid.

22. J. Andrew Hall to Brown, July 27, 1912, Presbyterian Mission Records, 1911–21, box 1, file 5; Howard W. Widdoes to Samuel S. Hough, November 11, 1910, United Brethren Mission Records; Widdoes, "Report for the First Quarter Conference Year 1911, Philippine Mission," ibid.

23. "Fourth of July Oration: Rev. Paul Dolts [*sic*] Makes Stirring Address," *Iloilo Enterprise*, July 6, 1910, in scrapbook, Doltz Papers; Charles N. Magill to Brown, July 7, 1910, Presbyterian Mission Records, reel 289; see also Hamilton to Brown, August 14, 1909, Presbyterian Mission Records, reel 289, and Sanford B. Kurtz to Hough [March or April?], 1910, United Brethren Mission Records.

24. Brent to Provost Macklem (copy), January 28, 1912, Brent Papers; *Mindanao Herald*, August 24, 1912, quoted in William Cameron Forbes, *The Philippine Islands*, 2 vols. (Boston: Houghton Mifflin, 1928), 2 : 196n.

25. James B. Rodgers, "Some Remnants of Pagan Belief among the Christianized Filipinos," in *Report of the Thirtieth Annual Lake Mohonk Conference*, October 23–25, 1912 (1912), pp. 149–53. The quotation is on p. 153. For Rossiter's remarks, see ibid., pp. 187–88. For a refutation of Rossiter and others who disparaged Filipino character, see M. M. Kalaw, ibid., pp. 189–91.

26. Marvin Rader to William F. Oldham, November 15, 1912, Methodist Mission Records, RG 43, file 66–12.

27. Oldham to William P. Eveland, November 19, 1912, ibid., RG 43, file 67; id. to Rader, December 10, 1913, ibid., file 66–12; see also id. to Rader (copy), November 20, 1912, ibid.

28. Information on the Philippine Society is found in Robert E. Speer to Dr. Reed, November 3, 1913, Presbyterian Mission Records, 1911–21, box 1, file 6, and in accompanying newspaper clippings and other enclosures; Brown to Members of the Board and Executive Council, May 9, 1913, ibid.; Brown to Lindley M. Garrison, March 26, 1913, B.I.A. file 1158; see also Stanley, *Nation in the Making*, p. 189.

29. Brent to Rivers, July 16, 1913, Brent Papers.

30. Oldham, *India, Malaysia, and the Philippines*, pp. 251–77. The quotations appear on pp. 266–67.

31. *Report of the Thirty-First Lake Mohonk Conference*, October 22–24, 1913 (1913), pp. 123–30; see also *Christian Advocate* 89 (June 11, 1914): 830.

32. Brent to J. T. Addison, February 3, 1913, Brent Papers; id. to the secretary of the Boston Anti-Imperialist League, March 29, 1913, in Forbes, *Philippine Islands*, 1 : 114; id. to Arthur C. A. Hall, March 18, 1913, Brent Papers.

33. New York *Tribune*, April 21, 1913, pp. 1, 3. Erving Winslow, the noted anti-imperialist, replied two days later to counter Brent's comment that imperialists and anti-imperialists were in fundamental agreement. The question of timing, which Brent dismissed as of little account, was crucial, Winslow argued convincingly. He went on: "We will not say ecclesiastics are affected by property interests, but at all events, such persons are strongly joining with banks and trusts, investors and salaried and pensioned officials, naval and military; sutlers and camp followers, in

exerting to-day influence of every kind and in every quarter and expending great sums of money for the destruction of Philippine independence. In view of these things, those who would preserve the principles of liberty in the Philippine Islands and the United States must join in urging instantly and with all their might: 'Now is the accepted time; now is the day of salvation!'" Ibid., April 24, 1913, p. 8.

34. Forbes, journal, April 3, 1913, 5:231, Forbes Papers.

35. Lindley M. Garrison to Woodrow Wilson, April 24, 1913, in Woodrow Wilson, *The Papers of Woodrow Wilson*, ed. Arthur S. Link, 36 vols. (Princeton: Princeton University Press), 27:454–56.

36. Charles Henry Brent, "National Awakening in the Philippines," *Report of the Thirty-First Lake Mohonk Conference*, p. 147.

37. Garrison to Wilson, June 13, 1913, in Wilson, *Papers*, 27:516. A week later Brent wrote Garrison suggesting that Forbes be retained as governor general for at least a year, so he could train his successor. Garrison's reply was noncommittal. Brent to Garrison, June 21, 1913, B.I.A. file 12848; Garrison to Brent, June 24, 1913, ibid.

38. Brent to the archbishop of Canterbury, July 15, 1913, Brent Papers; id. to Rivers, July 16, 1913, ibid.

39. Stanley, *Nation in the Making*, pp. 200–201.

40. Brent to James Bryce (copy), July 23, 1913, Brent Papers; Brent to Murray Bartlett, July 23, 1913, ibid.

41. Brent to Bryce, July 23, 1913; Forbes, journal, August 10, 1913, 5:291.

42. Stanley, *Nation in the Making*, pp. 200–203.

43. Brent, "National Awakening in the Philippines," pp. 144–48. A similar address Brent made that same month at the Episcopal General Convention received much greater public notice than the Lake Mohonk address. See New York *Tribune*, October 12, 1913, p. 7.

44. Leslie Wolfe to Kershner, January 19, 1914, Kershner Papers; J. M. Groves, "Annual Report Year Ending September 30, 1913," YMCA Records; id. to Sherwood Eddy, July 29, 1914, ibid.

45. *Journal of the Seventh Annual Session of the Philippine Islands Annual Conference* (1913), p. 26; Eveland to Oldham, June 13, 1914, Methodist Mission Records, RG 43, file 67.

46. John H. Lamb to Brown, September 10, 1913, Presbyterian Mission Records, 1911–21, box 1, file 7.

47. Ibid.

48. Presbyterian Missionaries of the Presbytery of Manila, "A Statement to the Public," [1913], ibid., file 6.

49. Rath to Brown, March 26, 1913, ibid., file 7; George William Wright to Brown, November 15, 1913, ibid.; J. Andrew Hall to A. W. Halsey, October 16, 1913, ibid., file 6; David S. Hibbard to Brown, August 28, 1913, ibid., file 7.

50. Marvin Rader, *Philippine Observer* 3 (March 1913): 5. For the fullest expression of Rader's views, see ibid. (August 1913): 8–9.

51. *Journal of the Seventh Annual Session of the Philippine Islands Annual Conference*, p. 70; Harry Farmer to Oldham, August 20, 1914, Mrs. Harry Farmer Materials.

52. *Philippine Observer* 6 (September 1916): 21, (January 1916): 8. For criticism of Harrison in 1915, see ibid., (March 1915): 8, (February 1915): 4.

53. Ernest T. Lyons to Frank Mason North, August 7, 1916, Methodist Mission Records, RG 43, file 66–9.

54. *Annual Report of the Board of Foreign Missions . . . for 1915* (1916), p. 166; Rader to Mr. Donohugh, October 24, 1916, Methodist Mission Records, RG 43, file 66–12.

55. Brent to Francis Burton Harrison (copy), June 5, 1914, Brent Papers.

56. Harrison to Brent, May 15, 1914, ibid.

57. Harrison to Brent, June 29, 1914, ibid; Brent to Forbes (copy), October 26, November 10, 1916, ibid.

58. Brent, "Sixteen Years in the Philippines," pp. 163–64.

59. Kershner to D. O. Cunningham, September 12, 1914, Kershner Papers; id. to A. E. Cory, December 31, 1914, ibid.

60. Hough to Wilson (copy), February 25, 1914, United Brethren Mission Records.

61. C. T. Sibley to Barton, November 27, 1914, American Board Mission Records; Frank C. Laubach to [W. E. Strong], August 16, 1916, ibid.; Frank C. Laubach, Report for 1917, ibid.

62. For example, George W. Dunlap to Robert E. Speer, April 17, 1919, Presbyterian Mission Records, 1911–21, box 1, file 13; Hall to Brown, March 29, 1916, ibid.

CHAPTER 8

1. Bishop Matthew Simpson, quoted in Philip D. Jordan, "Immigrants, Methodists, and a 'Conservative' Social Gospel, 1865–1908," *Methodist History* 17 (October 1978): 16.

2. Cyrus Foss, quoted ibid., p. 17.

3. Gerald H. Anderson, "Providence and Politics behind Protestant Missionary Beginnings in the Philippines," in *Studies in Philippine Church History*, ed. Anderson, p. 289.

4. Ray Allen Billington, *The Far Western Frontier 1830–1860* (New York: Harper & Row, 1956), p. 83; R. Pierce Beaver, *Church, State, and the American Indians: Two and a Half Centuries of Partnership between Protestant Churches and Government* (St. Louis: Concordia Publishing House, 1966), pp. 122–76; Sydney F. Alhstrom, *A Religious History of the American People* (New Haven: Yale University Press, 1972), p. 861. The policy remained in effect for a decade.

5. Jordan, "Immigrants, Methodists, and a 'Conservative' Social Gospel," p. 37. In 1882 the society declared that the "work of the missionary and the patriot is one."

6. Quoted in *The Report of the Philippines Mission of the Presbyterian Church in the U.S.A. 1904* (Manila: Methodist Publishing House, 1905), p. 5; Anderson, "Missionary Beginnings in the Philippines," pp. 289–90.

7. "The Lord has gone before us in placing these islands under the control of the United States so that liberty and freedom, and the right to worship as they may see

fit, might be given to these downtrodden people." L. V. Finster, "From the Philippines," *Advent Review and Sabbath Herald* 86 (November 4, 1909): 26; see also id., "Manila, Philippine Islands," *Union Conference Record* 13 (May 24, 1909).

8. Senate Committee on the Philippines, *Hearings on Affairs in the Philippines*, 57th Cong., 1st Sess., 1902, S. Doc. 331, p. 2672; see also Thoburn's remarks in "Annual Meeting of the General Missionary Committee," *Christian Advocate* 76 (November 28, 1901): 1904. For a modern expression of the providential viewpoint, see Arthur Leonard Tuggy, *The Philippine Church: Growth in a Changing Society* (Grand Rapids, Mich.: William B. Eerdmans, 1971), pp. 97–98.

9. Quoted in Moots, *Pioneer "Amerianas,"* p. 13.

10. W. H. Lingle to Frank F. Ellinwood, January 17, 1899, Presbyterian Mission Records, reel 287. The board paid no heed to Lingle's view. "Biography of Widdoes," p. 25.

11. *Annual Report of the Missionary Society . . . for 1902* (1903), p. 281; *Minutes of the Eleventh Session of the Malaysia Mission Conference of the Methodist Episcopal Church, 1903* (Singapore: American Mission Press, 1903), p. 36; Charles Henry Brent to Arthur S. Hall (copy), "Lent 2," 1908, Brent Papers.

12. William F. Oldham and James B. Rodgers for the Evangelical Union, March 25, 1905, Presbyterian Mission Records, reel 288.

13. Brent to William Howard Taft, April 14, 1902, Taft Papers, reel 35; Brent to W. A. Leonard, October 26, 1901, Brent Papers. The following year Brent wrote, "For God and country is the watchword of this outpost of the Church's work." Brent to John W. Wood, September 20, 1902, Episcopal Mission Records.

14. Homer C. Stuntz to Taft, July 27, 1906, Taft Papers, reel 602; [Bruce L. Kershner], "The Mission and the Government," paper read on December 31, 1907, at the seventh annual conference of the Philippine Mission of the Disciples of Christ, Kershner Papers.

15. Pentecost, *Protestantism in the Philippines*, p. 14.

16. "Government Success," *Philippine Observer* 3 (June 1913): 12–13; *Annual Report of the Board of Foreign Missions . . . for 1915* (1916), p. 178.

17. "Liberties Unappreciated," *Philippine Christian Advocate* 8 (November 1908): [3].

18. McKee, "Alliance Missions," p. 303; Paul Doltz, "The American Volunteer," manuscript, Paul Doltz Correspondence, Presbyterian Historical Society.

19. This theme was a common one. See, for example, "Bishop Thoburn's Instructive Words," *Christian Advocate* 76 (August 29, 1905): 1056; Eric Lund to Henry C. Mabie, October 4, 1900, Baptist Mission Records, reel 80; Bessie White, "God's Providence in the Entering of the Philippines," *Christian and Missionary Alliance* 25 (September 1, 1900): 119; Charles W. Briggs to E. R. Merriam, April 11, 1901, Baptist Mission Records, reel 181.

20. Homer C. Stuntz, *The Philippine Mission of the Methodist Episcopal Church* (New York: Missionary Society of the Methodist Episcopal Church, n.d.), p. 16; Brown, *Report of a Visitation*, p. 85; see also "A Missionary for the Philippines," *Christian and Missionary Alliance* 22 (April 1899): 145.

21. Presbyterian David S. Hibbard, for example, wrote, "If things are as 'eminently satisfactory'" as General Otis claimed, "it does not require much to satisfy

the General." In Panay, Hibbard added, the Filipino soldiers were disciplined and had "the sympathy of almost all the natives." Hibbard to Ellinwood, July 24, 1900, Presbyterian Mission Records, reel 287. See also Bessie White, "The Philippines from a Missionary Standpoint," *Christian and Missionary Alliance* 29 (March 24, 1900): 1.

22. Stuntz, *Philippines and the Far East*, p. 135

23. Charles Henry Brent, "American Democracy in the Orient," manuscript enclosed in Brent to Taft, April 6, 1905, B.I.A. file 12848. At least one missionary, Presbyterian Leonard P. Davidson, did use the term *American-Filipino war*. Quoted in Condict, *Old Glory and the Gospel in the Philippines*, p. 65.

24. Briggs to [ ], March 7, 1902, Baptist Mission Records, reel 181.

25. Charles Henry Brent, "Various Notes on Matters Philippine," October 24, 1905, Episcopal Mission Records; see also Ellen T. Hicks, "An Experiment in Nursing: A Belated Story," *Spirit of Missions* 71 (April 1905): 320–21; Forbes, journal, August 4, 1905, 1:272–73, Forbes Papers; Ellen T. Hicks to Brent (copy), July 30, 1905, Johnston Papers.

26. Z[erah] C. Collins, "With the Y.M.C.A. in the Spanish-American War in the Philippines," Collins biographical file, YMCA Records.

27. Rodgers to Ellinwood, August 28, 1899, Presbyterian Mission Correspondence, reel 287; Stuntz, *Philippines and the Far East*, p. 136.

28. David S. Hibbard to Ellinwood, July 24, 1900, Presbyterian Mission Records, reel 287; J. Andrew Hall to Ellinwood, November 1, 1900, ibid. Hibbard complained that the army had been "carefully feeding and housing the prisoners, and making them as comfortable as they are in their own homes." Hibbard to Ellinwood, October 23, 1900, ibid.

29. Rodgers to Ellinwood, January 21, 1901, ibid., reel 288.

30. Peter G. Gowing, *Mandate in Moroland: The American Government of Muslim Filipinos 1899–1920* (Quezon City, P.I.: Philippine Center of Advanced Studies, 1977), pp. 35, 36.

31. Rodgers to Ellinwood, January 11, 1900, Presbyterian Mission Records, reel 287; McKee, "Alliance Missions," p. 307. The Alliance supported its missionary and urged that the agreement "which, instead of bringing peace, can only bring more bitter misunderstanding and evil" be overturned. *Christian and Missionary Alliance* 29 (August 23, 1902): 106. When the Bates agreement was abrogated unilaterally in 1904, the missionaries were presumably gratified.

32. For a contrary view that contends the military viewed Protestant missions as an unsettling factor and preferred to cultivate relations with the Catholics, see Parker, "Church and State in the Philippines 1898–1906," pp. 195, 262–63; Dean, *Cross of Christ in Bolo-land*, pp. 49–50.

33. "Bishop Thoburn's Instructive Words," p. 1056; Apilado, "Revolution, Colonialism, and Mission," p. 129.

34. "Sees pagans in Fifth Avenue as in Luzon," clipping, *New York Tribune*, October 18, 1913, B.I.A. file 12848. All the Moro had learned from Western nations, Brent wrote shortly thereafter, was "that we are able to kill him." Brent to Henry L. Higginson (copy), February 3, 1914, Brent Papers. Brent attempted, apparently without success, to get congressional support for better medical services for the

Moros. So devoted did he become in later years to humanitarian work among the Muslim Filipinos that he directed that any memorial gifts received upon his death be used to assist such efforts. Brent to Mabel T. Boardman (copy), March 26, 1914, Brent Papers; Sen. G. M. Hitchcock to Boardman (copy), May 13, 1914, Brent Papers; Zabriskie, *Bishop Brent*, p. 73.

35. E. H. Gates, *Advent Review and Sabbath Herald* 83 (May 10, 1906): 11.
36. Cited in Rodgers to F. M. Bond, March 16, 1904, Presbyterian Mission Records, reel 288.
37. Stealy B. Rossiter, "The Philippines before and after the Occupation, May 1, 1898," ibid., reel 289; L. V. Finster to A. G. Daniells, August 23, 1911, Seventh-day Adventist Records, RG 11 (Presidential), Incoming Letters 1911-F; Henry W. Warren, "The United States in the Philippines," *Christian Advocate* 79 (December 15, 1904): 2032. For other comments lauding American efforts to improve public health, see Rodgers to Ellinwood, March 26, 1902, Presbyterian Mission Records, reel 288; Robert W. Carter to Arthur J. Brown, October 27, 1907, ibid., reel 289.
38. J. M. Groves to W. D. Murray, June 30, 1909, YMCA Records. "Publish nothing which may compromise the administration or officials," a YMCA official admonished John R. Mott. [W. A. Tener] to John R. Mott, September 1, 1908, ibid.
39. Samuel S. Hough, quoted in "Biography of Widdoes," p. 249.
40. *Annual Report of the Missionary Society . . . for 1904* (1905), p. 273; Alex A. Pieters to Ellinwood, April 29, 1903, Presbyterian Mission Records, reel 288; Charles W. Briggs, "The Pulahanes in Panay," *Missionary Review of the World* 34 (July 1911): 515.
41. For example, Arthur W. Prautch, "A Crime, Not a Blunder," Methodist Mission Records; id., "Marriage Question in the Philippines," December 28, 1899, ibid.; David S. Hibbard to Ellinwood, December 29, 1899, Presbyterian Mission Records, reel 287; Dean, *Cross of Christ in Bolo-land*, pp. 49–50. On the questionable validity of the criticism, see Rodgers to Ellinwood, February 6, 1900, Presbyterian Mission Records; Donald Dean Parker, "Church and State in the Philippines 1896–1906," *Philippine Social Science Review* 10 (1938): 381–82.
42. Archibald A. Forshee to Thomas A. Barbour, June 19, 1905, Baptist Mission Records, reel 188. When the commission witnessed the crowning of Nuestra Señora, a Disciples missionary wrote resignedly, "but, with Teddy and Taft back of him [Smith], I am decidedly in the minority." Kershner to Hanna, October 9, 1907, Kershner Papers.
43. Forbes, journal, January 14, 1913, 5:174.
44. Walter C. Clapp to John W. Wood, July 9, 1908, Episcopal Mission Records; Brent to Wood, November 21, 1908, ibid; J. M. Groves to Sherwood Eddy, June 29, 1914, YMCA Records. Worcester's reputation changed, however, at least in some important Protestant circles. No one doubted his intellectual abilities, and by 1912 Brent felt that the commissioner had "a genuine and self sacrificing love for the primitive folk." Brent to W. C. Rivers, October 21, 1912, Brent Papers; see also Frank C. Laubach to J. L. Barton, March 27, 1916, American Board Mission Records. Worcester, for his part, counted Brent among his friends and in 1914 endorsed the bishop's efforts to organize a nondenominational "Christian peace work" among the Moros. Dean C. Worcester, *The Philippines Past and Present*, 2

vols. (New York: Macmillan, 1914), 2:643. Worcester's endorsement is referred to in Edward H. Fallows to Hamilton Holt (copy), August 18, 1914, Brent Papers. When the commissioner resigned in 1913, the publication of the Disciples mission observed, surely incorrectly, that Americans reacted with "almost universal regret." "This and That," *Philippine Christian* 13 (September 10, 1913): 1.

45. G. A. Irvin, "Malay Peninsula and the Philippines," *Advent Review and Sabbath Herald* 82 (June 15, 1905): 14; Peter G. Gowing, "The White Man and the Moro: A Comparison of Spanish and American Policies toward Muslim Filipinos," *Solidarity* 6 (March 1971): 40.

46. Robert F. Black to Judson Smith, May 14, 1903, American Board Mission Records. A favor that must have been especially meaningful to the missionary involved Colonel James G. Harbord's decision to order a constabulary physician to remain in Davao to assist with the birth of the Blacks' child. The physician may well have saved Mrs. Black's life. Black to Smith, July 3, 1905, ibid.

47. "Address by Major Henry Gilheuser, Governor of the District of Davao, October 13, 1911," ibid.; Laubach to Barton, December 28, 1915, ibid.; id. to Enoch F. Bell, January 6, 1916, ibid.

48. Brent to John W. Wood, August 8, 1903, Episcopal Mission Correspondence; Irving Spencer to Wood, May 15, 1904, ibid.

49. Perhaps Bruce Kershner of the Disciples mission expressed most persuasively the advantages mission brought to the government. At a time "when the premonition of Oriental power and invasion" was "creeping like a chill up the spine of the West," he wrote in a reflective paper, it behooved the missionary community to foster conservative change only. As the promoters of carefully controlled change, Kershner thought, the missionary and the government were surely allies. For like the government, the missionary was "holding back the billows which may break with desolating power upon his own people. . . . He feels that he is the one whose hand is upon the balance wheel of a nation and his influence is the same as kings, emperors, or presidents." Bruce L. Kershner, "Missionary Inspiration," manuscript [1911?] given to Stephen J. Cory, Kershner Papers.

50. See, for example, James B. Rodgers to Taft, March 22, 1905, and Taft to Rodgers, February 10, 1906, B.I.A. file 12662; Brent, "Church in the Philippine Islands: A Trip through Northern Luzon," p. 792.

51. Homer C. Stuntz, "Governor William Howard Taft, of the Philippines," *Christian Advocate* 76 (August 29, 1901): 1380; Stuntz to Adna B. Leonard, December 24, 1903, Methodist Mission Records; Kenton J. Clymer, "Religion and American Imperialism: Methodist Missionaries in the Philippine Islands, 1899–1913," *Pacific Historical Review* 69 (February 1980): 40.

52. Neill, *Colonialism and Christian Mission*, p. 93.

53. Robert T. Handy, *A Christian America: Protestant Hopes and Historical Realities* (New York: Oxford University Press, 1971), pp. 38–40, 101–5. The quotation is on p. 101. George W. Wright to Arthur J. Brown, April 13, 1905, Presbyterian Mission Records, reel 288; Charles N. Magill to Brown, July 7, 1910, ibid., reel 289.

54. Laubach to Barton, May 6, 1915, American Board Mission Records; Charles W. Briggs, Report, January 16, 1907, Baptist Mission Records, reel 181; Marvin Rader to Leonard, March 17, 1911, Methodist Mission Records.

55. Rodgers to Ellinwood, March 5, 1899, Presbyterian Mission Records, reel 287; Walter O. McIntyre to Brown, October 21, 1903, ibid., reel 288.

56. Charles L. Maxfield to Miss Laclaurin, December 27, 1904, Baptist Mission Records, reel 194; Farmer, journal, May 8, 1904, August 26, December 19, 1905, pp. 21–22, 95–96, 143.

57. Stuntz to Roosevelt, February 2, 1907, B.I.A. file 4213–1. The B.I.A., which investigated Stuntz's "rather bitter complaint," found it to be without substance. Unsigned B.I.A. memorandum, n.d., ibid.

58. W. H. Hanna, "Religious Liberty in the Philippines," *Christian Evangelist* 45 (September 10, 1908): 1161; David O. Lund, quoted in Elizabeth White Jansen, "A Visit to Zamboanga, Philippines," *Christian and Missionary Alliance* 32 (May 8, 1909): 90; Laubach to J. L. Barton, May 6, 1915, American Board Mission Records.

59. See, for example, Leon C. Hills to Ellinwood, January 13, 1902, Presbyterian Mission Records, reel 288.

60. L. B. Hilles to Dr. Sauber (copy), August 20, 1903, ibid. If such a policy ever existed, it was quickly rescinded or ignored, for during their travels missionaries regularly lodged with American school teachers. See, for example, Farmer, journal, passim.

61. *Annual Report of the Missionary Society . . . for 1904*, p. 273. It seems likely that Atkinson was not very sympathetic with Protestant missionary work, for he once wrote that "The prospects as to Protestant work . . . are not very encouraging." Fred W. Atkinson, *The Philippine Islands* (Boston: Ginn & Co., 1905), p. 225.

62. *Pearl of the Orient* 3 (October 1906): 38.

63. H. W. Langheim to Arthur J. Brown, May 26, 1909, Presbyterian Mission Records, reel 289; Robert W. Carter to Dr. Halsey, October 5, 1909, ibid.

64. Brown, *Report of a Visitation*, pp. 53–54.

65. In 1909 Brown received sharply differing assessments from Presbyterian missionaries. George W. Wright strongly defended the government's school policy and claimed that relations with teachers were "most cordial and happy," whereas H. W. Langheim and Charles Hamilton disagreed. They felt that the policy was enforced only in cases involving Protestant teachers and, in any event, raised serious constitutional problems. Wright to Brown, May 18, 1909, Presbyterian Mission Records, reel 289; Langheim to Brown, May 26, 1909, ibid.; Hamilton to Brown, August 20, 1909, ibid.

66. "Philippine [Mission] Minutes, 1910," ibid., reel 290.

67. Brown, *Report of a Visitation*, p. 54; Laubach to Barton, May 6, 1915, American Board Mission Records. For similar expressions, see Rader to Leonard, March 17, 1911, Methodist Mission Records; Charles Maxfield to "friends," February 2, 1912, Baptist Mission Records, reel 198; [Eric Lund,] "Schools in the Philippines," manuscript enclosed in Lund to Barbour, March 28, 1906, Baptist Mission Records, reel 197.

68. For example, Laubach, *People of the Philippines*, pp. 333–34.

69. Maxfield to "friends," February 2, 1912, Baptist Mission Records, reel 198; galley proofs of J. L. McLaughlin's report of April 1907 to the American Bible Society enclosed in William I. Haven to Taft, April 3, 1907, B.I.A. file 1158.

70. For example, Farmer, journal, February 7, 1906, pp. 176–77; Robert W. Car-

ter to Brown, October 27, 1907, Presbyterian Mission Records, reel 289. Carter noted the "active opposition" to Protestant work "from government officials."

71. Stuntz to Roosevelt, December 4, 1904, B.I.A. file 11980; Bruce L. Kershner to W. H. Hanna (copy), October 9, 1907, Kershner Papers; J. L. McElhany, *Advent Review and Sabbath Herald* 84 (December 12, 1907): 19–20. The missions were also angered a few years later when the government helped reconstruct the town of Antipolo. See "This and That," *Philippine Christian* 8 (October 10, 1913): [1].

72. Charles W. Briggs to editor, May 21, 1908, "Unjust and Perilous Favoritism," clipping, *The Examiner*, July 9, [1908], p. 794, B.I.A. file 2396; James A. Graham to Brown, December 18, 1907, Presbyterian Mission Records, reel 289.

73. Harry Farmer to William F. Oldham, October 5, 1908, Mrs. Harry Farmer Materials.

74. For a fuller treatment of this matter, see Clymer, "Religion and American Imperialism," pp. 42–43.

75. "Philippine [Mission] Minutes," January and December 1910, Presbyterian Mission Records, reel 290; Presbyterian Philippine Mission reports of Bohol Station and Camarines Station, both received December 29, 1911, Philippine Mission Records 1911–21, box 1, file 2.

76. Frank W. Warne, "The Canteen in the Philippine Islands," *Christian Advocate* 76 (February 7, 1901): 212.

77. Statements made in August and September 1902, B.I.A. file 2396.

78. Walter C. Clapp to Arthur S. Lloyd, August 12, 1902, Episcopal Mission Records; Brent to E. F. Baldwin, July 24, 1903, Brent Papers; Zabriskie, *Brent*, pp. 54–55; Adolph Wislizenus to Brent, January 31, 1910, Brent Papers; Brent to Wislizenus, February 21, 1910, ibid.

79. James M. Thoburn, "Opium Monopoly in the Philippines," memorandum of a hearing of July 9, 1903, before Elihu Root, B.I.A. file 1023–44. For other protests, see Methodist Episcopal Mission of the Philippine Islands to Wilbur Crafts, May 2, 1903, B.I.A. file 1023–17, and "Report of the American Church in Manila of the [Presbyterian] Philippine Mission, 1903," Presbyterian Mission Records, reel 290.

80. Roosevelt to Taft (telegram), June 9, 1903, B.I.A. file 1023–24.

81. *Official Journal of the Second Annual Session of the Philippine Islands Mission Conference* (1906), p. 48; see also Parker, "Church and State in the Philippines, 1896–1906" (diss.), pp. 271–72.

82. Mercer G. Johnston to Henry C. Ide (letterbook copy), July 26, 1905, Johnston Papers, box 39.

83. Johnston to Ide, May 9, 1906, ibid. For a sketch of Brown and his activities, see Lewis E. Gleeck, Jr., *The Manila Americans (1901–1964)* (Manila: Carmelo & Bauermann, 1977), pp. 10–11.

84. Ide to Johnston, May 15, 1906, Johnston Papers, box 38.

85. Johnston to G. A. Miller (letterbook copy), June 7 [1906], ibid., box 39.

86. "The Moral Progress League in Manila," *Christian Advocate* 81 (August 30, 1906): 1319.

87. Ide to Johnston, June 28, 1906, Johnston Papers, box 38; Johnston to Richard E. Armstrong (letterbook copy), July 6, 1906, ibid., box 39; Johnston to Lewis B. Hilles, July 10, 1906, ibid.

88. *Manila Times*, July 16, 1906, pp. 1–2, quotation at p. 2. Forbes resented Brent's charges, in spite of his friendship with the bishop. Forbes, journal, July 3 and August 2, 1906, 2:60, 62.

89. W. A. Kinkaid to Johnston, July 17, 1906, Johnston Papers, box 38.

90. Forbes, journal, February 5, 1908, 2:396.

91. "The Government and Gambling in the Philippines," unidentified clipping enclosed in Mrs. Stephen L. Baldwin to Theodore Roosevelt, July 31, 1908, B.I.A. file 6633; Forbes, journal, February 21, 1908, 2:402; "Extracts from minutes of the meeting of the Evangelical Union held in the Methodist Church, February 15th, 1908," Johnston Papers, box 38; Mercer G. Johnston, Stealy B. Rossiter, and Isaac B. Harper to Philippines Carnival Association, n.d., ibid.

92. James F. Smith to the Evangelical Union, February 13, 1908, Johnston Papers, box 38; Forbes, journal, February 5, 1908, 2:408. Forbes wrote that he, the governor general, and General Wood all wanted the cockpit stopped, if possible.

93. Smith to the Evangelical Union, February 13, 1908, Johnston Papers, box 38.

94. "Extracts from Minutes of the Evangelical Union . . . February 15, 1908," ibid.; Johnston to Smith (letterbook copy), February 17, 1908, ibid., box 39.

95. For example, Johnston to Fernando M. Guerrero, February 17, 1908, ibid.

96. Forbes to Johnston, February 20, 1908, ibid., box 38; Mercer Johnston, *A Covenant with Death, an Agreement with Hell*, sermon preached at the Cathedral of St. Mary and St. John in Manila on February 23, 1908, printed copy in B.I.A. file 6633.

97. Johnston to Roosevelt (telegram), February 24, 1908, B.I.A. file 6633; Evangelical Union to Roosevelt (telegram), February 24, 1908, ibid. Copies of both telegrams are in Johnston Papers.

98. Forbes, journal, February 21, March 3, 1908, 2:402–3, 408.

99. Taft to Johnston (cable), February 28, 1908, B.I.A. file 6633.

100. Johnston to Ernest A. Rayner (letterbook copy), March 2, 1908, Johnston Papers, box 39.

101. *Missions in the Philippines* (Boston: American Baptist Missionary Union, [1906]), p. 40; H. H. Steinmetz, "A Social Gospel for the Philippines," *Pearl of the Orient* 10 (July 1913): 3–8. Methodist Harry Farmer also surmised that the government had lost interest in helping the poor. See Harry Farmer, "Contending for Religious Liberty," *Philippine Christian Advocate* 7 (July 1908): 6–8.

102. Clapp to Wood, May 22, 1904, Episcopal Mission Records; Brent, quoted in *Manila Times*, November 16, 1907, p. 3, citing *Washington Post*, October 9, 1907; [Arthur Seldon] Lloyd, "To Bontoc and Back Again," *Spirit of Mission* 72 (May 1908): 367.

103. Steinmetz, "A Social Gospel for the Philippines," pp. 3–8.

104. Brent to Mrs. George Monks (copy), April 27, 1907, Brent Papers.

105. Quoted in Daniel R. Williams, *The Odyssey of the Philippine Commission* (Chicago: A. C. McClurg, 1913), p. 350.

106. See, for example, Michael V. Metallo, "American Missionaries, Sun Yat-sen, and the Chinese Revolution," *Pacific Historical Review* 47 (May 1978): 266.

107. Quoted in American Board of Commissioners for Foreign Missions, *Missions in the Philippines*, p. 18.

CHAPTER 9

1. "Bishop Thoburn's Instructive Words," p. 1056; Walter C. Clapp to the *Spirit of Missions*, November 20, 1901, Episcopal Mission Records; David S. Hibbard to Frank F. Ellinwood, June 6, 1899, Presbyterian Mission Records, reel 287.

2. Leon C. Hills to Ellinwood, February 15, 1902, Presbyterian Mission Records, reel 288; *Minutes of the Fourth Session of the District Conference of the Philippine Islands* (1903), p. 19; Stealy B. Rossiter to Arthur J. Brown, February 28, 1904, Presbyterian Mission Records, reel 288.

3. Charles F. Rath to Brown, April 18, 1904, January 11, 1905, Presbyterian Mission Records, reel 188.

4. Charles Henry Brent to Arthur Seldon Lloyd, May 28, 1907, Episcopal Mission Records; William F. Oldham, "An Opportunity at Manila," *Christian Advocate* 78 (April 19, 1906): 565.

5. Lewis B. Hilles to Dr. Sauber, May 14, 1904, Presbyterian Mission Records, reel 288.

6. *Journal of the First Annual Session of the Philippine Islands Mission Conference* (1905), p. 48; Bruce L. Kershner and Ethel S. Kershner to Nell B. Ford, February 28, 1906, Kershner Papers; J. M. Groves, "Annual Report: October 1, 1910–September 30, 1911," p. 8, YMCA Records.

7. Remsen S. Ogilby to Brent, September 5, 1910, Brent Papers; H. H. Steinmetz, "Vacation Ramblings," *Pearl of the Orient* 11 (July 1914): 6.

8. [Bruce L. Kershner?] "Central Notes," [1910,] Kershner Papers; Myron B. Marshall to Brent, December 10, 1909, Brent Papers; Steinmetz, "Vacation Ramblings," p. 5.

9. Brent to John W. Wood, March 28, 1906, Episcopal Mission Records; Brent to Wood, April 26, 1909, ibid.; Elwood S. Brown, "Annual Report: October 1, 1912 to October 1, 1913. Physical Department—Y.M.C.A. of Manila," p. 13, YMCA Records. The club life of Manila is described in Gleeck, *The Manila Americans*, pp. 63–72.

10. Brown, "Annual Report: October 1, 1912, to October 1, 1913," Physical Department, p. 13; "The Church and the Young Americans in Manila," *Spirit of Missions* 71 (February 1906): 86–87.

11. Kenneth P. MacDonald to Brown, May 3, 1912, Presbyterian Mission Records, 1911–21, box 1, file 5; "Station Report of Camarines Station, November 1911-September 1912," ibid., file 4.

12. Elwood S. Brown, "Annual Report of the Year Ending September 30, 1917," p. 3, YMCA Records.

13. Varg, *Missionaries, Chinese, and Diplomats*, p. 84; Neill, *Colonialism and Christian Missions*, pp. 85–86; Arthur Schlesinger, Jr., "The Missionary Enterprise and Theories of Imperialism," in *The Missionary Enterprise in China and America*, ed. John K. Fairbank (Cambridge: Harvard University Press, 1974), pp. 342–46.

14. Quoted in Schlesinger, "The Missionary Enterprise," p. 343.

15. "The Appeal from Our Brethren in the East," *Advent Review and Sabbath Herald* 92 (October 14, 1915): 10; unidentified newspaper clipping with a letter from Paul Doltz to Mr. Craven, April 29, 1910, scrapbook, Doltz Papers.

16. James B. Rodgers, essay accompanying Rodgers to Ellinwood, October 4, 1899, Presbyterian Mission Records, reel 287; Brown, *Report of a Visitation*, p. 30; Leonard P. Davidson to Ellinwood, May 28, 1901, Presbyterian Mission Records, reel 288.

17. Pentecost, "Protestantism in the Philippine Islands," p. 11; J. Andrew Hall to Brown, June 8, 1908, ibid., reel 289.

18. Farmer, journal, June 10, 1905, pp. 135–36; "Some Boys and Girls in the Philippines," *Spirit of Missions* 75 (April 1910): 287.

19. Charles T. Sibley to Dr. Creegan, March 17, 1909, American Board Mission Records; id. and Annie E. Sibley to James L. Barton, March 27, 1908, ibid.

20. Sibley and Sibley to Barton, March 27, 1908, ibid.; C. Sibley to Barton, April 22, May 17, November 7, 1910, ibid. Little materialized along these lines, however, for the American Board was unable or unwilling to support such undertakings. The board's failure led to severe criticism by missionaries who arrived later.

21. Robert L. Black to Judson Smith, March 30, 1906, ibid.; Sibley and Sibley to Barton, May 8, 1908, ibid.; C. Sibley to Barton, August 11, 1909, ibid.; Frank C. Laubach to Enoch F. Bell, December 9, 1916, ibid. If the missionaries maintained good relations with most planters in Mindanao and seldom accused them of mistreating the people, the limited evidence from Cebu suggests a contrary perception. There Fred Jansen reported that field workers were poorly paid and that the American foremen on the plantations were generally "of a rough and rather brutal class." Given this kind of treatment, Jansen encouraged Filipino laborers to go to Hawaii where he thought conditions were considerably better and where the planters treated their laborers kindly. Fred Jansen to Brown, July 13, 1910, Presbyterian Mission Records, reel 289.

22. James M. Thoburn, diary, March 2, 1899, microfilm, Allegheny College Library, Meadville, Pa.; Charles W. Briggs to [ ], March 7, 1902, Baptist Mission Records, reel 181; id. to Thomas S. Barbour, April 21, 1902, ibid.

23. W. O. Valentine to Barbour, November 1, 1904, Baptist Mission Records, reel 211; Brent to Wood, September 20, 1902, Episcopal Mission Records; Zabriskie, *Bishop Brent*, p. 77.

24. Black to Judson Smith, July 3, 1905, American Board Mission Records.

25. *Philippine Observer* 3 (July 1913): 5; 4 (January 1914): 5; D. W. Le Lacheur, "Manila and the Philippines," *Christian and Missionary Alliance* 26 (March 30, 1901): 170.

26. Hibbard to Ellinwood, December 29, 1899, Presbyterian Mission Records, reel 287; George W. Wright, "Albay Impressions," *Philippine Presbyterian* 2 (January 1911): 4.

27. Manuscript accompanying Brent to Wood, July 15, 1904, Episcopal Mission Records; Brent, "American Democracy in the Philippines," p. 11, manuscript enclosed with Brent to William Howard Taft, April 6, 1905, B.I.A. file 12848.

28. M. G. Bailey, "The Work of Travelling Secretary: Importance, Methods, and Result," included in "Second Conference of Secretaries of the Y.M.C.A.," manuscript, p. 23, YMCA Records.

29. J. L. McLaughlin, "Five Years in the Philippines," *Christian Advocate* 80 (August 10, 1905): 1286; Le Lacheur, "Manila and the Philippines," p. 170; Frank W.

Warne, "The Canteen in the Philippine Islands," *Christian Advocate* 76 (February 7, 1901): 212–13.

30. Davidson to Ellinwood, May 28, 1901, Presbyterian Mission Records, reel 288; J. C. Webb, "Temperance," in "Second Conference of Secretaries of the Y.M.C.A," p. 17; *Journal of the Fifth Annual Session of the Philippine Islands Annual Conference* (1912), p. 80.

31. Hibbard to Ellinwood, August 7, 1899, Presbyterian Mission Records, reel 287; Sanford B. Kurtz to editor, July 8, 1902, *Woman's Evangel* 21 (September 1902): 147–48.

32. Black to Smith, January 16, 1904, American Board Mission Records; C. Sibley to Barton, August 11, 1909, ibid.; Edwin S. Eby to editor, July 24, 1902, *Woman's Evangel* 21 (October 1902): 161. (In the passage quoted, Eby was actually quoting a Manila newspaper.)

33. Ernest S. Lyons, in *Annual Report of the Board of Foreign Missions . . . for 1909* (1910), p. 354; Rambo, "Christian and Missionary Alliance in the Philippines," p. 65.

34. On irreligiosity, see Moots, *Pioneer "Americanas*," p. 57. "There were many soldiers who hated anything that savored of Christianity," Moots wrote.

35. Hibbard to Ellinwood, August 7, 1899, Presbyterian Mission Records, reel 287; Rath to Brown, n.d., received June 27, 1904, ibid., reel 288.

36. Rodgers, "Five Years of Protestant Work in the Philippine Islands," p. 7.

37. Sanford B. Kurtz to editor, December 24, 1902, *Woman's Evangel* 22 (June 1903): 105; Charles W. Briggs, Report of January 22, 1904, Baptist Mission Records, reel 181; Clymer, "Religion and American Imperialism," pp. 39–40.

38. Brent to H. R. Talbot (copy), March 5, 1902, Brent Papers; Brent to Lloyd, January 12, 1903, Episcopal Mission Records.

39. For example, Brent to Henry Yates Saterlee, January 26, 1907, Brent Papers; Brent to Leonard Wood (copy), November 22, 1907, ibid.; Brent to W. C. Rivers, November 25, 1907, ibid.

40. Brent to Rivers (copy), November 25, 1907, ibid.; Brent to Arthur C. A. Hall (copy), [January 6,] 1908, ibid.

41. Briggs, Report of January 22, 1904; "Malay Peninsula and the Philippines," p. 14.

42. James B. Rodgers, "Back among the Filipinos," clipping, *Utica Daily Press*, September 25, 1906, Presbyterian Mission Records, reel 289; Brent to Sam Drury, November 16, 1909, Brent Papers.

43. J. M. Groves, "Annual Report . . . Year Ending September 10, 1914," YMCA Records.

44. Ernest T. Lyons to Frank Mason North, August 7, 1916, Methodist Mission Records; J. Andrew Hall to A. W. Halsey, October 16, 1913, Presbyterian Mission Records, 1911–21, box 1, file 6.

45. Brent to Mrs. George Monks (copy), February 16, 1903, Brent Papers; Brent, "Church in the Philippine Islands: A Trip through Northern Luzon," p. 795; see also Brent to Wood, February 12, 1903, Episcopal Mission Records.

46. Irving Spencer, "Bagobo Land," *Spirit of Missions* 70 (May 1905): 388; Charles Henry Brent, "Kalinga," *Spirit of Missions* 80 (October 1915): 674, 676.

47. Laubach to Barton, December 28, 1915, American Board Mission Records; Brent, "Sixteen Years in the Philippines," p. 184; see also Laubach to Enoch F. Bell, March 11, 1916, American Board Mission Records.
48. George W. Wright to Brown, May 18, 1909, PresbyterianMission Records, reel 287; "Philippine Events of Note," *Pearl of the Orient* 3 (October 1906): 38; Brent to William Lawrence (copy), April 26, 1905, Brent Papers; Brent to Wood, April 20, 1905, Episcopal Mission Records.
49. Robert W. Carter to Brown, October 27, 1907, Presbyterian Mission Records, reel 287.
50. Brent to Wood, April 22, July 29, 1907, Episcopal Mission Records. On Saleeby, see Gowing, *Mandate in Moroland*, passim.
51. J. M. Groves, "Annual Report: October 1, 1910–September 30, 1911," p. 8, YMCA Records; William F. Oldham to Homer C. Stuntz (copy), April 15, 1905, Mrs. Harry Farmer Materials; *Annual Report of the Board of Foreign Missions . . . for 1908* (1909), p. 363.
52. "Biography of Widdoes," p. 83; Black to Smith, January 16, 1904, American Board Mission Records; C. Sibley to Barton, August 11, 1909, ibid.
53. Laubach to Barton, July, 5, 1915, American Board Mission Records; Archibald A. Forshee to "Brother Wood," August 17, 1910, Baptist Mission Records, reel 188.
54. Charles R. Hamilton to Brown (copy), August 14, 1909, Presbyterian Mission Records, reel 289; Eric Lund, "A Little Common Sense," *Pearl of the Orient* 7 (July 1910): 33–34.
55. Zerah C. Collins, untitled essay, n.d., YMCA Records; *Annual Report of the Board of Foreign Missions . . . for 1915* (1916), p. 166.
56. A. E. Bigelow, "Some Incongruities," *Pearl of the Orient* 5 (October 1908): 9–10; Brent to Wood, July 15, 1904, Episcopal Mission Records; Brent to Monks, February 16, 1903, Brent Papers.
57. Reverend and Mrs. C. N. Magill to Friends, June 11, 1906, Presbyterian Mission Records, reel 289; E. H. Gates, "Manila, Philippine Islands," *Union Conference Record* 10 (January 28, 1907): 3. For a similar assessment by the leading Disciples missionary, see Kershner to Abe McLean, July 31, 1906, Kershner Papers.
58. Charles R. Hamilton, "A Visiting Pastor in Tayabas," *Philippine Presbyterian* 3 (April 1912): 6; see also Farmer, journal, passim.
59. George W. Wright to Brown, May 8, 1909, Presbyterian Mission Records, reel 289; "Biography of Widdoes," p. 81; Black to Smith, July 17, 1903, American Board Mission Records; Black to Barton, January 31, 1907, ibid.
60. Daniel H. Klinefelter, *Annual Report of the Board of Foreign Missions . . . for 1910* (1911), p. 345.
61. Leon C. Hills to Ellinwood, December 16, 1901, Presbyterian Mission Records, reel 288.
62. Black to Smith, February 2, 1903, American Board Mission Records; Stuntz, in *Annual Report of the Missionary Society . . . for 1904* (1905), p. 273; W. H. Hanna to Kershner, September 21, 1907, Kershner Papers.
63. Ernest J. Pace to Samuel S. Hough, June 1, 1911, United Brethren Mission Records; Eric Lund, "A Little Common Sense," p. 35.

64. Gates, "Manila, Philippine Islands," p. 3; id., "Philippines Islands," *Advent Review and Sabbath Herald* 84 (March 28, 1907): 19.

65. Mrs. M. S. Caldwell to T. E. Bowen, August 11, 1908, Seventh-day Adventist Records, RG 21 (Secretariat), Incoming Letters: Foreign, 1908-C.

66. Elbridge M. Adams, *News Letter for the Asiatic Division* 2 (November 1, 1913): 9; id., "The Philippine Islands," *Advent Review and Sabbath Herald* 90 (December 11, 1913): 1193.

67. Lund, "A Little Common Sense," p. 34; Farmer, journal, May 1904, August 26, 1905, pp. 21–22, 143; Rodgers to Courtenay H. Fenn, September 15, 1902, Presbyterian Mission Records, reel 288; Laubach to Barton, May 6, 1915, American Board Mission Records.

68. Lund, "A Little Common Sense," p. 34; Farmer, journal, October 30, 1904, p. 75; Robert W. Carter to A. W. Halsey, October 5, 1909, Presbyterian Mission Records, reel 289; "The Opportunity of the American Teacher," *Philippine Christian* 7 (August 1910): [4].

69. For example, Herbert M. Damon to B. Winget, August 22, 1908, August 8, 1909, Free Methodist Mission Records; Forshee to Brother Wood, August 17, 1910, Baptist Mission Records, reel 188.

70. Hilles to Brown, August 4, 1908, Presbyterian Mission Records, reel 289; W. H. Hanna to Kershner, September 21, 1907, Kershner Papers.

CONCLUSION

1. Stanley, *Nation in the Making*, p. 277. A recent work that emphasizes the powerful impact of American cultural ideas on the Philippines is Fred Poole and Max Vanzi, *Revolution in the Philippines: The United States in a Hall of Cracked Mirrors* (New York: McGraw-Hill, 1984).

2. May, *Social Engineering in the Philippines*, p. xxiv. Other works that emphasize the limited nature of the American impact on the islands include Theodore Friend, *Between Two Empires: The Ordeal of the Philippines 1929–1946* (New Haven: Yale University Press, 1965), and Owen, ed., *Compadre Colonialism*.

3. Renato Constantino, *The Miseducation of the Filipino*, pamphlet (Manila: Erehwon Bookstores, [1966]).

4. The estimate is based on statistics compiled by Frank C. Laubach; see *People of the Philippines*, pp. 483–84. Laubach's statistics exclude the Episcopalians and the Christian and Missionary Alliance. There were, in addition, about 20,700 members in the schismatic Protestant churches; and the Iglesia ni Kristo, an indigenous church, had perhaps 5,000 members by 1925. See Tuggy, *Iglesia ni Cristo*, p. 222. Today the Iglesia ni Kristo has perhaps 500,000 members and is still growing rapidly.

5. *Minutes of the Fifth Annual Session of the District Conference of the Philippines of the Methodist Episcopal Church* (1904), p. 22.

6. See, for example, Gerald H. Anderson and Peter G. Gowing, "The Philippines: Bulwark of the Church in Asia," in *Christ and Crisis in Southeast Asia*, ed. Gerald H. Anderson (New York: Friendship Press, 1968), p. 153. It should also be

noted that some Protestant influences were at work in the formation of the Philippine Independent Church (*Iglesia Filipina Independiente*), which at its peak claimed the allegiance of as much as one-third of the population. Today the Church has 3 or 4 percent; it maintains a connection with the Episcopal Church. The major force behind the Church's formation, however, was Philippine nationalism.

7. Hermogenes Cera, Jr., "The Impact of Evangelical Faith upon Philippine Culture" (B.D. thesis, Union Theological Seminary, Dasmariñas, Cavite, P.I., 1958), especially pp. 58–61. Anthropological studies of the effects of Protestantism in specific areas of the Philippines include F. Landa Jocano, "Conversion and the Patterning of Christian Experience in Malitbog, Central Panay, Philippines," in *Acculturation in the Philippines: Essays on Changing Societies*, ed. Peter G. Gowing and William Henry Scott (Quezon City: New Day Publishers, 1971), pp. 43–72; and John J. Carroll, "Magic and Religion," in *Philippine Institutions*, ed. John J. Carroll et al. (Manila: Solidaridad Publishing House, 1970), pp. 40–74.

8. Gouverneur F. Mosher to John W. Wood, August 13, 1920, Episcopal Mission Records.

9. Clifford E. Barry Nobes to Artley B. Parson, May 22, 1940, ibid.; *Diocesan Chronicle: Missionary District of the Philippine Islands* 20 (March 1940): 3; ibid., 21 (August 1940): 102, (September 1940): 1–2.

10. Cornelio M. Ferrer, "How to Survive in the Ministry," p. 63, Ferrer Papers.

11. Dionisio D. Alejandro, *From Darkness to Light: A Brief Chronical of the Beginnings and Spread of Methodism in the Philippines* (n.p.: United Methodist Church [P.I.], 1974), p. 16; Cornelio M. Ferrer and Paul Locke A. Granadosin, "The Episcopal Address: Philippine Central Conference, The United Methodist Church, November 29, 1972," mimeographed, Ferrer Papers.

12. See, for example, *The Human Rights Advocate* 1 (Fourth Quarter, 1983). This publication originates with the UCCP's Human Rights Desk and is published in Manila.

13. For a discussion of Protestants and martial law, see Robert L. Youngblood, "The Protestant Church in the Philippines' New Society," *Bulletin of Concerned Asian Scholars* 12 (July-September 1980): 19–29. The same author analyzes Roman Catholic attitudes in "Church Opposition to Martial Law in the Philippines," *Asian Survey* 58 (May 1978): 505–20.

Selected Bibliography

PRIMARY SOURCES

1. Manuscript Material

American Baptist Missionary Union. Correspondence and Reports. American Baptist Historical Society, Rochester, New York.

American Board of Commissioners for Foreign Missions. Correspondence and Reports. Houghton Library, Harvard University.

"Biography of H. W. Widdoes." United Brethren Mission Records, United Methodist Archives, Lake Junaluska, North Carolina.

Black, Robert F. "Otao Po: A Salutation from Mindanao." American Board Mission Records, August 1905.

Brent, Charles Henry. Papers. Manuscript Division, Library of Congress, Washington, D.C.

Brent, Charles Henry. "A Study of Missions among a Primitive People." Episcopal Mission Records.

Bureau of Insular Affairs. Records of the Bureau of Insular Affairs Relating to the Philippine Islands 1898–1935. National Archives, Washington, D.C.

Compagno, Dorothy U. "Distribution in the Philippine Islands, 1898–1932." American Bible Society Historical Essay #15, Part VI-J, 1967. American Bible Society Archives, New York.

Doltz, Paul. Papers. Presbyterian Historical Society, Philadelphia, Pennsylvania.

Episcopal Church. Philippine Mission Correspondence and Reports. Archives and Historical Collections of the Episcopal Church, Austin, Texas.

Farmer, Harry. "Private Journal of Harry Farmer: Beginnings of Methodism in the Agno Valley Area, the Philippines, 1904–1907." United Methodist Headquarters, Manila.

Farmer, Mrs. Harry. Mrs. Harry Farmer Materials. Record Group 43, box 339, United Methodist Archives, Lake Junaluska, North Carolina.

Ferrer, Cornelio M. Papers. United Methodist Archives, Lake Junaluska, North Carolina.

Forbes, W. Cameron. "Journal of W. Cameron Forbes." W. Cameron Forbes Papers, Houghton Library, Harvard University.

Free Methodist Church. Records of the General Missionary Board. Free Methodist
World Headquarters, Winona Lake, Indiana.

Hall, Joseph Andrew. "Philippine Life and Character." Presbyterian Historical Society, Philadelphia, Pennsylvania.

Johnston, Mercer Green. Papers. Manuscript Division, Library of Congress, Washington, D.C.

Kershner, Bruce L. Papers. Disciples of Christ Historical Society, Nashville, Tennessee. (All letters and reports in the Kershner collection are typewritten
copies.)

Methodist Episcopal Church. Philippine Mission Correspondence and Reports.
United Methodist Archives, Lake Junaluska, North Carolina.

Parrish, Rebecca. Papers. In possession of United Methodist Bishop Paul Locke A.
Granadosin, Baguio City, Philippines.

Presbyterian Church, U.S.A., Board of Foreign Missions. Record Group 85. Secretaries' file, Philippine Mission Correspondence and Reports, 1898–1910. Presbyterian Historical Society, Philadelphia, Pennsylvania. Microfilm series, reels
287–89.

Presbyterian Church, U.S.A., Board of Foreign Missions. Record Group 85. Secretaries' file, Philippine Mission Correspondence and Reports, 1911–1921. Presbyterian Historical Society, Philadelphia, Pennsylvania.

Presbyterian Church, U.S.A., Board of Foreign Missions. Minutes. Presbyterian
Historical Society, Philadelphia, Pennsylvania.

Seventh-day Adventist Church. Correspondence and Reports. Archives of the
General Conference of Seventh-day Adventists, Washington, D.C.

"The Story of Rev. and Mrs. S. D. Lommasson: Lifetime Missionaries to the
Philippine Islands." Lommasson file, Christian and Missionary Alliance Headquarters, Nyack, New York.

Taft, William Howard. Papers. Manuscript Division, Library of Congress, Washington, D.C. Microfilm series.

Thoburn, James M. Diary. Allegheny College Library, Meadville, Pennsylvania.
Microfilm.

United Brethren in Christ Church, Board of Missions. Philippine Islands, 1907–
1922, Correspondence and Reports. United Methodist Archives, Lake
Junaluska, North Carolina.

Williams, Hermon P. Papers. Disciples of Christ Historical Society, Nashville,
Tennessee.

Young Men's Christian Association. Correspondence and Reports. Historical Library of the YMCA, New York, New York.

2. Published Official Records

Annual Report of the Board of Foreign Missions of the Methodist Episcopal Church,
1899–1916.

Annual Report of the Christian and Missionary Alliance, 1899–1916.

Annual Report of the Missionary Society of the Methodist Episcopal Church, 1899–1916.

Bibliography

Minutes of the Annual Session of the District Conference of the Philippines of the Metho-dist Episcopal Church, 1900–1904.

Minutes of the Annual Session of the Malaysia Mission Conference of the Methodist Epis-copal Church, 1900–1904.

Official Journal of the Annual Session of the Philippine Islands Annual Conference of the Methodist Episcopal Church, 1908–17.

Official Journal and Report of the Annual Session of the Philippine Islands District Conference, Malaysia Annual Conference of the Methodist Episcopal Church, 1900–1904.

Official Journal of the Annual Session of the Philippine Islands Mission Conference of the Methodist Episcopal Church, 1905–8.

Official Report of the Annual Session of the Woman's Conference of the Philippine Islands Mission of the Methodist Episcopal Church, 1913–17.

The Report of the Philippines Mission of the Presbyterian Church in the U.S.A. 1904. Manila: Printed at the Methodist Publishing House, 1905.

3. Publications by Philippine Missionaries and Missionary Spokesmen, 1899–1916

"Bishop Thoburn's Instructive Words." *Christian Advocate* 76 (August 29, 1905).

Brent, Charles Henry. *Adventures for God*. New York: Longmans, Green, & Company, 1905.

———. "The Church in the Philippine Islands." *Spirit of Missions* 68 (September 1903): 633–39.

———. "The Church in the Philippines: A Trip through Northern Luzon." *Spirit of Missions* 68 (November 1903): 788–95.

———. "Religious Conditions in the Philippine Islands." *Spirit of Missions* 69 (September 1904): 658–69.

———. "Sixteen Years in the Philippines." *Spirit of Missions* 83 (March 1918): 163–85.

Briggs, Charles W. *The Progressing Philippines*. Philadelphia: Griffith & Rowland Press, 1913.

Brown, Arthur J. *The New Era in the Philippines*. Chicago and New York: Fleming H. Revell, 1903.

———. *Memoirs of a Centenarian*, edited by William N. Wysham. New York: World Horizons, 1957.

———. *One Hundred Years: A History of the Foreign Missionary Work of the Pres-byterian Church in the U.S.A., With Some Account of Countries, People and the Policies and Problems of Modern Missions*. Chicago and New York: Fleming H. Revell Company, 1936.

———. *Report of a Visitation of the Philippine Mission of the Board of Foreign Missions of the Presbyterian Church in the United States of America*. New York: Board of Foreign Missions of the Presbyterian Church in the United States of America, 1902.

———. *The Why and How of Foreign Missions*. 3d ed. New York: Laymen's Mission-ary Movement, 1908.

Condict, Alice Byram. *Old Glory and the Gospel in the Philippines: Notes Gathered during Professional and Missionary Work.* Chicago and New York: Fleming H. Revell Company, 1902.

Dean, John Marvin. *The Cross of Christ in Bolo-land.* Chicago and New York: Fleming H. Revell Company, 1902.

Devins, John B. *An Observer in the Philippines.* Boston: American Tract Society, 1905.

Farmer, Harry. *The Philippine Mission of the Methodist Episcopal Church.* New York: Board of Foreign Missions of the Methodist Episcopal Church, 1910.

Hibbard, David S. *Making a Nation: The Changing Philippines.* New York: Presbyterian Board of Foreign Missions, 1926.

Higdon, Elmer K., and Higdon, I. W. *From Carabao to Clipper.* New York: Friendship Press, 1941.

Kershner, Bruce L. *The Head Hunter and Other Stories of the Philippines.* Cincinnati: Powell & White, 1921.

Laubach, Frank C. The Crucial Spot: Mindanao. N.p., n.d. Pamphlet, American Board Mission Records.

———. *The People of the Philippines: Their Religious Progress and Preparation for Spiritual Leadership in the Far East.* New York: George H. Doran Company, 1925.

Lerrigo, P. H. J. *Anita: A Tale of the Philippines.* Philadelphia: Judson Press, 1925.

Lund, Hulda Frykman. "The Philippines as a Mission Field." *Christian and Missionary Alliance* 34 (September 3, 1910): 361–63; (September 10, 1910): 377–79.

Mathews, G. M., and Hough, S. S. *The Call of China and the Islands: Report of the Foreign Deputation, 1911–1912, for Every Member of the United Brethren Church.* Dayton, Ohio: Foreign Missionary Society, United Brethren in Christ, n.d.

McKee, John. "Alliance Missions." *Christian and Missionary Alliance* 31 (October 31, 1903): 303, 307.

Munger, Henry W. "After Twenty-Five Years." *Missions* 16 (December 1925): 657–59.

———. *Christ and the Filipino Soul: A History of the Philippine Baptists.* N.p., 1967.

Moots, Cornelia Chillson. *Pioneer "Americanas"; or, First Methodist Missionaries in the Philippines.* N.p.: The Author, 1903.

Oldham, William F. *India, Malaysia, and the Philippines: A Practical Study in Mission.* New York: Eaton & Mains, 1914.

———. "The Philippine Situation." *Christian Advocate* 84 (May 6, 1909): 701–2.

———. *Thoburn: Called of God.* New York: Methodist Book Concern, 1918.

Pentecost, George F. *Protestantism in the Philippines.* N.p., n.d. Sermon preached in Manila, December 21, 1902. Presbyterian Historical Society.

Rodgers, James B. *Forty Years in the Philippines: A History of the Philippine Mission of the Presbyterian Church in the United States of America, 1899–1939.* New York: Board of Foreign Missions of the Presbyterian Church in the United States of America, 1940.

———. *Lessons from Five Years of Protestant Work in the Philippine Islands.* N.p., March 15, 1905. Portions of this paper were read at the Evangelical Union in Manila, March 16, 1905. Presbyterian Mission Records, reel 288.

———. "One Score Years." In *Twenty Years of Presbyterian Work in the Philippines.* N.p., n.d.

Bibliography

Stuntz, Homer C. *The Philippines and the Far East.* Cincinnati: Jennings & Pye, 1904.

Thoburn, James M. *India and Malaysia.* Cincinnati: Cranston & Curtis, 1892.

Warne, Frank W. "The People of the Philippine Islands." *Christian Advocate* 76 (January 17, 1901): 94–95.

SECONDARY SOURCES

1. The Context

Agoncillo, Teodoro A. *Malolos: The Crisis of the Republic.* Quezon City: University of the Philippines Press, 1960.

Alfonso, Oscar M. *Theodore Roosevelt and The Philippines 1897–1909.* Quezon City: University of the Philippines Press, 1970; New York: Oriole Editions, 1974.

Campbell, Charles S. *The Transformation of American Foreign Relations 1865–1900.* New York: Harper & Row, 1976.

Corpuz, Onofre D. *The Philippines.* Englewood Cliffs, New Jersey: Prentice-Hall, 1965.

Cruz, Romeo V. *America's Colonial Desk and the Philippines, 1898–1934.* Quezon City: University of the Philippines Press, 1974.

de la Costa, Horacio. *The Background of Nationalism and Other Essays.* Manila: Solidaridad Publishing House, 1965.

Forbes, W. Cameron. *The Philippine Islands.* 2 vols. Boston: Houghton Mifflin, 1928.

Gleek, Jr., Lewis F. *Americans on the Philippine Frontiers.* Manila: Carmelo & Bauermann, 1974.

———. *The Manila Americans (1901–1964).* Manila: Carmelo & Bauermann, 1977.

Gowing, Peter G. *Mandate in Moroland: The American Government of Muslim Filipinos 1899–1920.* Quezon City: Philippine Center for Advanced Studies, 1977.

Hayden, Joseph Ralston. *The Philippines: A Study in National Development.* New York: Macmillan, 1942.

Ileto, Reynaldo C. *Pasyon and Revolution: Popular Movements in the Philippines, 1840–1910.* Manila: Ateneo de Manila Press, 1981.

Larkin, John A. *The Pampangans: Colonial Society in a Philippine Province.* Berkeley: University of California Press, 1972.

LeRoy, James D. *The Americans in the Philippines.* Boston: Houghton Mifflin, 1914.

McCoy, Alfred W., and de Jesus, Edilberto C., eds. *Philippine Social History: Global Trade and Local Transformations.* Manila: Ateneo de Manila Press; Honolulu: University of Hawaii Press, 1982.

May, Glenn A. *Social Engineering in the Philippines: The Aims and Impact of American Colonial Policy, 1900–1913.* Westport, Connecticut: Greenwood Press, 1980.

———. "Social Engineering in the Philippines. The Aims and Execution of American Educational Policy, 1900–1913." *Philippine Studies* 24 (1976): 135–83.

Miller, Stuart Creighton. *"Benevolent Assimilation:" The American Conquest of the Philippines, 1899–1903.* New Haven: Yale University Press, 1982.

Onorato, Michael P. *A Brief Review of American Interests in Philippine Development, and Other Essays.* Revised edition. Manila: MCS Enterprises, 1972.

Owen, Norman, ed. *Compadre Colonialism: The Philippines Under American Rule.* Ann Arbor: University of Michigan Center for South and Southeast Asian Studies, 1971.

Perkins, Whitney T. *Denial of Empire: The United States and Its Dependencies.* Leyden: A. W. Sythoff, 1962.

Pratt, Julius W. *America's Colonial Experiment: How the United States Gained, Governed, and in Part Gave Away a Colonial Empire.* New York: Prentice-Hall, 1950.

Salamanca, Bonifacio S. *The Filipino Reaction to American Rule, 1901–1913.* [Hamden, Conn.:] Shoe String Press, 1968.

Schumacher, John N. *The Propaganda Movement: 1880–1895.* Manila: Solidaridad Publishing House, 1973.

Stanley, Peter W. "The Forgotten Philippines." In *American–East Asian Relations: A Survey,* edited by Ernest May and James C. Thomson, Jr., pp. 291–316. Cambridge: Harvard University Press, 1972.

———. *A Nation in the Making: The Philippines and the United States, 1899–1921.* Cambridge: Harvard University Press, 1974.

———, ed. *Reappraising an Empire: New Perspectives on Philippine American History.* Cambridge: Harvard University Press, 1984.

Steinberg, David Joel. *The Philippines: A Singular and Plural Place.* Boulder: Westview Press, 1982.

Thomson, James C., Jr., Stanley, Peter W., and Perry, John Curtis. *Sentimental Imperialists: The American Experience in East Asia.* New York: Harper & Row, 1981.

Welch, Jr., Richard F. *Response to Imperialism: The United States and the Philippine-American War, 1899–1902.* Chapel Hill: University of North Carolina Press, 1979.

Wolff, Leon. *Little Brown Brother: How the United States Purchased and Pacified the Philippine Islands at the Century's Turn.* Garden City, New York: Doubleday, 1960.

2. Material about Missionaries, Missions, Churches, and Other Religious Subjects

Achutegui, Pedro S. de, and Bernad, Miguel A. *Religious Revolution in the Philippines: The Life and Times of Gregorio Aglipay 1860–1960.* 2d ed. 3 vols. Manila: Ateneo de Manila Press, 1961.

———. "Brent, Herzog, Morayta and Aglipay." *Philippine Studies* 8 (July 1960): 568–83.

Alejandro, Dionisio D. *From Darkness to Light: A Brief Chronical of the Beginnings and Spread of Methodism in the Philippines.* N.p.: Philippine Central Conference, Board of Communications and Publications, United Methodist Church [Philippines], 1974.

Anderson, Gerald H., ed. *Studies in Philippine Church History.* Ithaca: Cornell University Press, 1969.

Apilado, Mariano C. "Revolution, Colonialism, and Mission: A Study of the Role of the Protestant Church in the United States' Rule of the Philippines, 1898–1928." Ph.D. dissertation, Vanderbilt University, 1976.

Barclay, Wade Crawford. *History of Methodist Missions: A Worldwide Church, 1896–1939.* New York: Board of Missions of the Methodist Church, 1957.

Beaver, R. Pierce. *Ecumenical Beginnings in the Protestant World Mission: A History of Comity.* New York: Thomas Nelson & Sons, 1962.

Binsted, Norman S. "The Philippine Independent Church (Iglesia Filipina Independiente)." *Historical Magazine of the Protestant Episcopal Church* 7 (September 1958): 209–46.

———. "Statement Concerning the Philippines Independent Church." *Historical Magazine of the Protestant Episcopal Church* 17 (June 1948): 138–39.

Cera, Hermogenes, Jr. "The Impact of Evangelical Faith upon Philippine Culture." B.D. thesis, Union Theological Seminary, Dasmariñas, Cavite, Philippines, 1958.

Clymer, Kenton J. "Methodist Missionaries and Roman Catholicism in the Philippines, 1899–1916. *Methodist History* 18 (April 1980): 171–78.

———. "Religion and American Imperialism: Methodist Missionaries in the Philippine Islands, 1899–1914." *Pacific Historical Review* 49 (February 1980): 29–50.

———. "The Episcopalian Missionary Encounter with Roman Catholicism in the Philippines, 1901–1916." *Philippine Studies* 28 (1980): 86–97.

———. "The Methodist Response to Philippine Nationalism, 1899–1916." *Church History* 17 (December 1978): 421–33.

Copplestone, J. Tremayne. *History of Methodist Missions: Twentieth Century Perspectives.* New York: Board of Global Ministries of the United Methodist Church, 1973.

Cullum, Leo A. "The Religion of the Y.M.C.A." *Philippine Studies* 1 (December 1953): 249–69.

de la Costa, Horacio. *The Jesuits in the Philippines 1581–1768.* Cambridge: Harvard University Press, 1967.

de los Reyes, Isabelo, Jr. "The Iglesia Filipina Independiente." *Historical Magazine of the Protestant Episcopal Church* 17 (June 1948): 132–37.

Deats, Richard L. *Nationalism and Christianity in the Philippines.* Dallas: Southern Methodist University Press, 1967.

———. *The Story of Methodism in the Philippines.* Manila: National Council of Churches in the Philippines for Union Theological Seminary, 1964.

Doeppers, Daniel. "The Evolution of the Geography of Religious Adherence in the Philippines before 1898." *Journal of Historical Geography* 2, no. 2 (1976): 95–110.

Doraisamy, Theodore R. *Oldham: Called of God.* Singapore: Methodist Book Room, 1979.

———. "Rescuing the Oldham Legend." *Methodist History* 18 (October 1979): 61–65.

Fairbank, John K., ed. *The Missionary Enterprise in China and America.* Cambridge: Harvard University Press, 1974.

Ferrer, Cornelio N. *Pastor to the Rural Philippines: An Autobiography.* Quezon City: New Day Publishers, 1974.

Fridell, Elmer A. *Baptists in Thailand and the Philippines*. Philadelphia: Judson Press, 1956.

Gowing, Peter G. *Islands under the Cross: The Story of the Church in the Philippines*. Manila: National Council of Churches in the Philippines, 1967.

————, and Scott, William Henry, eds. *Acculturation in the Philippines: Essays on Changing Societies*. Quezon City: New Day Publishers, 1971.

Isham, Mary. *Valorous Ventures: A Record of Sixty and Six Years of the Women's Foreign Missionary Society, Methodist Episcopal Church*. Boston: Women's Foreign Missionary Society, Methodist Episcopal Church, 1936.

Kavanagh, Joseph J. "The 'Iglesia ni Cristo.'" *Philippine Studies* 3 (March 1955): 19–42.

Latourette, Kenneth Scott. *A History of the Expansion of Christianity*. Vol. 5. *The Great Century in the Americas, Australia, Asia, and Africa A.D. 1800-A.D. 1914*. New York: Harper & Brothers, 1943.

McLean, Archibald. *The History of the Foreign Christian Missionary Society*. Chicago and New York: Fleming H. Revell Company, 1919.

Neill, Stephen. *Colonialism and Christian Missions*. New York: McGraw-Hill Book Company, 1966.

Osias, Camilo, and Lorenzana, Avelina. *Evangelical Christianity in the Philippines*. Dayton, Ohio: United Brethren Publishing House, 1931.

Parker, Donald Dean. "Church and State in the Philippines 1896–1906." Ph.D. dissertation, University of Chicago, 1936.

Piggin, Stuart. "Assessing Nineteenth-Century Missionary Motivation: Some Considerations of Theory and Method." In *Religious Motivation: Biographical and Sociological Problems for the Church Historian*, edited by Derek Baker. Oxford, England: Basil Blackwell for the Ecclesiastical Historical Society, 1978, pp. 327–38.

Portuondo, Emma J. "The Impact of Bishop Charles Henry Brent upon American Colonial and Foreign Policy, 1901–1917." Ph.D. dissertation, Catholic University, 1969.

Rabe, Valentin H. *The Home Base of American China Missions, 1880–1920*. Cambridge: Council on East Asian Studies, Harvard University, 1978.

Rambo, David L. "The Christian and Missionary Alliance in the Philippines, 1901–70." Ph.D. dissertation, New York University, 1974.

Reilly, Michael C. "Charles Henry Brent: Philippine Missionary and Ecumenist." *Philippine Studies* 24 (1976): 303–25.

Reuter, Frank T. *Catholic Influence on American Colonial Policies, 1898–1904*. Austin: University of Texas Press, 1967.

Roberts, Walter N. *The Filipino Church: The Story of the Development of an Indigenous Evangelical Church in the Philippine Islands as Revealed in the Work of 'The Church of the United Brethren in Christ.'* Dayton, Ohio: Foreign Missionary Society and the Women's Missionary Association, United Brethren in Christ, 1936.

Schumacher, John N. *The Revolutionary Clergy: The Filipino Clergy and the Nationalist Movement, 1850–1903*. Manila: Ateneo de Manila Press, 1981.

Scott, William Henry. *Hollow Ships on a Wine-Dark Sea and Other Essays.* Quezon City: New Day Publishers, 1976.

――――. "Staunton of Sagada: Christian Civilizer." *Historical Magazine of the Protestant Episcopal Church* 31 (December 1962): 305–39.

Sitoy, Jr., T. Valentino. "An Aborted Spanish Protestant Mission to the Philippines." *Silliman Journal* 15 (1968): 243–80.

――――. "Nineteenth Century Evangelical Beginnings in the Philippines." *South East Asia Journal of Theology* 9 (October 1967): 42–55.

Stipp, F. V. "The Disciples of Christ in the Philippines." D.D. thesis, Yale University, 1927.

Thomas, Ivor B. "American Imperialism in the Philippines: A Congregationalist Justification." *Silliman Journal* 20 (1973): 373–403.

Torres, Cristina Evangelista. "A Study of Church and State Relations in the First Decade of American Rule: The American Catholic Hierarchy and the American Colonial Government 1898–1910." M.A. thesis, University of the Philippines, 1977.

Tuggy, Arthur Leonard. *Iglesia ni Cristo: A Study in Independent Church Dynamics.* Quezon City: Conservative Baptist Publishing, Inc., 1976.

――――. *The Philippine Church: Growth in a Changing Society.* Grand Rapids, Michigan: William B. Eerdmans Publishing Company, 1971.

Varg, Paul A. *Missionaries, Chinese and Diplomats: The American Protestant Missionary Movement in China, 1890–1952.* Princeton: Princeton University Press, 1958.

von der Mehden, Fred R. *Religion and Nationalism in Southeast Asia: Burma, Indonesia, The Philippines.* Madison: University of Wisconsin Press, 1968.

Warren, Lee Donald. *Isles of Opportunity: Progress and Possibilities in the Philippines.* Washington, D.C.: Review & Herald Publishing Association, 1928.

Welch, Jr., Richard F. "Organized Religion and the Philippine–American War, 1899–1902." *Mid-America* 55 (July 1973): 184–206.

Zabriskie, Alexander C. *Bishop Brent: Crusader for Christian Unity.* Philadelphia: Westminster Press, 1948.

Index

Abel, William, 7
Adams, Elbridge M., 60, 128–29
Aglipay, Gregorio, 116–23, 195, 231n39; seeks episcopal consecration, 121–22; Disciples on, 230n24
Aglipayano schism. *See* Aglipay, Gregorio; *Iglesia Filipina Independiente*
Aguis, Ambrose, 111
Alejandro, D. D., 196
Allison, William B.: on Philippine Assembly, 134
American Bible Society, 4–5, 34
American expansionism, 2–4, 11
Aquinaldo, Emilio, 2, 4, 115, 120, 156, 168
Aquino, Benigno, 197
Araneta, Gregorio, 74
Ashbaugh, Floyd, 26
athletics: missionaries on, 85–86
Atkinson, Fred W., 163–64; on missionaries, 242n61
Aurora, Manuel, 123–26

Bagobos, 69–70; F. Laubach on, 219n48
Barbour, Thomas S., 30, 43, 210n41
Barrows, David Prescott, 91, 164; and missionaries, 185
Bartlett, Murray, 123
Bates, John C., 158
Bates Agreement (Treaty), of 1899, 158, 239n31
Beaver, R. Pierce: on comity, 32–33, 35
Bell, J. Franklin, 180
Beveridge, Albert: on Philippine Assembly, 134
Biak-na-bato, peace of, 1
Black, Mrs. Robert F., 205n57
Black, Robert F., 7, 25, 37, 49, 50, 70, 84, 161, 205n57, 212, 241n46; on Filipinos, 76,

90; on immorality, 78; on independence, 150; on planters, 179; on soldiers, 180; on government officials, 186
Bolton, E. C., 184–85
Brent, Charles Henry, 6, 8, 16–17, 18, 20, 21, 24, 27, 38, 51–54, 77, 91, 93, 104, 141, 150, 155, 160, 161–62, 166, 167, 182, 203n21, 204n23, 213nn83–84, 223n108, 235nn8, 33, 236nn37, 43; on Moros, 21, 71–72, 159; on missionaries' hardships, 26–27; on H. Stuntz, 52; on Protestantism, 54; on Igorots, 68–69. 84; on Bagobos, 70; on Negritos, 71; on Filipinos, 74–75, 76; on immorality, 78; on M. Johnston, 105; on Catholics, 106–13; on nationalism, 115; and G. Aglipay, 117, 120–23; on Philippine Assembly, 135, 139; on independence, 140, 142–44; and C. Hughes, 148; and F. Harrison, 148, 184; leaves Philippines, 149; on W. Wilson, 149; on Philippine-American War, 157; and Moral Progress League, 169; on American colonial government, 172; on British colonialism, 172–73; on Americans in the Philippines, 175; on clubs, 176; on soldiers, 180, 181; and W. Taft, 183; and W. Forbes, 184; on T. Hunt, 184; on D. Barrows, 185; on F. Carpenter, 185; on N. Saleeby, 185–86; on teachers, 187; on Calaagans, 217n20; on Filipino Catholic clergy, 227n63; and T. Roosevelt, 234n5; on D. Worcester, 240n44
Briggs, Charles W., 16, 26, 29–31, 32, 43, 45–49 passim, 65, 130, 165, 205n54, 206n66, 210n41, 211nn52, 57, 61; on *Iglesia Filipina Independiente*, 230n27; on Ilocanos and Visayans, 67; on Filipinos, 81–83; on Catholics, 97–98, 224n18; on

261

Index

Filipino Academy of Social Sciences, 168
Finster, L. V., 7, 60–61, 128; on Catholics, 223n6
Finster, Mrs. L. V., 25
Fonacier, Santiago, 118
Forbes, William Cameron, 107, 141, 142, 143–44, 148, 166, 169, 236n37, 244n92; on missionaries, 153, 160, 170–71, 184; and C. Brent, 184
Foreman, John, 157, 182; on soldiers, 181
Forshee, Archibald A., 32

gambling: missionaries on, 77, 82–83, 85–86
Garrison, Lindley M., 123, 142–43, 146, 231n39, 236n37
Gates, Elbridge H., 60, 215n112, 233n6
Gilheuser, Henry, 161
Glunz, Charles, 20–21, 86
Gomez Dominador, 126
Goodell, Mrs. Willard A., 25
Goodell, Willard A., 25
Goodrich, Jay C., 5, 34, 38
Gowing, Peter G.: on comity, 35; on missionaries and government, 161
Grant, Ulysses S., 154
Great Britain, 4
Groves, J. M., 90, 91; on government officials, 186; on Filipinos, 215n3

Hale, W. G., 185
Halford, Elijah, 34, 38
Hall, J. Andrew, 19, 41–46 passim, 48, 52, 65, 131, 139; on Filipinos, 89; on Philippine-American War, 158; on keeping the Sabbath, 178; on F. Harrison, 184
Hamilton, Charles R., 57, 85, 214n101, 245n65; on teachers, 187–88
Hampton Institute, 86
Hanna, W. F., 56
Harbord, James G., 241n46
Harrison, Francis Burton, 144, 146; and missionaries, 147, 184; and C. Brent, 148
Harty, Jeremias J., 111, 168; and YMCA, 104
Hartzell, Corwin Francis, 12
Hayes, Mrs. Rutherford B., 154
Herkert, Ella, 24
Hibbard, David S., 37, 42, 50, 65, 84–85, 86, 137, 180, 209n27; on comity, 39; on Catholics, 99; and Aglipayanos, 117–18; on Americans in the Philippines, 174; on

soldiers, 181; on Philippine-American War, 238n21, 239n28
Hicks, Ellen T.: on Philippine-American War, 157
Higdon, Elmer K.: on nationalism, 115
Hijalda, Narcisco, 120, 122
Hillis, Lewis B., 38, 45; on teachers, 189
Hills, Leon C., 25, 45; on Americans in the Philippines, 174
Hodgkin, Henry T., 22
Huddleston, Oscar, 24, 26, 55; on Catholics, 102
Hughes, Charles Evans, 148, 149
Hughes, Robert P., 180
Hunt, T. M., 184
Huse, S. S., Jr.: on Catholicism, 224n10

Ide, Henry C., 167; and missionaries, 184
Iglesia Evangelica Metodista en las Islas Filipinas (IEMELIF), 125–27
Iglesia Evangelica Unida de Cristo, 131
Iglesia Filipina Independiente, 5, 116–23, 194–95, 230n27, 250n6
Iglesia ni Kristo, 127–29
Igorots, 3, 194; missionaries on, 67–70, 84, 87–88, 217n16; defined, 216n10
Ilocanos: missionaries on, 67, 216n8
immorality: missionaries on, 78–79
indolence: missionaries on, 79
industrial education, 86–88
Irwin, G. A., 215n112
Isham, Mary: on Filipinos, 81

J. G. White Company, 178
Jansen, Fred, 40; on Tagalogs and Visayans, 67; on Filipinos, 8; on planters, 246n21
Jaro Industrial School for Boys, 87
Johnson, E. Finley, 90–91
Johnson, Mordecai, 22
Johnston, Mercer G., 8, 12, 16–17, 21, 24, 25, 27–29, 53, 106, 107, 108, 110; on Catholics, 105–6; on C. Brent, 109; on G. Aglipay, 120; on gambling, 167–71
Jones Bill, 8, 140, 147, 148
Jones, William A., 140, 142

Kershner, Bruce L., 11, 15, 18, 22, 25, 55–57, 57–59, 124, 132–33, 155, 214n93; on Filipinos, 72, 74, 76, 89, 90; on immorality,

Note on the Author

Kenton J. Clymer holds a Ph.D. from the University of Michigan (1970). He held a Fulbright-Hays lectureship in the Philippines in 1977–78 and during the summers of 1977 and 1978 was a guest participant in the Luce Foundation workshops on Philippine-American history held at Harvard University. He has received numerous research grants from the American Philosophical Society and the University Research Institute of the University of Texas at El Paso. He is the author of *John Hay: The Gentleman as Diplomat* and of articles about missionaries and the Philippines that have appeared in scholarly journals. Clymer is professor of history at the University of Texas at El Paso.